# Global Civil
# Society

# Global Civil Society

## Dimensions of the Nonprofit Sector

Volume Two

**Lester M. Salamon,
S. Wojciech Sokolowski,
and Associates**

Published in association with
the Johns Hopkins Comparative
Nonprofit Sector Project

Kumarian
Press, Inc.

*Global Civil Society: Dimensions of the Nonprofit Sector,* Volume Two

Published 2004 in the United States of America by Kumarian Press, Inc.
1294 Blue Hills Avenue, Bloomfield, CT 06002 USA

The text of this book is set in 10/12 Sabon.

Production and design by ediType, Yorktown Heights, N.Y.
Proofread by Bob Land

Printed in Canada by Transcontinental Printing. Text printed with vegetable oil–based ink.

∞ The paper used in this publication meets the minimum requirements of the American National Standard for Information Sciences–Permanence of Paper for Printed Library Materials, ANSI Z39.48–1984

Library of Congress Control Number: 2001368367
ISBN 1-56549-184-X

13  12  11  10  09  08  07  06  05  04      10  9  8  7  6  5  4  3  2  1      First Printing 2004

*This book is dedicated to the memory of*
Andrew Kiondo *and* Bazaara Nyangabyaki,
*dedicated scholars and pioneering explorers*
*of the civil society sector in Africa,*
*with appreciation for their friendship*
*and contributions to this work.*

# Contents

# Tables and Figures

## 1. Global Civil Society: An Overview

## 2. Measuring Civil Society: The Johns Hopkins Global Civil Society Index

## 3. Kenya

## 4. South Africa

## 9. The Philippines

## 10. South Korea

## 11. Egypt

## Appendix A. Comparative Tables

# Foreword

It is in the nature of civil society that few of us see the need to comprehend it as a whole. Civil society is, after all, essentially about individuals coming together for some shared specific purpose. As long as we can freely play out our associational lives, is that not enough?

Thanks to the work of the Johns Hopkins Comparative Nonprofit Sector Project over the past dozen years, we know definitively that this is anything but enough. The Project has given us the facts and figures that guide us to the greater-than-the-sum-of-the-parts aggregates of all of our individual efforts. The implications are massive.

Let me tell you a true story to illustrate the power of this project. Anyone who has ever lived or worked in Pakistan knows experientially that there is a phenomenal ethic of giving and voluntary caring. Its actuality, however, was not understood. Inspired by the work that the Comparative Nonprofit Sector Project had done in other countries, the Aga Khan Foundation and the Project initiated empirical research on giving and volunteering. The findings arrived with the force of revelation: private giving by ordinary citizens was five times the amount of international aid grants coming into the country. The effect of this and a host of other findings galvanized a sense of self-reliance. This bred a further conviction, "If we can do this, we can do so much more to tackle our social ills."

Riding this social optimism, the Aga Khan Foundation convened a national consultative process that culminated in a law providing liberal tax breaks for givers. To ensure that the impetus was not lost, a new organization was established with a mission to promote indigenous philanthropy for sustainable development. Today, the Pakistan Centre for Philanthropy is a vibrant national organization with a lengthening record of innovative programming, including a management standards certification service.

None of this would have been possible without the Johns Hopkins Comparative Nonprofit Sector Project.

Lester Salamon and his meticulous associates in 36 countries have, quite simply, provided the wherewithal to defend and increase civil society across the world. It is now up to us to use this magnificent volume like a societal mirror. The Project reflects the empirical outlines of our associational features, prompting the kind of understandings that can lead to leaps forward, great and small.

DAVID BONBRIGHT

*London, March 2004*

# Preface

A dramatic associational revolution has been under way throughout the world for the past several decades, a massive upsurge of organized private, voluntary activity, of nonprofit or civil society organizations seeking to alleviate want, deliver health care and education, provide social services, and give voice to a multitude of cultural, artistic, religious, ethnic, social, and environmental concerns.

Until recently, however, this global associational revolution was largely invisible to policymakers, the media, the academic community, and the public at large. Indeed, even activists within the civil society sector have been unaware of its dimensions or scope.

To help fill this gap in knowledge and understanding, a small group of colleagues joined with me in the early 1990s to create the Johns Hopkins Comparative Nonprofit Sector Project. Thanks to the assistance of a number of courageous funders, this Project has expanded into a worldwide effort to document the scope, structure, composition, financing, and impact of the world's civil society sector. This project has already generated 52 books, more than 250 published articles, and hundreds of working papers, country reports, and presentations. In the process, it has changed fundamentally our understanding of the third sector and the role it plays in countries from Australia to Argentina, and from Kenya to Korea.

The present book represents the second volume in what we hope will become a regular series of books summarizing the major empirical findings of this work on the scope and structure of the civil society sector around the world. Its principal purpose is to report on our effort to extend the work of this project to the countries of Africa, the Middle East, and South Asia. In addition, it reports on three countries for which data were not available at the time the first volume went to press. Finally, the volume seeks to put the individual country findings into context. It does this, first, through a comparative overview chapter that discusses the major cross-national findings in 36 countries; and, second, through a chapter that introduces a new "global civil society index" (GCSI) designed to pull the various dimensions of civil society together in a coherent way and show how different countries rank in terms of them.

As the introductory chapter and methodological appendix make clear, we use the terms "civil society sector" or "civil society organization" throughout this volume to refer to the broad array of organizations that are essentially private, i.e., outside the institutional structures of government;

that are not primarily commercial and do not distribute profits to their directors or "owners"; that are self-governing; and that people are free to join or support voluntarily. This definition was formulated in collaboration with teams of researchers and advisors from around the world and has been used successfully to guide field work in over 40 countries. Informal as well as formally constituted organizations are included within this definition as are religious as well as secular organizations. In addition, our effort to gauge the activities of these organizations includes the informal input of volunteers as well as the more formal effort of paid staff, both part-time and full-time.

The Johns Hopkins Comparative Nonprofit Sector Project has been a collaborative effort throughout, and I am grateful to the extraordinary team of colleagues who have joined together to formulate the basic concepts that have guided our work and to generate the information reported here. Special thanks are due, first of all, to the Local Associates noted on the Contributors List and in Appendix C, and the numerous scholars they have mobilized, for making us aware of the special features of the civil society sector in their countries and for helping us adapt our basic approach to capture these realities in a meaningful way.

Thanks are also due to my colleagues in the Johns Hopkins Center for Civil Society Studies who contributed enormously to this product. This Center seeks to encourage the development and effective operation of nonprofit, philanthropic, or "civil society" organizations through a combination of research, training, and information-sharing both in the United States and throughout the world. Key colleagues who contributed to this volume include Wojciech Sokolowski, who has overseen the data assembly for our Comparative Nonprofit Sector Project from the outset; Regina List, who coordinated much of the "Phase IIB" effort that is the focus of this report; Stefan Toepler, who coordinated the data gathering in the Middle Eastern countries; Leslie Hems, who coordinated the data gathering in Pakistan; Mimi Bilzor, who managed the extraordinarily complex editorial process required for this publication with amazing precision and skill; and Eileen Hairel, Claudine Holaska, and Sarah Parkinson, who read and re-read drafts, assembled and re-assembled graphics, and checked and re-checked data to ensure consistency and accuracy throughout.

Finally, I gratefully acknowledge the financial support provided by the organizations listed in Appendix E and the advice and counsel provided by the numerous experts on the nonprofit sector and philanthropy who have served on the national and international advisory committees to this project reported in Appendix D. Special thanks for the Phase IIB work reported on here is due to the Ford Foundation, both the national office and the regional offices in the Philippines, East Africa, and India; the David and Lucile Packard Foundation; the Aga Khan Foundation; and the Charles Stewart Mott Foundation.

None of these people or organizations, nor any others with which I am affiliated, bears responsibility for any errors of fact or interpretation that this document might contain, however. That responsibility is mine alone, and I accept it gladly.

Finally, two African scholars began this journey toward increasing the visibility of the civil society sector in their countries with us but passed away before their pioneering efforts could see the full light of day. Andrew Kiondo of Tanzania, and Bazaara Nyangabyaki of Uganda, were tremendously dedicated and effective students of the third sector both in their own countries and in the East African region more generally. They brought to this project, as to the rest of their work, a deep commitment not only to the third sector, but also to the norms of objective social research. Their passing is a loss not only to this project, but also to the cause of scholarly research in this field, both in Africa and the world. We therefore dedicate this book to their memory.

LESTER M. SALAMON

*Annapolis, Maryland*
*May 9, 2004*

# Contributors

*Gian Paolo Barbetta* is Professor of Economics and the Economics of Nonprofit Organizations at the Catholic University of Milan. He is also a member of the Agenzia per le Onlus, the public agency in charge of regulation and control of the Italian nonprofit sector.

*John-Jean Barya* is a Senior Research Fellow and former Executive Director of the Centre for Basic Research, and an Associate Professor of Law at Makerere University, Kampala, Uganda. He has published and has research interests in the areas of civil society and the nonprofit sector, constitutionalism, democracy and the state, labor law, and industrial relations as well as social policy issues.

*Ledivina V. Cariño,* Local Associate for the Philippines, is a Professor at the National College of Public Administration and Governance of the University of the Philippines-Diliman. She holds a doctoral degree in Sociology from Indiana University.

*Stefano Cima* is head of research in the field of nonprofit organizations at the Istituto per la Ricerca Sociale in Milan, Italy.

*Ramón L. Fernan III* is Deputy Director of the Philippine Nonprofit Sector Project. He is an environmental advocate who has worked for various nonprofit and nongovernmental organizations.

*Aisha Ghaus-Pasha* is a consultant to the Department of Economic and Social Affairs, United Nations. She previously was co–project leader of the Pakistani CNP team and Deputy Managing Director of the Social Policy and Development Centre in Karachi. She has a Ph.D. in Economics, and her research interests include social development, public policy, governance, and macroeconomics.

*Hashem El-Husseini,* Local Associate for Lebanon, is professor in the faculty of information and Ph.D. advisor in the faculty of sociology at the Lebanese University. He holds a doctoral degree in Social Psychology from the University of Paris. His most recent publication is *La mentalité tribale* (Lebanese University, 2003).

*Muhammad Asif Iqbal,* Principal Researcher and Project Manager for the Pakistani project team, is Principal Specialist at the Social Policy and Development Centre, Karachi. He holds master's degrees in Economics and in Public Policy and Administration.

*Ku-Hyun Jung* is President of Samsung Economic Research Institute in Seoul, Korea. He taught at the School of Business, Yonsei University in Seoul. He recently co-edited *Civil Society Response to Asian Crisis* (Institute of East and West Studies, 2002). He has a B.A. from Seoul National University and a Ph.D. from the University of Michigan.

*Amani Kandil,* Local Associate for Egypt, is Executive Director of the Arab Network for NGOs. She has published books and articles on civil society in the Arab World, and currently is working on developing a strategy for civil society in Egypt. She holds a Ph.D. in Political Science.

*Karuti Kanyinga,* co–Local Associate for Kenya, is a Senior Research Fellow at the Institute for Development Studies, Nairobi, Kenya. He holds a Ph.D. in Political Science from Roskilde University in Denmark. He has written extensively on the politics of development and civil society in Kenya.

*David Lameck Kibikyo,* co–Local Associate for Uganda, is a Research Associate with the Centre for Basic Research in Uganda. He currently is working on his Ph.D. in Institutional Frameworks for Industrialization at Roskilde University in Denmark.

*Andrew Kiondo,* Local Associate for Tanzania, was a Professor of Political Science at the University of Dar-es-Salaam. He passed away in October 2003 as the manuscript for this book was being completed. His last work was editing a book on Civil Society and Governance in Tanzania.

*Ewa Leś,* Local Associate for Poland, is Professor of Political Science at Warsaw University; Chair of the Research Center on Non-Profit Organizations at the Institute of Political Studies, Polish Academy of Science; and Director of the Postgraduate Programme of NGOs Management at Collegium Civitas, Polish Academy of Science. She has published several books on philanthropy and the voluntary sector in Eastern Europe.

*Regina A. List,* former Research Projects Manager at the Johns Hopkins Center for Civil Society Studies and also Coordinator for Developing Countries for the Comparative Nonprofit Sector Project, is a co-author of *Global Civil Society: Dimensions of the Nonprofit Sector, Volume One* and *Cross-border Philanthropy.* She holds an M.A. in International Development from the American University.

*Håkon Lorentzen,* Local Associate for Norway, is Research Director at the Institute for Social Research in Oslo. He holds a doctoral degree in Sociology. His research focuses on the relation between state and voluntary associations in Norway, and his most recent book is *The Modernization of Civil Society.*

*Winnie V. Mitullah,* co–Local Associate for Kenya, is a researcher and lecturer at the Institute for Development Studies, University of Nairobi.

She holds a Ph.D. in Political Science and Public Administration. Her research interests include urban development and housing, the informal urban economy, politics, institutions, governance, and the role of stakeholders in development. Her most recent publication is *Promoting Land Rights in Africa: How Do NGOs Make a Difference?*

*Sławomir Nałęcz,* co–Local Associate for Poland, works in the Nonprofit Research Laboratory at the Institute of Political Studies, Polish Academy of Sciences, and is a lecturer at Collegium Civitas on theory and methods of research on civil society. He is a graduate of Warsaw University and is completing his Ph.D. dissertation, "Social Impact of the Nonprofit Sector in III Republic of Poland: Do Nonprofits Change Us into Citizens?"

*Laurean Ndumbaro,* co–Local Associate for Tanzania, is Senior Lecturer in the Department of Political Science at the University of Dar-es-Salaam. He holds a Ph.D. in Political Science from the University of Florida. He is currently working on civil society and democratization in Tanzania.

*Bazaara Nyangabyaki,* who served as Local Associate for Uganda, passed away as this volume was being prepared for print. He was Executive Director of the Centre for Basic Research in Kampala. He received his masters in Political Science from Makerere University, Kampala and completed his Ph.D. in Political Science at Queen's University in Ontario, Canada. He published numerous articles on land policy, food security, the role of civil society, and most recently, on decentralization.

*Walter Odhiambo* is a Research Fellow at the Institute for Development Studies, University of Nairobi, and has been a member of the technical team for the Kenya Human Development Report for the last two years. He holds a Ph.D. in Economics from the University of Hohenheim, Germany. His research interests are agricultural development, poverty, and institutional economics.

*Tae-Kyu Park,* Local Associate for South Korea, is a Professor of Economics at Yonsei University in Seoul and also president of the Korean Association of Nonprofit Organization Research. He holds a doctoral degree in Economics from Indiana University. His recent research has focused on philanthropy, charitable giving, volunteering, and corporate social responsibility, as well as public finance, expenditure, and taxation.

*Rachel H. Racelis* is a volunteer consultant for the Philippine Nonprofit Sector Project. She earned her doctorate in Economics from the University of Hawaii and is currently Associate Professor at the School of Urban and Regional Planning of the University of the Philippines, Diliman.

*Bev Russell* is Managing Director of Social Surveys, which she founded 16 years ago, and has research experience in both the United Kingdom and South Africa. She recently co-authored *The Size and Scope of the Non-profit*

*Sector in South Africa* and wrote a chapter for inclusion in the 2003 UNDP Sustainable Development Report.

*Salama Saidi,* Local Associate for Morocco, is a researcher in social sciences and former Regional Advisor of the United Nations for North Africa and the Middle East. She is currently an international consultant and President of the Rawabit Association for NGO Training Research and Communication. She holds a Ph.D. in Demography from the University of Pennsylvania and an M.A. in Economics from Temple University in Philadelphia.

*Lester M. Salamon* is the Director of the Johns Hopkins Comparative Nonprofit Sector Project. A Professor at Johns Hopkins University, he was the founding director of the Johns Hopkins Institute for Policy Studies and currently directs the Johns Hopkins Center for Civil Society Studies. He is the author or editor of numerous books and articles including *The State of Nonprofit America* (Brookings, 2002) and *The Tools of Government: A Guide to the New Governance* (Oxford, 2002). Dr. Salamon received his B.A. degree in Economics and Policy Studies from Princeton University and his Ph.D. in Government from Harvard University.

*Per Selle,* co–Local Associate for Norway, is Professor of Comparative Politics at the University of Bergen and Senior Researcher at the Stein Rokkan Centre for Social Studies, Bergen. He holds doctoral and master degrees in Political Science from the University of Bergen. Recent publications include *Investigating Social Capital: Comparative Perspectives on Civil Society, Participation and Governance* (Sage, 2004, with Sanjeev Prakash).

*Karl Henrik Sivesind* is a Senior Researcher at the Institute for Social Research in Oslo, and was formerly Associate Professor in Sociology at the University of Oslo. He holds doctoral and master's degrees in Sociology from the University of Oslo. Recent publications include *The Voluntary Sector in Norway: Composition, Changes, and Causes* (Institute for Social Research, 2002).

*S. Wojciech Sokolowski* is Senior Research Associate for the Comparative Nonprofit Sector Project at Johns Hopkins University. He received his Ph.D. in Sociology from Rutgers University, an M.A. in Philosophy from the Lublin Catholic University in Poland, and an M.A. in Sociology from San Jose State University. He is the author of *Civil Society and the Professions in Eastern Europe: Social Change and Organization in Poland* (Plenum/Kluwer, 2001), and a co-author of *Measuring Volunteering: A Practical Toolkit* (Independent Sector/United Nations Volunteers, 2001) and *Global Civil Society: Dimensions of the Nonprofit Sector,* Volume One, as well as a contributor to several edited volumes and academic journals.

*S.S. Srivastava,* is the Principal Researcher for the Comparative Nonprofit Sector Project in India and is based at PRIA in New Delhi. He was formerly the Director General of the Central Statistical Organization in India. Previously, he worked in the Indian Statistical Service and has also taught at universities in India and the United States. He holds master's and doctoral degrees in Statistics with a specialization in Econometrics.

*Mark Swilling,* Local Associate for South Africa, heads up the Sustainable Development Division in the School of Public Management and Planning at the University of Stellenbosch, and is Academic Director of the Sustainability Institute. He research interests include sustainable cities, civil society, and social movements, as well as development finance, sustainable agriculture, and land reform.

*Rajesh Tandon,* Local Associate for India, is the founding president of PRIA, a voluntary organization providing support to grassroots initiatives in South Asia. He has published a number of articles, manuals, and books and has been associated with numerous national and international organizations such as Civicus, World Bank, Commonwealth Foundation, Forum International de Montreal, International Forum on Capacity Building, and the Rajiv Gandhi Institute of Contemporary Studies.

*Stefan Toepler* worked on several aspects of the Johns Hopkins Comparative Nonprofit Sector Project from 1995 to 2002, including overseeing the work in Central and Eastern Europe and the Middle East. Currently, he teaches nonprofit management in the Department of Public and International Affairs at George Mason University in Virginia. He received his doctorate in Business and Economics from the Free University of Berlin, Germany.

*Dag Wollebæk* is a doctoral student at the Department of Comparative Politics, University of Bergen. His recent publications include "Does Participation in Voluntary Associations Contribute to Social Capital? The Impact of Intensity, Scope and Type" in *Nonprofit and Voluntary Sector Quarterly* (2002, with Per Selle).

*Nereo Zamaro* is director of the Unit on public and private institutions at ISTAT, the Italian statistical office.

# Part One

# **OVERVIEW**

# Chapter 1

# Global Civil Society:
# An Overview

### Lester M. Salamon, S. Wojciech Sokolowski,
### and Regina List

## Introduction

A "global associational revolution" is under way around the world, a massive upsurge of organized private, voluntary activity in virtually every corner of the globe.[1] The product of new communications technologies, significant popular demands for greater opportunity, dissatisfaction with the operations of both the market and the state in coping with the inter-related social and economic challenges of our day, the availability of external assistance, and a variety of other factors, this associational revolution has focused new attention, and new energy, on the broad range of social institutions that occupy the social space between the market and the state. Known variously as the "nonprofit," the "voluntary," the "civil society," the "third," the "social economy," the "NGO," or the "charitable" sector, this set of institutions includes within it a sometimes bewildering array of entities — hospitals, universities, social clubs, professional organizations, day care centers, grassroots development organizations, health clinics, environmental groups, family counseling agencies, self-help groups, religious congregations, sports clubs, job training centers, human rights organizations, community associations, soup kitchens, homeless shelters, and many more.

Because of their unique combination of private structure and public purpose, their generally smaller scale, their connections to citizens, their flexibility, and their capacity to tap private initiative in support of public purposes, these organizations are being looked to increasingly to perform a number of critical functions: to help deliver vital human services, such as health, education, counseling, and aid to the poor, often in partnership with the state and the market; to empower the disadvantaged and bring unaddressed problems to public attention; to give expression to artistic, religious, cultural, ethnic, social, and recreational impulses; to build community

3

and foster those bonds of trust and reciprocity that are necessary for political stability and economic prosperity; and generally to mobilize individual initiative in the pursuit of the common good.

Despite their growing presence and importance, however, these "civil society organizations"[2] have long been the lost continent on the social landscape of our world. Only recently have they attracted serious attention in policy circles or the press, and academic interest in them has also surfaced only in recent years. For much of our recent history, social and political discourse has been dominated by a "two-sector model" that acknowledges the existence of only two social spheres outside of the family unit — the market and the state, or business and government. This was reinforced by statistical conventions that have kept this "third sector" of civil society organizations largely invisible in official economic statistics.[3] Even the most basic information about these organizations — their numbers, size, activities, economic weight, finances, and role — has consequently been lacking in most countries, while deeper understanding of the factors that contribute to their growth and decline has been almost nonexistent. As a consequence, the civil society sector's ability to participate in the significant policy debates now under way has been seriously hampered and its potential for contributing to the solution of pressing problems too often challenged or ignored.

The present volume is intended to fill this gap in knowledge, at least in part. More specifically, it reports on the latest findings of the Johns Hopkins Comparative Nonprofit Sector Project, the major project we have had under way around the world to bring the civil society sector into better empirical and conceptual focus. Previous publications have summarized the basic findings of this project with respect to 22 countries in Europe, Asia, North America, and Latin America.[4] The present volume extends the analysis to an additional 14 countries, most of them in Africa, the Middle East, and South Asia. In addition, it introduces a novel "global civil society index" intended to provide a convenient way to summarize the welter of data we are beginning to collect and use it to gauge the progress of civil society development among countries.

This overview chapter sets the context both for the index description in Chapter 2, and for the individual country chapters that follow. To do so, it first introduces the objectives and approach of this project, including the definition of the "civil society sector" that has guided our work. It then presents an overview of the major cross-national findings, integrating the new countries into the previous work of the project. Finally, it profiles a number of different regional groupings of countries that the data seem to suggest. These groupings make clear that the civil society sector, while sharing commonalities across countries, also takes rather different forms in different places.

# The Johns Hopkins Comparative
# Nonprofit Sector Project: Objectives and Approach

The work presented in this book is the product of a unique international collaboration engaging some 150 researchers in countries throughout the world. Begun in 1991, this project initially focused on thirteen countries—eight developed and five developing—and has since been extended to more than forty countries.

## Objectives

From the outset, this project has sought to accomplish five principal objectives:

- First, to *document* the scope, structure, financing, and role of the civil society sector for the first time in solid empirical terms in a significant number of countries representing different geographic regions, cultural and historical traditions, and levels of development;

- Second, to *explain* why this sector varies in size, composition, character, and role from place to place and identify the factors that seem to encourage or retard its development, including differences in history, legal arrangements, religious backgrounds, cultures, socioeconomic structures, and patterns of government policy;

- Third, to *evaluate* the impact these organizations are having and the contributions they make, as well as the drawbacks they entail;

- Fourth, to *improve awareness* of this set of institutions by disseminating the results of the work; and

- Fifth, to *build local capacity* to carry on the work in the future.

## Approach

To pursue these objectives, we formulated an approach that is:

- *Comparative,* covering countries at different levels of development and with a wide assortment of religious, cultural, and political traditions. This comparative approach was a central feature of the project's methodology. Far from obscuring differences, systematic comparison is the only way to identify what the differences among various countries actually are. As one analyst has put it: "Thinking without comparison is unthinkable. And, in the absence of comparison, so is all scientific thought and scientific research."[5] Carefully and sensitively done, comparison is thus not simply a technique for understanding others; it is also a necessary step toward understanding oneself.

  Accordingly, we have undertaken work in more than 40 countries representing all the inhabited continents and most of the world's major religions. As of this writing, results have been generated in 36 of these. As

**Table 1.1.** Country coverage of the Johns Hopkins
Comparative Nonprofit Sector Project

| Developed Countries | | Developing Countries | |
|---|---|---|---|
| Australia | Italy | Argentina | Pakistan |
| Austria | Japan | Brazil | Peru |
| Belgium | Netherlands | Colombia | Philippines |
| Finland | Norway | Egypt | South Africa |
| France | Spain | India | South Korea |
| Germany | Sweden | Kenya | Tanzania |
| Ireland | United States | Mexico | Uganda |
| Israel | United Kingdom | Morocco | |

| Transitional Countries | |
|---|---|
| Czech Republic | Romania |
| Hungary | Slovakia |
| Poland | |

noted in Table 1.1, this includes 16 advanced, industrial countries span-
ning North America, Western Europe, and Asia; 15 developing countries
spread across Latin America, Africa, the Middle East, and South Asia;
and 5 transitional countries of Central and Eastern Europe. This gives
the project a wide range of experiences on which to draw in formulating
its portrait of the world's third sector and assessing the explanations for
its varying patterns of development. It also provided a convenient basis
for cross-checking results from place to place.

• *Systematic,* utilizing a common definition of the entities to be included
  and a common classification system for differentiating among them. Comparison is only possible if reasonable care is taken in specifying what is
  to be compared. Given the conceptual ambiguity, lack of knowledge, and
  ideological overtones that exist in this field, this task naturally had to be
  approached with care. As outlined more fully below, our approach was
  to proceed in a bottom-up fashion, building up our definition and classification from the actual experiences of the project countries. The goal
  throughout was to formulate a definition that is sufficiently broad to encompass the diverse array of entities embraced within this sector in the
  varied countries we were covering yet sharp enough to differentiate these

entities from those that comprise the market and the state, the two other major sectors into which social life has traditionally been divided.

- *Collaborative,* relying extensively on local analysts to root our definitions and analysis in the solid ground of local knowledge and ensure the local experience to carry the work forward in the future. Accordingly, we recruited a principal Local Associate in each country to assist us in all phases of project work (see Appendix C). This included not only data collection and data analysis, but also the formulation of the project's basic conceptual equipment — its working definition, treatment of borderline organizations, classification system, and data-collection strategies. Local Associates met regularly throughout the life of the project to formulate research strategies, review progress, and fine-tune the approach. These individuals in turn recruited colleagues to assist in the effort. The result was a project team that has engaged at least 150 local researchers around the world in the development and execution of the project's basic tasks.

- *Consultative,* involving the active participation of local civil society activists, government leaders, the press, and the business community in order to further ensure that the work in each country was responsive to the particular conditions of the country and that the results could be understood and disseminated locally. To achieve this, we organized Advisory Committees in each project country and at the international level (see Appendix D for the membership of the Advisory Committees). These committees reviewed all aspects of the project approach, assisted in the interpretation of the results, and helped publicize the findings and think through their implications. Altogether, more than 600 nonprofit, philanthropic, government, and business leaders have taken part in the project through these Advisory Committees.

- *Empirical,* moving wherever possible beyond subjective impressions to develop a body of empirical data on this set of organizations. Obviously, not all facets of the civil society sector can be captured in empirical terms, and some components of the project, such as the legal analysis, the historical analysis, and the impact analysis, consequently used more qualitative techniques, including case studies, focus groups, and literature review. Nevertheless, given the general confusion that exists in many places about the real scope and structure of this sector, we felt it important to develop as reasonable as possible a set of empirical measures of the overall level of effort that civil society organizations mobilize in each country, the distribution of this effort among various activities, including both service activities and more expressive activities (e.g., policy advocacy, environmental protection, and arts and culture), and the sources of support for this activity. This required the formulation of a set of research protocols defining the data items being sought and suggesting ways to secure the needed data. It also required the tailoring of these protocols to the realities of the individual countries, a process that was accomplished in collaboration with our Local Associates, as noted more fully below.

## Definition and classification

Given the comparative and empirical nature of this inquiry, the task of developing a coherent definition of the entities of interest to us took on special importance and therefore deserves special comment. This is particularly true given the somewhat contested nature of the central concepts defining this field. Broadly speaking, three types of definitions of the entities that comprise the third or civil society sector were available to us, each associated with a particular set of terms.[6] One of these is an essentially *economic definition* that focuses on the *source of organizational support*. According to this definition, a civil society organization is one that receives the predominant portion of its revenue from private contributions, not from market transactions or government support. Terms such as "voluntary sector," "charitable sector," or "nonprofit sector" are sometimes used to convey this sense.

A second set of definitions focuses on the *legal status* of the organization. According to this definition, a civil society organization is one that takes a particular legal form (e.g., an association or a foundation) or that is exempted from some or all of a country's taxes. Terms such as "associations" or "tax-exempt organizations" are often used to convey this sense.

Finally, a third set of definitions focuses on the *purposes* such organizations pursue. According to this definition, a civil society organization is one that promotes the public good, encourages empowerment and participation, or seeks to address the structural roots of poverty and distress. Terms such as "civil society" or "NGO" or "charity" are often used to convey this sense.

Each of these definitions has its advantages. Nevertheless, we found them all inadequate for the kind of cross-national comparative inquiry we wanted to launch. The economic definition puts too much stress on the revenue sources of civil society organizations, downplaying other features that these organizations share, such as their use of volunteers, their social missions, and their not-for-profit character. By restricting the scope of this sector to organizations that rely chiefly on private philanthropic support, it turns out to exclude a substantial portion of the organizations commonly perceived to be part of the civil society sector. The legal definition, by contrast, is difficult to apply comparatively because each country has its own legal structure, making it difficult to find the comparable classes of entities in the legal frameworks of different countries. And purpose definitions, while appealing, are too nebulous and subjective to apply in a cross-national analysis, especially since different countries, or different groups of people within countries, have different ideas about what constitutes a valid "public purpose," and it is often difficult to determine whether a particular organization is actually pursuing its avowed purpose anyway. What is more, this kind of definition raises the danger of creating tautologies by making the sector's pursuit of public purposes true *by definition,* rendering it impossible to disprove.

### The structural-operational definition

In view of these difficulties, we adopted a bottom-up, inductive approach to defining the civil society sector, building up our definition from the actual experiences of the broad range of countries embraced within our project. In particular, we first solicited from our Local Associates a roadmap of the kinds of entities that would reasonably be included in the third or civil society sector in their respective countries. We then lined these roadmaps up against each other to see where they overlapped and identified the basic characteristics of the entities that fell into this overlapping area. Finally, we made note of the "gray areas" that existed on the fringes of this core concept and created a process for Local Associates to consult with us to determine how to treat entities that occupied these gray areas.

Out of this process emerged a consensus on five structural-operational features that defined the entities at the center of our concern. For the purpose of this project, therefore, we defined the civil society sector as composed of entities that are:

- *Organized,* i.e., they have some structure and regularity to their operations, whether or not they are formally constituted or legally registered. This means that our definition embraces informal, i.e., nonregistered, groups as well as formally registered ones. What is important is not whether the group is legally or formally recognized but that it have some organizational permanence and regularity as reflected in regular meetings, a membership, and some structure of procedures for making decisions that participants recognize as legitimate.

- *Private,* i.e., they are not part of the apparatus of the state, even though they may receive support from governmental sources. This feature differentiates our approach from the economic definitions noted above that exclude organizations from the civil society sector if they receive significant public sector support.

- *Not profit-distributing,* i.e., they are not primarily commercial in purpose and do not distribute profits to a set of directors, stockholders, or managers. Civil society organizations can generate surpluses in the course of their operations, but any such surpluses must be reinvested in the objectives of the organization. This criterion serves as a proxy for the "public purpose" criterion used in some definitions of civil society, but it does so without having to specify in advance and for all countries what valid "public purposes" are. Rather, it leaves these decisions to the people involved on the theory that if there are people in a country who voluntarily support an organization without hope of receiving a share of any profit the organization generates, this is strong evidence that they must see some public purpose to the organization. This criterion also usefully differentiates civil society organizations from for-profit businesses.

- *Self-governing,* i.e., they have their own mechanisms for internal governance, are able to cease operations on their own authority, and are fundamentally in control of their own affairs.
- *Voluntary,* i.e., membership or participation in them is not legally required or otherwise compulsory. As noted above, this criterion also helped relate our definition to the concept of public purpose, but in a way that allows each country's citizens to define for themselves what they consider to be a valid public purpose by virtue of their decisions to take part on their own initiative in the organizations affected.

Obviously, like any definition, this one cannot eliminate all gray areas or borderline cases. As these were identified, efforts were made to interpret them in the context of the basic thrust of the definition, and clarifications were issued as appropriate. Thus, for example, the "not profit-distributing" criterion was included to differentiate civil society organizations from private business firms, as well as from the large-scale cooperative and mutual enterprises that dominate the banking and insurance industries in many European countries. But when it became clear that this criterion inadvertently threatened to exclude as well an important class of community-based cooperatives serving essentially anti-poverty purposes in Latin America and elsewhere in the developing world, language was added to make clear that the latter institutions could be included.

The "structural-operational" definition has been tested in every country included in the project. The definition has proved to be sufficiently broad to encompass the great variety of entities commonly considered to be part of the third or civil society sector in both developed and developing countries, yet sufficiently sharp to distinguish these institutions from those in the other two major sectors — business and government. The result is a definition that encompasses *informal* as well as *formal* organizations; *religious* as well as *secular* organizations;[7] organizations with paid staff and those staffed entirely by volunteers; and organizations performing essentially *expressive* functions — such as advocacy, cultural expression, community organizing, environmental protection, human rights, religion, representation of interests, and political expression — as well as those performing essentially *service* functions — such as the provision of health, education, or welfare services. While the definition does not embrace individual forms of citizen action such as voting and writing to legislators, it nevertheless embraces most organized forms, including social movements and community-based cooperative activities serving fundamentally solidarity objectives, such as the *stokvels,* or revolving credit associations, in Africa. Intentionally excluded, however, are government agencies, private businesses, and commercial cooperatives and mutuals.[8]

For the sake of convenience, we will generally use the term "civil society organizations" or "civil society sector" to refer to the institutions that meet this five-fold structural-operational definition. To be sure, this term is often used in a broader sense to encompass individual citizen activity as well.[9] To emphasize our focus on the more collective and organized forms of civil society, we will generally use the term "civil society organization" or "civil society sector" rather than simply "civil society" to depict the range of social phenomena that is the focus of our attention. This term has gained the widest acceptance internationally to refer to the organizations with which we are concerned. Other terms that will occasionally be used interchangeably to refer to the same set of entities will be "nonprofit sector," "nonprofit organizations," "third sector," and "voluntary organizations." Each of these terms carries its own baggage, but the "civil society" term seems the closest to gaining truly universal usage and has the advantage of avoiding the negative connotations associated with the terms "nonprofit" or "nongovernmental."

## International Classification of Nonprofit Organizations

As a further aid to depicting the entities embraced within our project definition, we formulated a classification scheme for differentiating these entities according to their primary activity. To do so, we adopted a method similar to that used for our definition. Beginning with the existing International Standard Industrial Classification (ISIC) used in most international economic statistics, we asked our Local Associates to report how well this classification fit the diverse realities of nonprofit activity in their countries. This input suggested the need to elaborate on the basic ISIC categories in a number of respects to capture the diversity of the civil society sector. Thus, for example, the broad health and human services category of ISIC was broken into a number of subcategories to differentiate better the range of civil society organization health and human-service activities that exist. So, too, a special "development" category was added to accommodate the "nongovernmental organizations," or NGOs, common in the developing world. These organizations pursue a broad range of development purposes and often utilize an empowerment strategy that blends service and expressive functions.

Out of this process emerged an International Classification of Nonprofit Organizations (ICNPO) that, as shown in Table 1.2, identifies 12 different categories of civil society organization activity. Included here are essentially service functions (which include education and research, community development and housing, health care, and social services) as well as more "expressive" functions (which include civic and advocacy; arts, culture, and recreation; environmental protection; and business, labor, and professional representation). Each of these categories in turn is further subdivided into subcategories (see Appendix B for a further specification of the resulting

**Table 1.2.** International Classification
of Nonprofit Organizations*

| Code | Field | Code | Field |
|------|-------|------|-------|
| 1 | Culture and recreation | 7 | Civic and advocacy |
| 2 | Education and research | 8 | Philanthropic intermediaries |
| 3 | Health | 9 | International |
| 4 | Social services | 10 | Religious congregations |
| 5 | Environment | 11 | Business and professional, unions |
| 6 | Development and housing | 12 | Not elsewhere classified (n.e.c.) |

* See Appendix B for additional detail.

classification system). All the types of civil society organizations covered by this classification system are included within the project's definition and are covered by the project. As will be noted more fully below, this classification structure makes it possible to draw some fairly fine-grained distinctions among the different types of civil society organizations. Like the basic definition, moreover, this classification system has been tested in more than 40 countries and found to be both workable and effective.

## Data sources and methodology

In order to ensure a reasonable degree of comparability in the basic data generated about the organizations identified above, we developed a data assembly approach that specified a common set of target data items, offered guidance on likely sources of such data, and then relied on Local Associates to formulate detailed strategies for generating the needed information in each country.

The principal focus in this basic descriptive portion of the project was on the overall scope and scale of civil society organization activity and the resources required to support it. Because it is a notoriously imprecise measure, we devoted little attention to the number of organizations and focused instead on variables more indicative of the level of effort these organizations mobilize. These included the number of workers, both paid and volunteer, expressed in full-time equivalent terms; the expenditures; the sources of revenue; and the primary activity.[10]

Broadly speaking, four types of data sources were employed to generate estimates of these key variables:

- Official economic statistics (e.g., employment surveys, population surveys), particularly those that included coverage of civil society organizations, giving, or volunteering. Where the civil society organizations were not separately identified in the data source, as was often the case, a variety of estimating techniques were used to determine the civil society organization share of particular industry aggregates;

- Data assembled by umbrella groups or intermediary associations representing various types of civil society organizations or industries in which civil society organizations are active;

- Specialized surveys of civil society organizations; and

- Population surveys, particularly those focusing on giving and volunteering.

The extent of reliance on these different types of sources varied greatly from country to country and even from field to field. Where existing data systems could be tapped to locate relevant information about a class of nonprofit organizations in a country, these were heavily mined. Where such data systems were inadequate or a class of organizations not covered by them, special surveys were carried out. Depending on the legal arrangements and registration systems in place, these surveys began with existing core lists of organizations or with lists that had to be built from the ground up. As the project moved its focus from areas with more developed data systems and more formalized civil society sectors to those with less developed data systems and less formal organizations, the extent of reliance on specially designed, bottom-up surveys naturally expanded. Thus, in Africa and Southeast Asia, detailed "snowball sampling" or "hypernetwork sampling" techniques were used to build profiles of the civil society sector from the ground up by going house to house or organization to organization in selected geographic areas, asking respondents about the organizations they belonged to or worked with, and continuing this process until no new organizations were encountered. (For more information on the various data assembly techniques used, see Appendix B.)

## Caveats

In interpreting the findings presented here, several features of the analysis should be borne in mind:

- Employment data — both paid and volunteer — are expressed in *full-time equivalent* (FTE) terms to make them comparable among countries and organizations. Thus, an organization that employs 20 half-time workers would have the same number of "full-time equivalent" workers (i.e., 10) as an organization that employs 10 people full-time. Similarly, an organization that employs 10 full-time paid workers would have the same "workforce" as an organization that engages 50 volunteers who work one day a week, or one-fifth time, each. Part-time workers, paid and volunteer, were converted to full-time equivalent terms by dividing the number of hours they work by the number of hours considered to represent a full-time job in the respective country.

- Unless otherwise noted, average figures reported here are unweighted averages in which the values of all countries are counted equally regardless of the size of the country or of its civil society sector. Where aggregate totals are more appropriate (e.g., to report the number of volunteers or paid workers as a share of the total employment in the target countries), weighted figures are used.

- Although data were collected at different *time periods* (1995 for most of the 22 countries in earlier reports and 1997 to 2000 for the new countries covered by this report), we have attempted to minimize the consequences of the different base years by focusing on the *relative* size of the civil society sector in a country rather than the *absolute* size since the relative size is not likely to change much over the three- or four-year period we are examining. Thus, for example, we measure the workforce of the civil society sector in a country as the *percent* of the economically active population that works for civil society organizations in either paid or volunteer positions.[11]

- As noted above, religious as well as secular organizations were included within the project's definition of the civil society sector, and an effort was made in most countries to capture the activity of both *religious worship organizations* (e.g., churches, mosques, synagogues, choirs, and religious study groups) and *religiously affiliated service organizations* (e.g., schools, hospitals, and homeless shelters). Generally, where a distinction between these two was possible, the affiliated service organizations were assigned to the relevant service field in which they chiefly operate (e.g., health, education, and social services). The organizations primarily engaged in religious worship, by contrast, were assigned to the special category of "religious congregations" (ICNPO Category 10). *Since comparable data on religious worship organizations could not be gathered in all countries, the cross-country comparisons here generally exclude the religious worship organizations (but not religiously affiliated service organizations).* However, where this exclusion affects the results significantly, we also note what difference the inclusion of religious worship organizations would make in the countries for which data are available.

- The revenues of civil society organizations come from a variety of sources. For the sake of convenience, we have grouped these into three categories: *fees,* which includes private payments for services, membership dues, and investment income; *philanthropy,* which includes individual giving, foundation giving, and corporate giving; and *government* or *public sector support,* which includes grants, contracts, and voucher or third-party payments from all levels of government, including government-financed social security systems that operate as quasi-nongovernmental organizations.

- Unless otherwise noted, *monetary values* are expressed in U.S. dollars at the exchange rate in effect as of the date for which data are reported.

- The number of countries covered varies somewhat by data availability. We have total employment and volunteering data for 36 countries, but have breakdowns by activity field for only 33 of them. Similarly, we have revenue data for 34 countries, but the revenue breakdown by field for only 33 countries. Finally, we have religious worship data for only 27 countries.

## Major Cross-National Findings

Five major findings emerge from this work on the scope, structure, financing, and role of the civil society sector in the 36 countries for which we have now assembled data.

### 1. A major economic force

In the first place, in addition to its social and political importance, the civil society sector turns out to be a considerable economic force in the countries we have examined, accounting for a significant share of national expenditures and employment. More specifically:

- **A $1.3 trillion industry.** The civil society sector had aggregate expenditures of $1.3 trillion as of the late 1990s. This represents 5.4 percent of the combined gross domestic product (GDP) of these countries (see Table 1.3).

- **The world's seventh largest economy.** To put these figures into context, if the civil society sector in these countries were a separate national economy, its expenditures would make it the seventh largest economy in the world, ahead of Italy, Brazil, Russia, Spain, and Canada and just behind France and the United Kingdom (see Table 1.4).

- **A major employer.** The civil society sector in these 36 countries is also a major employer, with a total aggregate workforce of 45.5 million full-time equivalent workers (paid and volunteer) including religious worship organizations. This means that civil society organizations employ:

  - On average, 4.4 percent of the economically active population, or an average of almost one out of every 20 economically active persons;

**Table 1.3.** The scale of the civil society sector,
36 countries, ca. 1995–2000

---

**$1.3 trillion in expenditures**
- 5.4% of combined GDP

**45.5 million FTE workforce***
- 25.3 million paid workers
- 20.2 million FTE volunteers
- 4.4% of the economically active population

**132 million people volunteering**
- 98 volunteers per 1,000 adult population

---

* Aggregate data include 4.5 million FTE workers in religion.

SOURCE: Johns Hopkins Comparative Nonprofit Sector Project

**Table 1.4.** If the civil society sector were a country . . .

| Country | GDP (trillion $) |
|---|---|
| United States | 7.2 |
| Japan | 5.1 |
| China | 2.8 |
| Germany | 2.2 |
| United Kingdom | 1.4 |
| France | 1.3 |
| **Civil society sector expenditures (36 countries)** | **1.3** |
| Italy | 1.1 |
| Brazil | 0.7 |
| Russia | 0.7 |
| Spain | 0.6 |
| Canada | 0.5 |

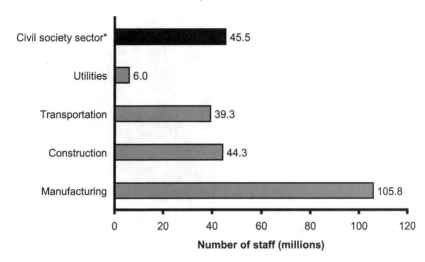

**Figure 1.1.** Civil society organization workforce in context, 36 countries

* Including volunteers.
SOURCE: Johns Hopkins Comparative Nonprofit Sector Project

- Nearly eight times more people than utilities (water and electricity) providers, about the same number of people as the construction industry, and nearly half as many people as manufacturing (see Figure 1.1).

## 2. Significant volunteer involvement

Of the 45.5 million FTE civil society organization workers in our 36 countries, over 20 million, or 44 percent, are volunteers, and over 25 million, or 56 percent, are paid workers (see Figure 1.2).[12] This demonstrates the ability of civil society organizations to mobilize sizable amounts of volunteer effort. Since most volunteers work fewer hours than paid workers, the actual number of people working in the civil society sector exceeds even these numbers. In fact, we estimate the actual number of people volunteering for civil society organizations in these 36 countries to be at least 132 million, or about 10 percent of the adult population in these countries.

## 3. Great variations among countries

While the civil society sector is a sizable force in a wide range of countries, there are considerable differences among countries.

- **Overall variation.** In the first place, countries vary greatly in the overall scale of their civil society organization workforce. Thus, as Figure 1.3

**Figure 1.2.** Civil society organization
paid vs. volunteer staff, 36 countries*

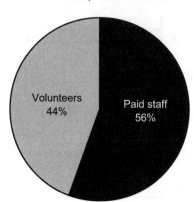

n = 45.5 million
* Weighted average.
SOURCE: Johns Hopkins Comparative Nonprofit Sector Project

makes clear, the civil society sector workforce — paid and volunteer —
varies from a high of 14.4 percent of the economically active population
in the Netherlands to a low of 0.4 percent in Mexico.[13]

- **Developed vs. developing and transitional countries.** A closer look at Figure 1.3 suggests that the civil society sector is relatively larger in the more developed countries. In fact, as Figure 1.4 shows, the civil society organization workforce in the developed countries is, on average, proportionally more than three times larger than that in the developing and transitional countries (7.4 percent vs. 1.9 percent of the economically active population, respectively).[14] This is so, moreover, even when account is taken of volunteer labor and not just paid employment.

  The relatively limited presence of civil society organizations in the developing and transitional countries does not, of course, necessarily mean the absence of helping relationships in these countries. To the contrary, many of these countries have strong traditions of familial, clan, or village networks that perform many of the same functions as civil society institutions. What is more, as Figure 1.3 also makes clear, there are considerable differences in the scale of civil society activity even among the less developed countries.

- **Variations in reliance on volunteers.** Not only do countries vary considerably in the overall size of their civil society sectors, but they also vary in the extent to which these organizations rely on paid as opposed to volunteer workers. While volunteers account, on average, for 38 percent of

**Figure 1.3.** Civil society organization workforce as a share of
the economically active population, by country

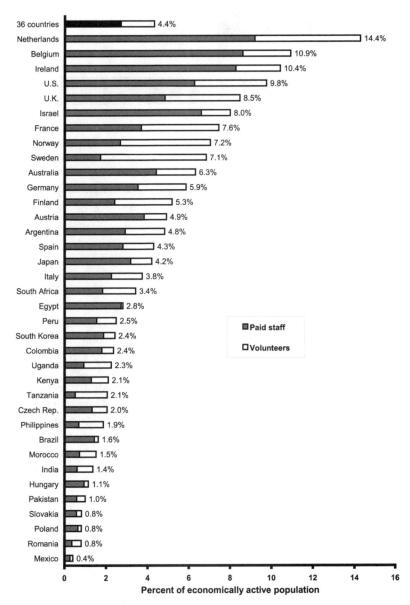

SOURCE: Johns Hopkins Comparative Nonprofit Sector Project

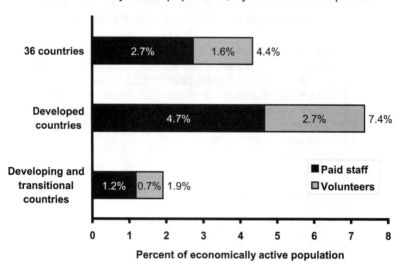

**Figure 1.4.** Civil society organization workforce as a share of the economically active population, by level of development

SOURCE: Johns Hopkins Comparative Nonprofit Sector Project

the civil society organization workforce among our 36 countries, reliance on volunteers varies considerably among individual countries — from a low of under 20 percent in Hungary, Israel, Brazil, and Egypt to a high of over 70 percent in Sweden and Tanzania (see Figure 1.5).[15]

Interestingly, the overall scale of volunteering tends to be higher in the developed countries than in the developing ones. Thus, as Figure 1.4 shows, volunteers represent 2.7 percent of the economically active population in developed countries compared to 0.7 percent in developing and transitional countries. But since the paid staff of civil society organizations also tends to be larger in the developed countries, the share that volunteers represent of the total civil society organization workforce turns out to be similar in these two groups of countries, as Figure 1.5 shows.

- **Paid employment and volunteering mutually reinforcing.** This finding poses a challenge to the widespread assumption that paid employment displaces spontaneous citizen initiatives and volunteering in civil society organizations, and that volunteers are a substitute for paid employees. In reality, however, the larger the paid civil society organization workforce, other things being equal, the larger the volunteer workforce, and vice versa. This is evident in Table 1.5, which shows the relationship between paid staff and volunteers in our 36 countries.

**Figure 1.5.** Volunteer share of civil society
organization workforce, by country

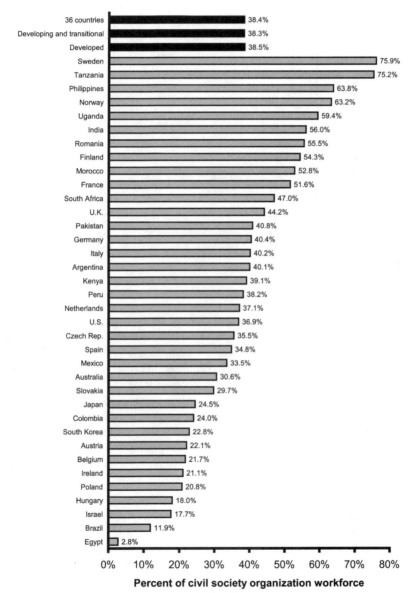

SOURCE: Johns Hopkins Comparative Nonprofit Sector Project

**Table 1.5.** Share of countries with high vs. low paid staff
and volunteers, 36 countries

| Paid Staff | Volunteer Staff | | |
|---|---|---|---|
| | below average | above average | Total |
| above average | 14%[a] | 25%[b] | 39% |
| below average | 53%[c] | 8%[d] | 61% |
| Total | 67% | 33% | 100% |

Countries represented by percentages above are as follows:

[a] Austria, Egypt, Israel, Japan, Spain

[b] Argentina, Australia, Belgium, France, Germany, Ireland, Netherlands, U.K., U.S.

[c] Brazil, Colombia, Czech Rep., Hungary, India, Italy, Kenya, Mexico, Morocco, Pakistan, Peru, Philippines, Poland, Romania, Slovakia, South Africa, South Korea, Tanzania, Uganda

[d] Finland, Norway, Sweden

As this table shows, in most of the countries, volunteer presence was high where paid staff presence was high and volunteer presence was low where paid staff presence was low. Specifically, in 19 of these countries, or 53 percent, both paid staff and volunteer presence were below average; while in 9 countries, or 25 percent, both paid staff and volunteer presence were above average. By contrast, in only 8 countries, or 22 percent, did the two types of labor move in the direction predicted by the conventional wisdom. This finding underscores the fact that volunteering is a social act, not simply an individual one. Volunteers have to be mobilized and recruited and their work structured to have its maximum impact. And for this, paid staff can be very helpful. In fact, in only three cases was low civil society organization paid employment associated with high volunteer input, and all three of these are the Nordic countries (Sweden, Finland, and Norway), where a distinctive pattern of civil society development has emerged, as we will see more fully below. This pattern reflects the long history of social movements in these countries coupled with the role that the state has assumed as both a provider and financier of social welfare services. To understand this more fully, it is useful to turn from this overview of the size of the civil society sector to an analysis of its composition.

## 4. More than service providers

Civil society organizations are not simply places of employment. What makes them significant are the functions they perform, and these functions are multiple.[16] For one thing, these organizations deliver a variety of human services, from health care and education to social services and community development. While disagreements exist over how distinctive civil society organization services are compared to those provided by businesses or governments, these organizations are well known for identifying and addressing unmet needs, for innovating, for delivering services of exceptional quality, and often for serving those in greatest need.

But provision of tangible services is only one function of the civil society sector. Also important is the sector's *advocacy* role, its role in identifying unaddressed problems and bringing them to public attention, in protecting basic human rights, and in giving voice to a wide assortment of social, political, environmental, ethnic, and community interests and concerns. The civil society sector is the natural home of social movements, and it functions as a critical social safety valve, permitting aggrieved groups to bring their concerns to broader public attention and to rally support to improve their circumstances.

Beyond political and policy concerns, the civil society sector also performs a broader *expressive function*, providing the vehicles through which an enormous variety of other sentiments and impulses — artistic, spiritual, cultural, ethnic, occupational, social, and recreational — also find expression. Opera companies, symphonies, soccer clubs, hobby associations, places of worship, fraternal societies, professional associations, book clubs, and Girl Scouts are just some of the manifestations of this expressive function. Through them, civil society organizations enrich human existence and contribute to the social and cultural vitality of community life.

Finally, these institutions are also important in *community building*, in creating what scholars are increasingly coming to call "social capital," those bonds of trust and reciprocity that seem to be crucial for a democratic polity and a market economy to function effectively. By establishing connections among individuals, involvement in associations teaches norms of cooperation that carry over into political and economic life.[17]

Gauging the extent to which civil society organizations engage in these various activities is difficult because many organizations are often involved in more than one. Nevertheless, it is possible to gain at least a rough first approximation by grouping organizations according to their principal activity and then assessing the level of effort each such activity absorbs.

To simplify this discussion, it is convenient to group the twelve activities identified in our International Classification of Nonprofit Organizations into two broad categories: (a) *service functions*, and (b) *expressive functions*.

- **Service functions** involve the delivery of direct services such as education, health, housing, economic development promotion, and the like.

- **Expressive functions** involve activities that provide avenues for the expression of cultural, spiritual, professional, or policy values, interests, and beliefs. Included here are cultural institutions, recreation groups, professional associations, advocacy groups, community organizations, environmental organizations, human rights groups, social movements, and the like.[18]

The distinction between expressive and service functions is far from perfect, of course, and many organizations are engaged in both. Nevertheless, the distinction helps clarify the roles that civil society organizations play.[19] In particular:

- **Service functions dominate in scale.** From the evidence available, it appears that the service functions of the civil society sector clearly absorb the lion's share of the activity. Excluding religious worship organizations, for which data were not available for all countries, an average of 64 percent of the total paid and volunteer full-time equivalent workforce of the civil society sector in the 33 countries for which we have activity data work for organizations primarily engaged in service functions (see Figure 1.6).[20]

- **Education and social services the dominant service functions.** Among the service activities of the civil society sector, education and social services clearly absorb the largest share of the effort, as Figure 1.6 also shows. About 43 percent of the civil society organization workforce — paid and volunteer — is engaged in these two service functions on average, with health accounting for another 14 percent.

- **Sizable involvement in expressive functions.** While the majority of civil society organization effort goes into organizations primarily engaged in service functions, a significant portion — amounting on average to almost a third of the workforce — goes into organizations primarily engaged in expressive functions, as Figure 1.6 also reveals. The most prominent fields here are culture and recreation and professional associations. These two account, respectively, for 19 percent and 7 percent of the workforce. By contrast, only 4 percent of the civil society organization workforce is engaged primarily in civic and advocacy activities and 2 percent in environmental protection. It is likely, however, that a substantial portion of the civil society organization workers employed in development organizations (7 percent of the workforce) are also engaged in empowerment activities along with some portion of the workers in other service fields.

- **Volunteer and paid staff roles differ markedly.** Volunteers and paid staff play markedly different roles in the operation of the civil society sector internationally.

**Figure 1.6.** Distribution of civil society sector workforce
by field and type of activity, 33 countries

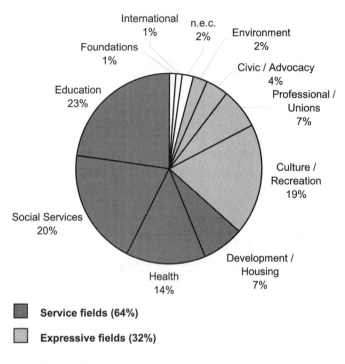

Service fields (64%)

Expressive fields (32%)

n.e.c.= not elsewhere classified
SOURCE: Johns Hopkins Comparative Nonprofit Sector Project

- In the first place, although both volunteers and paid staff are primarily engaged in service functions, paid staff are more heavily involved in these functions than are volunteers. Thus, while 73 percent of paid staff effort, on average, is devoted to service functions, only 53 percent of the volunteer effort is (see Figure 1.7).

- By contrast, only 24 percent of paid staff time is devoted to the expressive functions compared to 41 percent of volunteer time. Particularly noticeable is the role that volunteers play in cultural and recreational activity, which absorbs about 25 percent of all volunteer time as compared to 13 percent of paid staff time.

- Volunteers are also much more actively engaged than paid staff in civic and advocacy activity and environmental protection, which together absorb 10 percent of all volunteer effort. Moreover, if we were to include the 8 percent of all volunteer effort devoted to development organizations, which also often perform an empowerment role, the

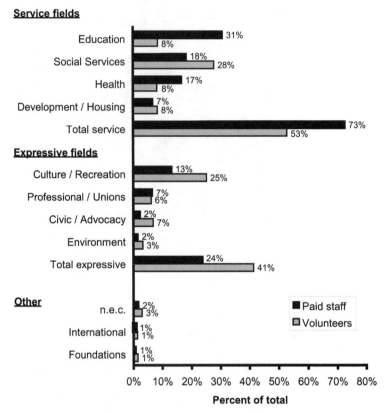

**Figure 1.7.** Distribution of civil society
organization workforce, by field, 33 countries

n.e.c.= not elsewhere classified
SOURCE: Johns Hopkins Comparative Nonprofit Sector Project

share of the volunteer effort going into expressive functions would
rise to nearly 50 percent.

– Even in their service functions, moreover, volunteers appear to concentrate their efforts in different fields than do paid staff. Thus, a sizable 28 percent of all volunteer effort is devoted to organizations providing social services, and 8 percent to organizations primarily engaged in development. The respective figures for paid staff are 18 and 7 percent. In fact, nearly half of all the work effort in these two fields is supplied by volunteers. Volunteers thus play an especially important role not only in maintaining the civil society sector's advocacy functions, but also in helping it maintain its long-standing commitment to social justice and development.

- **Inclusion of religious-worship organizations.** This picture of the principal activities of civil society organizations changes only partly when we take account of religious worship organizations. In the 27 countries for which we have religious workforce data, these organizations engage an average of 8 percent of the total civil society organization workforce, paid and volunteer. Including these workers boosts the expressive share of total civil society organization employment in these countries from 30 to 38 percent. As in other expressive fields, volunteers are an especially important part of this religious organization workforce. Reflecting this, religious congregations account for an average of only 5 percent of civil society paid staff time in these countries compared to 13 percent of the volunteer time.

- **Variations by country.** As reflected in Figure 1.8, the service functions of the civil society sector absorb the largest share of the civil society organization workforce in all but 6 of 33 countries. What is more, there does not seem to be a marked difference between the developed and the developing and transitional countries. In both groups, just over 60 percent of all civil society organization workers — paid and volunteer — work for service-oriented organizations.

  Beyond this aggregate level, however, some interesting variations are apparent in the structure of civil society employment between developed and developing and transitional countries:

  - First, in the developed countries, most of paid staff (nearly 80 percent) perform service functions while volunteer staff (49 percent) tend to focus on expressive functions. In the developing and transitional countries, however, paid and volunteer effort alike goes mostly into service functions (67 and 60 percent, respectively). This difference may result from the availability of government funding of the service functions of the third sector in the developed countries, a point we will return to below. By contrast, in the developing and transitional countries, less public funding is available, and these functions must be handled more fully by volunteers.

  - Second, the composition of the service functions performed by civil society organizations differs markedly between these two groups of countries. In particular, organizations engaged in development work absorb a significantly higher proportion of the civil society organization workforce in the developing and transitional countries than in the developed ones (9 percent vs. 5 percent) (see Appendix Table A.3). In the African countries, this figure reaches 18 percent of the civil society organization workforce. This is significant because, as we have noted, these development organizations often have a distinct empowerment orientation that differentiates them from the more assistance-oriented

**Figure 1.8.** Civil society organization workforce in service and expressive roles, by country

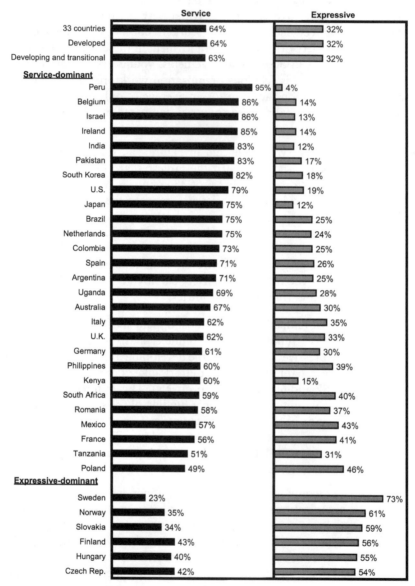

Percent of total workforce

SOURCE: Johns Hopkins Comparative Nonprofit Sector Project

service agencies in fields such as education and health. Coupled with the 29 percent of the civil society organization workforce occupied in expressive functions, this suggests an especially marked grassroots tilt to civil society activity in this region.

- **Two deviations.** Two other deviations from the general pattern of service dominance among the activities of civil society organizations are evident in the data presented in Figure 1.8. The first of these relates to the Nordic countries of Finland, Norway, and Sweden. The second relates to the countries of Central and Eastern Europe (the Czech Republic, Hungary, Slovakia, and, to a slightly lesser extent, Poland). In both of these groups of countries, organizations primarily engaged in expressive activities absorb a larger share of the civil society organization workforce than do those engaged in the service functions. As we will note more fully below, the most likely explanation for this is that in both groups of countries the state assumed a dominant position in both the financing and delivery of social welfare services, leaving less room for private, civil society organizations.

  - In Central Europe this was a product of the imposition of a Soviet-style regime in the aftermath of World War II. While this regime concentrated social welfare services in the hands of the state and discouraged, or prohibited, the emergence of independent civic organizations, it did sanction professional, sports, and recreational organizations, many of which survived into the post-Communist era.

  - In the Nordic countries, by contrast, a robust network of grassroots labor and social-movement organizations took shape during the late 19th century and pushed through a substantial program of social welfare protections financed and delivered by the state. This limited the need for active civil society involvement in service provision but left behind a vibrant heritage of citizen-based civil society activity in advocacy, recreation, and related expressive fields.

    While the structure of the civil society sector in these two groups of countries is similar, however, the scale of the sector differs widely. In particular, the civil society sector in the Central and Eastern European countries remained quite small nearly a decade after the overthrow of the Soviet-type regimes. By contrast, in the Nordic countries, a sizable civil society sector operates to this day, though it is largely staffed by volunteers and engaged in a variety of cultural, recreational, and expressive functions.

What these findings make clear is that the structure and character of the civil society sector differ markedly from country to country. More than that, these features provide an extraordinary reflection of a country's broader social, political, and cultural history.

**Figure 1.9.** Sources of civil society organization revenue, 34 countries

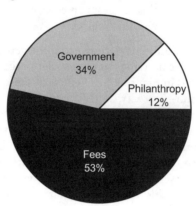

SOURCE: Johns Hopkins Comparative Nonprofit Sector Project

## 5. Not a substitute for government

A fifth key finding of this research relates to the financing of civil society organizations throughout the world. Perhaps the central conclusion here is that private philanthropy accounts for a smaller share of civil society organization revenue than is commonly thought. In particular:

- **Fees are the dominant source of revenue.** In the 34 countries for which revenue data are available,[21] over half (53 percent) of civil society organization income comes, on average, not from private philanthropy but from fees and charges for the services that these organizations provide and the related commercial income they receive from investments, dues, and other commercial sources (see Figure 1.9).

- **Significant public sector support.** Nor is philanthropy the second largest source of civil society organization revenue internationally. That distinction belongs, rather, to government or the public sector. An average of 34 percent of all civil society organization revenue comes from public sector sources, either through grants and contracts or reimbursement payments made by governmental agencies or quasi-nongovernmental organizations such as publicly financed social security and health agencies.

- **Limited role of private philanthropy.** Private giving from all sources — individuals, foundations, and corporations — accounts for a much smaller 12 percent of total civil society organization revenue in the countries we have examined, or approximately one-third as much as government and less than one-fourth as much as fees and charges.

- **Fee dominance holds in most fields.** This pattern of fee dominance in the revenue base of civil society organizations is fairly consistent among the different fields of activity, although the extent of the dominance does vary. More specifically:

  - *Fees are the largest income source in eight fields.* In 8 of the 12 fields of civil society organization activity identified in our classification system, fees are the major source of income. In six of these (professional organizations, culture, development and housing, foundations, education, and other) fees account for half or more of total revenue; and in two others (environment and civic and advocacy), fees constitute the largest single source of revenue even though they account for something less than half of the total (see Figure 1.10). This is understandable enough in the cases of professional organizations, and recreation and culture, where membership fees provide important sources of revenue. In the development field, the explanation lies in the inclusion of substantial numbers of housing organizations, many of which collect rent or other payments from occupants. So far as foundations are concerned, over half of their revenue (52 percent) derives from earnings on endowments, which are treated here as fee income. In the case of education organizations, the fees take the form of tuition payments, while for environmental and civic organizations they likely take the form of membership dues.[22]

  - *Public sector–dominant fields.* In 2 of the 12 major fields of civil society organization action — health and social services — the dominant source of income is not fees and charges but public sector support. In the case of health organizations, government provides half of the funds. Among social service organizations, government accounts for 42 percent of the funding, fees for 38 percent, and private philanthropy for 19 percent.

  - *Private philanthropy–dominant fields.* In only two fields — religion and international assistance — is private philanthropy the dominant source of income, and in one of these, international assistance, government support is a very close second (34 percent from government vs. 38 percent from philanthropy).

- **Variations among countries.** As with other facets of the civil society sector, the revenue structure varies considerably among countries, as shown in Figure 1.11.

  - *Fee-dominant countries.* In 24 of the 34 countries, fees are the major source of civil society organization revenue. Interestingly, this pattern is especially marked among the developing and transitional countries, which also have the smallest civil society sectors. Thus, the Philippines, Mexico, Kenya, Brazil, Argentina, South Korea, Colombia, and

**Figure 1.10.** Sources of civil society
organization revenue, by field, 33 countries

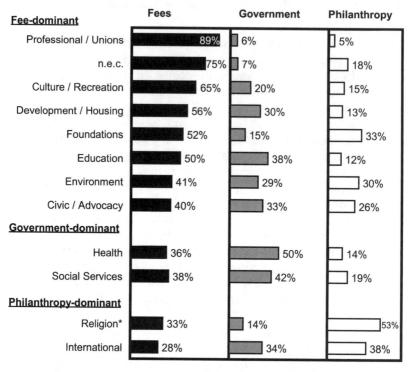

n.e.c.= not elsewhere classified
* 27-country average.
SOURCE: Johns Hopkins Comparative Nonprofit Sector Project

Peru have the highest levels of reliance on fees and charges. Indeed, for the developing and transitional countries as a whole, fees average 61 percent of civil society organization income, compared to only 45 percent for the developed countries. By contrast, government provides only 22 percent of civil society revenue in the developing and transitional countries compared to 48 percent in the developed ones. This paradoxical result underlines the dual character of the civil society sector in these countries, with a substantial portion of the sector providing services to a better-off clientele willing and able to pay for the often superior education, health, and related services that civil society organizations can offer; and a smaller development and empowerment-oriented component with relatively limited public sector and fee support.

**Figure 1.11.** Sources of civil society
organization revenue, by country

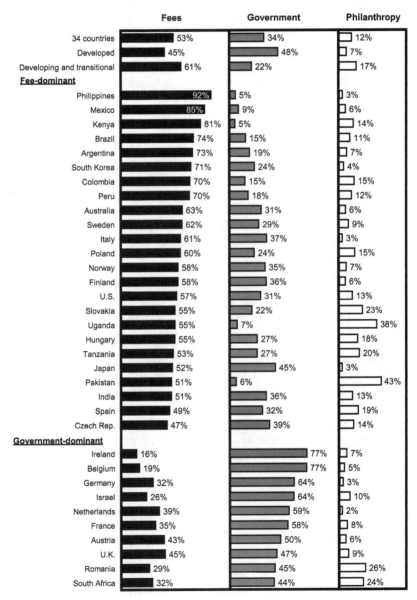

Percent of total revenue

SOURCE: Johns Hopkins Comparative Nonprofit Sector Project

- *Government-dominant pattern.* In the remaining countries, public sector support is the largest source of civil society organization revenue, accounting for over 60 percent of the total in four of them. This pattern is especially marked in the developed countries of Western Europe, at least those outside of Scandinavia — such as Ireland, Belgium, Germany, the Netherlands, France, Austria, and the United Kingdom — as well as in Israel, which follows a similar Western European social democratic tradition. What this makes clear is that outside of Scandinavia, the Western European welfare state has actually operated quite differently than is commonly assumed. Instead of creating a "classic" welfare state characterized by government provision of a full range of social welfare services, Western European countries more often created a welfare *partnership* in which the state finances welfare services but relies heavily on private civil society organizations for their delivery. Far from displacing civil society organizations, the growth of state-financed social welfare actually helped stimulate their growth. Not surprisingly, therefore, these countries have the largest civil society sectors of all the countries we have examined. Government thus emerges from these data as a major source of civil society organization development and growth.

- **Inclusion of volunteering boosts private philanthropy's share of revenue.** The picture of civil society organization revenue portrayed above changes somewhat when the contributions of time represented by volunteers are added to the contributions of money and treated as part of philanthropy.[23]

  - *Aggregate picture.* In the first place, as shown in Figure 1.12, the inclusion of volunteers in the revenue stream of civil society organizations boosts the average philanthropic share of total revenue from 12 to 31 percent. This reflects the fact that contributions of time, even when valued conservatively at the average wage in the fields in which volunteering occurs, are twice as large as contributions of money or material. With volunteer time included, private philanthropy climbs into second place in the support base of the civil society sector globally, ahead of public sector payments, though still behind fees and charges.

  - *Variations among fields.* The inclusion of volunteer time as part of private philanthropy makes private philanthropy the largest single source of civil society organization income in 7 of the 12 fields — religion (73 percent of income from contributions of time and money), international aid (60 percent), environment and civic/advocacy (57 percent each), foundations (56 percent), culture and recreation (45 percent), and social services (43 percent) (see Figure 1.13). These data make clear the substantial contribution that volunteer activity makes to the overall operation of the civil society sector, significantly expanding the

**Figure 1.12.** Sources of civil society
organization support (with volunteers), 34 countries

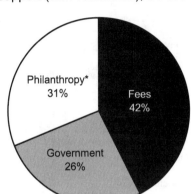

\* Includes the value of volunteer time.

SOURCE: Johns Hopkins Comparative Nonprofit Sector Project

resources the sector commands and making philanthropy a far more important source of sector support than cash revenue alone would suggest. This is particularly true with regard to the expressive functions such as religion, civic and advocacy activity, and recreation and culture where volunteer input is especially marked; but it holds as well in the service field most closely associated with the sector's social justice mission — social services.

- *Variations among countries.* The inclusion of volunteer time in the revenue base of the civil society sector also alters the picture of sector finance among countries, though less so. As noted in Figure 1.14, even with volunteer time included, fees remain the dominant source of civil society organization revenue in 18 of our 34 countries. What is more, the developing and transitional countries continue to head this list, with an average of 50 percent of their income from fees, compared to only 34 percent among the developed countries. At the same time, the number of countries in which philanthropy becomes the major source of civil society income swells from zero to nine. Especially notable is the sizable role of philanthropy in the Nordic countries of Sweden and Norway once volunteer inputs are included. This reflects the substantial volunteer presence in the workforce of the civil society sector in these countries mentioned earlier. Also notable, however, is the substantial boost that philanthropic support receives from the inclusion of volunteer effort in the five developing countries of Tanzania, Uganda,

**Figure 1.13.** Sources of civil society organization support,
by field, including volunteer time, 32 countries

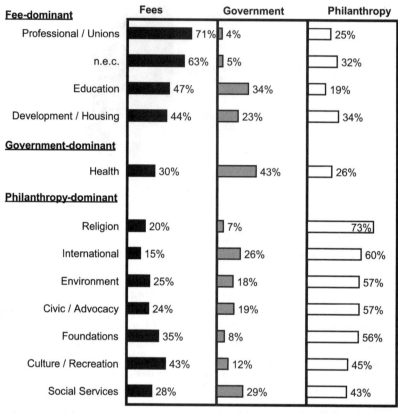

n.e.c.= not elsewhere classified
SOURCE: Johns Hopkins Comparative Nonprofit Sector Project

Pakistan, South Africa, and India with the Philippines not far behind. This suggests the substantial popular base for civil society activity in these countries.

## Regional Patterns

From the discussion so far, it should be clear that significant differences exist in the scope, structure, role, and financing of civil society activity in different countries. To an important extent, these differences are country-specific

## Figure 1.14. Sources of civil society organization support (with volunteers), by country

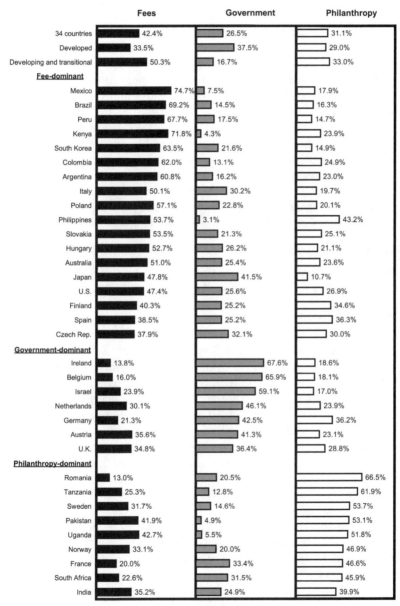

Percent of total revenue

SOURCE: Johns Hopkins Comparative Nonprofit Sector Project

and reflect the particular cultural, social, political, and economic histories of the different countries. At the same time, a number of patterns are also evident that go well beyond the simple distinction between developed and developing countries that we have drawn so far.[24] While any such grouping is necessarily somewhat arbitrary, we find it useful to divide the developed countries we have examined into four sociopolitical subgroups, and to divide the developing and transitional countries into three regional subgroups plus a fourth "other" category. While these groupings are partly geographical, they also reflect aspects of the social and political development of the respective countries. Table 1.6 summarizes the groupings that seem to emerge from the data.

The discussion below summarizes some of the salient features of the civil society sector in these clusters of countries and suggests some of the factors that may help explain them. Obviously, this brief overview cannot do justice to the complex set of factors that lies behind the shape of the civil society sector in each country, let alone each cluster; nonetheless it can at least suggest the rich insights and questions that can flow from the portrayal of the civil society sector made possible by our data.

## Developed countries

Among the more developed countries covered by our work, at least four more or less distinct patterns of civil society evolution seem apparent.

### The Anglo-Saxon cluster

The first of these patterns embraces three countries within our sample — the United Kingdom, the United States, and Australia — that share a high level of economic development and a common historical association with the Anglo-Saxon political and legal tradition. These countries have also historically shared a common approach to social policy characterized by a relatively small, hands-off role for the state and significant reliance instead on private, charitable activity. Although government involvement in social welfare provision in these countries has expanded in more recent decades — most notably in the United Kingdom in the aftermath of World War II — these have all been relatively reluctant welfare states that have retained a considerable level of reliance on private charity even as public social welfare involvement has grown.

Reflecting this tradition, civil society organizations occupy a significant role in these countries. Indeed, as shown in Figure 1.15, this group of countries boasts the largest average civil society sector workforce of any of the clusters we have identified — an average of 8.2 percent of the economically active population, or nearly double the all-country average.

A number of other features of the civil society sector in these countries are also notable. One is the sizable volunteer presence, almost twice the all-country average (see Table 1.7). A second is the heavy focus of these

**Table 1.6.** Sociopolitical clusters of countries

| Developed countries | Developing and transitional countries |
|---|---|
| **Anglo-Saxon** | **Latin America** |
| Australia | Argentina |
| United Kingdom | Brazil |
| United States | Colombia |
| | Mexico |
| **Nordic Welfare States** | Peru |
| Finland | |
| Norway | **Africa** |
| Sweden | Kenya |
| | South Africa |
| **European-Style Welfare Partnerships** | Tanzania |
| | Uganda |
| Austria | |
| Belgium | **Central and Eastern Europe** |
| France | Czech Republic |
| Germany | Hungary |
| Ireland | Poland |
| Israel | Romania |
| Italy | Slovakia |
| Netherlands | |
| Spain | **Other Developing** |
| | Egypt |
| **Asian Industrialized** | India |
| Japan | Morocco |
| South Korea | Pakistan |
| | Philippines |

organizations on essentially service functions (especially among paid staff), though the exact service field in which they concentrate differs from country to country — health services in the United States and education in the United Kingdom and Australia.

Finally, the civil society sector in these countries also has a distinctive revenue structure. Contrary to popular mythologies, private charity constitutes a relatively small share of total civil society organization revenue even in these countries — 9 percent overall compared to an overall average of 12 percent in our 34-country sample. The largest source of civil society organization income in this set of countries is fees and charges, which is above the all-country average, though the United Kingdom deviates from

**Figure 1.15.** Civil society organization workforce as a share of the economically active population, by country cluster

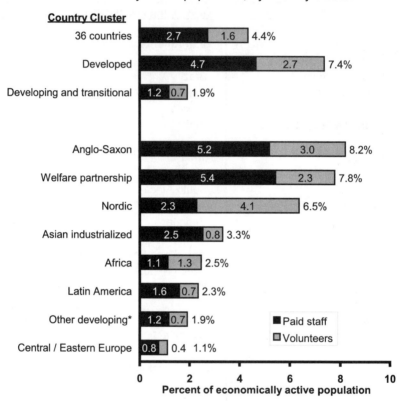

* Egypt, India, Morocco, Pakistan, and the Philippines
SOURCE: Johns Hopkins Comparative Nonprofit Sector Project

this pattern due to its significant departure from the traditional Anglo-Saxon or liberal pattern in the immediate aftermath of World War II when a partial welfare state was created there. The United Kingdom thus represents a hybrid between the traditional Anglo-Saxon pattern and the continental European one, as we will see more fully below.

The overall contours of civil society sector revenue do not change in these countries when volunteer effort is factored into the equation. Volunteer inputs boost the philanthropy share of income from 9 to 26 percent, but philanthropy still lags behind fees and public sector support.

*Nordic welfare states*

A quite different civil society sector reality is evident in the three Scandinavian countries of Finland, Norway, and Sweden. As reflected in Figure 1.15

**Table 1.7.** Anglo-Saxon pattern

| | All countries* | Anglo - Saxon | Australia | U.K. | U.S. |
|---|---|---|---|---|---|
| **Workforce** [1] | | | | | |
| FTE paid | **2.7%** | **5.2%** | 4.4% | 4.8% | 6.3% |
| FTE volunteers | **1.6%** | **3.0%** | 1.9% | 3.6% | 3.5% |
| FTE total | **4.4%** | **8.2%** | 6.3% | 8.5% | 9.8% |
| **Composition of workforce** [2,4] | | | | | |
| Service | **64%** | **69%** | 67% | 62% | 79% |
| Expressive | **32%** | **27%** | 30% | 33% | 19% |
| Other | **4%** | **3%** | 3% | 5% | 2% |
| **Cash revenues** [3,4] | | | | | |
| Fees | **53%** | **55%** | 63% | 45% | 57% |
| Government | **34%** | **36%** | 31% | 47% | 31% |
| Philanthropy | **12%** | **9%** | 6% | 9% | 13% |
| **Total support (with volunteers)** [4,5] | | | | | |
| Fees | **42%** | **44%** | 51% | 35% | 47% |
| Government | **26%** | **29%** | 25% | 36% | 26% |
| Philanthropy | **31%** | **26%** | 24% | 29% | 27% |

\* Workforce: 36 countries; composition: 33 countries;
revenues and total support: 34 countries

[1] As percent of economically active population

[2] As percent of total nonprofit workforce (paid staff and volunteers)

[3] As percent of total nonprofit cash revenues

[4] Percentages may not add to 100% due to rounding

[5] As percent of total cash and volunteer support

SOURCE: Johns Hopkins Comparative Nonprofit Sector Project

and Table 1.8, the civil society sector in these countries is larger than the all-country average, but this is largely due to the sizable volunteer workforce that the sector mobilizes. By contrast, the paid civil society organization workforce — at 2.3 percent of the economically active population — is below the all-country average. This reflects the broad welfare-state policies adopted in these countries in the first half of the 20th century and the limited reliance placed on private philanthropy and private civil society organizations to deliver basic social and human services. But this does not mean that no civil society sector exists in these countries, as is sometimes supposed. Rather, a rich social movement history has long characterized

### Table 1.8. Nordic pattern

| | All countries* | Nordic | Finland | Norway | Sweden |
|---|---|---|---|---|---|
| **Workforce** [1] | | | | | |
| FTE paid | **2.7%** | **2.3%** | 2.4% | 2.7% | 1.7% |
| FTE volunteers | **1.6%** | **4.1%** | 2.8% | 4.4% | 5.1% |
| FTE total | **4.4%** | **6.5%** | 5.3% | 7.2% | 7.1% |
| **Composition of workforce** [2,4] | | | | | |
| Service | **64%** | **34%** | 43% | 35% | 23% |
| Expressive | **32%** | **64%** | 56% | 61% | 73% |
| Other | **4%** | **3%** | 1% | 3% | 4% |
| **Cash revenues** [3,4] | | | | | |
| Fees | **53%** | **59%** | 58% | 58% | 62% |
| Government | **34%** | **33%** | 36% | 35% | 29% |
| Philanthropy | **12%** | **7%** | 6% | 7% | 9% |
| **Total support (with volunteers)** [4,5] | | | | | |
| Fees | **42%** | **35%** | 40% | 33% | 32% |
| Government | **26%** | **20%** | 25% | 20% | 15% |
| Philanthropy | **31%** | **45%** | 35% | 47% | 54% |

\* Workforce: 36 countries; composition: 33 countries; revenues and total support: 34 countries

[1] As percent of economically active population

[2] As percent of total nonprofit workforce (paid staff and volunteers)

[3] As percent of total nonprofit cash revenues

[4] Percentages may not add to 100% due to rounding

[5] As percent of total cash and volunteer support

SOURCE: Johns Hopkins Comparative Nonprofit Sector Project

these countries, giving rise to strong advocacy and professional organizations. What is more, voluntary activity has deep roots in Nordic sports and recreational life.[25] This explains the sizable volunteer component of the civil society sector in the Nordic countries (4.1 percent of the economically active population vs. the all-country average of 1.6 percent). Perhaps because of this also, the revenue structure of the Nordic civil society sector differs considerably from the all-country average, at least with volunteers included. With volunteer input excluded, fees, most likely in the form of membership dues, dominate the fiscal structure of the civil society sector in these countries, with government support in second place. Once volunteer input is factored in, however, philanthropy — most of it contributions of time — jumps into first place, accounting for 45 percent of the support. In short, the Nordic pattern features a large civil society sector staffed mainly by volunteers and engaged mostly in expressive rather than service functions.

### European-style welfare partnerships

Elsewhere in Western Europe, the structure, composition, and financing of the civil society sector differ markedly from both the classic Nordic pattern and the Anglo-Saxon one. As reflected in Figure 1.15 and Table 1.9, the civil society sector in these countries is generally quite large, averaging 7.8 percent of the economically active population and exceeding 10 percent in three of the countries (Belgium, Ireland, and the Netherlands). Much of this labor force is paid, moreover. In fact, the paid civil society organization labor force in these countries is higher on average than in any of the other groupings (5.4 percent of the economically active population vs. 2.7 percent for the all-country average).

The ability of the civil society sector to support this labor force is due, moreover, to the substantial levels of public sector support available to it. Nearly 60 percent of civil society sector revenue, on average, comes from the public sector in these countries, well above the all-country average. In fact, the public sector accounts for 50 percent or more of civil society organization revenue in seven of these countries (Austria, Belgium, France, Germany, Ireland, Israel, and the Netherlands). Consistent with this general pattern, moreover, most of the sizable civil society organization labor force in these countries is engaged in service functions, particularly social welfare services such as education (25 percent), social services (23 percent), and health (20 percent).

These features reflect the distinctive way in which the welfare state evolved in these countries. As in the Nordic countries, popular pressures for social welfare protections led to more extensive, and earlier, government involvement in the social welfare field than in the Anglo-Saxon countries. Though this is commonly viewed as having created a "classic" welfare state, something else seems to have occurred in fact. In large part due to the power of organized religion, particularly the Catholic Church, the state chose, or was persuaded, to funnel social welfare protections extensively through private, voluntary groups, many of them religiously affiliated, rather than delivering the services itself.

The result was an extensive pattern of partnership between the state and the organized civil society sector. In Germany, this partnership was formalized in the principle of "subsidiarity" built into the basic social welfare laws. Under this principle, state authorities are obliged to turn first to the "free welfare associations" to solve social problems. In the Netherlands, a

**Table 1.9.** European-style welfare partnership pattern

| | All countries* | Welfare partnership | Austria | Belgium | France | Germany | Ireland | Israel | Italy | Netherlands | Spain |
|---|---|---|---|---|---|---|---|---|---|---|---|
| **Workforce [1]** | | | | | | | | | | | |
| FTE paid | **2.7%** | **5.4%** | 3.8% | 8.6% | 3.7% | 3.5% | 8.3% | 6.6% | 2.3% | 9.2% | 2.8% |
| FTE volunteers | **1.6%** | **2.3%** | 1.1% | 2.3% | 3.7% | 2.3% | 2.1% | 1.4% | 1.5% | 5.1% | 1.5% |
| FTE total | **4.4%** | **7.8%** | 4.9% | 10.9% | 7.6% | 5.9% | 10.4% | 8.0% | 3.8% | 14.4% | 4.3% |
| **Composition of workforce [2,4]** | | | | | | | | | | | |
| Service | **64%** | **73%** | - | 86% | 56% | 61% | 85% | 86% | 62% | 75% | 71% |
| Expressive | **32%** | **24%** | - | 14% | 41% | 30% | 14% | 13% | 35% | 24% | 26% |
| Other | **4%** | **3%** | - | 1% | 3% | 9% | 1% | 2% | 3% | 1% | 3% |
| **Cash revenues [3,4]** | | | | | | | | | | | |
| Fees | **53%** | **35%** | 43% | 19% | 35% | 32% | 16% | 26% | 61% | 39% | 49% |
| Government | **34%** | **58%** | 50% | 77% | 58% | 64% | 77% | 64% | 37% | 59% | 32% |
| Philanthropy | **12%** | **7%** | 6% | 5% | 8% | 3% | 7% | 10% | 3% | 2% | 19% |
| **Total support (with volunteers) [4,5]** | | | | | | | | | | | |
| Fees | **42%** | **28%** | 36% | 16% | 20% | 21% | 14% | 24% | 50% | 30% | 38% |
| Government | **26%** | **46%** | 41% | 66% | 33% | 43% | 68% | 59% | 30% | 46% | 25% |
| Philanthropy | **31%** | **27%** | 23% | 18% | 47% | 36% | 19% | 17% | 20% | 24% | 36% |

* Workforce: 36 countries; composition: 33 countries; revenues and total support: 34 countries
[1] As percent of economically active population
[2] As percent of total nonprofit workforce (paid staff and volunteers)
[3] As percent of total nonprofit cash revenues
[4] Percentages may not add to 100% due to rounding
[5] As percent of total cash and volunteer support
SOURCE: Johns Hopkins Comparative Nonprofit Sector Project

similar pattern emerged out of the conflict between secularists and those committed to value-based education in the early 20th century. The result was a compromise under which the state financed universal education but through payments to private nonprofit schools, many of them with religious or ideological orientations. This arrangement was then extended to other social benefits, creating a widespread pattern of "pillarization" under which state support was provided to various "pillars" of private institutions. This pattern is also evident in Israel, which was strongly influenced by the Western European social democratic tradition, but which has also had an influential religious community as well as a labor movement accustomed to handling important social welfare functions. France presents an interesting variant on the general theme: though it initially followed a path much closer to the Nordic one, the decentralization policies introduced there in the early 1980s led to a significant growth of civil society institutions when local governments found themselves responsible for a variety of human service functions for which they were not staffed and turned to civil society organizations for assistance.[26]

The upshot is a distinctive Western European–style welfare partnership pattern characterized by a large civil society sector staffed mostly by paid employees, heavily engaged in service provision, and extensively financed by tax revenue. To be sure, this pattern is not equally present in all of the Western European countries, as the cases of Spain and Italy show.[27] Nevertheless, it is the dominant pattern in this region.

### The Asian industrialized model

Japan and South Korea have pursued a different path in the evolution of their civil society sectors as compared with either the Anglo-Saxon or Western European countries, though there are also important differences between them in the extent to which they have moved along this path. The civil society sector in these countries is considerably smaller than in the other advanced, industrial societies, engaging only 3.3 percent of the economically active population on average compared to the all-country average of 4.4 percent, though the overall scale is much larger in Japan than in South Korea (see Figure 1.15 and Table 1.10). To the extent that civil society activity exists in these countries, moreover, it is heavily service oriented, much of it in the health and education fields. Reflecting this, fees are the dominant source of civil society organization revenue, accounting for 62 percent on average, though in Japan government support is a close second.

This pattern reflects the distinctive path that industrialization has taken in both of these countries, and in much of Asia more generally. In particular, government has aggressively promoted rapid industrialization while supplying the bare minimum of social protections and generally discouraging, or at least not actively promoting, the development of civil society institutions

**Table 1.10.** Asian industrialized pattern

| | All countries* | Asian industrialized | Japan | South Korea |
|---|---|---|---|---|
| **Workforce** [1] | | | | |
| FTE paid | 2.7% | 2.5% | 3.2% | 1.9% |
| FTE volunteers | 1.6% | 0.8% | 1.0% | 0.6% |
| FTE total | 4.4% | 3.3% | 4.2% | 2.4% |
| **Composition of workforce** [2,4] | | | | |
| Service | 64% | 78% | 75% | 82% |
| Expressive | 32% | 15% | 12% | 18% |
| Other | 4% | 7% | 13% | 0% |
| **Cash revenues** [3,4] | | | | |
| Fees | 53% | 62% | 52% | 71% |
| Government | 34% | 35% | 45% | 24% |
| Philanthropy | 12% | 3% | 3% | 4% |
| **Total support (with volunteers)** [4,5] | | | | |
| Fees | 42% | 56% | 48% | 64% |
| Government | 26% | 32% | 42% | 22% |
| Philanthropy | 31% | 13% | 11% | 15% |

\* Workforce: 36 countries; composition: 33 countries; revenues and total support: 34 countries

[1] As percent of economically active population

[2] As percent of total nonprofit workforce (paid staff and volunteers)

[3] As percent of total nonprofit cash revenues

[4] Percentages may not add to 100% due to rounding

[5] As percent of total cash and volunteer support

SOURCE: Johns Hopkins Comparative Nonprofit Sector Project

through which citizens could mobilize effective protests. Although some private charitable organizations took root in these countries, they emerged in large part from the work of Western missionaries, chiefly in the fields of education, health, and social services. The resulting institutions have had to rely heavily on private fees to survive, however, except where government agencies have embraced them to help fulfill public priorities. In these latter situations, however, government bureaucracies have exerted an unusual level of control over the institutions to make sure they adhere to authorized governmental priorities.[28] The result has been a generally small and passive civil society sector, though recent years have witnessed important new stirrings.

## Developing and transitional countries

Civil society sector development has taken a somewhat different course in the developing and transitional countries of Africa, South Asia, the Middle East, Latin America, and Central and Eastern Europe. In some respects, the development of the civil society sector in these countries has been more robust in recent years than in any of the other regions covered here, the product of expanding communications technologies, frustrations with state-centered approaches to development, and new efforts to empower the rural poor.[29] Despite this, however, civil society organizations still engage a smaller proportion of the economically active populations in these countries than in the more developed regions of the world. One reason for this may be the rural character of these societies and the resulting retention of traditional forms of social assistance relying on clan and family relationships rather than voluntary organization. To the extent that such relationships still operate, the need for more institutionalized structures, whether formal or informal, is reduced. So, too, traditional clientelistic systems of social control and modern authoritarian political regimes have often conspired to limit the space available for the development of independent organizations that might threaten the social and political status quo. With historically small urban middle class populations and large numbers of marginalized rural poor, these countries have not historically provided a fertile soil for the growth of civil society institutions.

Reflecting these forces, the average size of the civil society sector in the developing and transitional countries is well below that of the all-country average (1.9 vs. 4.4 percent of the economically active population), as reflected in Figure 1.15. Interestingly, the volunteer component of the civil society organization workforce in these countries is also well below the all-country average, suggesting that the absence of paid staff hinders rather than helps the mobilization of volunteers.

Another distinguishing feature of the civil society sector in these countries is the relatively low level of government support available to it (22 percent vs. 34 percent for all countries) (see Table 1.11). These organizations therefore have to depend more heavily on fees and private philanthropy than their counterparts elsewhere, with much of the latter coming from international sources. Even with volunteer effort included, fees remain the dominant source of civil society organization income in these countries.

While the civil society sectors in the developing and transitional countries share a number of common features, they also differ from each other in important respects. These differences are clearly apparent at the country level, but significant regional variations are also apparent.

**Table 1.11.** Developing and transitional country pattern

| | All countries* | Developing and transitional |
|---|---|---|
| **Workforce** [1] | | |
| FTE paid | 2.7% | 1.2% |
| FTE volunteers | 1.6% | 0.7% |
| FTE total | 4.4% | 1.9% |
| **Composition of workforce** [2, 4] | | |
| Service | 64% | 63% |
| Expressive | 32% | 32% |
| Other | 4% | 5% |
| **Cash revenues** [3, 4] | | |
| Fees | 53% | 61% |
| Government | 34% | 22% |
| Philanthropy | 12% | 17% |
| **Total support (with volunteers)** [4, 5] | | |
| Fees | 42% | 50% |
| Government | 26% | 17% |
| Philanthropy | 31% | 33% |

\* Workforce: 36 countries; composition: 33 countries; revenues and total support: 34 countries
[1] As percent of economically active population
[2] As percent of total nonprofit workforce (paid staff and volunteers)
[3] As percent of total nonprofit cash revenues
[4] Percentages may not add to 100% due to rounding
[5] As percent of total cash and volunteer support
SOURCE: Johns Hopkins Comparative Nonprofit Sector Project

## The Latin American model

The civil society sector in Latin America is slightly larger than the developing and transitional country average, though this is largely due to the inclusion of Argentina, which has a civil society sector on a par with that in many Western European countries (see Table 1.12). Volunteers play an unusually small part in the workforce of the Latin American civil society sector, accounting for 0.7 percent of the economically active population on average. This may be related to the role that civil society organizations play in this region. That role, as reflected in the data, is heavily oriented to service functions, and particularly education, which absorbs a third of the total civil

**Table 1.12.** Latin American pattern

| | All countries* | Developing and transitional | Latin America | Argentina | Brazil | Colombia | Mexico | Peru |
|---|---|---|---|---|---|---|---|---|
| **Workforce** [1] | | | | | | | | |
| FTE paid | 2.7% | 1.2% | 1.6% | 2.9% | 1.4% | 1.8% | 0.3% | 1.5% |
| FTE volunteers | 1.6% | 0.7% | 0.7% | 1.9% | 0.2% | 0.6% | 0.1% | 0.9% |
| FTE total | 4.4% | 1.9% | 2.3% | 4.8% | 1.6% | 2.4% | 0.4% | 2.5% |
| **Composition of workforce** [2,4] | | | | | | | | |
| Service | 64% | 63% | 74% | 71% | 75% | 73% | 57% | 95% |
| Expressive | 32% | 32% | 24% | 25% | 25% | 25% | 43% | 4% |
| Other | 4% | 5% | 2% | 4% | 1% | 2% | 1% | 1% |
| **Cash revenues** [3,4] | | | | | | | | |
| Fees | 53% | 61% | 74% | 73% | 74% | 70% | 85% | 70% |
| Government | 34% | 22% | 15% | 19% | 15% | 15% | 9% | 18% |
| Philanthropy | 12% | 17% | 10% | 7% | 11% | 15% | 6% | 12% |
| **Total support (with volunteers)** [4,5] | | | | | | | | |
| Fees | 42% | 50% | 67% | 61% | 69% | 62% | 75% | 68% |
| Government | 26% | 17% | 14% | 16% | 15% | 13% | 7% | 18% |
| Philanthropy | 31% | 33% | 19% | 23% | 16% | 25% | 18% | 15% |

* Workforce: 36 countries; composition: 33 countries; revenues and total support: 34 countries
[1] As percent of economically active population
[2] As percent of total nonprofit workforce (paid staff and volunteers)
[3] As percent of total nonprofit cash revenues
[4] Percentages may not add to 100% due to rounding
[5] As percent of total cash and volunteer support
SOURCE: Johns Hopkins Comparative Nonprofit Sector Project

society organization workforce and 44 percent of the paid workers. While some of this represents religious education open to all, a significant portion also reflects elite private education. Reflecting this, fees and charges constitute an unusually large share (74 percent) of total civil society sector revenue in Latin America. Even with the value of volunteering included in the revenue base of the region's civil society organizations, fees account for two-thirds of the support. By contrast, government support — at 14 percent of the revenue — is unusually low, making it difficult for civil society organizations to extend their reach to those in greatest need. While there is clear evidence of the emergence of advocacy and empowerment-oriented organizations, these institutions maintain a wary coexistence with the more substantial educational institutions and church-related assistance agencies.

### The African pattern

A considerably different civil society reality is evident in the countries of southern and eastern Africa (South Africa, Kenya, Tanzania, and Uganda). The civil society sector appears quite robust in these countries, engaging as much as 3.4 percent of the economically active population in South Africa and averaging 2.5 percent overall, well above the developing and transitional country average (see Table 1.13). What is more, volunteers account for over half of the civil society organization workforce in this region, perhaps reflecting the strong traditions of informal ties along tribal and village lines that have long characterized the region. Also notable is the composition of the civil society sector workforce in southern and eastern Africa. Although 60 percent of this workforce is engaged in service activities — about on a par with the all-country average — a large component of this (18 percent of the workforce) works with development organizations, which tend to be more advocacy and empowerment-oriented than traditional charitable service institutions. Coupled with the 29 percent of other civil society organization workers engaged in essentially expressive functions in Africa, this means that nearly half of the civil society organization workforce in Africa has some empowerment or other expressive function, well above the all-country average. This suggests a substantially larger empowerment character to the African civil society sector, perhaps as a byproduct of the struggle for independence from colonial rule or, in the case of South Africa, against the apartheid regime.

The scale of the African civil society sector remains constrained, however, by the limited financial support it has available. Particularly notable, as in other developing regions, has been the limited availability of public sector funding, which has played so significant a role in the growth of civil society organizations in the developed world. Only 21 percent of civil society organization revenue comes from government in the African countries, although here wide variations are evident among countries, with South

## Table 1.13. African pattern

| | All countries* | Developing and transitional | Africa | Kenya | South Africa | Tanzania | Uganda |
|---|---|---|---|---|---|---|---|
| **Workforce** [1] | | | | | | | |
| FTE paid | 2.7% | 1.2% | 1.1% | 1.3% | 1.8% | 0.5% | 0.9% |
| FTE volunteers | 1.6% | 0.7% | 1.3% | 0.8% | 1.6% | 1.5% | 1.3% |
| FTE total | 4.4% | 1.9% | 2.5% | 2.1% | 3.4% | 2.1% | 2.3% |
| **Composition of workforce** [2,4] | | | | | | | |
| Service | 64% | 63% | 60% | 60% | 59% | 51% | 69% |
| Expressive | 32% | 32% | 29% | 15% | 40% | 31% | 28% |
| Other | 4% | 5% | 12% | 25% | 0% | 17% | 4% |
| **Cash revenues** [3,4] | | | | | | | |
| Fees | 53% | 61% | 55% | 81% | 32% | 53% | 55% |
| Government | 34% | 22% | 21% | 5% | 44% | 27% | 7% |
| Philanthropy | 12% | 17% | 24% | 14% | 24% | 20% | 38% |
| **Total support (with volunteers)** [4,5] | | | | | | | |
| Fees | 42% | 50% | 41% | 72% | 23% | 25% | 43% |
| Government | 26% | 17% | 14% | 4% | 31% | 13% | 6% |
| Philanthropy | 31% | 33% | 46% | 24% | 46% | 62% | 52% |

* Workforce: 36 countries; composition: 33 countries; revenues and total support: 34 countries

[1] As percent of economically active population
[2] As percent of total nonprofit workforce (paid staff and volunteers)
[3] As percent of total nonprofit cash revenues
[4] Percentages may not add to 100% due to rounding
[5] As percent of total cash and volunteer support
SOURCE: Johns Hopkins Comparative Nonprofit Sector Project

African organizations recording over 40 percent of their funding from public sources, and Kenyan organizations recording 5 percent. However, private philanthropy surges into first place as a source of revenue once the value of volunteer time is included, at least in Uganda, South Africa, and Tanzania. These data suggest the considerable popular support that the civil society sector has generated in southern and eastern Africa and the substantial record of self-help it has helped to foster.

## The Central and Eastern European model

Central and Eastern Europe exhibits yet another pattern of civil society sector development, one reflecting the powerful influence on these societies and their civil society sectors of the Soviet-style regimes that came to power in the aftermath of World War II. Most notable, perhaps, is the quite small scale of the civil society sector in these countries — engaging only one-fourth as large a proportion of the economically active population as the all-country average. Indeed, as shown in Figure 1.15, the civil society sector in these countries is smaller than in any of the other regions we have examined, including the developing countries of Africa and Latin America. Also notable is the relatively large presence of expressive activity within what little civil society sectors exist in these countries. This is likely a reflection of the social welfare policies of the Soviet-era governments, which relied on direct provision of the most important social services by the "workers' state" and discouraged reliance on private voluntary organizations, including those affiliated with religious groups. The civil society sector in these countries was limited largely to sports, recreational, and professional associations, which remained under state control. In the aftermath of the collapse of the state socialist regimes, a number of these sanctioned organizations were able to make the transition into nonprofit status, often with the aid of captured state resources (buildings, equipment, and occasionally subsidies), and their relatively sizable presence is reflected in the data.

One particularly ironic byproduct of this peculiar history of civil society development in Central and Eastern Europe is the relatively high level of reliance on philanthropic support on the part of the region's civil society organizations. Ironically, despite its socialist past, philanthropy constitutes a larger share of the revenue of civil society organizations in this region than in most other regions (20 percent vs. an all-country average of 12 percent) (see Table 1.14). There are several factors accounting for this. When state enterprises were transformed into private firms, they spun off into civil society organizations many of the health and recreational services they previously provided to their workers free of cost, but they continued some degree of financial or in-kind support to these activities. Since these state enterprises became private firms, however, this support shows up in our data as private charity. What is more, many public health care institutions established foundations to collect "donations" in lieu of fees for services

**Table 1.14.** Central and Eastern European pattern

| | All countries* | Developing and transitional | Central / Eastern Europe | Czech Rep. | Hungary | Poland | Romania | Slovakia |
|---|---|---|---|---|---|---|---|---|
| **Workforce** [1] | | | | | | | | |
| FTE paid | **2.7%** | **1.2%** | **0.8%** | 1.3% | 0.9% | 0.6% | 0.4% | 0.6% |
| FTE volunteers | **1.6%** | **0.7%** | **0.4%** | 0.7% | 0.2% | 0.2% | 0.4% | 0.2% |
| FTE total | **4.4%** | **1.9%** | **1.1%** | 2.0% | 1.1% | 0.8% | 0.8% | 0.8% |
| **Composition of workforce** [2,4] | | | | | | | | |
| Service | **64%** | **63%** | **45%** | 42% | 40% | 49% | 58% | 34% |
| Expressive | **32%** | **32%** | **50%** | 54% | 55% | 46% | 37% | 59% |
| Other | **4%** | **5%** | **5%** | 4% | 5% | 4% | 5% | 8% |
| **Cash revenues** [3,4] | | | | | | | | |
| Fees | **53%** | **61%** | **49%** | 47% | 55% | 60% | 29% | 55% |
| Government | **34%** | **22%** | **31%** | 39% | 27% | 24% | 45% | 22% |
| Philanthropy | **12%** | **17%** | **20%** | 14% | 18% | 15% | 26% | 23% |
| **Total support (with volunteers)** [4,5] | | | | | | | | |
| Fees | **42%** | **50%** | **43%** | 38% | 53% | 57% | 13% | 54% |
| Government | **26%** | **17%** | **25%** | 32% | 26% | 23% | 21% | 21% |
| Philanthropy | **31%** | **33%** | **33%** | 30% | 21% | 20% | 66% | 25% |

* Workforce: 36 countries; composition: 33 countries; revenues and total support: 34 countries

[1] As percent of economically active population

[2] As percent of total nonprofit workforce (paid staff and volunteers)

[3] As percent of total nonprofit cash revenues

[4] Percentages may not add to 100% due to rounding

[5] As percent of total cash and volunteer support

SOURCE: Johns Hopkins Comparative Nonprofit Sector Project

(which they could not legally charge). Finally, during the transition period, Eastern Europe was a major recipient of foreign assistance, often distributed by private organizations, some of which supported activities of civil society organizations.

### Other developing countries

The remaining five developing countries — Egypt, India, Morocco, Pakistan, and the Philippines — do not truly form a coherent grouping. To be sure, three of them are heavily Islamic countries with significant recent histories of authoritarian rule. Unfortunately, however, the data available on two of them — Egypt and Morocco — are not sufficient to permit us to draw any but the most tentative conclusions about what this pattern might entail. What does seem clear, at least from the data on India and Pakistan, and the limited data available on Morocco, is that the civil society sector in these countries is relatively small, well below that in the developing and transitional countries as a whole. This is consistent with a history of authoritarian politics and a cultural tradition that fuses political and religious authority, leaving little room for the emergence of a truly autonomous sphere of organized citizen activity. The India and Pakistan data, which show an unusually high involvement of civil society organizations in service activities and relatively limited involvement in expressive functions, also support this interpretation. Although Egypt seems to deviate from this pattern as reflected in the rather sizable 2.8 percent of the economically active population engaged in civil society activity there, much of this employment represents state workers seconded to civil society social welfare organizations (see Table 1.15). In fact, the Egyptian state has maintained a highly distrustful attitude toward its civil society institutions.[30] One other notable feature of the civil society sector in these countries, at least as illustrated by Pakistan, is the unusual level of private philanthropic support that the country's limited civil society organizations receive. Part of this may result from foreign gifts channeled through institutions such as the Aga Khan Foundation. But part of it likely reflects the strong Islamic tradition of *zakat,* or charitable tithing, which puts a special premium on charitable donations in Islamic society.[31] By contrast, the level of private philanthropy in India is rather low, while the size of government support is on a par with the all-country average.

The Philippines differs markedly from the other four countries in this grouping. A heavily Catholic country with a long history of colonization by major European powers, the Philippines resembles the Latin American countries examined above. Not surprisingly, therefore, its civil society sector also bears striking resemblance to the Latin American pattern. This is evident in the concentration of the Philippines civil society organization workforce in services, particularly education (66 percent of paid staff vs. the Latin American average of 44 percent), the prominence of fees and service charges in civil society revenues (92 percent vs. the Latin American average of 74 percent),

**Table 1.15.** Other developing countries

| | All countries* | Developing and transitional | Egypt | India | Morocco | Pakistan | Philippines |
|---|---|---|---|---|---|---|---|
| **Workforce** [1] | | | | | | | |
| FTE paid | 2.7% | 1.2% | 2.7% | 0.6% | 0.7% | 0.6% | 0.7% |
| FTE volunteer | 1.6% | 0.7% | 0.1% | 0.8% | 0.8% | 0.4% | 1.2% |
| FTE total | 4.4% | 1.9% | 2.8% | 1.4% | 1.5% | 1.0% | 1.9% |
| **Composition of workforce** [2,4] | | | | | | | |
| Service | 64% | 63% | - | 83% | - | 83% | 60% |
| Expressive | 32% | 32% | - | 12% | - | 17% | 39% |
| Other | 4% | 5% | - | 5% | - | 0% | 1% |
| **Cash revenues** [3,4] | | | | | | | |
| Fees | 53% | 61% | - | 51% | - | 51% | 92% |
| Government | 34% | 22% | - | 36% | - | 6% | 5% |
| Philanthropy | 12% | 17% | - | 13% | - | 43% | 3% |
| **Total support (with volunteers)** [4,5] | | | | | | | |
| Fees | 42% | 50% | - | 35% | - | 42% | 54% |
| Government | 26% | 17% | - | 25% | - | 5% | 3% |
| Philanthropy | 31% | 33% | - | 40% | - | 53% | 43% |

* Workforce: 36 countries; composition: 33 countries; revenues and total support: 34 countries

[1] As percent of economically active population

[2] As percent of total nonprofit workforce (paid staff and volunteers)

[3] As percent of total nonprofit cash revenues

[4] Percentages may not add to 100% due to rounding

[5] As percent of total cash and volunteer support

SOURCE: Johns Hopkins Comparative Nonprofit Sector Project

and the heavy reliance on volunteers in social service provision (84 percent of the total workforce in this field vs. the Latin American average of 56 percent). At the same time, the Philippines civil society sector also reflects the country's recent history of citizen protest against corrupt and authoritarian government as manifested in the above-average civil society organization workforce engaged in expressive functions.

## Conclusions and Implications

The civil society sector is thus a major social and economic force in countries throughout the world. Once considered to be present only in a handful of countries, these organizations turn out to be a significant presence in virtually every country and region.

At the same time, important variations are present in the size, composition, and financing of this set of institutions from country to country. These variations reflect the distinctive cultures, traditions, and political histories of the different places. Indeed, one of the strengths of the comparative approach that we have adopted is precisely that it highlights these differences and brings them into better focus. Nevertheless, the ubiquity of civil society organizations remains a central conclusion to emerge from this work.

To say that the civil society sector is a major global force is not, however, to say that it does not face important challenges. To the contrary, the challenges are often enormous. They involve issues of basic visibility and legitimacy, of sustainability, of effectiveness, and of forging the workable partnerships with other sectors that real progress on complex social and economic problems increasingly requires.

To cope with these problems, concerted efforts will be needed. But underlying all such efforts must be a better base of knowledge about this elusive set of institutions. While we harbor no illusions that the work represented here closes all the gaps that exist, we hope it offers a useful foundation on which others can build.

## Notes

1. Lester M. Salamon, "The Rise of the Nonprofit Sector," *Foreign Affairs,* Vol. 74, no. 3 (July/August 1994).

2. We will use the term "civil society organization" or "civil society sector" to refer to this broad range of institutions. This is one of several terms that have been used to depict such institutions, but it appears to be the one that is gaining the greatest currency internationally. Although some would reserve this term for just a subset of all such private, nongovernmental, non-market institutions — namely those engaged in advocacy and empowerment activities — we believe that a strong case can be made for its use more generally to depict the broader class of organizations. We draw a distinction between "civil society organizations" and "civil society," however.

The former relates to a class of organizations. The latter is a more general term that embraces as well such features as the rule of law, the existence of a free press, and the relationships among sectors in a society. For a more concrete definition of what we mean by "civil society organizations" and the "civil society sector," see note 9 below.

3. The System of National Accounts (SNA), the guidance system for international economic statistics, essentially assigns most nonprofit institutions to the corporate or government sectors based on their principal source of revenue. See: Lester M. Salamon and Helmut K. Anheier, "Nonprofit Institutions in the Household Sector," in *Household Accounting Experience in Concepts and Compilation,* Vol. I (New York: United Nations, 2000), 275–99; and Lester M. Salamon, Gabriel Rudney, and Helmut K. Anheier, "Nonprofit Institutions in the System of National Accounts: Country Applications of SNA Guidelines," *Voluntas,* Vol. 4, no. 4 (1993): 486–501. A new handbook based on the work of this project has now been issued by the United Nations Statistics Division calling on national statistical offices to create a "satellite account" that will present a more complete view of the nonprofit sector. See: United Nations, *Handbook on Non-Profit Institutions in the System of National Accounts* (New York: United Nations, 2003).

4. For a summary of the results of the first phase of project work, focusing on eight countries, see: Lester M. Salamon and Helmut K. Anheier, *The Emerging Sector: An Overview* (Baltimore, MD: Johns Hopkins Institute for Policy Studies, 1994), republished as *The Emerging Nonprofit Sector,* Vol. 1 in the Johns Hopkins Nonprofit Sector Series (Manchester, U.K.: Manchester University Press, 1996). More detailed results are available in a series of books published in the Johns Hopkins Nonprofit Sector Series by Manchester University Press. Results of the second phase of project work, covering 22 countries, can be found in: Lester M. Salamon, Helmut K. Anheier, Regina List, S. Wojciech Sokolowski, Stefan Toepler, and Associates, *Global Civil Society: Dimensions of the Nonprofit Sector* (Baltimore, MD: Johns Hopkins Center for Civil Society Studies, 1999). For a complete list of the products of the Johns Hopkins Comparative Nonprofit Sector Project, please contact the Center for Civil Society Studies as noted on the back cover of this book. Project results are also available on our Web site at: www.jhu.edu/ccss.

5. Quoted in Charles Ragin, *The Comparative Method* (Berkeley, CA: University of California Press, 1987), 1.

6. For further detail on these alternative definitions and their limitations, see: Lester M. Salamon and Helmut K. Anheier, "In Search of the Nonprofit Sector: The Question of Definitions," in *Defining the Nonprofit Sector: A Cross-national Analysis,* ed. Lester M. Salamon and Helmut K. Anheier (Manchester, U.K.: Manchester University Press, 1997).

7. Religious organizations can take at least two different forms: (1) places of religious worship, and (2) service organizations such as schools and hospitals with a religious affiliation. Both of these are included within the project's definition of a civil society organization, though, as noted below, where it was possible to differentiate the two, the religiously affiliated service organizations were grouped together with other service organizations in the relevant field and the religious worship organizations identified separately. Not all countries were able to collect information on the religious worship organizations, however.

8. Since data on the large mutual and cooperative institutions is fairly readily available, those interested in the broader "social economy" definition, which includes these entities, can easily add them to the data reported here to generate a picture of the broader "social economy." For a discussion of the "social economy" concept, see: Jacques Defourny and Patrick Develtere, "The Social Economy: The Worldwide Making of a Third Sector," in *L'economie sociale au Nord et au Sud,* ed. Jacques Defourny, Patrick Develtere, and Bénédicte Fonteneau (Paris: Université de Boeck, 1999).

9. For an illustration of the confusion attending the "civil society" concept, see: Alan Fowler, "Civil Society Research Findings from a Global Perspective: A Case for Redressing Bias, Asymmetry, and Bifurcation," *Voluntas,* Vol. 13, no. 3 (September 2002), 287–300. Although claiming to use a different concept than the one adopted here, Fowler defines civil society in terms quite consistent with the definition adopted in this project — i.e., "an arena of voluntary formal and informal collective citizen engagement distinct from families, state, and profit-seeking institutions." The emphasis on "collective" engagement in this definition is similar to our focus on organizations.

10. See the Caveats section for a discussion of the full-time equivalent conversion. Other components of the project examined additional facets of the civil society sector in the target countries such as the legal framework, the history, religious and cultural traditions, and the policy context.

11. Readers of our previous reports will note that the basis of comparison used here differs slightly from that used previously. In particular, we compare nonprofit employment here to the *economically active population* in the countries covered rather than to the *nonagricultural workforce* as in previous reports. This change was made necessary because of the huge size of the agricultural workforce, the large informal economy, and the resulting relatively small size of the formally recorded "workforce" in many of the countries now covered by the project. In India, for example, no more than 10 percent of the economically active population — i.e., the population of working age that is able to work — is recorded in government documents as part of the formal "labor force." This change in the base of the percentages means that the relative size of the nonprofit sector reported here appears lower than that reported in previous reports for some of the countries covered. This is so because the "economically active population" is generally larger than the "nonagricultural labor force," the base used for the earlier figures. "Economically active population" is essentially the population of working age that is not institutionalized or otherwise unavailable for productive work, whether they are formally employed, self-employed, producing for their own consumption, or looking for work. See: International Labor Organization, *Current International Recommendations on Labour Statistics* (Geneva: International Labour Organization, 1988).

12. This is a weighted average considering the aggregate number of paid and volunteer workers (including those in religious worship organizations). As will be noted more fully below, the unweighted average differs slightly because the countries with the larger nonprofit sectors also tend to have higher numbers of volunteers. The unweighted average volunteer share of nonprofit employment is thus 38 percent.

13. As noted earlier, the figures reported here appear lower than in our earlier publications. This is not due to any change in the relative size of the civil society

organization workforce in our original 22 countries, but rather to our decision to compare this workforce to the "economically active population" rather than the "nonagricultural workforce" as before. For an explanation of this decision, see note 11.

14. The distinction between developed and developing countries here is based on the classification found in the World Bank's *World Development Report* (New York: Oxford University Press, 2001), which in turn is based on per capita gross national product (GNP). All countries classified as "high income" (1999 per capita GNP of $9,266 or more) are considered here as "developed," whereas all countries falling below that level are classified as "developing" and "transitional" (for a detailed list, see Table 1.1).

15. The 38 percent figure reported here is an unweighted average and therefore differs from the weighted average of 44 percent reported in Figure 1.3. For further elaboration on this distinction, see the 2nd bullet point in the Caveats section above.

16. For an elaboration on these functions, see: Lester M. Salamon, *America's Nonprofit Sector: A Primer, Second Edition* (New York: The Foundation Center, 1999), 15–17.

17. See, for example: James S. Coleman, *Foundations of Social Theory* (Cambridge, MA: Harvard University Press, 1990), 300–321; Robert Putnam, *Making Democracy Work: Civic Traditions in Modern Italy* (Princeton, NJ: Princeton University Press, 1993), 83–116, 163–185.

18. While religious worship organizations are also included in the expressive category, we could not include them here due to data limitations. However, religiously affiliated service organizations are included. For more information, see Appendix B.

19. To some extent this distinction may correspond to that sometimes drawn between civil society organizations that are primarily agencies of assistance, and those that are fundamentally agencies of empowerment seeking to change the relations of power thought to create the need for assistance. See, for example: Julie Fisher, *The Road from Rio: Sustainable Development and the Nongovernmental Movement in the Third World* (Westport, CT: Praeger, 1993); John P. Lewis, *Strengthening the Poor: What Have We Learned* (New Brunswick, NJ: Transaction Books, 1988); Jude Howell and Jenny Pearce, *Civil Society and Development: A Critical Exploration* (Boulder, CO: Lynne Rienner, 2001).

20. Comparative figures do not include religious worship organizations because data on these organizations were not available for all countries. However, religiously affiliated service organizations are included. For more information, see Appendix B.

21. Revenue data could not be collected in Egypt and Morocco.

22. Some of these dues could reasonably be considered philanthropic contributions on the part of members committed to the values being promoted by the organizations, though they are treated here as dues.

23. For purposes of these calculations, volunteer time is valued at the average wage in the respective country in the fields in which volunteering takes place.

24. For an earlier effort to identify and explain patterns of third sector development among countries, see: Lester M. Salamon and Helmut K. Anheier, "Social Origins of Civil Society: Explaining the Nonprofit Sector Cross-Nationally," *Voluntas,* Vol. 9, no. 3 (1998): 213–248. For a more complete account, see Lester M.

Salamon and S. Wojciech Sokolowski, *Social Origins of Civil Society* (New York: Cambridge University Press, forthcoming).

25. Tommy Lundström and Filip Wijkström, *The Nonprofit Sector in Sweden* (Manchester, U.K.: Manchester University Press, 1998).

26. For further detail on these cases, see: Lester M. Salamon et al., *Global Civil Society: Dimensions of the Nonprofit Sector* (Baltimore, MD: Johns Hopkins Center for Civil Society Studies, 1999); Helmut K. Anheier and Wolfgang Seibel, *The Nonprofit Sector in Germany* (Manchester, U.K.: Manchester University Press, 1997); Edith Archambault, *The Nonprofit Sector in France* (Manchester, U.K.: Manchester University Press, 1997); Ary Burger, Paul Dekker, Tymen van der Ploeg, and Wino van Veen, *Defining the Nonprofit Sector: The Netherlands* (Baltimore, MD: Johns Hopkins Institute for Policy Studies, 1997); and Ralph M. Kramer, *Voluntary Agencies in the Welfare State* (Berkeley, CA: University of California Press, 1981).

27. One possible explanation for these deviations is the greater power that the state secured vis-à-vis the church in these two countries. For further exploration of these points, see: Lester M. Salamon and S. Wojciech Sokolowski, *Social Origins of Civil Society* (New York: Cambridge University Press, forthcoming).

28. Takeyoshi Amenomori, "Japan," in *Defining the Nonprofit Sector*, ed. Lester M. Salamon and Helmut K. Anheier (Manchester, U.K.: Manchester University Press, 1997), 188–214; Tadashi Yamamoto, "The State and the Nonprofit Sector in Japan," in *The Nonprofit Sector in Japan*, ed. Tadashi Yamamoto (Manchester, U.K.: Manchester University Press, 1998), 119–144.

29. See, for example, Julie Fisher, *The Road from Rio: Sustainable Development and the Nongovernmental Movement in the Third World* (Westport, CT: Praeger, 1993).

30. See, for example, Amani Kandil, "The Nonprofit Sector in Egypt," in *The Nonprofit Sector in the Developing World*, ed. Helmut K. Anheier and Lester M. Salamon (Manchester, U.K.: Manchester University Press, 1998), 149–51.

31. Amani Kandil, *Civil Society in the Islamic World* (Washington, D.C.: Civicus, 1995).

## Chapter 2

# Measuring Civil Society: The Johns Hopkins Global Civil Society Index*

Lester M. Salamon and S. Wojciech Sokolowski

## Introduction

Recent research suggesting a link between the presence of civil society organizations and both economic progress and democratic governance have made the health and vitality of the civil society sector increasingly a matter of practical, and not simply academic, concern.[1] This has led to efforts on the part of private foundations, national governments, and multinational institutions to promote civil society and encourage its development.[2]

But how can the success of such efforts be gauged? More generally, how can we measure the health and vitality of the civil society sector from place to place or country to country?

From the discussion in the previous chapter, it should be clear that no single dimension will suffice. Civil society is a complex phenomenon with multiple dimensions.[3] Even when we focus on civil society *organizations* or *sectors,* as we do throughout this book, we discover that they come in a variety of shapes and configurations and that they vary in size, composition, financing, activities, and operations. Under these circumstances, no single facet of civil society can suffice to convey this sector's aggregate character and role. Yet, without some way to capture this complex reality in summary form, we will remain unable to represent it effectively or assess the efforts to promote its development.

Fortunately, social scientists have devised a technique for coming to terms with complex social phenomena of this sort without losing sight of their multiple dimensions. That technique is index construction.

*We are grateful to Andrew Green, Kathryn Chinnock, Nereo Zamaro, Jack Quarter, and Laurie Mook for helpful comments on an earlier draft of this chapter.

Indexes combine the multiple dimensions of a complex phenomenon into a composite measure that can be easily understood and systematically analyzed. The Human Development Index created by the United Nations Development Program, for example, provides a summary measure of human development using three broad dimensions — life expectancy, knowledge, and standard of living — each of which is measured against international experience.[4] Freedom House similarly produces an annual index of global political rights and liberties based on a lengthy checklist of questions.[5] More recently, a set of Millennium Development Goals has been established to measure progress toward achieving "development" in countries throughout the world. And a number of scholars have formulated indexes to measure the prevalence of democracy.[6] Indeed, an entire subfield of statistics exists to guide such index construction.[7]

Although some quite promising efforts have recently been made to formulate a "civil society index," these efforts have so far been constrained by the absence of solid empirical measures of the civil society phenomenon. As a consequence, the efforts have had to rely on essentially subjective measures or focus on relatively narrow facets of the overall phenomenon.[8] This has put efforts to promote civil society into jeopardy because of the apparent indeterminacy of the underlying phenomenon.

Thanks to the sizable body of data on the civil society sector assembled through the Johns Hopkins Comparative Nonprofit Sector Project, however, an opportunity now exists to create a more objectively grounded "global civil society index." What is more, the recent acceptance by the United Nations Statistical Commission of the new *Handbook on Nonprofit Institutions in the System of National Accounts,*[9] which holds the promise of making data comparable to that generated by the Johns Hopkins project available on a more or less permanent basis for an even broader range of countries, the possibility exists for creating an index that can be updated on a regular basis into the future. The result would be a powerful tool for helping policymakers in both the public and private sectors chart the consequences of their efforts to promote the development of civil society, as well as a vehicle for keeping the health of civil society in the forefront of public concern.

The purpose of this chapter is to lay out the contours of a new Global Civil Society Index that builds on this new body of data. In addition, it tests this index by applying it to the countries for which we now have solid empirical data through the Hopkins project. The result is the first systematic, empirical ranking of countries in terms of the level of development of their civil society sectors.

To pursue this purpose, the discussion here falls into four parts. Part I sets the stage by outlining the key considerations that must go into the design of any effective index. Part II shows how we took account of these considerations in designing our proposed Global Civil Society Index. Part III presents the results of the application of this index to the 34 countries for which we now have complete data. Part IV then evaluates the index in terms of the criteria we have identified and notes some of the uses to which this index can be put and the next steps that will be needed to extend its reach.

Needless to say, given the complexity of the civil society concept, we have no illusions that the index presented here will be the last word, or even *our* last word, on how to measure the progress of civil society development. Hopefully, however, it will identify some of the criteria that any such index must meet and provide a foundation on which others can build.

# I. The Challenge of Index Construction: The Criteria

Fundamentally, index construction involves three basic tasks: first, *conceptualization,* which involves the specification of the basic meaning of the phenomenon being measured; second, *operationalization,* which involves the identification of concrete indicators in terms of which the phenomenon can be measured; and third, *aggregation,* which involves assembling these separate indicators into a composite score that can be benchmarked in a meaningful way.

While there is no one "right" way to carry out these tasks and construct an effective index, experts on index construction have identified a number of criteria to guide index development and to differentiate more reliable from less reliable indexes.[10] If a civil society index is to be credible, it must therefore meet these standards as well. More specifically, five such criteria seem especially important:

## Conceptual clarity

In the first place, to be effective, an index must begin with a clear understanding of the concept it is seeking to measure. This is difficult because indexes are often used where the underlying concept is complex, with multiple dimensions and enormous variations from place to place. The task, therefore, is to find a definition that is broad enough to capture the diverse manifestations of the phenomenon in different social settings yet precise enough to differentiate it from other phenomena with which it may be related.

Experts in index construction recommend dealing with this dilemma by identifying a "basic 'minimal' common understanding" of the target concept "based on meaningful international and intercultural dialogues"[11] and by focusing on its "leading indicators." Otherwise, the concept becomes so broad that it begins to merge with other social phenomena, creating serious dangers of misperception and misspecification.

## Validity

To move from effective conceptualization to effective operationalization, indexes must identify tangible indicators for the phenomenon being measured. To be meaningful, however, such measures need to be valid reflections of the underlying concept. This means that indicators cannot be chosen randomly or on the basis of hunches or wishful assumptions. Rather, there must be some demonstrable connection, backed up by a convincing body of theory, linking the indicator to the phenomenon being examined.

## Reliability/objectivity

Not only must the indicators used in an index be valid, they must also be reliable. This means that they must be measurable in reasonably objective terms and not based merely on the subjective views of particular informants. Otherwise, repeated measures of the same indicators will yield different results depending on who does the measurement or who this person consults.

## Comparability

To be most effective, indexes must also facilitate comparisons. Indeed, indexes are pre-eminently vehicles for comparison, both across time and space. They thus make it possible to assess change over time and to understand one's own situation better by showing how it compares with the situation elsewhere. For this to be possible, however, the indicators built into an index must be similar from place to place, and must be measured in a similar fashion. This constitutes an additional argument against purely subjective measures since observers in one country are rarely in a position to correlate their judgments and scores on particular indicators with those of observers in other places. The demands of comparability thus reinforce those resulting from the need for reliability in putting a premium on objective indicators in constructing an effective index.

## Utility

Finally, to be effective, indexes must be useable. This requires a reasonable degree of comprehensibility, workability, and analytical power. Overly abstract indicators or indexes that include more indicators than are strictly required can thus undercut the utility of an index by making it impossible to gather the required information or diluting the central concepts. What is more, indexes should be capable of driving action. This requires that they focus on significant phenomena and embody the most salient and important dimensions of these phenomena so that the consequences of scoring high or low are clear.

Given these five criteria, the task of constructing a Global Civil Society Index thus boiled down to devising a suitably clear conceptualization of the civil society sector, identifying valid and understandable indicators of it, finding ways to measure these indicators objectively in a cross-national setting, and then aggregating and benchmarking these indicators. In the next section, we describe how we have addressed these tasks.

# II. Applying the Criteria: The Johns Hopkins Global Civil Society Index

As noted earlier, index construction essentially involves three key steps: conceptualization, operationalization, and aggregation. In this section we review how these steps were carried out in the construction of a Global Civil Society Index that meets the criteria identified above.

## Conceptualization: toward a working definition of civil society

As noted earlier, the first step in constructing an index is to clarify the basic concept being measured. This is a special challenge in the case of civil society because this concept is so hotly contested. Indeed, few concepts in modern social science have had more meanings attached to them. From its early origins in the Scottish Enlightenment, through its use by Hegel, to its recent reincarnations in the work of Antonio Gramsci and in the struggles for independence from Soviet rule in Central Europe, the concept of civil society has been mobilized to refer to everything from private economic activity, to family life, to popular political action outside the control of the state.[12]

While disputes rage about the outer boundaries of the civil society concept, there seems to be a reasonable consensus about its central core. That core consists of the basic private associational life of a society — the private associations and organizations that operate more or less outside the confines of the state and business, as well as of the family, though they may receive aid and support from all of these.[13] Such "intermediary" institutions function as the social glue of society. They bring people together for joint activity without the need for official auspices. They thus provide vehicles for individual initiative for the common good, or at least for the common good as perceived by some reasonable segment of the community.[14]

To meet the requirement for conceptual clarity called for in an effective index, this associational phenomenon seems the most reasonable to use as the core of the civil society concept. Such an approach is consistent with the advice in the index construction literature to focus on a "basic, common understanding" of the phenomenon under investigation.

But which social institutions are properly considered part of civil society for these purposes? And how can they be identified and singled out from other social institutions?

As detailed in the previous chapter, our approach to this question was to build on the experiences of the diverse countries covered by our work through precisely the kind of "meaningful intercultural dialogue" recommended in the literature. Thus, as discussed in Chapter 1, we adopted an inductive, bottom-up approach, asking our local associates to identify the major types of organizations commonly considered to be part of "civil society" or any of its related organizational namesakes (e.g., third sector, NGOs, nonprofit organizations, and voluntary organizations) in their respective countries. We then extracted the common features of the entities so identified.[15] Out of this process emerged a consensus on a set of "structural" or "operational" features that seemed to define the organizational core of civil society in all of the countries in which we worked, which included both developed and developing countries representing all of the inhabited continents and most of the world's major religious traditions. So conceived, civil society is defined here as:

> *The set of (1) formal or informal organizations or structured relationships among people that are (2) private (i.e., not part of the apparatus of the state), (3) not profit-distributing, (4) self-governing, and (5) voluntarily constituted and supported.*

Included within this definition are both legally constituted organizations and informal groups, social clubs and professional associations, human service agencies and community organizations, service providers, and advocacy groups of every imaginable type. The focus on organizations thus gives some concreteness to the definition while still accommodating a significant range of variation in the types of entities that are included.[16]

## Operationalization: from concept to indicators

Conceptualization is only the first step toward formulating a valid and reliable index. Equally important is converting the concept into operational terms by identifying the concept's major dimensions, specifying concrete indicators for each such dimension, and then subjecting the resulting indicators to measurement.

Generally speaking, there are two broad approaches to this task. The first is *data-driven;* it consists of gathering data on each of a wide assortment of factors thought to be associated with a concept and then testing to see which are actually correlated with each other.[17] The second is *theory-driven;* it begins with the underlying phenomenon and conceptualizes the features that best exemplify it, even though these features may be quite divergent.

For a variety of reasons, we utilized the theory-driven approach here. This approach is far more economical since it identifies the relevant dimensions through a conceptual process rather than a complex process of "factor analysis," and therefore does not require as much data. What is more, it promises greater validity since it focuses only on dimensions thought to be central to the underlying concept.

More specifically, our research identified a number of key features of global civil society that seemed important to accommodate in any meaningful civil society index:

- The presence of informal as well as formal organizations;
- The mobilization of significant voluntary effort in addition to paid employment;
- A diverse fiscal base that includes fees, charges, and public sector support in addition to philanthropy and private giving;
- The importance of contextual factors, such as an enabling legal environment and a climate of popular support, in shaping the sector's development;
- The variety of functions these organizations perform, including both "expressive" functions and "service" functions; and
- The diverse forms that civil society takes in different countries and regions.

To embrace these various features, we focused our attention not on a single dimension of the civil society sector, but rather on three different ones:

- First, its *capacity* or scale;
- Second, its *sustainability* or staying power; and
- Third, its *impact,* the contribution it makes to the societies in which it operates.

For each dimension, moreover, we utilized a variety of indicators in order to capture the different forms that these various dimensions take in different places. The discussion below details the rationale for these three dimensions and outlines the indicators we have identified for each.

## Capacity

The most basic dimension of civil society is its scale or capacity. Capacity is fundamentally a measure of the size of the civil society sector in a country. But more than that, it is a measure of the effort or activity this sector mobilizes.

Traditionally, this dimension has been measured in terms of the number of organizations or associations in a country, either in the aggregate or on a per capita or per 1,000 population basis. Unfortunately, however, this straightforward approach can produce enormous distortions because of the significant variations in registration requirements and record-keeping systems from place to place, not to mention the vast differences in the relative sizes of organizations. What is more, counts of organizations typically underestimate the more informal organizations, which often do not appear on government registries.

Accordingly, we rejected counts of organizations as a way to capture the scale or capacity of the civil society sector and focused instead on four other indicators that reflect better the level of effort that these organizations generate:

- *The extent of paid employment,* measured as the number of full-time equivalent paid workers as a share of the country's economically active population.

   Employees represent perhaps the most tangible indicator of the effort that civil society organizations mobilize. What is more, employment data are commonly generated by economic statistics agencies as part of their normal work, even though civil society organization employment is rarely broken out separately in the data sources. We were able to remedy this through a variety of procedures as part of the Johns Hopkins Comparative Nonprofit Sector Project, as detailed more fully in the previous chapter and in Appendix B.

   The number of paid workers was converted into "full-time equivalent" terms because of the substantial number of part-time workers in the civil society sector.[18] The full-time equivalent workforce was expressed as a share of the economically active population in order to take account of the variations in the overall size of different countries.[19]

- *The extent of volunteer employment,* similarly measured as the number of full-time equivalent volunteers as a share of the country's economically active population.

   The inclusion of volunteers reflects the substantial role such workers play in the activities of civil society organizations. Indeed, as noted elsewhere in this volume, volunteers account for over 40 percent of the full-time equivalent workforce of the civil society sector, and in many countries this figure is far higher. Data on volunteer effort were collected through population surveys carried out as part of our Comparative Nonprofit Sector Project. These surveys sought data on the number of volunteer hours by field of activity. Volunteer effort was then converted into full-time equivalent terms using the same process as was used for paid workers and expressed as a share of the economically active population to adjust for differences in the overall size of countries.

- *The amount of charitable contributions,* expressed as a share of the gross domestic product.

   Civil society organizations mobilize not only workers, both paid and volunteer, but also financial resources. Of particular interest in measuring the capacity of the civil society sector are the philanthropic contributions these organizations generate. These contributions truly represent additional resources that civil society organizations bring to the fields in which they operate. By contrast, the other forms of revenue they generate would likely exist even if civil society organizations were not in existence to receive them. Service fees, for example, would go to for-profit or other providers, and government payments could be used to support for-profit provision or provision by government agencies themselves. By contrast, civil society organizations almost alone mobilize private charitable contributions, and these contributions would not likely be devoted to the purposes that these organizations serve if the organizations did not exist to generate and channel them. Hence they constitute a measure of the extra capacity mobilized by these organizations.

The measure of philanthropic contributions used here is *the value of all individual, business, and foundation donations to civil society organizations computed as a percentage of the gross domestic product* to control for variations in the size of different countries. Data on such contributions were collected for most countries covered by the Johns Hopkins Comparative Nonprofit Sector Project using a combination of special surveys and existing data on transfer payments. The new U.N. *Handbook on Nonprofit Institutions in the System of National Accounts* makes the collection of such data a part of the recommended nonprofit institutions (NPI) satellite account process.

- *The degree of diversification of the civil society sector,* measured in terms of the distribution of the nonprofit workforce among different fields of activity.

  A final measure of the capacity of the civil society sector focuses on the level of diversification the sector has achieved. Other things being equal, a civil society sector that is active in a wide variety of fields is stronger and more capable than one that is active in only a narrow range of fields.

  To measure this dimension of civil society capacity, we computed a civil society "fractionalization index" for each country based on the distribution of paid and volunteer employment among the twelve different fields of civil society organization activity identified in the International Classification of Nonprofit Organizations used in our work. The fractionalization index measures the likelihood that any two randomly selected civil society organization workers — paid or volunteer — will work in *different* fields in a particular country. The higher this index, the more dispersed the civil society sector.

As shown in Annex A at the end of this chapter, the 34 countries on which we have generated data as part of the Johns Hopkins Comparative Nonprofit Sector Project vary considerably along each of these indicators of the *capacity* of the civil society sector. Thus, the paid civil society workforce varies from a high of 9.21 percent of the economically active population in the Netherlands to a low of 0.26 percent in Mexico, with an average of 2.78 percent and a standard deviation of 2.47 percent. Volunteering similarly varies from a high of 5.11 percent of the economically active population in Sweden to a low of 0.13 percent in Mexico, with an average of 1.68 percent and a standard deviation of 1.41 percent. The fact that countries rank differently in terms of these different indicators confirms that our index is achieving its goals of taking account of the different forms that the civil society sector takes in different places.

### Sustainability

As important as the scale or strength of the civil society sector at a point in time is its ability to sustain itself over time. To sustain themselves, organizations must, at a minimum, secure the resources they need to operate. But such resources are not only financial. They are also human. What is more, sustainability requires a broader environment that is enabling and supportive. These considerations lead to a concept of sustainability that embraces a number of crucial indicators:

- *Self-generated income.* As detailed in the previous chapter, a crucial factor in determining the ability of civil society organizations to sustain themselves is their ability to attract their own sources of revenue through fees, venture activities, dues from their members, or earnings from the resources they command. To be sure, some of these forms of income are available to for-profit firms as well, and too heavy a reliance on them can lead civil society organizations to sacrifice their special character. Nevertheless, a meaningful level of self-generated income appears to be crucial for civil society organization sustainability.

  For the purposes of our index, we measure such self-generated income as *the total amount of fees, proceeds from the sale of goods, membership dues, and investment income received by civil society organizations in a country computed as a share of the civil society sector's total revenue.* This measure is thus independent of the overall size of the civil society sector, which is captured in the capacity measure. Data on civil society organization revenue were compiled on 34 countries as part of the Johns Hopkins Comparative Nonprofit Sector Project. Through the satellite account process outlined in the U.N. *Handbook on Nonprofit Institutions in the System of National Accounts,* such data should soon become available on a larger group of countries as well.

- *Government support.* Also important to the sustainability of the civil society sector around the world has been public sector support. Indeed, as Chapter 1 has shown, the presence of government support has been one of the chief factors explaining the significant scale of the civil society sector in many Western European countries.[20] While not without its risks, government support tends to stabilize the financial base of the civil society sector and thereby contribute to its sustainability and growth.

  The measure of government support used here is *the total amount of government grants, contracts, and reimbursement payments made to civil* society organizations as a share of total civil society sector revenue. The inclusion of public sector reimbursement payments is especially important since such payments are quite large in many countries yet often get recorded as fees or service revenue in official statistics even though they originate with the public sector.

Data on such government support were collected on 34 countries as part of our Comparative Nonprofit Sector Project and are scheduled to be collected under the U.N. *Handbook on Nonprofit Institutions in the System of National Accounts* for all countries that implement this *Handbook*.

- *Popular support as reflected in the number of people volunteering.* Not only does civil society organization sustainability depend on a steady flow of financial support, but also it requires a significant level of popular support.

  One measure of the civil society sector's popular support is the membership it mobilizes. However, not all civil society organizations are membership-based. A more effective measure of popular support is therefore the volunteer activity that these organizations are able to mobilize. Volunteer involvement speaks to the enthusiasm these organizations are able to muster among citizens.

  Volunteer activity was already included in our "capacity" dimension above. However, the measure used there was a capacity measure — volunteer hours were calculated, converted into full-time equivalent workers, and expressed as a percent of the economically active population. Measured more directly as the sheer number of people involved, without taking account of the time they devote, volunteering can also serve as an indicator of popular support. It is this measure that we use here, adjusting for the size of the country by expressing the number of people volunteering as a share of the adult population.

- *Legal environment.* Finally, the viability of the civil society sector in a country is affected by the broader policy environment in which these organizations operate. Especially important here is the legal environment, the set of laws and regulations governing the operations of civil society organizations.

  The legal environment can affect the sustainability of civil society organizations in two different ways, however.[21] In the first place, it can affect the *demand* for such organizations, or the likelihood that citizens will rely on them for important functions. It does this by affecting the degree of confidence people have in these organizations. This is particularly important in settings where civil society traditions are weak or sentiments of trust strained. In the second place, however, the legal environment can affect the *supply* of civil society organizations. It does this by determining the tax or other incentives they enjoy as well as the hurdles they have to surmount to secure legal status. The more cumbersome it is to establish civil society organizations as legal entities, the less likely it is that people will be inclined to do so.

To gauge this facet of civil society, we constructed a special Civil Society Legal Environment Scale. This scale consists of two components: first, a *demand* component containing six types of legal provisions thought to affect the trust that people can have in civil society organizations (e.g., legal provisions that clarify the governance requirements for these organizations, prohibit the distribution of profits, and require transparency in their operations); and second, a *supply* component consisting of fourteen legal provisions thought to affect the ease with which civil society organizations can form and operate (e.g., registration requirements, minimum membership or asset requirements, registration procedures, and provisions for special tax treatment for the organizations or for donors to them).

A coding system was devised to rate the provisions of the legal codes of various countries in terms of these two dimensions. Drawing on detailed memoranda produced by legal experts in the countries covered by the Johns Hopkins Comparative Nonprofit Sector Project, we then applied this coding system to the legal codes of the project countries. The resulting scores were then verified with local experts and summed to form separate "demand" and "supply" legal environment scores for each country.[22]

Because legal codes are not enforced uniformly in all parts of the world, we also introduced a measure designed to adjust the *de jure* provisions of the law for the *de facto* operation of country legal systems. For this purpose, we drew on work under way at the World Bank on "governance indicators" for countries throughout the world.[23] More specifically, we used an average of two indicators proposed in this World Bank work: (1) the "government effectiveness" index, designed to measure the capacity of government to enforce laws; and (2) the "rule of law" index, designed to measure the extent to which laws are followed and enforced.[24] By "weighting" the *de jure* provisions of law by this composite measure of country inclination and capacity to enforce the law, we have a more precise indicator of the legal environment for civil society organizations in a country.

Annex B summarizes these various measures of civil society sector *sustainability* for the 34 countries on which we have so far generated data. As is shown there, each of the measures of sustainability varies considerably from country to country. Thus, for example, government payments to civil society organizations as a share of total civil society revenue range from a high of 77 percent in Ireland to a low of 5 to 6 percent in the Philippines, Kenya, and Pakistan. Volunteer participation varies from a high of 52 percent of the adult population in Norway to less than 1 percent in Japan, Mexico, and Pakistan.

## Impact

Ultimately, what is important about civil society organizations is not just their capacity or their ability to sustain themselves, but the impact of their activities. We want to know what contribution the civil society sector is making to social, economic, and political life.

However, this dimension is exceedingly difficult to measure in a meaningful way, if for no other reason than that the activities of the civil society sector are so broad and encompassing. Finding a common metric in which to express the contribution of civil society organizations engaged in community organizing, health care delivery, education, human rights advocacy, artistic expression, and protection from homelessness is almost impossible. Not only do these organizations operate in widely divergent fields, but also their *modus operandi* varies widely. Thus, some organizations operate by providing concrete services while others engage in advocacy or provide vehicles for expression of cultural, recreational, professional, ethnic, or other interests. A measure of impact that focuses only on the service functions of this set of organizations would thus ignore some of the most crucial functions these organizations perform. Yet these latter functions are often the most difficult to capture in operational terms.

To get around these obstacles, we focused on a set of four "proxy" indicators of the impact of civil society organizations. Two of these implicitly focus on the service functions of the sector while the other two tap broader expressive and representational roles. In addition, we developed a measure of civil society organization performance of five critical social roles, though we were only able to apply this measure to 19 of our 34 countries. More specifically, the impact measures include:

- *Economic contribution,* as measured by "value added." The first measure of the impact of the civil society sector is the overall contribution this sector makes to the production of value in the economy. Economists use the concept of "value added" to gauge the economic contribution of particular industries or economic sectors. "Value added" represents the net contribution that a set of institutions makes to the total output of the economy after factoring out the value already embodied in the resources or materials these institutions use to produce their output (e.g., factoring out the steel that automobile manufacturers use to produce their cars).

  In the case of civil society organizations, where profits are not generated, the value added can be roughly approximated by the value of the labor inputs. We therefore estimated the value added by civil society organizations as the wages of the sector's paid workers plus the imputed wages of its volunteers, both computed as a share of the country's gross domestic product to control for the differing sizes of national economies.[25]

- *Human service contribution,* as measured by the nonprofit share of total employment in key human service fields. A second measure of the contribution of civil society organizations focuses more squarely on the services that these organizations generate. Here our approach was to calculate the share that civil society organizations represent of the total employment in each of a number of major service fields in which these organizations operate. More specifically, we focused on four such fields (health, education, social services, and culture and recreation). Nonprofit employment in these four fields was computed as a share of total employment in these fields.[26]

- *Contribution to advocacy and expression,* as measured by the amount of civil society organization paid and volunteer staff effort devoted to these activities. Since civil society organizations perform crucial expressive and advocacy functions in addition to their service functions, it was important to include these functions as well in our measure of civil society organization impacts. For this purpose, we focused on the scale of the human resources — paid and volunteer — that civil society organizations mobilize for expressive activities — i.e., advocacy, professional associations, labor unions, environmental protection, and culture and recreation. This was calculated as a share of the adult population in order to adjust for variations in country size.

- *Popular commitment,* as reflected in the extent of organizational memberships. As a fourth indicator of civil society impact, we sought to include a measure of the popular commitment to civil society organizations. This was done on the theory that the sector's impact includes the extent to which it has penetrated the hearts and minds of the populace.

  The ideal way to assess this dimension of civil society impact would be to tap public attitudes toward the civil society sector. Unfortunately, empirical data of this sort do not exist for a sufficient range of countries. As a substitute, we therefore used the share of the adult population reporting membership in civil society organizations as reflected in the World Values Survey. While, as noted above, not all civil society organizations are membership based, the willingness to join civil society organizations nevertheless provides a measure of the popular acceptance of these organizations.

- *Performance of key roles,* as reflected in field studies. Finally, to gain a more in-depth understanding of the performance and contributions of the civil society sector, we undertook a series of field studies in major fields of nonprofit activity to assess the extent to which these organizations were actually performing the functions claimed for them in the literature. These functions include service provision, especially for disadvantaged populations; innovation; advocacy; community-building; and value guardianship. Based on field reports provided by local associates on the basis of interviews and focus groups, scores were assigned to the civil society sector in particular fields in each country to reflect how they performed in terms of each of these functions. These scores were then averaged across fields for each country and an average "role performance score" derived. Since these data could only be assembled in 19 countries, however, we ultimately did not incorporate them into the index calculations reported below, though we did assess what difference it would make in the countries for which we do have data.

Annex C presents the raw data recording how the 34 countries on which we have data scored on four indicators of impact. As this table shows, countries vary considerably along these dimensions of impact, and not always in the same direction. Thus, the Netherlands leads the group in terms of value added and the service role, but Sweden and Norway jump ahead when the focus shifts to the expressive role.

## Aggregation: from indicators to index

The final step in constructing an index is to assemble the various indicators into a composite score and calibrate this against a fixed standard. Since each dimension has different components, and each component is measured in a different way, this step involves its own complexities. This is especially true since there is no "natural" or ideal state of civil society and therefore no given standard against which different countries can be compared.

To accomplish this final task, three steps were required: first, the separate indicators identified above had to be "normalized" by expressing them in terms of a common measuring system (equivalent to converting separate national currencies into a common currency for purposes of comparison); second, the normalized scores for each of the indicators had to be assembled into composite measures for each of our three dimensions (capacity, sustainability, and impact); and finally, the scores for the three dimensions had to be assembled into an overall composite index score for each country.

### Normalizing the indicators

Because each of the indicators for each of the dimensions of our proposed index is measured in a different way, it was necessary to devise a way to convert them to a common standard in order to combine them into an overall dimension score. However, as noted above, since there is no generally accepted standard of what an "ideal" civil society sector looks like, and therefore no standard measure against which to compare each indicator, we opted for an experiential standard based on the record of the countries on which we have assembled data through the Johns Hopkins Comparative Nonprofit Sector Project. As noted earlier, these countries represent, by design, a diverse mixture of regions, levels of development, cultural and religious traditions, and historical evolution. While it would be foolhardy to claim that they "represent" all the countries in the world, they nevertheless reflect a good portion of the known variations in civil society scale and development and therefore a reasonable starting point for normalization.

To normalize the different indicators in our index, therefore, we computed each country's score on each indicator *as a percent of the maximum score for that indicator among all the countries on which we have data*. The resulting percent became that country's score on that indicator. For each indicator, therefore, we have a score that potentially ranges from 0 to 100, with 100 representing not some abstract ideal but the maximum reported on that indicator for the countries on which we have data. As updated data on these countries, or new data on additional countries, become available, this maximum value could change. However, our intent is to keep the standard fixed for a minimum period (e.g., five years) so that it will be possible to measure change against a fixed standard. If the maximum observed value for any indicator does change over time, it will be relatively easy to recalibrate the "old" values to the ones based on the "new" standard for longitudinal comparisons.

## Aggregating the indicators into dimensions

Once all the indicators were converted into a common measure stretching from 0 to 100, it was possible to aggregate the dimensions to create average scores for each of the three dimensions in our index — capacity, sustainability, and impact. This was important because, as noted earlier, no one indicator adequately captures the essence of each dimension. It was therefore necessary to create aggregate measures made up of several different indicators.

Generally speaking, our aggregation method consisted of computing a simple average of the indicator scores. In one place, however, we felt it appropriate to weight an indicator twice in order to avoid potential bias in the index. Specifically, in the calculation of the Sustainability Score, we double-weighted volunteer participation. This was done to counteract the effect of having several indicators in the index that essentially reflect the size of the more formal components of the civil society sector (e.g., the nonprofit share of service employment), and it seemed important to balance this by double weighting one of the few measures (volunteer participation) that tapped the more informal components of the sector.[27]

## Aggregating the dimensions into an index

The final step in the aggregation process was to assemble the three dimensions into an overall index. To do this, we followed the same procedure that we used to compile the dimensions; i.e., we computed the average of the three dimensions. Like the scores on the separate dimensions, this composite score potentially varies from 0 to 100, with 0 representing the lowest possible and 100 representing the closest to the maximum value on all of the separate dimensions of the index.[28]

## III. The Global Civil Society Index: Initial Results

As a first application of this Global Civil Society Index, we calculated the scores that resulted from applying the index to the 34 countries for which we have fairly complete data from the Johns Hopkins Comparative Nonprofit Sector Project and other relevant data sources.

The results of this exercise are reported in Table 2.1 below. This table records the Hopkins Global Civil Society Index (GCSI) scores for each country on each of the three major dimensions of our index, and then the composite score.

A number of important observations flow from these results:

- First, and most obviously, this table demonstrates that the GCSI is workable, that the components can be measured empirically, and that real results can be generated. Given the obstacles that have stood in the way of accurate measurement in this field, this is no small accomplishment in and of itself.

- Second, it is notable that no country achieves a score of 100 on any of the dimensions of the GCSI, or on the overall index. This underlines the multi-dimensionality of the civil society phenomenon and the fact that some countries score higher on some dimensions than others. It also makes clear that even using the "experiential" standard that we have adopted, no country has an "ideal" civil society sector even when measured in experiential terms.

- Third, not only does no country achieve a 100 on any dimension but also no country tops the list on all dimensions. Thus, while the Netherlands ends up with the highest overall GCSI score, it falls behind Norway, the United Kingdom, and Sweden on the Sustainability Score.

- Fourth, the data reported in Table 2.1 demonstrate the success that the GCSI has in capturing the different dimensions of the civil society phenomenon. Thus, countries do not automatically sweep the index by having a large, formal, civil society service sector. Rather, several countries with small civil society sectors as measured in terms of paid employment (e.g., Norway and Sweden) nevertheless score quite high on the aggregate GCSI, contrary to much of the conventional wisdom about the Nordic welfare state. This is so because the GCSI deliberately takes account of facets of civil society activity other than those reflected in paid

**Table 2.1.** Global Civil Society Index: country scores

| Country | Capacity | Sustain-ability | Impact | Total |
|---|---|---|---|---|
| Netherlands | 79 | 54 | 89 | 74 |
| Norway | 55 | 82 | 59 | 65 |
| United States | 76 | 54 | 54 | 61 |
| Sweden | 58 | 56 | 67 | 60 |
| United Kingdom | 66 | 60 | 50 | 58 |
| Belgium | 65 | 45 | 60 | 57 |
| Israel | 70 | 42 | 50 | 54 |
| Ireland | 64 | 45 | 52 | 54 |
| Australia | 51 | 46 | 49 | 49 |
| France | 56 | 46 | 44 | 49 |
| Finland | 48 | 42 | 50 | 47 |
| Germany | 47 | 45 | 47 | 46 |
| Spain | 54 | 37 | 30 | 40 |
| Argentina | 48 | 35 | 36 | 40 |
| Tanzania | 45 | 32 | 38 | 39 |
| South Africa | 44 | 35 | 33 | 37 |
| Uganda | 44 | 37 | 30 | 37 |
| Austria | 35 | 42 | 34 | 37 |
| Japan | 38 | 34 | 35 | 36 |
| South Korea | 32 | 38 | 36 | 35 |
| Italy | 38 | 37 | 25 | 33 |
| Kenya | 41 | 28 | 29 | 33 |
| Czech Republic | 34 | 35 | 25 | 31 |
| Hungary | 38 | 32 | 20 | 30 |
| Brazil | 30 | 31 | 26 | 29 |
| Colombia | 37 | 26 | 22 | 28 |
| Peru | 32 | 30 | 22 | 28 |
| Philippines | 30 | 35 | 17 | 27 |
| India | 27 | 30 | 20 | 26 |
| Poland | 30 | 38 | 7 | 25 |
| Slovakia | 32 | 28 | 13 | 24 |
| Mexico | 23 | 29 | 19 | 24 |
| Romania | 27 | 26 | 14 | 22 |
| Pakistan | 26 | 19 | 12 | 19 |

SOURCE: Johns Hopkins Comparative Nonprofit Sector Project

employment. One reflection of this is the fact that the correlations among the different indicators and dimensions are significant but far from unitary, as shown in Annex D. In fact, this is one of the advantages of the "theory-led" approach that guided our index construction: it allows us to embrace within our index and measure the many distinctly different dimensions that the civil society concept embodies. As a result, Norway, which has a relatively small paid-staff nonprofit sector, nevertheless ranks above the United States in its overall GCSI score, and Sweden is not far behind it. What is more, many developing countries, such as Tanzania, South Africa, and Uganda, rank quite close behind developed countries such as France, Germany, and Spain. The GCSI thus seems to accommodate the diversity of the civil society phenomenon quite well. Countries can score high on the index with rather different types of civil society structures. Put somewhat differently, the index is not biased toward any particular type of civil society structure.

- Fifth, while there are multiple opportunities for countries to score high on this index, the index does serve to differentiate countries in terms of the extent of civil society development. In fact, some interesting patterns emerge. Thus, as reflected in Table 2.2 below, the developed countries tend to have higher GCSI scores than the developing and transitional ones, though the difference is somewhat less extensive than might have been expected (average score of 51 vs. 30). Similarly, important variations in GCSI scores are evident by country cluster. Interestingly, the cluster with the highest average GCSI score is the Nordic cluster, followed closely by the Anglo-Saxon cluster made up of the United Kingdom, the United States, and Australia. The "welfare partnership" countries of Western Europe rank third. The countries of Africa rank next highest in average GCSI score, ahead of the Asian industrial cluster (Japan and South Korea), as well as the Latin American, Central and Eastern European, and other developing country clusters.[29]

## IV. Evaluating the Global Civil Society Index

At the outset of this chapter, we identified five basic criteria for judging indexes of the sort we have constructed here: conceptual clarity, validity, reliability, comparability, and utility. As we pointed out there, every index involves complex trade-offs among these objectives. The pursuit of conceptual breadth, for example, can lead to a loss of validity and reliability as efforts are made to capture amorphous features that require the use of highly subjective indicators. The relevant test for any index, therefore, is not whether it achieves some perfect ideal but rather how well it has balanced these competing considerations.

**Table 2.2.** Global Civil Society Index: country cluster scores

| Country cluster | Capacity | Sustain-ability | Impact | Total |
|---|---|---|---|---|
| 34 countries | 45 | 39 | 36 | 40 |
| Developed countries | 56 | 48 | 50 | 51 |
| Developing and transitional | 34 | 31 | 23 | 30 |
| Anglo-Saxon | 64 | 54 | 51 | 56 |
| Nordic | 54 | 60 | 59 | 58 |
| Welfare partnership | 56 | 44 | 48 | 49 |
| Asian industrialized | 35 | 36 | 36 | 35 |
| Latin America | 34 | 30 | 25 | 30 |
| Africa | 44 | 33 | 33 | 36 |
| Other developing | 28 | 28 | 17 | 24 |
| Central / Eastern Europe | 32 | 32 | 16 | 27 |

SOURCE: Johns Hopkins Comparative Nonprofit Sector Project

How well does the Hopkins Global Civil Society Index outlined here meet this test? To what extent has it struck the appropriate balance among the competing criteria? The answer, we believe, is generally quite well and far better than the other efforts that have so far become available. The Hopkins GCSI scores especially well in terms of its validity, reliability, and comparability. While it purchases these advantages at some cost in terms of conceptual breadth, it nevertheless enjoys considerable conceptual clarity and utility as well. This section examines these judgments a bit more closely in order to clarify the strengths, as well as the inevitable limitations, of this index.

## Conceptual clarity

As noted earlier, the foundation of any successful index must be a clear understanding of the concept being examined. Since such concepts frequently have multiple dimensions, the basic definition must be broad enough to encompass the different dimensions yet narrow enough to differentiate the concept from other related phenomena. The literature on index construction suggests balancing these concerns by focusing on the "basic minimal" understanding of the concept and the "leading indicators" of its presence.

We have generally followed this advice by focusing our index on the organizational manifestations of civil society, though taking pains to include within this conceptualization informal and non-registered organizations as well as formal and registered ones, and the activities of volunteers and members as well as those of paid staff. Our contention has been that private, non-profit-distributing organizations, whether formal or informal, that individuals choose to join on a non-compulsory basis form the core of civil society. While other manifestations, such as spontaneous citizen action or attitudes of civility, may also be important, these are far more amorphous and difficult to capture in objective terms and therefore unwise to use as the base of an index that seeks to be reliable and objective. By focusing on the organizational core of the concept but consciously including within this the related voluntary citizen activity that associations mobilize, we have sought to achieve the best of both worlds.

From the evidence presented in Table 2.1, it appears that the GCSI has achieved its objective in creating an index with sufficient conceptual breadth to encompass a variety of manifestations of the civil society concept while still focusing on a core that has solid analytical meaning. Just as there are many paths to civil society, so there are many routes to a robust ranking on this civil society index.

## Validity and reliability

In addition to its conceptual strengths, the index developed here enjoys considerable validity and reliability. As noted earlier, validity is the degree of fit between the phenomenon being measured and the indicators used to measure it, while reliability is the degree of objectivity of the measures, the likelihood that two independent observers using the same methods will reach roughly the same conclusion about the presence or absence of the phenomenon.

We believe the GCSI ranks quite high in terms of these criteria. So far as validity is concerned, the three dimensions in terms of which this index assesses the health and vitality of civil society — capacity, sustainability, and impact — are central features of the civil society phenomenon. Any effective index seeking to gauge the health and vitality of civil society in a country will likely begin with these basic features. What is more, we have taken care to utilize multiple indicators of each of these dimensions in order to capture the varied forms that civil society organizations can assume, and the different functions they perform, from place to place. Thus, as noted above, while the index focuses on the organizational core of civil society, it includes informal as well as formal organizations. In addition, it explicitly captures the more informal dimensions of even the formal organizations as manifested in the involvement of volunteers and members and the engagement in expressive as well as service functions. This makes it possible to square the focus on organizations with the commonsense understanding of civil society as a mechanism for engaging citizen energies for a variety of social, political, and related purposes.

As noted above, moreover, the index seems to work the way we hoped, producing high "scores" for a wide assortment of national manifestations of the basic civil society phenomenon, including some, like the Netherlands and the United States, where the sector includes sizable formal organizations employing numerous paid workers engaged in basic service functions; and others, like Norway and Sweden, where it more commonly takes the form of associations relying heavily on volunteers and members performing essentially expressive functions.

Not only does the GCSI achieve a high degree of validity, but also it uses indicators that are objectively derived and therefore generally reliable — numbers of paid staff, numbers of volunteers, revenue structures, legal structures, and the like. This differentiates it markedly from other indexes currently available in the field, which rely much more heavily on subjective judgments or much more narrow portions of the field. This is a particular strength in a field so dominated by ideological disputation and mythology, and in which the collection of subjective judgments can often achieve no more than to systematize, and hence legitimize, prevailing misconceptions. To be sure, data sources in this field are far from perfect and considerable work remains to achieve the level of reliability that is desirable. But the types of indicators used in the GCSI nevertheless hold enormous promise as a way to generate objective measures of the strength and vitality of civil society among countries and over time. In the process, it provides a way to challenge prevailing myths. Indeed, even our preliminary test of this index demonstrates this capability, challenging, for example, the widespread view that the American nonprofit sector is the most highly developed in the world, or that the Scandinavian countries lack vibrant civil society sectors.

## Comparability

In addition to scoring high in terms of validity and reliability, the GCSI also achieves a high degree of comparability. This is a considerable accomplishment in a field as diverse and contested as this one, and it results from the close association of this index with a basic conceptualization of civil society formulated through a collaborative process engaging teams of researchers in over 40 countries throughout the world. What is more, this conceptualization was tested on the ground in these countries and found to work. In addition, the data on most of the crucial indicators used in the index were actually assembled as part of this cross-national inquiry and were known to produce reliable cross-national measures. Comparability was thus "hard-wired" into this index at its inception. Where comparative data were not available through our Comparative Nonprofit Sector Project, other comparable data were identified (e.g., data on membership in civil society organizations secured from the World Values Survey). Perhaps the best evidence of the comparability of the GCSI is that it was possible for us to apply it comparatively to over 30 countries that differ by region, religious orientation, level of development, governance structure, culture, and history, and to generate meaningful results.

This is not to say that the GCSI is fully developed even in its current form, and it would be wrong to read too much into small differences of a point or two in country scores. Nevertheless, the overall picture portrayed by the index likely calls attention to real differences in the overall health and vitality of the civil society sector from place to place. As such, it is a vast improvement over what is currently available.

## Utility

The final test of an index is its utility and usability. This requires, at a minimum, that the index be comprehensible. Equally important, the indicators it calls for must actually be available. Finally, the index must have relevance to valid analytical or policy concerns.

Here as well, the GCSI scores high. The basic dimensions in terms of which civil society is measured in this index (capacity, sustainability, and impact) are straightforward concepts. While some of the indicators of these dimensions are necessarily indirect (e.g., measuring impact in terms of the civil society share of total employment in a field rather than more directly in terms of service outputs), none is so abstract as to be unrecognizable. To the contrary, they tend to be fairly straightforward and concrete. What is more, the likelihood is high that most of the indicators will be available for a broad range of countries over the foreseeable future. For one thing, as we have already shown, most are already available for the countries covered by the Johns Hopkins Comparative Nonprofit Sector Project. What is more, the data are likely to be updated and made available for a growing number of countries due to the recent adoption by the United Nations Statistical Commission of the *Handbook on Nonprofit Institutions in the System of National Accounts*.[30] This *Handbook* calls on statistical offices throughout the world to assemble "satellite accounts" that pull together data on the employment, expenditures, assets, receipts, and activities of nonprofit institutions on a regular basis, and to incorporate as well data on the volunteer activity that these organizations mobilize. Virtually all of the variables incorporated in the GCSI will therefore be available once these "NPI satellite accounts" are produced. This makes the construction of this index readily doable over the long run in an increasing range of countries, though efforts are still needed to persuade national statistical offices to adopt this *Handbook*.

Not only is the GCSI doable, however, it also holds considerable policy, diagnostic, and analytical promise. Armed with this index, sector leaders and national policymakers will be able to gauge not only where their countries stand vis-à-vis other countries in the development of the civil society sector, but also what steps might usefully be taken to improve the situation. For example, Japan (overall index score 36), scores particularly low on the sustainability dimension. This suggests that efforts to boost the civil society sector in that country should concentrate mainly on improving sustainability, which means changes in the legal environment and in citizen engagement. In the same vein, Spain's civil society sector has considerable capacity (as evidenced by a score of 54), but rather unimpressive impact and sustainability scores (30 and 37, respectively). This implies that Spain's civil society sector is performing below its capacity, which suggests directions for improvement.

In addition, students of civil society will be able to use this index to test theories relating the presence or absence of civil society to such factors as economic growth, popular well-being, and democratic practice. The fact that the index was constructed in a way that deliberately kept most of these presumed consequences of civil society out of the index should add to its analytical value. Analysts can therefore test their theories without worrying about potential tautologies resulting from the inclusion in the index of relationships they want to use the index to test.

## Conclusion

Civil society has become a matter of increased analytical and policy concern throughout the world. National governments, international organizations, private foundations, and third-sector organizations have sought to promote civil society in the hope that it will contribute to democratization, poverty alleviation, and the accumulation of social capital.

For all the attention it has attracted, however, civil society remains an elusive concept, and an even more elusive reality. Little agreement exists about how to define the concept, let alone how to measure its presence or absence.

The Johns Hopkins Global Civil Society Index outlined here will doubtless not be the last word on index development in this field. As new data become available, improvements will become possible in some of the measures it incorporates. In addition, refinements may be possible in some of the basic concepts. In both respects — conceptual and empirical — we encourage colleagues to join in this process of refinement. Nevertheless, we are convinced that the index presented here constitutes an important step forward in giving empirical expression to the civil society concept and thus in transforming it into a more useful concept for both analysis and policy choice.

## Notes

1. James T. Coleman, *Foundations of Social Theory* (Cambridge, MA: Harvard University Press, 1990); Robert D. Putnam, Robert Leonardi, and Raffaella Y. Nanetti, *Making Democracy Work: Civic Traditions in Modern Italy* (Princeton, NJ: Princeton University Press, 1993); Francis Fukuyama, *Trust: Social Virtues and*

*the Creation of Prosperity* (New York: Simon and Schuster, 1995); Julie Fisher, *Non-governments: NGOs and the Political Development of the Third World* (West Hartford, CT: Kumarian Press, 1998); Ewan Ferlie (ed.), *The New Public Management in Action* (Oxford: Oxford University Press, 1996); Michael Edwards and David Hulme (eds.), *Beyond the Magic Bullet: NGO Performance and Accountability in the Post-Cold War World* (London: Macmillan, 1995); Anthony Giddens, *The Third Way and Its Critics* (London: Polity Press, 1999).

2. Marina Ottaway and Thomas Carothers (eds.), *Funding Virtue: Civil Society Aid and Democracy Promotion* (Washington, D.C.: Carnegie Endowment for International Peace, 2000).

3. John Keane, *Civil Society and the State* (New York: Verso, 1988); Jean L. Cohen and Andrew Arato, *Civil Society and Political Theory* (Cambridge, MA: MIT Press, 1992); Adam B. Seligman, *The Idea of Civil Society* (New York: The Free Press, 1992).

4. United Nations Development Program, *Human Development Report 2002: Deepening Democracy in a Fragmented World* (New York: Oxford University Press, 2002), 253.

5. Freedom House, *Annual Survey of Freedom Country Scores, 1972–73 to 1999–2000*. Retrieved April 19, 2004, from the Freedom House Web site: http://www.freedomhouse.org/ratings/index.htm.

6. See, for example, Zehra F. Arat, *Democracy and Human Rights in Developing Countries* (Boulder, CO: Lynne Rienner Publishers, 1991); Axel Hadenius, *Democracy and Development* (Cambridge, U.K.: Cambridge University Press, 1992); Gerardo L. Munck and Jay Verkuilen, "Conceptualizing and Measuring Democracy: Evaluating Alternative Indices," *Comparative Political Studies*, Vol. 35, No. 1 (February 2002): 5–34.

7. Earl Babbie, *The Practice of Social Research* (Belmont, CA: Wadsworth Publishing Co., 1992), 165–189, 444–447.

8. Two examples of civil society indexes based on essentially subjective measures are the U.S. Agency for International Development's NGO Sustainability Index, which relies on estimates made by local USAID officials of seven facets of the civil society sector in selected Central European countries; and CIVICUS' Diamond, which utilizes a series of interviews and focus groups to portray civil society in different countries along four dimensions (structure, environment, values, and impact). Anheier and Stares formulate a more empirical set of measures but focused exclusively on a relatively narrow band of cross-national civil society organizations, while Green has developed a measure that uses as a proxy for civil society the legal environment for this set of organizations. See: United States Agency for International Development, *The NGO Sustainability Index* (Washington, D.C.: U.S. Agency for International Development, 2001); Volkhart Finn Heinrich and Kumi Naidoo, "From Impossibility to Reality: A Reflection and Position Paper on the Civicus Index on Civil Society Project, 1999–2001," *Civicus Index on Civil Society Occasional Paper* Series, Vol. I, Issue 1 (Frankfurt, Germany: CIVICUS, 2001); Helmut K. Anheier and Sally Stares, "Introducing the Global Civil Society Index," in *Global Civil Society 2002*, ed. Marlies Glasius, Mary Kaldor, and Helmut Anheier (New York: Oxford University Press, 2002), 241–254; and Andrew Green, "Comparative

Development of Post-Communist Civil Societies," *Europe-Asia Studies,* Vol. 54, no. 3 (May 2002): 455–471.

9. United Nations, Department of Economic and Social Affairs, Statistics Division, *Handbook on Nonprofit Institutions in the System of National Accounts,* Studies in Methods, Series F, no. 91, Handbook on National Accounting (New York: United Nations, 2003).

10. Gerardo L. Munck and Jay Verkuilen, "Conceptualizing and Measuring Democracy: Evaluating Alternative Indices," *Comparative Political Studies,* Vol. 35, No. 1 (February 2002): 5–34; Earl Babbie, *The Practice of Social Research* (Belmont, CA: Wadsworth Publishing Co., 1992), 129–134.

11. Dirk Berg-Schlosser, *Indicators of Democratization and Good Governance —Strengths and Weaknesses.* Retrieved April 21, 2004, from the Deutsche Gesellschaft für Technische Zusammenarbeit (GTZ) Governance Web site: http://www.gtz.de/governance/download/BergSchlosser.doc.

12. Adam B. Seligman, *The Idea of Civil Society* (New York: The Free Press, 1992); Jean L. Cohen and Andrew Arato, *Civil Society and Political Theory* (Cambridge, MA: MIT Press, 1992); Jude Howell and Jenny Pearce, *Civil Society and Development: A Critical Exploration* (Boulder, CO: Lynne Rienner Publishers, 2001).

13. Alternative conceptualizations would extend the concept of civil society to embrace the rule of law, the presence of an independent press, public attitudes, and individual political mobilization outside the realm of organizations (see, for example, Miguel Darcy de Oliveira and Rajesh Tandon, "An Emerging Global Civil Society," in *Citizens: Strengthening Global Civil Society,* coordinated by Miguel Darcy de Oliveira and Rajesh Tandon [Washington, D.C.: Civicus, 1994]). Many of these facets are difficult to capture, however, while others run the danger of confusing the concept of civil society with other social concepts, such as democracy, with which it is sometimes associated. Indeed, some of the alternative conceptions can confuse the concept of civil society with very uncivil forms of social action. For example, mass mobilization of citizens into political life without the intervening presence of associations has been associated with the rise of totalitarianism, not civil society (William Kornhauser, *The Politics of Mass Society* [Glencoe, IL: Free Press, 1959]).

14. See, for example, Peter L. Berger and Richard J. Neuhaus, *To Empower People: The Role of Mediating Structures in Public Policy* (Washington, D.C.: American Enterprise Institute for Public Policy Research, 1977); Robert Nisbet, *The Quest for Community: A Study in the Ethics of Order and Freedom* (New York: Oxford University Press, 1953); Alexis de Tocqueville [1835], *Democracy in America,* The Henry Reeves Text, Vol. 2 (New York: Vintage Books, 1945), 268.

15. For further detail on this process, see Chapter 1.

16. For an alternative definition of the organizational core of "civil society" that includes mutuals and cooperatives, see: Jacques Defourny, Patrick Develtere, and Bénédicte Fonteneau, *L'économie sociale au Nord et au Sud* (Paris: Université de Boeck, 1999). As noted in Chapter 1, our definition accommodates those cooperatives and mutuals serving community development purposes but excludes more commercially oriented institutions of this type.

17. In this approach, known as "factor analysis," regression coefficients are computed on a large set of possible indicators of a phenomenon, and the indicators with high "factor loadings," or standardized regression coefficients, are considered to be the best candidates for including in an index of the phenomenon in question. A consistency (or reliability) measure (Cronbach's Alpha) tells how well a set of indicators measures a single unidimensional construct. The closer this measure is to 1, the higher the average inter-correlation or internal consistency of the tested items.

18. To compute the number of full-time equivalent workers, we multiplied the number of part-time workers by the average hours such workers devote and divided the result by the number of hours in an average full-time job over the course of a year. This quotient was then added to the number of full-time workers to yield the total full-time equivalent workforce.

19. We use the "economically active population" rather than the "labor force" as the denominator to adjust for the relative size of different countries in view of the limitations of "labor force" data in countries with a large informal economy, since official labor force statistics typically do not include informal workers.

20. See also Lester M. Salamon, Helmut K. Anheier, Regina List, Stefan Toepler, S. Wojciech Sokolowski, and Associates, *Global Civil Society: Dimensions of the Nonprofit Sector* (Baltimore, MD: The Johns Hopkins Center for Civil Society Studies, 1999).

21. For further detail, see Lester M. Salamon and Stefan Toepler, "The Influence of the Legal Environment on the Development of the Nonprofit Sector," *Working Paper Series, Johns Hopkins Center for Civil Society Studies,* No. 17 (2000).

22. For more details, see Salamon and Toepler, "The Influence of the Legal Environment on the Development of the Nonprofit Sector" (2000). For an alternative scale rating the legal environment for the third sector in Central Europe, see Andrew Green, "Comparative Development of Post-Communist Civil Societies," *Europe-Asia Studies* 54, no. 3 (2002): 455–471.

23. Daniel Kaufmann, Aart Kraay, and Massimo Mastruzzi, "Governance Matters III: Governance Indicators for 1996–2002," Mimeo. (Washington, D.C.: The World Bank, 2003).

24. Operationally, this was done by computing the average of these two scores for our target countries, normalizing this by computing each country's score as a percent of the maximum observed score for all countries, multiplying this by the sum of the demand and supply legal scores discussed above, and then normalizing this product by computing each country's score as a percent of the maximum score for all countries. This procedure thus produces a measure of the *de jure* legal environment as reflected in written law weighted by the capacity and inclination of the country's government to enforce the law. We are indebted to Dr. Andrew Green for the suggestion to incorporate this measure of *de facto* legal operation.

25. This method does not include capital income (such as interest on land, structures and equipment), for which we do not have data. However, in the case of nonprofit institutions this component is relatively small, accounting for only about 8 percent of the net value added of the nonprofit sector in the United States, and probably less in the developing countries (Robert Eisner, "The Total Incomes System of Accounts," *Survey of Current Business* (January 1985): 24–48. The method used

here to compute the value added by civil society is thus very probably a conservative estimate. See also: United Nations, Department of Economic and Social Affairs, Statistics Division, *Handbook on Nonprofit Institutions in the System of National Accounts* (New York: United Nations, 2003), Annex A3, 132–145.

26. An alternative approach would be to calculate the proportion of the services in each of these fields that civil society organizations account for — e.g., the proportion of hospital stays, enrolled students, nursing home slots, cultural events. However, it is virtually impossible to secure a complete set of such indicators, and any subset is open to dispute as being biased for or against these organizations. A measure using the proxy of employment, while hardly perfect, avoids many of these dilemmas.

27. As indicated in note 24 above, the computation of the "legal context" score in the sustainability dimension was a bit more complex than this since the supply and demand scores first had to be added together, normalized, and then multiplied by the normalized scores for the "government effectiveness" and "rule of law" measures to yield a normalized legal context score that embraced both the de jure and the de facto aspects of the legal environment. For further detail, see note 13 above.

28. In practice, a score of zero is highly improbable since it would mean the virtual total absence of any vestige of a civil society sector or associated phenomena (e.g., legal framework) in a particular country.

29. Interestingly, the replacement of the membership-based impact measure with a measure based on a direct assessment of role performance in several representative fields does not affect these results significantly. With the role performance measure included, several countries rise in the rankings, but only marginally. Thus the United Kingdom, Ireland, France, and Peru move up on this basis, while the United States, Israel, Australia, and Colombia decline marginally.

30. United Nations, Department of Economic and Social Affairs, Statistics Division, *Handbook on Nonprofit Institutions in the System of National Accounts.* Studies in Methods, Series F, no. 91, Handbook on National Accounting (New York: United Nations, 2003).

**Annex A.** GCSI capacity dimension components

| Country | Paid employment | Volunteers | Workforce dispersion | Private giving |
|---|---|---|---|---|
| | % of econ. active pop. | | Index | % of GDP |
| Argentina | 2.93% | 1.90% | 82.1% | 0.38% |
| Australia | 4.43% | 1.90% | 82.5% | 0.34% |
| Austria | 3.84% | 1.07% | 55.9% | 0.17% |
| Belgium | 8.62% | 2.32% | 77.7% | 0.44% |
| Brazil | 1.43% | 0.19% | 77.8% | 0.17% |
| Colombia | 1.79% | 0.56% | 83.8% | 0.32% |
| Czech Republic | 1.32% | 0.72% | 81.2% | 0.23% |
| Finland | 2.42% | 2.77% | 80.4% | 0.28% |
| France | 3.70% | 3.75% | 79.8% | 0.28% |
| Germany | 3.54% | 2.33% | 82.4% | 0.13% |
| Hungary | 0.94% | 0.21% | 79.7% | 0.60% |
| India | 0.60% | 0.76% | 71.4% | 0.09% |
| Ireland | 8.28% | 2.15% | 72.9% | 0.55% |
| Israel | 6.61% | 1.40% | 72.0% | 1.29% |
| Italy | 2.26% | 1.49% | 81.4% | 0.09% |
| Japan | 3.19% | 1.02% | 77.9% | 0.14% |
| Kenya | 1.29% | 0.82% | 83.6% | 0.54% |
| Mexico | 0.26% | 0.13% | 75.5% | 0.04% |
| Netherlands | 9.21% | 5.07% | 78.7% | 0.37% |
| Norway | 2.69% | 4.35% | 77.1% | 0.26% |
| Pakistan | 0.59% | 0.40% | 64.4% | 0.22% |
| Peru | 1.55% | 0.94% | 64.0% | 0.26% |
| Philippines | 0.68% | 1.18% | 76.8% | 0.04% |
| Poland | 0.64% | 0.17% | 78.8% | 0.28% |
| Romania | 0.35% | 0.44% | 78.0% | 0.10% |
| Slovakia | 0.57% | 0.24% | 78.9% | 0.36% |
| South Africa | 1.84% | 1.59% | 82.9% | 0.43% |
| South Korea | 1.88% | 0.55% | 73.2% | 0.18% |
| Spain | 2.82% | 1.48% | 81.5% | 0.87% |
| Sweden | 1.74% | 5.11% | 74.0% | 0.40% |
| Tanzania | 0.52% | 1.54% | 89.3% | 0.60% |
| Uganda | 0.92% | 1.33% | 80.2% | 0.64% |
| United Kingdom | 4.84% | 3.63% | 81.0% | 0.62% |
| United States | 6.28% | 3.49% | 78.6% | 1.01% |
| **Average** | **2.78%** | **1.68%** | **77.5%** | **0.37%** |
| **Std. deviation** | **2.47%** | **1.41%** | **6.4%** | **0.28%** |
| **Maximum** | **9.21%** | **5.11%** | **89.3%** | **1.29%** |

SOURCES:
Johns Hopkins Comparative Nonprofit Sector Project
International Labour Organization (http://laborsta.ilo.org)

## **Annex B.** GCSI sustainability dimension components

| Country | Government payments | Fees | Persons volunteering | Legal environment | | | |
|---|---|---|---|---|---|---|---|
| | % of revenue | | % of adult pop. | Demand | Supply | Gov't effect. | Rule of law |
| Argentina | 19.5% | 73.1% | 7.6% | 7 | 17 | 2.87 | 2.76 |
| Australia | 31.2% | 62.5% | 12.9% | 6 | 22 | 4.21 | 4.39 |
| Austria | 50.4% | 43.5% | 8.3% | 8 | 17 | 4.05 | 4.49 |
| Belgium | 76.8% | 18.6% | 9.7% | 6 | 24 | 3.80 | 3.93 |
| Brazil | 15.5% | 73.8% | 5.8% | 3 | 19 | 2.33 | 2.33 |
| Colombia | 14.9% | 70.2% | 4.8% | 8 | 5 | 2.56 | 1.95 |
| Czech Republic | 39.4% | 46.6% | 4.5% | 6 | 22 | 3.16 | 3.11 |
| Finland | 36.2% | 57.9% | 7.8% | 7 | 19 | 4.27 | 4.51 |
| France | 57.8% | 34.6% | 14.0% | 4 | 21 | 4.02 | 4.00 |
| Germany | 64.3% | 32.3% | 10.3% | 8 | 17 | 4.16 | 4.35 |
| Hungary | 27.1% | 54.6% | 3.3% | 8 | 18 | 3.11 | 3.20 |
| India | 36.1% | 51.0% | 2.4% | 7 | 17 | 2.36 | 2.60 |
| Ireland | 77.2% | 15.8% | 10.6% | 7 | 19 | 4.09 | 4.24 |
| Israel | 63.9% | 25.8% | 6.2% | 10 | 24 | 3.49 | 3.60 |
| Italy | 36.6% | 60.6% | 4.1% | 5 | 21 | 3.36 | 3.46 |
| Japan | 45.2% | 52.1% | 0.5% | 6 | 16 | 3.61 | 4.12 |
| Kenya | 4.8% | 81.0% | 5.7% | 6 | 18 | 1.81 | 1.62 |
| Mexico | 8.5% | 85.2% | 0.1% | 8 | 21 | 2.53 | 2.26 |
| Netherlands | 59.0% | 38.6% | 15.5% | 7 | 26 | 4.70 | 4.43 |
| Norway | 35.0% | 58.1% | 52.2% | 10 | 26 | 4.42 | 4.60 |
| Pakistan | 6.0% | 51.1% | 0.2% | 7 | 17 | 1.96 | 1.94 |
| Peru | 18.1% | 69.8% | 4.7% | 7 | 17 | 2.52 | 2.12 |
| Philippines | 5.2% | 91.6% | 6.0% | 9 | 19 | 2.66 | 2.43 |
| Poland | 24.1% | 60.4% | 11.9% | 8 | 18 | 3.16 | 3.01 |
| Romania | 45.0% | 28.5% | 1.8% | 7 | 20 | 1.92 | 2.24 |
| Slovakia | 21.9% | 54.9% | 3.6% | 8 | 15 | 2.63 | 2.62 |
| South Africa | 44.2% | 31.7% | 9.3% | 9 | 18 | 2.68 | 2.77 |
| South Korea | 24.3% | 71.4% | 3.4% | 9 | 25 | 2.98 | 3.29 |
| Spain | 32.1% | 49.0% | 5.1% | 8 | 20 | 4.16 | 3.76 |
| Sweden | 28.7% | 62.3% | 28.4% | 7 | 18 | 4.28 | 4.44 |
| Tanzania | 27.0% | 53.1% | 11.1% | 5 | 16 | 1.78 | 2.03 |
| Uganda | 7.1% | 54.7% | 23.5% | 5 | 15 | 2.30 | 2.03 |
| United Kingdom | 46.7% | 44.6% | 30.4% | 10 | 17 | 4.58 | 4.44 |
| United States | 30.5% | 56.6% | 21.7% | 10 | 23 | 4.18 | 4.23 |
| **Average** | **34.1%** | **53.4%** | **10.2%** | **7.2** | **19.0** | | |
| **Std. deviation** | **19.9%** | **18.2%** | **10.6%** | **1.7** | **3.9** | | |
| **Maximum** | **77.2%** | **91.6%** | **52.2%** | **10** | **26** | | |

Values in shaded areas are imputed.
SOURCES:
Johns Hopkins Comparative Nonprofit Sector Project
United States Census Bureau
World Values Survey, 1991 and 1995 (computer files)

## Annex C. GCSI impact dimension components

| Country | Value added | Nonprofit service share | Workforce in expressive fields | Organization membership |
|---|---|---|---|---|
| | % of GDP | % of total empl. | % of adult pop. | Index |
| Argentina | 3.21% | 41.2% | 0.67% | 0.424 |
| Australia | 3.88% | 33.8% | 1.23% | 0.811 |
| Austria | 2.40% | 26.3% | 0.62% | 0.617 |
| Belgium | 7.09% | 64.6% | 0.75% | 0.700 |
| Brazil | 0.86% | 18.4% | 0.26% | 0.630 |
| Colombia | 1.46% | 15.4% | 0.39% | 0.419 |
| Czech Republic | 1.09% | 10.3% | 0.74% | 0.549 |
| Finland | 3.83% | 25.5% | 1.87% | 0.810 |
| France | 5.01% | 28.5% | 1.74% | 0.447 |
| Germany | 4.53% | 33.8% | 1.06% | 0.712 |
| Hungary | 0.85% | 3.9% | 0.36% | 0.549 |
| India | 0.55% | 19.7% | 0.11% | 0.462 |
| Ireland | 6.30% | 57.0% | 0.73% | 0.576 |
| Israel | 7.26% | 41.1% | 0.60% | 0.655 |
| Italy | 1.85% | 21.9% | 0.67% | 0.375 |
| Japan | 2.70% | 46.0% | 0.32% | 0.456 |
| Kenya | 1.25% | 15.6% | 0.26% | 0.763 |
| Mexico | 0.25% | 3.6% | 0.10% | 0.655 |
| Netherlands | 11.18% | 76.4% | 2.00% | 0.993 |
| Norway | 4.10% | 26.0% | 2.81% | 0.846 |
| Pakistan | 0.27% | 19.7% | 0.09% | 0.191 |
| Peru | 1.07% | 19.7% | 0.06% | 0.509 |
| Philippines | 1.47% | 4.3% | 0.42% | 0.388 |
| Poland | 0.54% | 5.8% | 0.23% | 0.108 |
| Romania | 0.56% | 8.3% | 0.17% | 0.351 |
| Slovakia | 0.47% | 5.0% | 0.33% | 0.336 |
| South Africa | 1.39% | 19.0% | 0.80% | 0.729 |
| South Korea | 3.14% | 30.7% | 0.27% | 0.694 |
| Spain | 3.33% | 29.9% | 0.57% | 0.347 |
| Sweden | 6.19% | 16.2% | 3.55% | 0.908 |
| Tanzania | 4.23% | 17.3% | 0.55% | 0.763 |
| Uganda | 0.80% | 16.4% | 0.57% | 0.763 |
| United Kingdom | 4.38% | 37.8% | 1.78% | 0.587 |
| United States | 4.53% | 46.2% | 1.24% | 0.791 |
| **Average** | **3.00%** | **26.0%** | **0.82%** | **0.586** |
| **Std. deviation** | **2.53%** | **17.6%** | **0.80%** | **0.206** |
| **Maximum** | **11.18%** | **76.4%** | **3.55%** | **0.993** |

Values in shaded areas are imputed.
SOURCES:
Johns Hopkins Comparative Nonprofit Sector Project
International Labour Organization (http://laborsta.ilo.org)
United States Census Bureau
World Values Survey, 1991 and 1995 (computer files)

**Annex D.** Global Civil Society Index: correlation matrices[a]

| Capacity | | | | |
| --- | --- | --- | --- | --- |
| | Paid | Volunteers | Dispersion | Giving |
| Paid employment | 1.00 | 0.57 | -0.06 | 0.43 |
| Volunteers | 0.57 | 1.00 | 0.13 | 0.22 |
| Dispersion | -0.06 | 0.13 | 1.00 | 0.17 |
| Private giving | 0.43 | 0.22 | 0.17 | 1.00 |

| Sustainability | | | | |
| --- | --- | --- | --- | --- |
| | Gov't payments | Fees | Legal environ. | Volunteer particip. |
| Gov't payments | 1.00 | -0.88 | 0.59 | 0.13 |
| Fees | -0.88 | 1.00 | -0.36 | -0.08 |
| Legal environment | 0.59 | -0.36 | 1.00 | 0.17 |
| Volunteer participation | 0.13 | -0.08 | 0.55 | 1.00 |

| Capacity | | | | |
| --- | --- | --- | --- | --- |
| | Value added | Market share | Expressive | Member-ship |
| Value added | 1.00 | 0.83 | 0.61 | 0.57 |
| Market share | 0.83 | 1.00 | 0.30 | 0.39 |
| Expressive | 0.61 | 0.30 | 1.00 | 0.17 |
| Membership | 0.57 | 0.39 | 0.58 | 1.00 |

| GCSI | | | |
| --- | --- | --- | --- |
| | Capacity | Sustain-ability | Impact |
| Capacity | 1.00 | 0.68 | 0.85 |
| Sustainability | 0.68 | 1.00 | 0.78 |
| Impact | 0.85 | 0.78 | 1.00 |

[a] Bivariate Pearson correlation coefficients, normalized variables

# Part Two

# AFRICA

# Chapter 3

# Kenya

Karuti Kanyinga, Winnie Mitullah,
Walter Odhiambo, S. Wojciech Sokolowski,
and Lester M. Salamon

## Introduction

Kenya has a rich tradition of philanthropy and voluntarism with roots in the communal relationships of a rural African society. This tradition was augmented, however, by a host of educational and social welfare institutions established by 19th-century Christian missionaries, by the social clubs created to serve the British colonial settlers, by the social-political and protest organizations that arose to combat British rule, and by the networks of self-help, or *harambee,* groups promoted by the first post-Independence government before the subsequent Moi government began a crackdown on civil society groups.

The upshot is a sizable and diverse civil society sector that includes indigenous grassroots associations and self-help groups, religiously affiliated organizations, foundations, health care centers, schools, welfare groups, political parties, business and professional associations, and secular nongovernmental organizations. These organizations employ well over a quarter of a million full-time equivalent workers, both paid and volunteer, and are engaged predominantly in service-oriented activities. Their main sources of support are service fees, charges, and membership dues.

These findings emerge from a body of work carried out by a Kenyan research team as part of the Johns Hopkins Comparative Nonprofit Sector Project.[1] This work sought both to analyze Kenyan civil society organizations and to compare and contrast them to those in other countries in a systematic way.[2] Our data cover not only larger nongovernmental organizations (NGOs) but also small community-based associations. The result is the first empirical overview of the Kenyan civil society sector and the first systematic comparison of Kenyan civil society realities to those elsewhere in the world.

**Table 3.1.** The civil society sector* in Kenya, ca. 2000

---

**$269.7 million in expenditures**

- 2.5% of the GDP

**290,948 full-time equivalent workers**

- 177,075 full-time equivalent paid employees
- 113,873 full-time equivalent volunteers
- 2.1% of the economically active population
- 16.3% of nonagricultural employment
- 42.6% of public employment

---

* Including religious worship organizations.

SOURCE: Johns Hopkins Comparative Nonprofit Sector Project

This chapter reports chiefly on the major descriptive findings of this project relating to the size, composition, and financing of the civil society sector in Kenya and other countries. Other reports from this project will fill in more of the history, legal position, and impact of these institutions. Most of the data reported here were generated from an expressly designed survey that used hypernetwork sampling techniques to capture unregistered, informal organizations, supplemented by information from various government sources. Additional research work, including a giving and volunteering survey, was also conducted by the project team. The year covered in this report is 2000. Unless otherwise noted, financial data are reported in U.S. dollars at the 2000 average exchange rate. For a more complete statement of the types of organizations included, see Chapter 1 and Appendix B.

## Principal Findings

### 1. A significant economic force

The civil society sector in Kenya (including religious worship organizations) is a sizeable economic force. More specifically:

- **A $270 million industry.** Civil society organizations in Kenya accounted for $270 million in expenditures as of 2000. This amount represents 2.5 percent of the nation's gross domestic product (GDP), as reported in Table 3.1.

- **A significant employer.** The workforce — paid and volunteer — behind these expenditures represents over 290,000 full-time equivalent (FTE) workers. This constitutes 2.1 percent of Kenya's economically active population, and 16.3 percent of its nonagricultural employment.

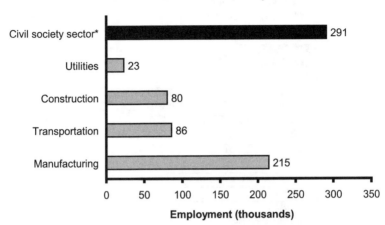

**Figure 3.1.** Civil society organization workforce in context, Kenya

Employment (thousands)

* Including volunteers
SOURCE: Johns Hopkins Comparative Nonprofit Sector Project

- **Outdistances major industries.** The civil society sector employs almost half (43 percent) as many people as the public sector (see Table 3.1), and outdistances major industries in Kenya. As Figure 3.1 shows, the civil society organization workforce — paid and volunteer — exceeds employment in the utilities, construction, transportation, and manufacturing sectors in Kenya.

- **Substantial volunteer input.** Of the 290,000 FTE civil society organization workers in Kenya, almost 114,000, or 39 percent, are volunteers. Our survey data suggest that the actual number of people who volunteer is significantly higher — almost 1.0 million people, or approximately 6 percent of the adult population — because on average volunteers work fewer than 65 hours per year (see Appendix Table A.2).

## 2. Similar to other developing countries

- **Slightly above most developing and transitional countries.** The Kenyan civil society organization workforce is larger than those in most other developing and transitional countries. As shown in Figure 3.2, excluding religious worship organizations, the civil society organization workforce — paid and volunteer — varies from a high of 14.4 percent of the economically active population in the Netherlands to a low of 0.4 percent in Mexico, with an average of 4.4 percent overall, and 1.9 percent in the developing and transitional countries.[3] The Kenyan figure is higher than the developing and transitional country average (2.1 vs. 1.9 percent).

**Figure 3.2.** Civil society organization workforce
as a share of the economically active population, by country

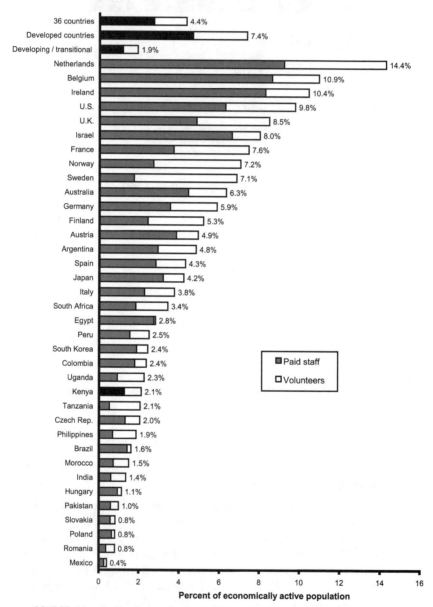

Percent of economically active population

SOURCE: Johns Hopkins Comparative Nonprofit Sector Project

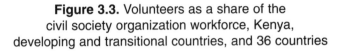

**Figure 3.3.** Volunteers as a share of the
civil society organization workforce, Kenya,
developing and transitional countries, and 36 countries

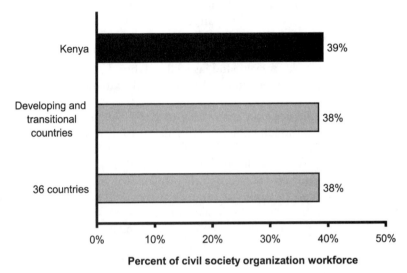

**Percent of civil society organization workforce**

SOURCE: Johns Hopkins Comparative Nonprofit Sector Project

- **Below the all-country average.** However, the civil society organization workforce in Kenya is much smaller than those in the developed countries. Consequently, it falls well below the all-country average (2.1 percent vs. 4.4 percent). The Kenyan civil society organization workforce is also smaller than the average for all the African countries covered in this project, which is 2.5 percent of the economically active population (see Chapter 1, Table 1.13).

- **Volunteer share of civil society organization workforce on a par with other countries.** As shown in Figure 3.3, volunteer participation in Kenya, which accounts for about 39 percent of the civil society sector workforce, is slightly above the developing and transitional country and all-country averages (38 percent each).

## 3. A complex history

The civil society sector in Kenya owes its origins to three major sources: African communal traditions and values, early Christian missionaries, and British colonization during the 19th century.

Before the 19th century, the peoples of Kenya lived in small rural communities organized along primary social groups, such as clans and lineages.

These communities developed institutions that provided a social safety net and emergency relief for members and that pooled resources to help each other. Perhaps the most characteristic feature of these early forms of social organization was their collectivistic nature, which emphasized the close connection among individuals and the larger community and the community's responsibility for each individual's well-being. The form of charity that existed during this time included mostly donations of needed goods, such as food, shelter, livestock, or even land, as well as labor. Providing such goods was viewed as a social obligation and an aspect of mutualism rather than a benevolent act.

The Christian missionaries who came to Kenya in the early 1840s introduced modern, although relatively informal institutions, such as schools, health care facilities, and churches. The first institution of this kind, a mission school run by the Church Mission Society at Rabai, was established in 1846.[4] These institutions focused on relief, social welfare, and provision of social services. However, existing traditional forms of social organization heavily influenced these forms of social assistance.

British colonization in 1895 brought other forms of nonprofit and philanthropic institutions to Kenya, including settler associations, social clubs, and sporting associations. These organizations were aimed primarily at promoting the welfare of the colonial settlers. However, traditional organizational forms, serving mainly the indigenous people, existed alongside the British-introduced institutions.

In response to the expropriation of native land and other forms of exploitation introduced by colonialism, a variety of indigenous organizations surfaced to resist colonial exploitation. These included political associations, such as the Kikuyu Central Association, the Taita Hills Association, and the North Kavirondo Association, as well as independent schools, churches, trade unions, and self-help groups. Some of these groups formed along ethnic lines because the colonial state confined their operations to their respective Native Reserves. This ethnicized the society and prevented the growth of nationwide groups.

Following World War II, the independence movement intensified with the return of the African soldiers who had fought in the war. This led to the emergence of militant political groups such as the Kenya Land Reform Army and the Mau Mau peasant movement, which was instrumental in the national liberation struggle in the 1950s leading to independence from colonial rule in 1963.

The Kenyatta government that emerged after Kenya gained independence in 1963 encouraged the growth of self-help groups and traditional forms of social solidarity as a means of mobilizing political support. These efforts led to the emergence of the *harambee* (pooling together) movement, which aimed to mobilize local populations and their resources to build schools, health facilities, community centers, and infrastructure.[5] Other types of civil society organizations, including trade unions, church-based entities, and economic interest groups, such as cooperatives and self-help women's groups, also enjoyed government support.

With the replacement of the Kenyatta government by the Moi administration in 1978, the cordial partnership and laissez-faire environment the civil society sector enjoyed gradually changed to a hostile and competitive one, particularly in the development and political arenas. In an attempt to consolidate its power and undermine opposition, the Moi government demobilized or marginalized many regional associations and consolidated its control over those entities that were allowed to operate (e.g., the *harambees*).[6] Some organizations, such as the umbrella women's body, *Maendeleo ya Wanawake,* were co-opted into the ruling party, the Kenya African National Union (KANU). The 1991 repeal of a constitutional clause outlawing opposition and the subsequent liberalization of the economy during the 1990s, however, led to a revival of the Kenyan civil society sector, as development organizations, a variety of women's groups, and professional and grassroots movement groups significantly broadened the sector's social base.

## 4. Strong presence of service organizations

Reflecting these historical influences, most of the Kenyan civil society sector workforce is engaged in service functions, such as community development and social services. Although expressive activities, which include advocacy, political organizing, labor and professional organizations, and culture and recreation seem less prominent, this is largely due to the fact that many primarily service-oriented organizations also perform advocacy functions. More specifically:

- **Service activities dominate.** As shown in Figure 3.4, 60 percent of all Kenyan civil society organization workers — paid and volunteer — are engaged in service activities.[7] This is comparable to the pattern found in the developing and transitional country and all-country averages (63 and 64 percent, respectively). However, a much larger share of this workforce is engaged in community development and housing activity in Kenya than the average for all countries or for just the developing and transitional countries (20 percent vs. 7 and 9 percent, respectively). Such a large share of development-oriented activities is characteristic of the African civil society sector (on average, 18 percent of the total workforce). On the other hand, education absorbs a smaller share of the civil society organization workforce in Kenya than the all-country or developing country averages (11 percent vs. 23 and 25 percent, respectively).

- **Small share of expressive activities.** By contrast, the share of the civil society sector workforce engaged in expressive activities in Kenya is quite small at only 15 percent. This is less than half of both the developing and transitional country and the all-country averages (32 percent each). What

**Figure 3.4.** Composition of the
civil society organization workforce, Kenya,
developing and transitional countries, and 33-country average

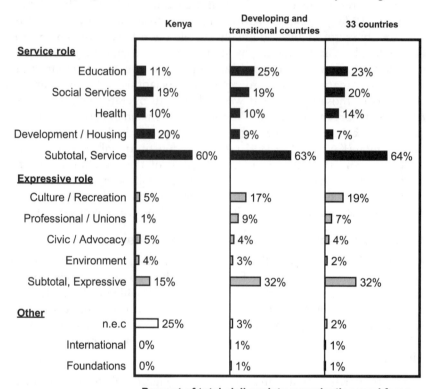

**Percent of total civil society organization workforce**

n.e.c.= not elsewhere classified
SOURCE: Johns Hopkins Comparative Nonprofit Sector Project

is more, Kenya engages significantly fewer people in expressive activities than the other African countries studied (15 vs. 29 percent, as noted in Chapter 1, Table 1.13).

• **Dual role of community development organizations.** In addition to the recent history of authoritarian rule, another possible explanation for the apparently low level of expressive activity on the part of Kenyan civil society organizations is the dual character of community development organizations in the African context. Although community development organizations were initially promoted by the colonial authorities to remedy social problems created by colonial exploitation, these organizations often served as the basis for political mobilization and empowerment of

**Figure 3.5.** Distribution of paid employees and volunteers between service and expressive activities in Kenya

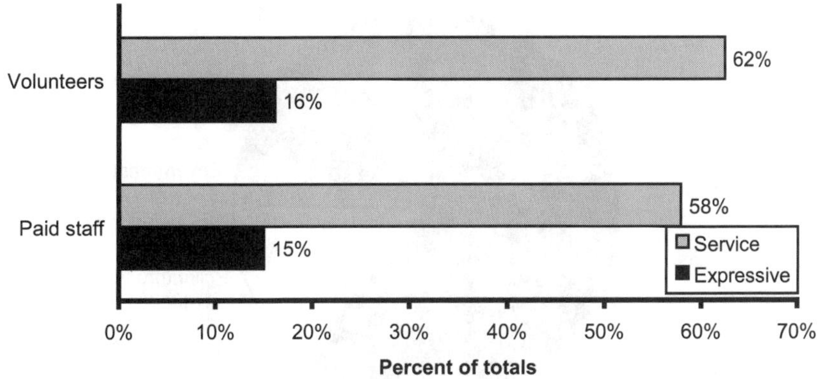

SOURCE: Johns Hopkins Comparative Nonprofit Sector Project

disenfranchised populations. They are therefore properly considered part of both the service and expressive components of the civil society sector in Africa. Including community development organizations in the expressive component would therefore increase the expressive share from 15 to 35 percent of Kenya's civil society sector workforce, moving it much closer to the developing and transitional country average.

- **Large share of "other" activities.** A unique feature of the Kenyan civil society sector is the sizable 25 percent of the workforce engaged in activities "not elsewhere classified." This group is primarily made up of organizations concentrating on agricultural activities and related rural development projects. Many of these organizations also probably belong in the development category. Including them there would increase the development share to almost 45 percent of the total civil society sector workforce.

- **Paid and volunteer staff distributed similarly.** The distribution of the civil society organization workforce in Kenya changes very little when paid staff and volunteers are examined separately. As shown in Figure 3.5, most (62 percent) volunteer staff time is concentrated in service functions. Similarly, most paid staff time (58 percent) is concentrated in service functions, too.

## 5. Revenue dominated by fees and charges

Fees, charges, and membership dues are the dominant source of civil society organization revenue in Kenya, outdistancing philanthropy and government support. In particular:

**Figure 3.6.** Sources of civil society
organization revenue in Kenya

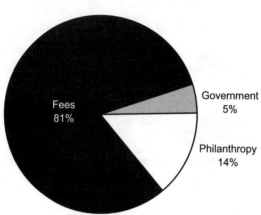

SOURCE: Johns Hopkins Comparative Nonprofit Sector Project

- **Fee dominance in Kenya.** About 81 percent of Kenyan civil society organizations' cash revenue comes from service fees, property income, and
  membership dues, as shown in Figure 3.6. Of the balance, 14 percent
  comes from all sources of private philanthropy, including individuals,
  foundations, corporations, and foreign donors; and 5 percent from the
  public sector.

- **Differs from international pattern.** This pattern of civil society organization revenue differs significantly from that found elsewhere.

  – The Kenyan civil society sector relies much more substantially on fees
    and dues than its counterparts elsewhere. As Figure 3.7 shows, the
    fee share of Kenyan civil society sector revenue is significantly larger
    than the developing and transitional country and all-country averages
    (81 percent vs. 61 and 53 percent, respectively).

  – At the same time, the Kenyan civil society sector receives a much
    smaller share of its support from the public sector than the other
    developing and transitional countries or the 34-country average (5 per-
    cent vs. 22 and 34 percent, respectively). This low level of public
    support can be explained, in part, by the post-colonial government's
    policy of encouraging traditional forms of self-help to offset short-
    falls in the government's ability to fund social development programs;
    and in part by the Moi government's outright hostility to civil society
    organizations.

**Figure 3.7.** Sources of civil society organization revenue,
Kenya, developing and transitional countries,
and 34-country average

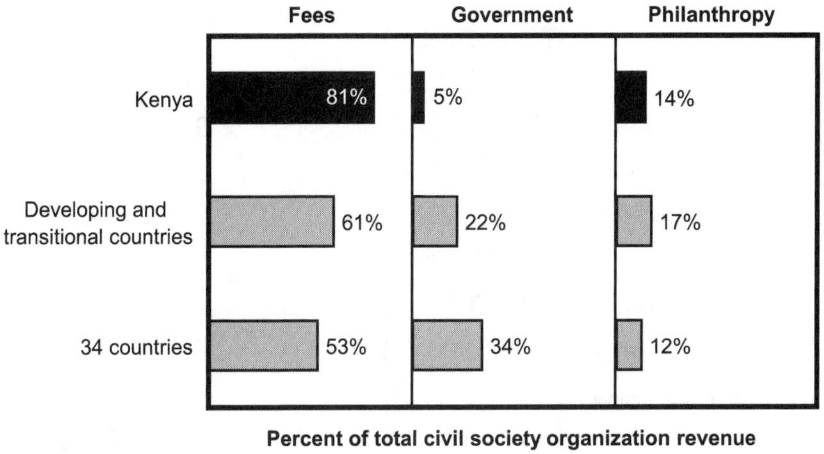

| | Fees | Government | Philanthropy |
|---|---|---|---|
| Kenya | 81% | 5% | 14% |
| Developing and transitional countries | 61% | 22% | 17% |
| 34 countries | 53% | 34% | 12% |

**Percent of total civil society organization revenue**

SOURCE: Johns Hopkins Comparative Nonprofit Sector Project

- Philanthropic giving in Kenya, at 14 percent of civil society sector revenue, is also less than the developing and transitional country average (17 percent), but above the all-country average (12 percent).

• **Support structure varies among fields.** The dominant position of fees and dues in the finances of Kenyan civil society organizations finds reflection in all but one field. However, the share of fee income varies from 49 percent in environmental protection to 100 percent in health. For only one type of organization — foundations and philanthropic intermediaries — does private giving account for the largest share of revenues (see Figure 3.8). Government payments are not the main income source in any field.

• **Volunteers change the revenue structure modestly.** This picture of the revenue structure of the Kenyan civil society sector changes moderately when the value of volunteer input is included. As Figure 3.9 demonstrates, with contributions of time treated as part of philanthropy, the philanthropy share of civil society support in Kenya increases from 14 to 24 percent. This is below the developing and transitional country average (33 percent) and the all-country average (31 percent), as well as other African countries (on average, 46 percent of the total civil society organization support, as shown in Chapter 1, Table 1.13).

**Figure 3.8.** Sources of civil society organization revenue, Kenya, by field

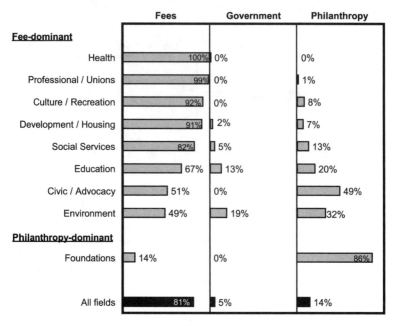

SOURCE: Johns Hopkins Comparative Nonprofit Sector Project

**Figure 3.9.** Sources of civil society organization support
including volunteers, Kenya, developing and
transitional countries, and 34-country average

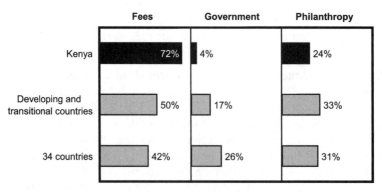

SOURCE: Johns Hopkins Comparative Nonprofit Sector Project

**Figure 3.10.** Sources of civil society organization support
in Kenya, including volunteers, by field

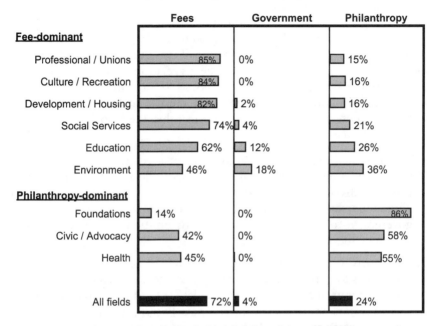

**Percent of total civil society organization support**

SOURCE: Johns Hopkins Comparative Nonprofit Sector Project

– With the value of volunteer input included, private philanthropy becomes the main source of support in three fields: foundations and
philanthropic intermediaries (86 percent), civic and advocacy activity (58 percent), and health (55 percent). This reflects the importance
of volunteer input in health care delivery in Kenya. In fact, nearly a
fifth of the volunteer workforce is concentrated in this field. All other
fields rely primarily on fee support (see Figure 3.10).

## Conclusions and Implications

Kenya thus has one of the largest civil society sectors among the developing
and transitional countries. Its workforce, a substantial part of which is volunteers, exceeds that of the country's entire manufacturing sector. The civil
society sector plays significant economic, political, and social roles in Kenya.
It provides important human services, especially in the area of community development, and empowers disadvantaged segments of the population,
such as women and the rural poor.

The Kenyan government's policy toward this sector has been somewhat ambivalent, however. Whereas the government views civil society organizations as potential partners in national development, it is often reluctant to let these organizations operate without constraints. In spite of an open-door policy, the government often closely monitors and controls the activity of civil society organizations through the use of law and provincial administration. No overall policy guides government's relationships with civil society organizations. As a result, the civil society sector in Kenya is not being fully utilized to assist both the government and international agencies in their efforts to promote national growth. To correct this, the following steps could usefully be taken:

- **Pluralism and democracy.** The government needs to make a clear commitment to securing a political environment that respects human rights, promotes freedoms, and enables civil society organizations to operate without unreasonable constraints. At the same time, there is a need for the government to recognize civil society organizations as legitimate actors in Kenya's development space.

- **Public-private partnership.** The government also needs to broaden the opportunities for partnership with the civil society sector. Such partnerships should operate under clearly defined roles for the public, private, and civil society sectors. In particular, the civil society sector needs to articulate its complementary role to both the public and the private sectors.

- **Capacity building.** The leadership of civil society organizations should make a commitment to building their organizational and professional capacity. The government and foreign agencies, such as international relief organizations and the World Bank, should provide the resources necessary for strengthening the organizational capacity of the civil society sector; this includes professional skill development as well as securing funding and in-kind support.

- **Building legitimacy through self-regulation.** The civil society sector needs to develop and enforce codes of conduct, accountability, and administration standards and to promote greater transparency in its own operations.

- **Information gathering and dissemination.** In order to foster public understanding of the civil society sector and its role in Kenyan society, there needs to be a sustained effort to produce reliable information about the sector's organizational capacity and output, as well as an unbiased assessment of the quality of its services and their social and economic impact.

The civil society sector has proven to be an important agent in facilitating economic development, providing relief and social services, and empowering disadvantaged social groups in Kenya. It is therefore crucial that this role be more fully recognized and utilized by both policymakers and foreign assistance agencies. To achieve that goal, however, it is essential to develop an accurate assessment of the civil society sector's capacities and needs. We hope that this chapter is a useful step towards this goal.

## Notes

1. The work in Kenya has been coordinated by Karuti Kanyinga and Winnie Mitullah. Sebastian Njagi served as the project assistant. Other researchers in the project were Walter Odhiambo, Lawrence Mute and Patrick Alila. The research team was aided, in turn, by a local advisory committee (see Appendix D for a list of committee members). The Johns Hopkins project was directed by Lester M. Salamon, and the work in Kenya was overseen by Leslie C. Hems and later by S. Wojciech Sokolowski.

2. The definitions and approaches used in the project were developed collaboratively with the cooperation of Kenyan researchers and researchers in other countries and were designed to be applicable to Kenya and other project countries. For a full description of this definition, the types of organizations included, and the methodology used, see Chapter 1 and Appendix B. For a full list of the other countries included, see Table 1.1.

3. Comparative figures do not include religious worship organizations because data on these organizations were not available for all countries. However, religiously affiliated service organizations are included. For more information, see Appendix B.

4. J.E. Otiende, "Education Since the Early Missionaries," in *Themes in Kenyan History,* ed. William R. Ochieng (Nairobi: East African Education Publishers, 1990), 145–155.

5. Karuti Kanyinga, "Ethnicity, Patronage and Class in a Local Arena: High and Low Politics in Kiambu, Kenya, 1982–1992," in *The New Local Level Politics in East Africa,* ed. Peter Gibbon (Uppsala, Sweden: Scandinavian Institute of African Studies, 1994), 88–117.

6. Stephen N. Ndegwa, *The Two Faces of Civil Society: NGOs and Politics in Africa* (West Hartford, CT: Kumarian Press, 1996).

7. Percentages displayed in figures may not add to 100 due to rounding.

# Chapter 4

# South Africa

Mark Swilling, Bev Russell,
S. Wojciech Sokolowski, and Lester M. Salamon

## Introduction

The civil society sector in South Africa has been shaped by two forces: the corporatist tradition of the Dutch settlers that gave civic associations a prominent role in the delivery of public welfare services, and the self-help spirit of the indigenous people. Under the apartheid regime, civic associations were incorporated into the social welfare system, which served the white population exclusively. Blacks, on the other hand, were cut off from any government assistance and forced to rely on their own organizations and networks. These indigenous organizations subsequently played an important role in political mobilization during the struggle against apartheid and the transition to democracy.

As a result of these influences, South Africa has a sizeable civil society sector that is dominated by service activities, but that also has a relatively large advocacy component. Its main sources of support — government payments and substantial volunteer input — are large by developing country standards.

These findings emerge from a body of work carried out by a South African research team as part of the Johns Hopkins Comparative Nonprofit Sector Project.[1] This work sought both to analyze South African civil society organizations and to compare and contrast them to those in other countries in a systematic way.[2] The result is the first empirical overview of the South African civil society sector and the first systematic comparison of South African civil society realities to those elsewhere in the world.[3]

This chapter reports chiefly on the major descriptive findings of this project relating to the size, composition, and financing of the civil society sector in South Africa and other countries. Other reports from this project fill in more of the history, legal position, and impact of this set of institutions. Most of the data reported here were generated from an expressly designed survey, which used hypernetwork sampling techniques to capture unregistered, informal organizations, supplemented by a sample derived from the

**Table 4.1.** The civil society sector* in South Africa, 1998

---

**$1.7 billion in expenditures**

- 1.3% of the GDP

**645,322 full-time equivalent workers**

- 328,327 full-time equivalent paid employees
- 316,995 full-time equivalent volunteers
- 4.0% of the economically active population
- 8.7% of nonagricultural employment
- 36.7% of public employment

---

* Including religious worship organizations.

SOURCE: Johns Hopkins Comparative Nonprofit Sector Project

PRODDER registry of nonprofit entities.[4] The year covered in this report is 1998. Additional research work, including a giving and volunteering survey, was also conducted by the project team. Unless otherwise noted, financial data are reported in U.S. dollars at the 1998 average exchange rate. For a more complete statement of the types of organizations included, see Chapter 1 and Appendix B.

# Principal Findings

## 1. A significant economic force

The size and economic significance of the civil society sector in South Africa is greater than previously thought. More specifically, the data assembled for South African civil society organizations in 1998 depict:

- **A $1.7 billion industry.** The civil society sector in South Africa accounted for $1.7 billion in expenditures, or 1.3 percent of the nation's gross domestic product (GDP), as reported in Table 4.1.

- **A significant employer.** Even more impressive is the workforce behind these expenditures, which numbers over 645,000 full-time equivalent (FTE) workers (including religious worship organizations). This represents 4.0 percent of the country's economically active population, and 8.7 percent of its nonagricultural employment.

- **A sector that outdistances many industries.** The civil society sector in South Africa engages a larger workforce than the nation's key industry, mining. As shown in Figure 4.1, it also outdistances utilities, transportation, and construction. What is more, this workforce equals half of that in the entire manufacturing sector.

**Figure 4.1.** Civil society organization workforce in context, South Africa

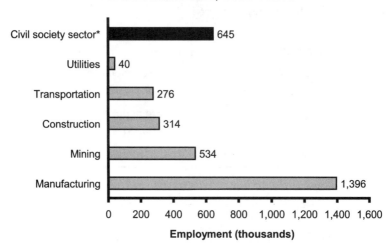

\* Including volunteers
SOURCE: Johns Hopkins Comparative Nonprofit Sector Project

- **Extensive volunteer input.** There are over 300,000 FTE volunteers in South Africa (see Table 4.1), which represents about 1.6 percent of the economically active population (see Appendix Table A.1). The actual number of people volunteering is actually even higher than this because most volunteers do not work full-time. We conservatively estimate that approximately 9.0 percent of South Africa's adult population, 2.7 million people in all, engage in volunteer work of some kind (see Appendix Table A.2).

## 2. South African civil society sector exceeds developing country average

- **One of the largest civil society sectors among developing and transitional countries.** The South African civil society organization workforce is the second largest among developing and transitional countries included in this study. As shown in Figure 4.2, excluding religious worship organizations, for which data are not available for all countries, the civil society organization workforce — paid and volunteer — varies from a high of 14.4 percent of the economically active population in the Netherlands to a low of 0.4 percent in Mexico, with an average of 4.4 percent overall.[5] The South African figure, at 3.4 percent, is higher than that of eighteen other developing and transitional countries included in this project, and is surpassed only by Argentina.

**Figure 4.2.** Civil society organization workforce
as a share of the economically active population, by country

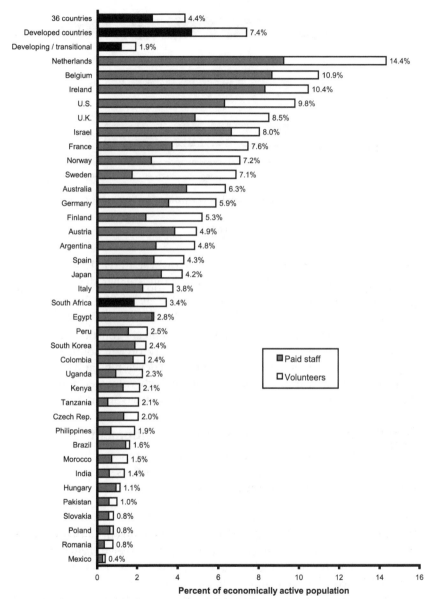

SOURCE: Johns Hopkins Comparative Nonprofit Sector Project

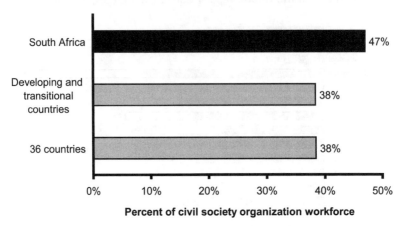

**Figure 4.3.** Volunteers as a share of the civil society organization workforce, South Africa, developing and transitional countries, and 36 countries

**Percent of civil society organization workforce**

SOURCE: Johns Hopkins Comparative Nonprofit Sector Project

- **Slightly below the international average.** However, the civil society organization workforce in South Africa is noticeably smaller than that in the developed countries (3.4 percent vs. 7.4 percent). Consequently, it also falls below the all-country average of 4.4 percent (see Figure 4.2).

- **Volunteer participation unusually high.** Volunteers constitute a particularly large share of the civil society sector workforce in South Africa (47 vs. 38 percent each for all countries and for all developing and transitional countries), as shown in Figure 4.3. Similar high volunteer participation rates were also found in the other African countries studied.

## 3. A complex history of civil society development

The key element in the development of the civil society sector in South Africa is race, and, to some extent, social class. Race and class divisions separated communities and diminished their ability to solve common problems. Separate organizations emerged to serve narrowly defined ethnic, cultural, and religious groups.[6]

The indigenous population of South Africa consisted of the Khoi and San communities, which formed loosely knit, highly egalitarian, nomadic groups; and Bantu tribes, which lived in pastoral communities with, in most cases, clearly articulated chieftain structures. However, these structures were prone to splitting into separate groups in response to harsh natural environments that were unsuited to sustaining large populations of hunter-gatherers and pastoralists. This tendency to self-organize to cope with life-threatening circumstances carried over into the modern civil society sector and manifests itself in the proliferation of separatist churches, unions, service and civic organizations, herbalist associations, and traditional tribal organizations.

Dutch colonization between 1652 and 1810 introduced farming and slavery to the area. In 1795, the British took control of the Cape Colony. British occupation created an entry for Northern charitable organizations and missions into South Africa. Christian missionaries, aiming to convert the indigenous peoples, eventually came to support the campaign against slavery and played a role in improving the treatment of black slaves and in their eventual emancipation. The British Abolition of the Slave Trade Act took effect in 1808, and the Emancipation Act was passed in 1834.

Rapid economic growth brought a massive influx of immigrants to South Africa. Each of these ethnic, cultural, and religious groups developed organizations to serve their own interests. However, these groups rarely united to fight for their common interests; rather, each acted individually to protect their own rights. In reaction to the growing British influence in the region, Afrikaners launched a number of associations to protect their interests, such as the Afrikaner Bond and the Boer Farmer's Protection Association.

Black organizations started to emerge in the late 19th century in response to increasing discrimination. For example, the "Ethiopian" church movement, which spun off from the Wesleyan Church in 1892, began to challenge white authority and provide leadership for African movements against racial separatism and in favor of African nationalism. The first African political association, Imbumba Yama Afrika, was formed in 1882, followed by the formation of the Native Electoral Association in 1884.

The formation of the Union of South Africa in 1910 and the industrialization that followed spurred a large-scale labor movement that resulted in new labor legislation granting trade union rights to all ethnic groups except Africans. In response, Africans formed the South African Native National Congress (SNNC) whose main mission was advocacy and representation of black interests in South Africa and abroad. It was later transformed into the African National Congress (ANC), the organization that played the leading role in the struggle against the apartheid regime.

These developments, in turn, strengthened the resistance of both English- and Afrikaans-speaking whites to the growing influence of non-whites. Afrikaner nationalism became a "civil religion" as it penetrated the Afrikaner community through an extensive network of Dutch Reformed churches, Federation of Afrikaans Cultural Associations (FAK), and affiliated organizations.

The policy of apartheid, initiated in 1948, led to further racial polarization of civil society organizations. Through its policy of selectively withholding financial support, the government implemented a systematic separation of community welfare organizations along racial and ethnic lines.

Legal obstacles were also raised against foreign funding of organizations perceived as opposing the state. These policies, compounded by ethnic, cultural, religious, and political divides within the civil society sector, led to extreme fragmentation of the sector, duplication of efforts, and inefficiency. This situation was further exacerbated by discriminatory provision of state support on the basis of the apartheid racial hierarchy in which the best quality services were provided to whites, with lesser quality for Coloureds and Indians, and virtually no services for native Africans.

In response to these policies, two types of organizations emerged in black civil society. The "organizations of survival," such as burial clubs, informal savings clubs (*stokvels*), trade unions, nonpolitical professional associations and unions, and sports clubs, aimed to provide collective sustenance within communities. The "organizations of resistance," consisting mainly of civic associations and trade unions, filled the vacuum created by government repression of political organizations. There was, however, overlap between the two because the latter arose only during periods of crisis and quite often emerged from and then sank back into the "survival organizations."

Among the many African organizations that were active in the antiapartheid struggle were the United Democratic Front (an ANC-allied organization), the Congress of South African Trade Unions, the National Education Union of South Africa, the South African Catholic Bishops' Conference, the South African Council of Churches, as well as local associations, such as the Soweto Civic Association, the Western Cape Civic Association, the Azanian People's Organization, the Port Elizabeth Black Civic Organization, and many others. The politicized positions and activities of these organizations blurred the division between political action and civil society in South Africa and created mass mobilization that eventually ended the apartheid regime through peaceful negotiations in 1994.

In 1994, the first democratically elected government committed itself to an extensive development program in the areas of social welfare, education, health, and housing to reverse the effects of apartheid. In addition to increased funding, the government bolstered its relationship with the civil society sector in policy development and implementation, engaging nongovernmental organizations in the funding and delivery of development projects in line with public policy agendas.

The post-apartheid government also actively engaged civil society organizations in the public policy process. The National Economic Development and Labour Council Act of 1994 and the Local Government Municipal Systems Act of 2000 institutionalized a decision-making process involving a wide set of economic and development policy issues at both the national and local government levels. These acts established a formal structure comprising four separate chambers with representation from government, trade unions, organized business, and community-based organizations.

**Figure 4.4.** Composition of the
civil society organization workforce, South Africa,
developing and transitional countries, and 33-country average

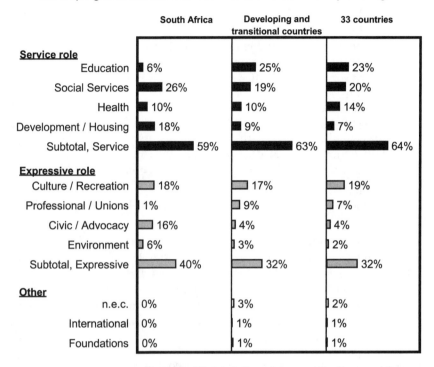

**Percent of total civil society organization workforce**

n.e.c.= not elsewhere classified
SOURCE: Johns Hopkins Comparative Nonprofit Sector Project

## 4. Strong presence of expressive organizations

Reflecting this diverse history, most of the South African civil society sector workforce is engaged in service functions, such as social services, health, or education; but expressive activities, which include culture/recreation and advocacy, are more salient than in most countries except those in Scandinavia and Eastern Europe. More specifically:

- **Service activities dominate.** As shown in Figure 4.4, about 59 percent of all South African civil society organization workers — paid and volunteer — are engaged in service activities.[7] But a sizable 40 percent are engaged in expressive functions such as culture/recreation and advocacy.

- **Relatively larger expressive component than elsewhere.** Reflecting its tradition of social movements, the South African civil society sector engages a larger share of its workforce in expressive functions than is the case elsewhere. Compared to the 40 percent of all civil society organization workers engaged in expressive functions in South Africa the average both internationally and for all developing and transitional countries is 32 percent.

- **Composition of service and expressive fields also differs in South Africa.** Not only do the respective sizes of the service and expressive functions of the civil society sector differ in South Africa, but so does their internal composition.

  - Thus, among the service fields, education and health absorb considerably smaller shares of the civil society organization workforce in South Africa than they do internationally (16 percent vs. 37 percent), whereas housing and development absorb a considerably larger share (18 percent vs. 7 percent). This likely reflects the prominent role of development-oriented "nongovernmental organizations" in the South African civil society sector.

  - Similarly, among the expressive fields, civic/advocacy and environmental functions absorb a larger share of the civil society organization workforce in South Africa than internationally (22 percent vs. 6 percent). By contrast, professional organizations absorb a considerably smaller share (1 percent vs. 7 percent). This pattern likely results from the significant role of civil rights and advocacy activities in the battle against apartheid.

- **Expressive functions even more pronounced if development organizations included.** The prominent position of expressive organizations in the South African civil society sector would be even more pronounced if development organizations were included among the expressive functions rather than the service functions. Such a regrouping makes sense in view of the dual role that many of these organizations play as agents both of service provision and empowerment of marginalized populations. With development organizations included, the expressive functions of the South African civil society sector would swell to 58 percent of the country's civil society organization workforce.

- **Paid and volunteer staff distributed differently.** This picture of the distribution of the civil society organization workforce in South Africa changes significantly when paid staff and volunteers are examined separately. As shown in Figure 4.5, more volunteer staff time is concentrated in expressive functions than service functions (56 percent vs. 44 percent), while more paid staff time is concentrated in service functions than expressive ones (73 percent versus 27 percent).

**Figure 4.5.** Distribution of paid employees and volunteers between service and expressive activities in South Africa

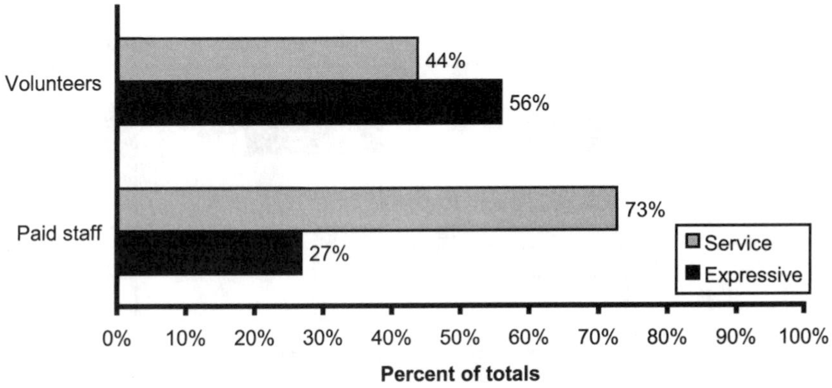

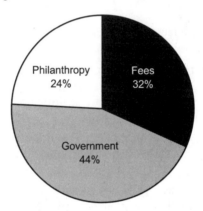

SOURCE: Johns Hopkins Comparative Nonprofit Sector Project

**Figure 4.6.** Sources of civil society organization revenue in South Africa

Philanthropy 24%
Fees 32%
Government 44%

SOURCE: Johns Hopkins Comparative Nonprofit Sector Project

## 5. Revenue dominated by government payments

Government payments are the dominant source of civil society organization revenue in South Africa, outdistancing philanthropy and fees and charges. In particular:

- **Government is the largest source of civil society revenue.** About 44 percent of all South African civil society organization cash revenue comes from government payments, as shown in Figure 4.6. Another 32 percent of

**Figure 4.7.** Sources of civil society organization revenue,
South Africa, developing and transitional countries,
and 34-country average

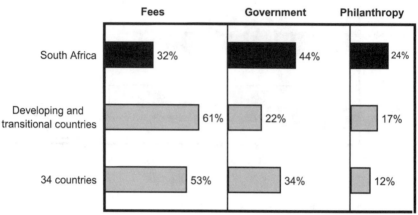

**Percent of total civil society organization revenue**

SOURCE: Johns Hopkins Comparative Nonprofit Sector Project

revenue comes from fees, and 24 percent comes from all sources of private philanthropy, including individuals, foundations, and corporations.

• **Differs from international pattern.** This pattern of civil society organization revenue differs significantly from that evident internationally, especially in other developing and transitional countries. It also differs from that evident elsewhere in Africa.

– The South African civil society sector relies much more substantially on government payments (both domestic and foreign) than its counterparts in other developing and transitional countries. As Figure 4.7 shows, the government share of South Africa's civil society sector revenue is twice as large as that in other developing and transitional countries (44 vs. 22 percent) and exceeds the all-country average by 10 percentage points. In fact, the government share of civil society organization revenue in South Africa is almost on a par with the developed country average (44 percent and 48 percent, as shown in Appendix Table A.4).

– The South African civil society sector also receives almost twice as much support from philanthropic giving than its counterparts internationally (24 percent vs. 12 percent). This high level of philanthropic support can be explained, in part, by the post-apartheid government policy of strong encouragement of corporate philanthropy to offset social disadvantages created by the apartheid regime, and in part by the

**Figure 4.8.** Sources of civil society organization revenue, South Africa, by field

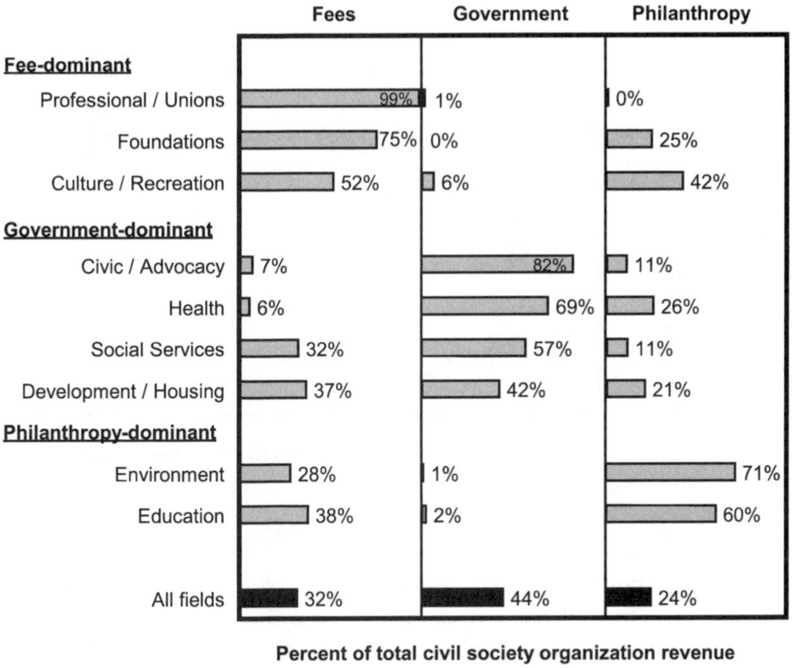

**Percent of total civil society organization revenue**

SOURCE: Johns Hopkins Comparative Nonprofit Sector Project

tradition of external support to South African civil society established during the apartheid period.

- Consequently, the South African civil society sector relies on fees and charges to a much lesser extent than most other countries, especially those in the developing and transitional group. Fees account for only 32 percent of civil society sector revenue in South Africa compared to 61 percent in developing and transitional countries, and 53 percent in all 34 countries (see Figure 4.7).

• **Support structure varies among fields.** The fee share of total revenue is naturally highest among professional associations and labor unions, where membership dues are the primary revenue source, as well as in foundations and culture. Government payments dominate revenue in health, social services, development, and especially in the civic and advocacy field where they account for 82 percent of all cash revenue (see Figure 4.8). Private philanthropy is the main income source in environmental protection and education.

**Figure 4.9.** Sources of civil society organization support including volunteers, South Africa, developing and transitional countries, and 34-country average

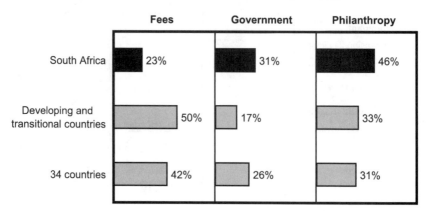

**Percent of total civil society organization support**

SOURCE: Johns Hopkins Comparative Nonprofit Sector Project

- **Volunteers significantly change the revenue structure.** The picture of the revenue structure of the South African civil society sector changes substantially when the value of volunteer input is included. As Figure 4.9 demonstrates, with volunteers included, private contributions of time and money constitute the largest source of civil society sector support in South Africa, accounting for 46 percent of the total. This is substantially above the developing and transitional country average (33 percent) and the all-country average (31 percent), but on a par with other African countries, which average 46 percent (see Table 1.13).

  - With the value of volunteer input included, private philanthropy becomes the main source of support in all fields except professional associations, which rely primarily on fee support, and health and social services, which rely predominantly on government payments (see Figure 4.10).

## Conclusions and Implications

The data reported in this study reveal for the first time the size of the civil society sector in South Africa and the social and political roles it plays. The study captured not only larger formally registered entities, but also less formal community-based organizations serving predominantly disadvantaged segments of the population.

**Figure 4.10.** Sources of civil society organization support
in South Africa, including volunteers, by field

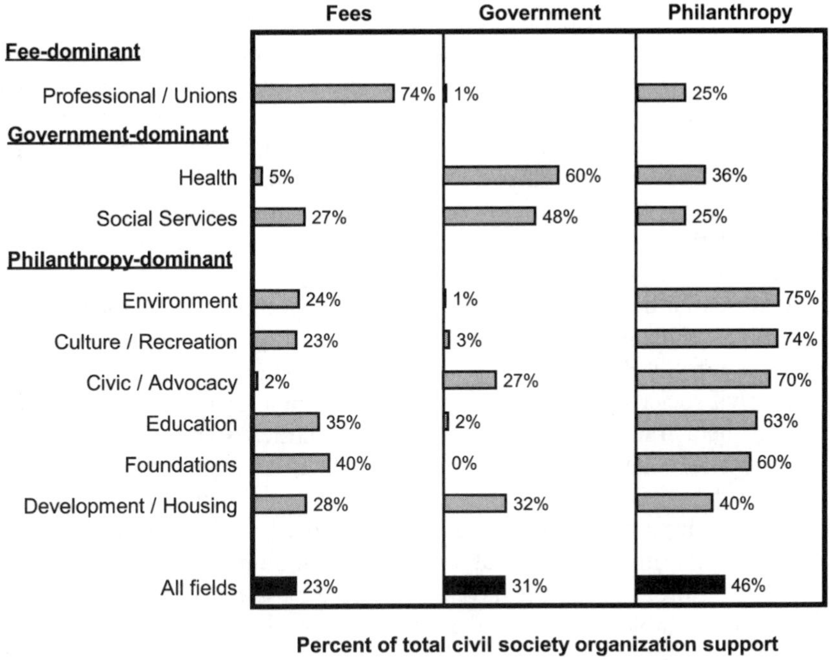

| | Fees | Government | Philanthropy |
|---|---|---|---|
| **Fee-dominant** | | | |
| Professional / Unions | 74% | 1% | 25% |
| **Government-dominant** | | | |
| Health | 5% | 60% | 36% |
| Social Services | 27% | 48% | 25% |
| **Philanthropy-dominant** | | | |
| Environment | 24% | 1% | 75% |
| Culture / Recreation | 23% | 3% | 74% |
| Civic / Advocacy | 2% | 27% | 70% |
| Education | 35% | 2% | 63% |
| Foundations | 40% | 0% | 60% |
| Development / Housing | 28% | 32% | 40% |
| All fields | 23% | 31% | 46% |

**Percent of total civil society organization support**

SOURCE: Johns Hopkins Comparative Nonprofit Sector Project

As the data show, the civil society sector engages a sizeable paid workforce and equally impressive volunteer staff, which together surpass employment in the key South African industry, mining. South Africa also boasts the second largest civil society sector among the developing and transitional countries covered by this project. While most of this workforce concentrates in service-oriented activities, especially social services and development/housing, the expressive activities (culture and advocacy) also absorb a substantial portion. Government payments constitute the main source of the civil society sector's revenues, but the private philanthropy share is quite high by international standards, and when the value of volunteer input is factored in, it represents the main source of support.

The shape of the civil society sector in South Africa is the product of the country's troubled history, marred by deep fractures along racial, ethnic, religious, and cultural lines. However, the post-apartheid democratic South Africa has provided ample room for the resulting extensive networks of civil society groups, while pursuing social welfare policies that favor growth of the civil society sector. The business sector has also committed itself to significant donations to the civil society sector as a component of its wider funding support for social responsibility projects.

Given the strong position of labor unions and advocacy groups in post-apartheid South Africa, policies stressing public-private cooperation and civil society involvement in service delivery and policymaking are likely to continue. The new democratic state and the civil society sector have negotiated an impressive and sophisticated public space that serves their respective interests. The state is able to harness the financial and organizational resources of the civil society sector to realize its development goals. The civil society sector, on the other hand, can access the financial resources of the state in a way that helps the organizations operate in the new democratic order.

At the same time, however, the civil society sector faces challenges that may substantially impact its growth and relationships with other institutions in the country. Perhaps the most important among them is the bifurcation of the civil society sector into formal and informal spheres inherited from the apartheid era. On the one hand, there are large, established (previously mainly white) health and social service organizations with a considerable capacity to deliver services to a broad variety of constituencies. On the other hand, there are a myriad less formal, community-based organizations serving poorer and more disadvantaged segments of South Africa's population. While these informal entities have limited access to financial resources, they retain considerable potential for mobilizing social movements against unpopular policy decisions. As the economic situation worsens, this bifurcation of the civil society sector may pose a danger to political stability. The fiscal constraints on the state and constraints on the expansion of social welfare spending may undermine the partnership between the civil society sector and the government and create fertile ground for social protest movements.

These challenges will affect the government–civil society sector relationship in the near future. In addressing them, it is important to remember that the civil society sector has proven to be a powerful moderating factor in the turbulent, conflict-ridden history of South Africa and will likely play a similar role in building a new democratic society. It is therefore crucial that that role be fully recognized and utilized by policymakers. To achieve that goal, it is essential not only to continue the current dialogue and cooperation between the public and civil society sectors, but also to create structures allowing a systematic and continuing assessment of the civil society sector's capacity and needs, as the research reported here has sought to do.

## Notes

1. The work in South Africa has been coordinated by Hanlie van Dyk-Robertson (Department of Public Service and Administration, Government of South Africa) and later by Mark Swilling (School of Public Management and Planning, University of

Stellenbosch), aided by Bev Russell (Social Surveys) who designed and executed data collection. The team was aided, in turn, by a local advisory committee (see Appendix D for a list of committee members). The Johns Hopkins project was directed by Lester M. Salamon, and the work in South Africa was overseen by S. Wojciech Sokolowski.

2. The definitions and approaches used in the project were developed collaboratively with the cooperation of South African researchers and researchers in other countries and were designed to be applicable to South Africa and other project countries. For a full description of this definition, the types of organizations included, and the methodology used, see Chapter 1 and Appendix B. For a full list of the other countries included, see Table 1.1.

3. The results of the Johns Hopkins Comparative Nonprofit Sector project have been simultaneously released in South Africa in a publication by Mark Swilling and Bev Russell, *The Size and Scope of the Non-profit Sector in South Africa* (Witwatersrand, South Africa: Graduate School of Public and Development Management, University of Witwatersrand and The Center for Civil Society, University of Natal, 2002).

4. PRODDER is the name of a directory of nonprofit organizations that is compiled and annually updated for publication by the Human Sciences Research Council, which is a government-funded social science research institute. The PRODDER Directory is published by the Human Sciences Research Council each year, and part of the costs are covered from advertising by organizations that are included in the Directory. The Directory simply lists the names and contact addresses of NGOs, with a brief description of the organization's core focus.

5. Comparative figures do not include religious worship organizations because data on these organizations were not available for all countries. However, religiously affiliated service organizations are included. For more information, see Appendix B.

6. This section draws on an unpublished report by Phiroshaw Camay and Anne J. Gordon, "Study on the History of the Nonprofit Sector in South Africa," submitted to the Johns Hopkins Center for Civil Society Studies (Baltimore, MD: 2000).

7. Percentages displayed in figures may not add to 100 due to rounding.

# Chapter 5

# Tanzania

Andrew Kiondo, Laurean Ndumbaro,
S. Wojciech Sokolowski, and Lester M. Salamon

## Introduction

Rooted in a strong tradition of tribal communalism, the civil society sector in Tanzania was amplified by German and British missionary activity and given modern expression in labor and peasant movements in the first half of the 20th century. Also at work in shaping the civil society sector has been the cultural and political diversity of the country, marked by Islamic, Asian, European, and African influences. However, political constraints and controls imposed by the nationalist government after independence and subsequent economic difficulties have impeded the sector's growth in Tanzania.

As a result, the civil society sector in Tanzania is a fairly significant force by developing and transitional country standards, but its size falls well below that of more economically developed countries. The Tanzanian civil society sector relies on volunteers to a much greater degree than those in most other countries for which data are available. While most of the civil society sector workforce concentrates on service delivery, expressive activities, especially environmental protection and culture and recreation, are also prominent. About half of the sector's revenue comes from fees, while the rest is split between government support and private philanthropy.

These findings emerge from a body of work carried out by a Tanzanian research team as part of the Johns Hopkins Comparative Nonprofit Sector Project.[1] This work sought both to analyze Tanzanian civil society organizations and to compare and contrast them to those in other countries in a systematic way.[2] The result is the first empirical overview of the Tanzanian civil society sector and the first systematic comparison of Tanzanian civil society realities to those elsewhere in the world.

This chapter reports chiefly on the major descriptive findings of this project relating to the size, composition, and financing of the civil society sector in Tanzania and other countries. Other reports from this project will fill in more of the history, legal position, and impact of this set of institutions. Most of the data reported here were generated from an expressly

**Table 5.1.** The civil society sector* in Tanzania, ca. 2000

---

**$259.3 million in expenditures**
- 2.9% of the GDP

**331,573 full-time equivalent workers**
- 82,192 full-time equivalent paid employees
- 249,381 full-time equivalent volunteers
- 2.1% of the economically active population
- 20.7% of nonagricultural employment

---

\* Including religious worship organizations.

SOURCE: Johns Hopkins Comparative Nonprofit Sector Project

designed survey, which used hypernetwork sampling techniques to capture unregistered, informal organizations in addition to more formal ones. Additional research work, including a giving and volunteering survey, was also conducted by the project team. The year covered in this report is 2000. Unless otherwise noted, financial data are reported in U.S. dollars at the 2000 average exchange rate. For a more complete statement of the types of organizations included, see Chapter 1 and Appendix B.

# Principal Findings

## 1. A significant economic force

The civil society sector is a significant economic force in Tanzania. More specifically:

- **A $260 million industry.** The civil society sector in Tanzania accounted for $260 million in expenditures. This figure represents 2.9 percent of the country's gross domestic product (GDP), as reported in Table 5.1.

- **A significant employer.** The workforce behind these expenditures represents over 331,000 full-time equivalent (FTE) workers (including religious worship organizations). This is equal to 2.1 percent of the country's economically active population and over 20 percent of its nonagricultural employment. To put this into context, the civil society sector workforce in Tanzania is half as large as the entire workforce in manufacturing.

- **Impressive volunteer input.** Volunteers represent three-quarters of the entire civil society organization workforce in Tanzania. Expressed in terms of full-time equivalent workers, volunteers constitute a workforce of a quarter of a million people (see Table 5.1). However, the actual number of people who volunteer is significantly higher because most volunteers do not work full-time. We estimate that as many as 2.1 million individuals, 11 percent of Tanzania's adult population, engage in volunteer work of some kind (see Appendix Table A.2).

## 2. Tanzanian civil society sector relatively larger than in other developing countries

- **Above the developing and transitional country average.** Measured as a share of the economically active population, the Tanzanian civil society organization workforce is larger than that in most other developing and transitional countries. As shown in Figure 5.1, excluding religious worship organizations, the civil society organization workforce — paid and volunteer — varies from a high of 14.4 percent of the economically active population in the Netherlands to a low of 0.4 percent in Mexico, with an average of 4.4 percent overall.[3] The Tanzanian figure, at 2.1 percent, is higher than those of eleven of the developing and transitional countries included in this project and above the developing and transitional country average (1.9 percent). However, the civil society organization workforce in Tanzania falls well below the average for all countries, which is 4.4 percent.

- **Volunteer workforce significantly larger than elsewhere.** The volunteer workforce in Tanzania, representing 1.5 percent of the economically active population, is significantly higher than that in other developing and transitional countries but on a par with the 36-country average (see Appendix Table A.1). Reflecting this, the share of volunteers in the civil society sector workforce in Tanzania is nearly twice as large as that elsewhere (75 vs. 38 percent for both developing and transitional countries and all countries) as shown in Figure 5.2. This is a result of vigorous mobilization efforts by community-based organizations and high unemployment. Many people, especially college graduates, see volunteering as an opportunity to gain job experience.

## 3. Brief history of civil society institutions in Tanzania

Tanzania emerged as a national entity in 1964 with the unification of two countries, the Republic of Tanganyika and the People's Republic of Zanzibar.[4] While the mainland of Tanganyika was inhabited by African tribes, the coastal areas were settled by Arabs around 1270 and became a center of the slave trade. The island sultanate of Zanzibar (and Pemba) was established in 1652 by the Omani Arabs, who also extended their control to the coastal areas of Tanganyika. The Germans first colonized Tanganyika in the 1880s, and the British replaced them at the end of World War I. Tanganyika gained national independence in 1961. The island of Zanzibar became a British protectorate in 1890 and gained national independence in 1963.

**Figure 5.1.** Civil society organization workforce
as a share of the economically active population, by country

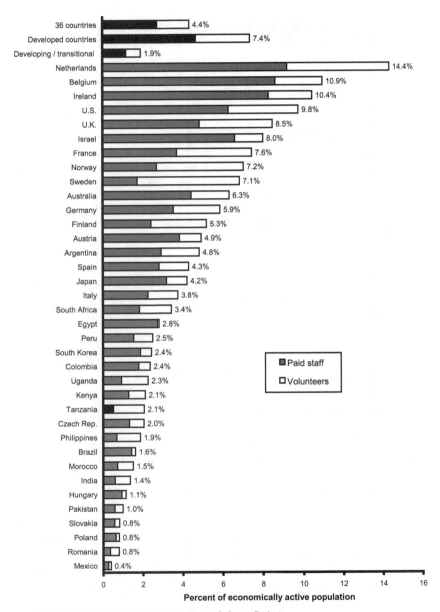

SOURCE: Johns Hopkins Comparative Nonprofit Sector Project

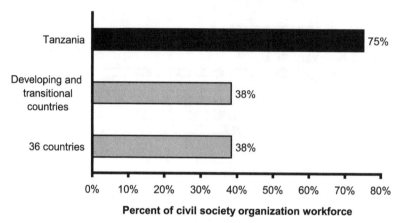

**Figure 5.2.** Volunteers as a share of the civil society organization workforce, Tanzania, developing and transitional countries, and 36 countries

SOURCE: Johns Hopkins Comparative Nonprofit Sector Project

The pre-colonial societies in what is now mainland Tanzania (formerly Tanganyika) developed elaborate forms of mutual self-help based on kinship and age-group membership (i.e., members of differing age groups performing distinct social functions). The most common form of social organization was rural communalism, but feudalism and slavery developed in coastal urban centers. Indigenous institutions were based on customary rights transferred from one generation to another and governed by the principles of reciprocity and redistribution of pooled resources based on need.

Civil society organizations in the modern sense were introduced by European missionaries in the mid-19th century. Missionary societies helped establish the first health care centers and schools. The German colonial authorities, which took control of Tanganyika in 1884, developed a three-tier educational system encompassing primary, central, and high schools serving mainly the coastal population. The formal education of the rural population was provided in cooperation with mission schools. By 1914, there were over 1,000 such schools providing instruction to over 110,000 students.

At the end of World War I, the Germans lost control of their African colonies to the British, who tended to relegate the provision of health and education to voluntary agencies and missions, while cutting government support for these programs. Urbanization and industrialization under British rule also led to the emergence of more formal civil society organizations, including trade unions, peasant cooperatives, civil servant associations, burial associations, and sports clubs. The unions and peasant cooperatives in particular played a major part in the movement for national independence during the 1940s. In the process, these organizations underwent considerable restructuring, which led to the creation of large umbrella organizations. The Victoria Federation of Cooperatives, for example, emerged as the largest cooperative organization in Sub-Saharan Africa.

Shortly after independence and the unification of Tanganyika and Zanzibar in 1964, the nationalist government of Julius Nyerere took steps to establish tight control of civil society organizations, especially labor unions. New registration requirements were introduced and the right to strike was outlawed. The government policy of agricultural development and self-reliance provided strong support to the peasant cooperative movement, but these organizations also came under tight government control. As a result, the relationship between the government and the civil society sector during this period was tenuous and marked by conflict.

Unsuccessful development policies, corruption, and mismanagement led to the economic collapse of the country and intensified internal tensions between the mainland and Islamic Zanzibar. These developments prompted Nyerere's resignation in 1985. His successor, Ali Hassan Mwinyi, introduced a multiparty system and economic reforms that allowed private enterprise. New institutions (e.g., the Advisory Board) were implemented to improve communication and collaboration between governmental agencies and civil society organizations. With the state impoverished and external donors frustrated by government shortcomings, increased reliance has been placed on civil society organizations.

## 4. Service activities prevail but expressive activities not far behind

Reflecting this history, while most of the Tanzanian civil society sector workforce is engaged in service functions, expressive functions also engage a substantial portion of the workforce. More specifically:

- **Service activities dominate.** As shown in Figure 5.3, 51 percent of all Tanzanian civil society organization workers — paid and volunteer — are engaged in service activities.[5] The workforce is more or less equally distributed among the four components that constitute the service field: social services (16 percent), community development and housing (13 percent), education (12 percent), and health (10 percent).

- **Smaller service focus than average.** The service focus of the Tanzanian civil society sector, though substantial, is still less pronounced than that in other developing and transitional countries (51 vs. 63 percent). The major reason for this is that a considerably smaller proportion of the civil society sector workforce in Tanzania is engaged in education compared to other developing and transitional countries (12 vs. 25 percent).

- **Average share of Tanzanian civil society workers engaged in expressive activities.** Thirty-one percent of Tanzanian civil society organization

**Figure 5.3.** Composition of the
civil society organization workforce, Tanzania,
developing and transitional countries, and 33-country average

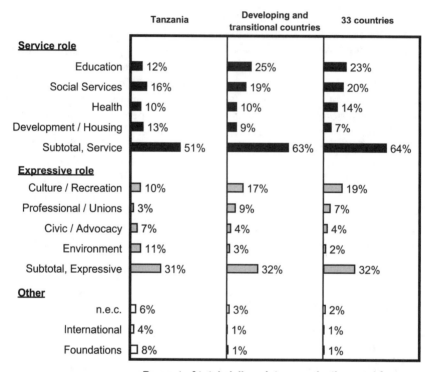

Percent of total civil society organization workforce

n.e.c.= not elsewhere classified
SOURCE: Johns Hopkins Comparative Nonprofit Sector Project

workers, paid and volunteer, are engaged in expressive activities. This is comparable to that in other countries (32 percent in both developing and transitional countries and internationally). At the same time, Tanzanian civil society organizations engage slightly more people in expressive activities than their counterparts in other African countries studied (31 vs. 29 percent) (see Table 1.13).

- **Inclusion of community development changes the picture.** The share of the Tanzanian civil society sector workforce engaged in expressive activities increases significantly if community development activities are included. In the African context, community development organizations often play a dual role of service provision and mobilization of disfranchised groups. With the community development field included,

**Figure 5.4.** Distribution of paid employees and volunteers between service and expressive activities in Tanzania

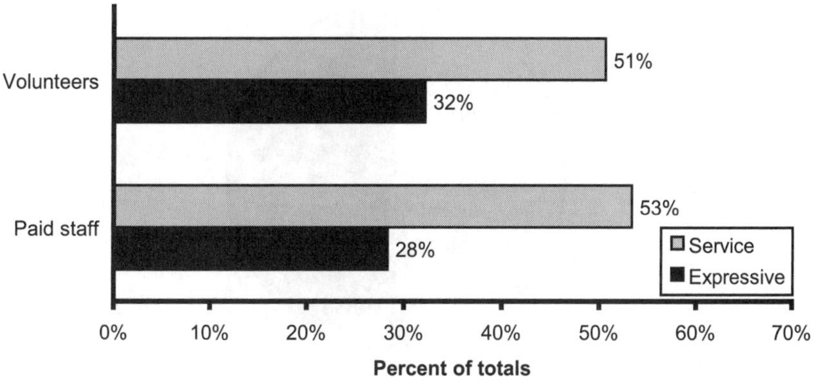

SOURCE: Johns Hopkins Comparative Nonprofit Sector Project

expressive activities account for 44 percent of the total civil society organization workforce in Tanzania.

- **Unusually high proportion of Tanzanian civil society organization workforce engaged in "other" functions.** A relatively sizable 18 percent of the Tanzanian civil society sector workforce is engaged in a variety of other functions including foundations, international activities, and organizations "not elsewhere classified." By contrast, these functions absorb only 5 percent of the civil society organization workforce on average in all developing and transitional countries and about 4 percent in all countries. This may be a result of the multi-purpose character of many civil society organizations in Tanzania. Also at work, however, may be the tendency of organizations to expand into new fields as donor priorities shift (e.g., the increased emphasis on HIV/AIDS programming). In addition, the concept of a foundation may have a different meaning in the Tanzanian context, where foundations may also be operating organizations.

- **Paid and volunteer staff distributed similarly.** The distribution of the civil society sector workforce in Tanzania changes very little when paid staff and volunteers are examined separately. As shown in Figure 5.4, comparable portions of volunteer staff time and paid staff time are concentrated in service functions (51 and 53 percent, respectively).

## 5. Revenue dominated by fees and charges

Fees, charges, and membership dues are the dominant source of civil society organization revenue in Tanzania, outdistancing philanthropy and government support. In particular:

**Figure 5.5.** Sources of civil society
organization revenue in Tanzania

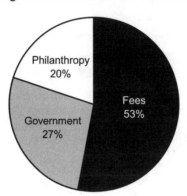

SOURCE: Johns Hopkins Comparative Nonprofit Sector Project

- **Fee dominance in Tanzania.** About 53 percent of all Tanzanian civil society organization cash revenue comes from service fees, property income, and membership dues, as shown in Figure 5.5. Only 20 percent of revenue comes from all sources of private philanthropy, including individuals, foundations, and corporations; and 27 percent comes from the public sector.

- **Revenue structure close to international averages.** This pattern of civil society organization revenue is similar to that found in other countries.

  - The fee share of civil society sector revenue in Tanzania is the same as the all-country average (53 percent), as Figure 5.6 shows. However, it falls below the developing and transitional country average (61 percent).

  - Government payments account for a slightly larger share of civil society sector revenue in Tanzania than in other developing and transitional countries (27 vs. 22 percent of total revenue), but Tanzania still falls below the all-country average of 34 percent in this area.

  - Private philanthropy also accounts for a somewhat larger portion of civil society sector support in Tanzania than the developed and transitional country average (20 vs. 17 percent of total revenue). This is due to the heavy reliance of many Tanzanian civil society organizations

**Figure 5.6.** Sources of civil society organization revenue,
Tanzania, developing and transitional countries,
and 34-country average

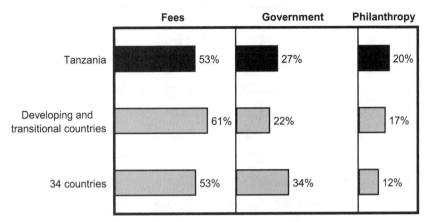

**Percent of total civil society organization revenue**

SOURCE: Johns Hopkins Comparative Nonprofit Sector Project

on foreign support, especially in the areas of environmental protection
and advocacy.

- **Fees dominate revenue in all fields.** Fees are the dominant revenue source
  for Tanzanian civil society organizations in all major fields (see Figure
  5.7). The fee share of total revenue is highest among professional organizations and unions (66 percent) and lowest in environmental protection
  (44 percent).

- **Volunteers change the revenue structure significantly.** The revenue structure of Tanzanian civil society organizations changes significantly when
  the value of volunteer input is included. As Figure 5.8 demonstrates,
  with volunteer inputs of time included, the philanthropic share of total
  support in Tanzanian civil society organizations increases to 62 percent.
  This is notably higher than the comparable shares in other African countries (on average, 46 percent) (see Table 1.13), as well as the developing
  and transitional country and all-country averages (33 and 31 percent,
  respectively).

  – With the value of volunteer input included, private philanthropy be-
    comes the main source of support for civil society organizations in all
    fields in Tanzania (see Figure 5.9).

**Figure 5.7.** Sources of civil society organization revenue, Tanzania, by field

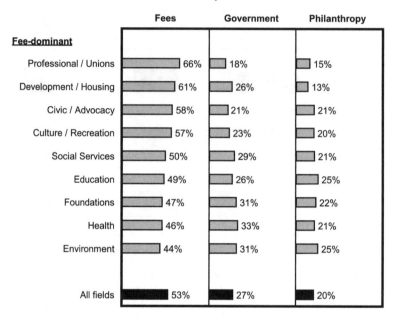

SOURCE: Johns Hopkins Comparative Nonprofit Sector Project

**Figure 5.8.** Sources of civil society organization support including volunteers, Tanzania, developing and transitional countries, and 34-country average

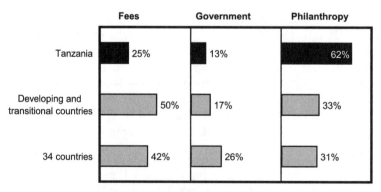

SOURCE: Johns Hopkins Comparative Nonprofit Sector Project

**Figure 5.9.** Sources of civil society organization support
in Tanzania, including volunteers, by field

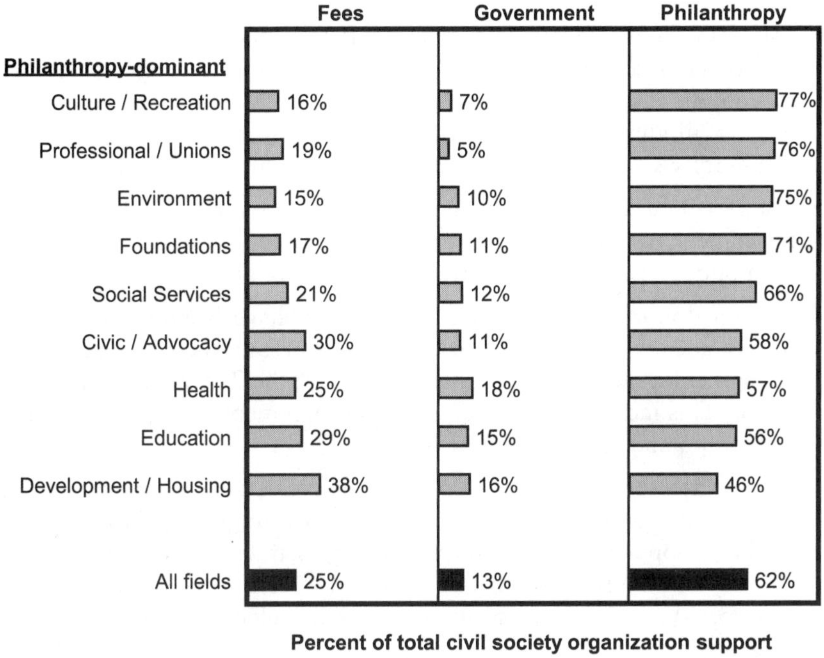

| | Fees | Government | Philanthropy |
|---|---|---|---|
| **Philanthropy-dominant** | | | |
| Culture / Recreation | 16% | 7% | 77% |
| Professional / Unions | 19% | 5% | 76% |
| Environment | 15% | 10% | 75% |
| Foundations | 17% | 11% | 71% |
| Social Services | 21% | 12% | 66% |
| Civic / Advocacy | 30% | 11% | 58% |
| Health | 25% | 18% | 57% |
| Education | 29% | 15% | 56% |
| Development / Housing | 38% | 16% | 46% |
| All fields | 25% | 13% | 62% |

**Percent of total civil society organization support**

SOURCE: Johns Hopkins Comparative Nonprofit Sector Project

## Conclusions and Implications

As this chapter demonstrates, the civil society sector in Tanzania has strong roots in the country's communal tradition and more recent labor and peasant movements, which may help to explain its substantial volunteer base. At the same time, the sector's development has been marred by heavy-handed government control, mutual suspicion, and even hostility. Although economic and political reforms that took place after 1985 substantially improved these relations, the legacy of mistrust still remains. As a result, the level of transparency, especially in reporting revenues and revealing revenue sources, is very low among Tanzania's civil society organizations, which seriously undermines public accountability and trust in the sector.

Despite these problems, the civil society sector in Tanzania has shown remarkable resilience. Perhaps the most visible sign of that resilience is that the sector has begun to play a more prominent role in assisting the government with economic development, environmental protection, and the AIDS

epidemic. However, the increased reliance on the civil society sector to address social and economic problems has created new challenges for both the
government and civil society organizations. Specifically:

- Given Tanzania's history of statism and heavy-handed government control of civil society organizations, the government needs to reaffirm
  its commitment to freedom of association and freedom of expression,
  which will allow civil society organizations to thrive and perform their
  community service functions without unreasonable interference.

- The restructuring of state-owned enterprises provides an opportunity to
  foster new partnerships with civil society organizations, provide them
  with public resources, and entrust them with public functions.

- Foreign donor agencies, which traditionally have been a major source
  of civil society support in Tanzania, need to retain their commitment to
  strengthening the organizational capacity of the Tanzanian civil society
  sector. This includes professional skill development, as well as provision
  of funding and in-kind support.

- Civil society organizations need to better define and communicate their
  mission and role in Tanzanian society and encourage people to contribute
  to their support. Rather than portraying itself as an alternative service
  delivery mechanism, which may threaten government departments, the
  civil society sector needs to emphasize its complementary role.

- The civil society sector needs to develop greater transparency and implement rules and procedures allowing for public accountability of its
  resources and activities.

- Finally, there needs to be a sustained effort to produce reliable information about the sector's organizational capacity and output, as well as an
  unbiased assessment of the quality of its services and their social and
  economic impact.

The civil society sector has proven to be an important agent of social
change and economic development in Tanzania. But it is crucial that this
role be more fully recognized and explicitly utilized by both domestic policy
makers and foreign assistance agencies. To achieve this goal, however, it
is essential to develop an accurate assessment of the civil society sector's
capacities and needs. We hope that this chapter takes a useful first step
toward this goal.

## Notes

1. The work in Tanzania was coordinated by Andrew Kiondo, who also super-
vised the data collection. The research team was aided, in turn, by a local advisory
committee (see Appendix D for a list of committee members). The Johns Hopkins

project was directed by Lester M. Salamon, and the work in Tanzania was overseen by Leslie C. Hems and later by S. Wojciech Sokolowski.

2. The definitions and approaches used in the project were developed collaboratively with the cooperation of Tanzanian researchers and researchers in other countries and were designed to be applicable to Tanzania and other project countries. For a full description of this definition, the types of organizations included, and the methodology used, see Chapter 1 and Appendix B. For a full list of the other countries included, see Table 1.1.

3. Comparative figures do not include religious worship organizations, because data on these organizations were not available for all countries. However, religiously affiliated service organizations are included. For more information, see Appendix B.

4. This section draws on the following sources: I.N. Kimambo and A.J. Temu, eds., *A History of Tanzania* (Nairobi: East African Publishing House, 1969); Thomas P. Ofcansky and Rodger Yeager, *Historical Dictionary of Tanzania,* 2nd edition (Lanham, MD: The Scarecrow Press, 1997); and Rodger Yeager, *Tanzania: An African Experiment* (Boulder, CO: Westview Press, 1989).

5. Percentages displayed in figures may not add to 100 due to rounding.

# Chapter 6

# Uganda

Bazaara Nyangabyaki, David Kibikyo, John-Jean Barya,
S. Wojciech Sokolowski, and Lester M. Salamon

## INTRODUCTION

The civil society sector of Uganda has a rich but varied history. Originally rooted in the deep traditions of communal activity that pre-dated the colonial era in this country, civil society activity underwent a significant change during the colonial era as Western missionaries, with encouragement from British colonial powers, established religiously affiliated schools and health facilities as part of their effort to convert the natives to Christianity. However, as discontent against colonial rule intensified in the aftermath of the Great Depression in the 1930s, at least some of these institutions, as well as community-based organizations established on a self-help basis, became the organizational base for a vibrant independence movement that finally succeeded in 1964.

In spite of pressure from civil society organizations, however, the early post-Independence period witnessed a significant expansion of the role of the state and the subjugation of independent civil society organization activity by a series of authoritarian regimes. Many of the service-providing colonial institutions survived during this period, however. In the 1980s and the 1990s, moreover, they were joined by a substantial number of newer nongovernmental organizations (NGOs) encouraged by a more tolerant regime that came to power during this period. More significantly, the adoption of structural adjustment economic programs and the resulting state disengagement from social service provision led to the emergence of NGOs to fill the gap.

Reflecting this history, Uganda boasts a quite sizable civil society sector, with a workforce that exceeds that of the public sector. Most of the civil society sector's workforce concentrates in the service fields, especially social services and community development, but a surprisingly large share of that capacity is also found in recreation and sports. Most of the sector's revenue comes from fees.

These findings emerge from a body of work carried out by a Ugandan research team as part of the Johns Hopkins Comparative Nonprofit Sector Project.[1] This work sought both to analyze Ugandan civil society organizations and to compare and contrast them to those in other countries in a systematic way.[2] The result is the first empirical overview of the Ugandan civil society sector and the first systematic comparison of Ugandan civil society realities to those elsewhere in the world.[3]

This chapter reports chiefly on the major descriptive findings of this project relating to the size and composition of the civil society sector in Uganda and other countries. Other reports will fill in more of the financing structure, history, legal position, and impact of these institutions. The data reported here were largely generated from National Social Security Fund records that contain employment data from major registered entities. They were supplemented, however, by data gathered by the Uganda Bureau of Statistics and by a supplementary organizational survey focusing on informal organizations conducted by the project team. The year covered by these data is 1998. Unless otherwise noted, financial data are reported in U.S. dollars at the 1998 average exchange rate. For a more complete statement of the types of organizations included, see Chapter 1 and Appendix B.

## Principal Findings

### 1. A sizeable economic force

The civil society sector in Uganda is relatively large, especially in comparison to other developing and transitional countries. More specifically:

- **An $89 million industry.** The Ugandan civil society sector accounted for about $89 million in expenditures as of 1998. This amount is equivalent to 1.4 percent of the nation's gross domestic product (GDP), as reported in Table 6.1.

- **A significant employer.** Even more important is the workforce behind these expenditures, which numbers over 230,000 full-time equivalent (FTE) workers (including those in religious worship activities). This represents 2.3 percent of the country's economically active population and 10.9 percent of its nonagricultural employment (see Table 6.1).

- **Larger than the public sector.** To put these figures in context, the civil society sector workforce in Uganda — paid and volunteer — is roughly one-and-a-half times that of the public sector workforce, and over half as large as that in all fields of manufacturing combined.

- **Significant volunteer presence.** Over half of the civil society organization workforce in Uganda is made up of volunteers. This volunteer workforce alone accounts for 1.3 percent of the country's economically active population (see Appendix Table A.1). In fact, volunteer involvement is more

**Table 6.1.** The civil society sector* in Uganda, ca. 1998

| |
|---|
| **$88.9 million in expenditures** |
| • 1.4% of the GDP |
| **231,181 full-time equivalent workers** |
| • 94,084 full-time equivalent paid employees |
| • 137,097 full-time equivalent volunteers |
| • 2.3% of the economically active population |
| • 10.9% of nonagricultural employment |
| • 138.9% of public employment |

\* Including religious worship organizations.

SOURCE: Johns Hopkins Comparative Nonprofit Sector Project

extensive than this suggests since most people devote only a small portion of their time to volunteer effort. A rough estimate puts the share of the population engaged in volunteer work at approximately 2.6 million people, or 23 percent of the adult population (vs. 10 percent for the all-country average) (see Appendix Table A.2).

## 2. Above-average civil society sector

• **Above the developing and transitional country average.** As shown in Figure 6.1, the civil society sector workforce — paid and volunteer — varies from a high of 14.4 percent of the economically active population in the Netherlands to a low of 0.4 percent in Mexico, with an average of 4.4 percent overall.[4] Although the Ugandan figure is about half that of the all-country average (2.3 vs. 4.4 percent, with religion excluded), it ranks above thirteen other developing and transitional countries and substantially exceeds the developing and transitional country average (2.3 vs. 1.9 percent).

• **Relatively high volunteer participation.** As noted earlier, volunteers account for 59 percent of the Ugandan civil society organization workforce. This is significantly higher than the developing and transitional country and all-country averages (38 percent each), as shown in Figure 6.2. Reflecting this, the scale of volunteer effort in Uganda, which translates into the equivalent of 1.3 percent of the economically active population, is nearly twice the developing and transitional country average of 0.7 percent and almost as high as the all-country average of 1.6 percent (see Table 1.13). This puts Uganda on a par with other African countries included in this study, where the volunteer labor force accounts for 1.3 percent of the economically active population on average.

**Figure 6.1.** Civil society organization workforce
as a share of the economically active population, by country

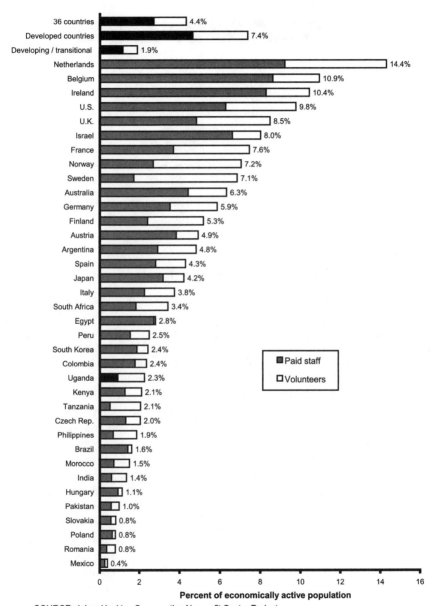

SOURCE: Johns Hopkins Comparative Nonprofit Sector Project

**Figure 6.2.** Volunteers as a share of the
civil society organization workforce, Uganda,
developing and transitional countries, and 36 countries

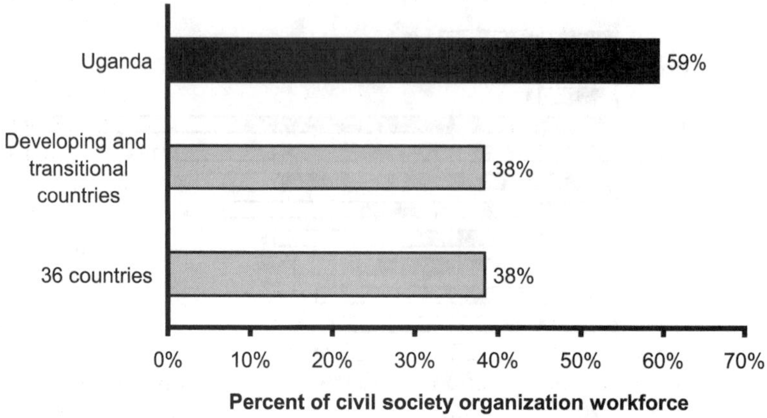

**Percent of civil society organization workforce**

SOURCE: Johns Hopkins Comparative Nonprofit Sector Project

## 3. The colonial roots of civil society development

The sizeable civil society sector in modern-day Uganda very likely reflects
the elaborate mutual self-help networks along clan, family, or neighborhood
lines evident in the pre-colonial society.

The first modern civil society organizations in Uganda were created by
missionaries in the late 1890s to help cope with diseases and famine brought
by the "pacification" and subjugation of the indigenous population. Catholic and Protestant missionaries built schools and hospitals both to provide
services and to establish Christianity and spread its practice throughout
the country.[5] Many of the schools established by the missionaries, such as
Kings College and Gayaza, Nabumali, and Mbarara High Schools, are still
in existence. Other organizations established in this period were designed to
minister to the medical and social needs of the colonial administrative staff
and members of the local elite.

Side-by-side with these missionary and colonial institutions, local populations formed their own institutions, partly to press reforms on the colonial
administration. For example, local clan leaders (*bataka*) formed the Bataka
Association to curb the excessive rents demanded by landowners and regain
control of land lost through privatization by British colonial authorities.[6]
In response to the Great Depression and World War II, British authorities
promoted a set of policies designed to stimulate community development
through voluntary self-help organizations and to respond to increased labor
militancy by creating unions that were controlled and guided by the state.[7]

Muslim organizations also began to emerge in the 1930s as a result of the growing Indian influence in the country. The most important organization was the East African Moslem Welfare Society, which was created in 1945 by the Aga Khan's Ismaili Community. This organization was able to negotiate with the government for recognition of Islamic laws and approval of schools, welfare services, and development agencies.[8]

Following independence in 1964 the ruling party, the Uganda People's Congress (UPC), centralized most existing grassroots organizations, such as youth and women's groups and trade unions, and used them as a platform to mobilize political support. Organizations that resisted integration were either marginalized or destroyed.[9] The political turbulence created by this power struggle, and the civil war triggered by the coup d'état of 1971 (Idi Amin overthrowing the UPC government of Milton Obote) and the 1979 war waged from Tanzania, leading to the downfall of Amin's regime and Obote's return to power, further politicized the civil society sector. Successive regimes made various attempts to extend their control over existing organizations, schools, and churches (both Christian and Muslim) and to destroy those perceived to be carrying out anti-government activities.[10]

The overthrow of the Obote government in 1985, and the emergence of a new regime under Yoweri Museveni, ushered in a more tolerant policy towards both domestic and foreign NGOs, resulting in a rapid growth of the civil society sector.[11] Also contributing to the growth of the civil society sector during this period were structural adjustment programs and retrenchment of public service employees, which led to an employment crisis. This crisis reduced employment opportunities in the public sector and stimulated many unemployed civil servants, former parastatal employees, and college graduates to start NGOs that could mediate between donor agencies and community-based groups.[12]

## 4. Strong presence of service organizations

The resulting civil society sector is an important provider of public services in Uganda. Mission hospitals are the main health service providers in the country, Parent Teacher Associations keep many schools running, and AIDS support groups play a major role in assisting victims of the AIDS epidemic. In the absence of private sector investment, civil society organizations are also active in developing rural infrastructure and providing microcredit to entrepreneurs.

Reflecting this, most of the Ugandan civil society sector workforce is engaged in service functions, especially social services and community development.

- **Service activities dominate.** As shown in Figure 6.3, about two-thirds (69 percent) of all Ugandan civil society organization workers, paid and volunteer, are engaged in service activities.[13] Of these, the largest share

**Figure 6.3.** Composition of the
civil society organization workforce, Uganda,
developing and transitional countries, and 33-country average

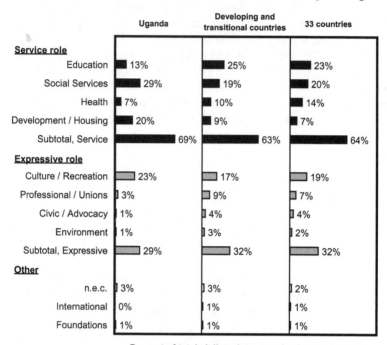

Percent of total civil society organization workforce

n.e.c.= not elsewhere classified
SOURCE: Johns Hopkins Comparative Nonprofit Sector Project

work in social services (29 percent). This service share of civil society
activities is slightly higher than the developing and transitional country
and all-country averages (63 and 64 percent, respectively).

- **Relatively small share of workers engaged in expressive activities.** About
  28 percent of civil society organization workers in Uganda, paid and
  volunteer, are engaged in expressive activities. This is below both the
  developing and transitional country and the all-country averages (32 percent each). However, the field that dominates these activities in Uganda is
  culture and recreation, including sports, which accounts for 23 percent of
  the civil society sector's workforce. This is well above the developing and
  transitional and all-country averages (17 and 19 percent, respectively).

- **Empowerment role of development organizations.** This picture of relatively limited civil society expressive activity changes dramatically if
  we include the work of the community development organizations in

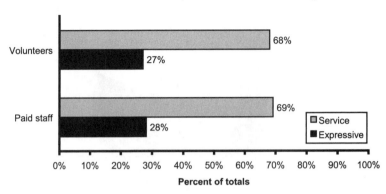

**Figure 6.4.** Distribution of paid employees and volunteers between service and expressive activities in Uganda

SOURCE: Johns Hopkins Comparative Nonprofit Sector Project

the expressive activities rather than the service one — on grounds that these organizations engage in a variety of essentially empowerment activities. Under these circumstances, the expressive share would increase to 48 percent, well above the all-country average.

- **Paid and volunteer staff distributed similarly.** The distribution of the civil society sector workforce between service and expressive functions in Uganda does not change significantly when paid staff and volunteers are examined separately. Thus, service activities absorb most of both paid and volunteer staff (69 and 68 percent, respectively), as Figure 6.4 demonstrates.

## 5. Revenue dominated by fees

Service fees and charges are the dominant source of civil society organization revenue in Uganda, outdistancing philanthropic giving and government support. In particular:

- **Fee dominance.** About 55 percent of all cash revenue of Ugandan civil society organizations comes from fees, as shown in Figure 6.5. About 38 percent comes from philanthropic giving, and only 7 percent comes the public sector.

- **Differs from international pattern.** This pattern of civil society organization revenue differs significantly from that found elsewhere.

  - The Ugandan civil society sector relies much more substantially on private philanthropy than its counterparts in other developing and transitional countries and internationally. As Figure 6.6 shows, the philanthropy share of the Ugandan civil society sector's revenue is two

**Figure 6.5.** Sources of civil society
organization revenue in Uganda

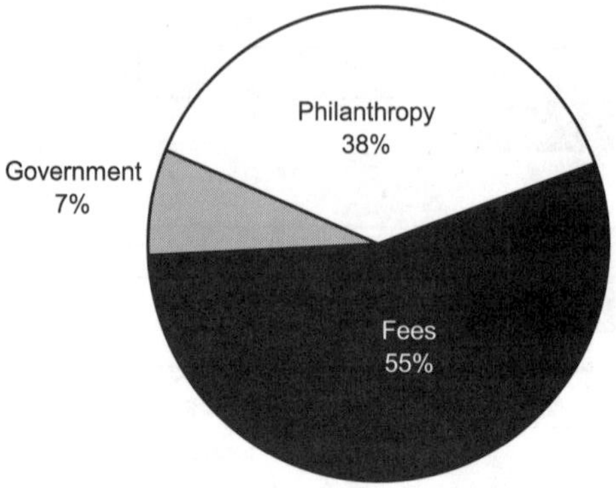

SOURCE: Johns Hopkins Comparative Nonprofit Sector Project

times larger than in other developing and transitional countries (38 vs.
17 percent) and three times larger than the all-country average (12 percent). In fact, the philanthropy share of civil society sector revenue in
Uganda is higher than in any of the countries we studied, and ranks
fourth (after Israel, the U.S., and Spain) as a share of GDP (see Appendix Table A.5). This likely reflects the significant financial support
that reaches Ugandan civil society organizations through international
nongovernmental organizations as well as the tendency of Ugandan
businesses to use philanthropy as a way to market their products.

– By contrast, the Ugandan civil society sector receives a much smaller
  fraction of its support from the public sector than that found on
  average in developing and transitional countries and internationally
  (7 percent vs. 22 and 34 percent, respectively).

– The 55 percent of civil society sector revenue in Uganda that comes
  from fees, charges, and membership dues is below the developing
  and transitional country average (61 percent), but on a par with the
  all-country average (53 percent). But much of this funding may actually originate with public funds passed through intermediaries as
  reimbursements for community services.

• **Support structure varies among fields.** Private philanthropy is the dominant revenue source in Uganda in four fields, ranging from 61 percent
  in health to 100 percent in civic and advocacy, as shown in Figure 6.7.
  Fees and dues are the dominant revenue source in four fields, ranging
  from 50 percent in culture and recreation to 100 percent in professional

**Figure 6.6.** Sources of civil society organization revenue,
Uganda, developing and transitional countries,
and 34-country average

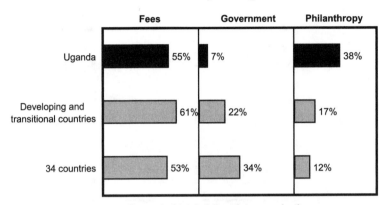

SOURCE: Johns Hopkins Comparative Nonprofit Sector Project

**Figure 6.7.** Sources of civil society organization revenue,
Uganda, by field

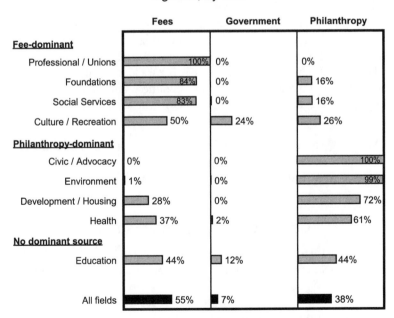

SOURCE: Johns Hopkins Comparative Nonprofit Sector Project

**Figure 6.8.** Sources of civil society organization support including volunteers, Uganda, developing and transitional countries, and 34-country average

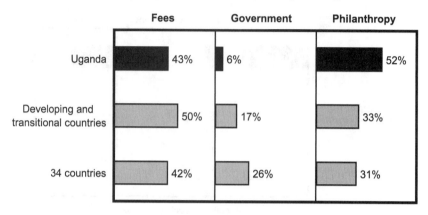

**Percent of total civil society organization support**

SOURCE: Johns Hopkins Comparative Nonprofit Sector Project

associations and unions. The funding of education is evenly split between philanthropy and fees (44 percent each).

• **Volunteers further increase the role of private philanthropy.** With the value of volunteer input included and treated as a form of philanthropy, the philanthropy share of total civil society organization support in Uganda climbs to 52 percent (see Figure 6.8). This is substantially above the developing and transitional country and all-country averages (33 and 31 percent, respectively), but below the level found in neighboring Tanzania (62 percent) (see Appendix Table A.4).

– With the value of volunteer input included, private philanthropy becomes the main source of support in all but two fields, professional associations and social services (see Figure 6.9).

## Conclusions and Implications

The picture of Uganda's civil society sector that emerges from this chapter is that of a sizeable economic force that employs significantly more people than the public sector. In fact, employment in civil society organizations is often viewed as an alternative to government employment by Ugandan civil servants and college graduates. Moreover, volunteering in Uganda is higher than in many other developing and transitional countries, with more than half of the civil society sector workforce composed of volunteers.

**Figure 6.9.** Sources of civil society organization support
in Uganda, including volunteers, by field

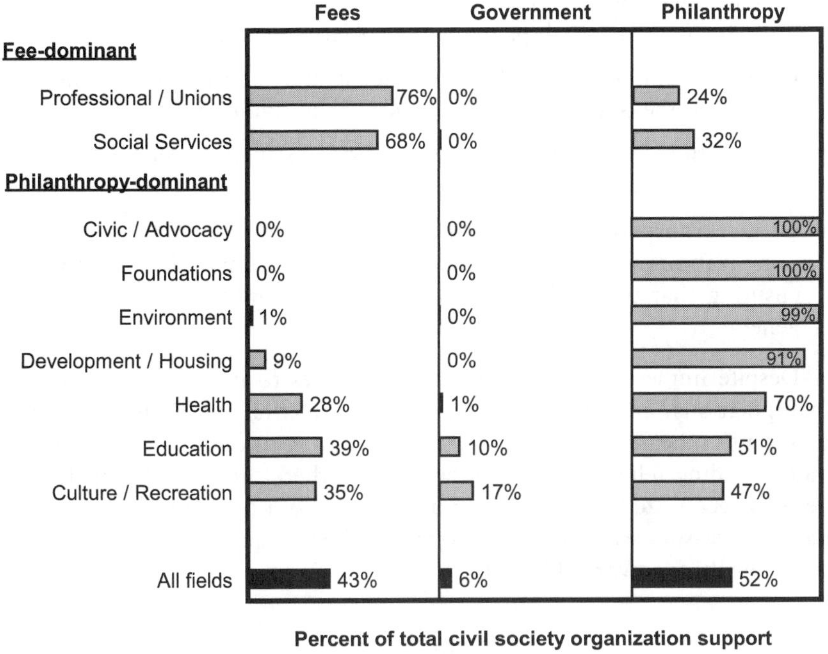

|  | Fees | Government | Philanthropy |
|---|---|---|---|
| **Fee-dominant** | | | |
| Professional / Unions | 76% | 0% | 24% |
| Social Services | 68% | 0% | 32% |
| **Philanthropy-dominant** | | | |
| Civic / Advocacy | 0% | 0% | 100% |
| Foundations | 0% | 0% | 100% |
| Environment | 1% | 0% | 99% |
| Development / Housing | 9% | 0% | 91% |
| Health | 28% | 1% | 70% |
| Education | 39% | 10% | 51% |
| Culture / Recreation | 35% | 17% | 47% |
| All fields | 43% | 6% | 52% |

**Percent of total civil society organization support**

SOURCE: Johns Hopkins Comparative Nonprofit Sector Project

The Ugandan civil society sector emerged during the turbulent post-independence period as an institutional player capable of supplementing government policies, and this potential has become even more apparent in more recent years as a result of structural adjustment policies that have led to a retrenchment in public sector employment and privatization of public enterprises (parastatals). At the same time, however, various regimes have tried to control civil society organizations and destroy or marginalize those that resisted. As a result, there is considerable mistrust of the government among civil society leaders.

Despite these tensions, the civil society sector in Uganda has great potential to assist the society, the government, and progressive international agencies in their efforts to rebuild the country and improve public health, especially by helping to control the AIDS epidemic that has ravaged the country. But to fully realize this potential, the civil society sector and the government need to build a better relationship with each other and with international agencies. This will require:

- A positive declaration by the government of its commitment to freedom of association and freedom of expression;

- A greater willingness on the part of the government to provide opportunities for real partnerships with civil society organizations;

- Greater commitment by the government and international agencies to strengthen the organizational capacity of the civil society sector;

- Clarification by civil society organizations of their mission and role in Ugandan society;

- Greater transparency and public accountability on the part of civil society organizations regarding both their financial affairs and their effectiveness, ensuring that they are accountable to their membership and society in general.

Despite numerous legal obstacles, challenges to its legitimacy, political manipulations, and at times even suppression, the civil society sector remains a significant force in Uganda, contributing to economic development and providing relief and social services. It is therefore crucial that this role be fully recognized and positively utilized by both policymakers and international assistance agencies. We hope that the data presented in this chapter will contribute toward this goal.

## Notes

1. The work in Uganda was coordinated by Bazaara Nyangabyaki, who passed away as this volume was being prepared for print. His work as the local associate was continued by John-Jean Barya. The research team was aided, in turn, by a local advisory committee (see Appendix D for a list of committee members). The Johns Hopkins project was directed by Lester M. Salamon, and the work in Uganda was overseen by Leslie C. Hems and later by S. Wojciech Sokolowski.

2. The definitions and approaches used in the project were developed collaboratively with the cooperation of Ugandan researchers and researchers in other countries and were designed to be applicable to Uganda and other project countries. For a full description of this definition, the types of organizations included, and the methodology used, see Chapter 1 and Appendix B. For a full list of the other countries included, see Table 1.1.

3. A preliminary version of the Uganda findings was published in Lester M. Salamon, S. Wojciech Sokolowski, and Regina List, *Global Civil Society, An Overview* (Baltimore, MD: The Johns Hopkins Comparative Nonprofit Sector Project, 2003). The findings reported here differ somewhat from these preliminary estimates and are based on survey results that only became available after the release of these preliminary estimates.

4. Comparative figures do not include religious worship organizations because data on these organizations were not available for all countries. However, religiously affiliated service organizations are included. For more information, see Appendix B.

5. J.C. Ssekamwa, *History and Development of Education in Uganda* (Kampala: Fountain Publishers, 1997).

6. Dan Mudoola, "The Young Basoga and Abataka Association: A Case Study in Chiefly Politics in Colonial Busoga," *The Uganda Journal* 38 (1976).

7. Michael P. Cowen and Robert W. Shenton, *Doctrines of Development* (London: Routledge, 1996); John-Jean Barya, *Workers and the Law in Uganda,* Working Paper No. 17 (Kampala: Centre for Basic Research, 1991).

8. Sallie Sima Kayunga, "Islamic Fundamentalism in Uganda: The Tabligh Youth Movement," in *Uganda: Studies in Living Conditions, Popular Movements and Constitutionalism,* ed. Mahmood Mamdani and Joe Oloka-Onyango (Kampala: Centre for Basic Research, 1994); Constantin François, "Muslims and Politics: The Attempts to Create Muslim National Organizations in Tanzania, Uganda and Kenya," in *Religion and Politics in East Africa: The Period Since Independence,* ed. Holger B. Hansen and Michael Twaddle (Kampala: Fountain Publishers, 1995).

9. Carolyn Day White, *The Role of Women as an Interest Group in the Ugandan Political System,* Master's Thesis (Kampala: Makerere University, 1973).

10. A.R. Nsimbabmbi, "The Politics of Education in Uganda, 1964–1970," *The Uganda Journal* 38 (1976); Holger B. Hansen and Michael Twaddle (eds.), *Religion and Politics in East Africa: The Period Since Independence* (Kampala: Fountain Publishers, 1995).

11. World Bank, "Republic of Uganda," in *The Role of Nongovernmental Organizations and Community-Based Groups in Poverty Alleviation,* World Bank Report No. 12262-UG (1994).

12. Zie Gariyo, "NGOs and Development in East Africa: The View from Below," paper presented at the Workshop on NGOs and Development: Performance and Accountability in the New World Order, University of Manchester (1994).

13. Percentages displayed in figures may not add to 100 due to rounding.

# Part Three

# ASIA

Chapter 7

# India

## S.S. Srivastava, Rajesh Tandon, S. Wojciech Sokolowski, and Lester M. Salamon

## Introduction

The roots of Indian civil society reach back to antiquity, when guilds and religious monasteries played a key role in the provision of social welfare, public services, education, and culture. This ancient tradition merged with Western influences during the period of British rule, creating a vibrant civil society sector promoting education, economic development, self-reliance, and empowerment. Today, this diverse set of institutions employs over 6 million full-time equivalent workers, about the same as paid employment in the entire manufacturing sector. Half of these workers are volunteers. This impressive workforce is engaged in a wide spectrum of activities ranging from education to rural development to human rights and advocacy.

These findings emerge from a body of work carried out by an Indian research team as part of the Johns Hopkins Comparative Nonprofit Sector Project.[1] This work sought both to analyze Indian civil society organizations and to compare and contrast them to those in other countries in a systematic way.[2] The data presented in this chapter are based on survey results obtained in five states. These results were then extrapolated to the country level. The upshot is the most comprehensive empirical overview to date of the Indian civil society sector and the first systematic comparison of that sector to those elsewhere in the world.[3]

This chapter reports chiefly on the major descriptive findings of this project relating to the size, composition, and financing of the civil society sector in India and other countries. Other reports will fill in more of the history, legal position, and impact of these institutions. Most of the data reported here come from detailed, neighborhood-based surveys designed and implemented by the Johns Hopkins Comparative Nonprofit Sector Project and the local research team. The base year for the estimates is 2000. Unless otherwise noted, financial data are reported in U.S. dollars at the 2000 average exchange rate. For a more complete statement of the types of organizations included, see Chapter 1 and Appendix B.

**Table 7.1.** The civil society sector* in India, 2000

---

**$2.8 billion in expenditures**

- 0.6% of the GDP

**6,035,000 full-time equivalent workers**

- 2,655,400 full-time equivalent paid employees
- 3,379,600 full-time equivalent volunteers
- 1.4% of the economically active population

---

* Religious worship organization figures not available.

SOURCE: Johns Hopkins Comparative Nonprofit Sector Project

# Principal Findings

## 1. A noteworthy economic force

The data assembled indicate that in the year 2000 Indian civil society organizations constituted a considerable economic force. More specifically:

- **A $2.8 billion industry.** The civil society sector in India accounted for approximately $2.8 billion in expenditures as of 2000, or about 0.6 percent of the nation's gross domestic product (GDP), as reported in Table 7.1.

- **A sizable employer.** About 6 million full-time equivalent (FTE) workers, roughly half of whom are volunteers, work in the Indian civil society sector. This represents 1.4 percent of the country's economically active population (see Table 7.1).

- **Outdistances key industries.** Civil society organizations in India thus engage a larger workforce — paid and volunteer — than many key industries in the country. This workforce exceeds the paid employment in utilities, construction, and transportation, and nearly equals that in the entire manufacturing sector (see Figure 7.1).[4]

## 2. A small civil society sector in comparative terms

Though large in absolute terms, the relative size of the civil society organization workforce in India is rather small when compared to international averages.

- **Significantly below the all-country average.** As shown in Figure 7.2, the civil society organization workforce — paid and volunteer — varies from a high of 14.4 percent of the economically active population in the Netherlands to a low of 0.4 percent in Mexico, with an average of 4.4 percent overall.[5] The Indian figure, at 1.4 percent, is thus well below the all-country average.

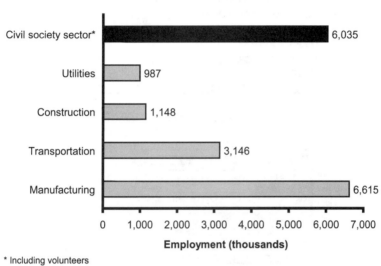

**Figure 7.1.** Civil society organization
workforce in context, India

* Including volunteers
SOURCE: Johns Hopkins Comparative Nonprofit Sector Project

- **Below the developing and transitional country average.** The Indian civil society organization workforce is also lower than the average for developing and transitional countries (1.4 vs. 1.9 percent) (see Figure 7.2). However, it is higher than that in neighboring Pakistan (1.4 vs. 1.0 percent).

- **Moderate volunteer participation.** It is estimated that about 16 million individuals in India engaged in volunteer work of some kind in 2000. This represents approximately 2 percent of India's adult population (see Appendix Table A.2). However, most volunteers work only a few hours a week, so these numbers translate into about 3.4 million full-time equivalent volunteers, or less than 1 percent of the economically active population. This is similar to the developing and transitional country average of 0.7 percent (see Appendix Table A.1). When computed as a share of the total civil society organization workforce (see Figure 7.3), volunteers in India account for a somewhat larger share than the developing and transitional country average (56 vs. 38 percent).

## 3. A long tradition of civil society institutions

As in many other developing and transitional countries, the historical development of civil society organizations falls into three distinct phases: pre-colonial, colonial, and post-colonial (national independence).[6] In the

**Figure 7.2.** Civil society organization workforce
as a share of the economically active population, by country

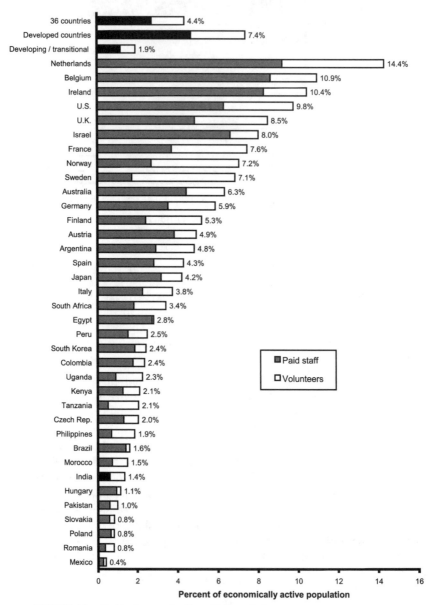

SOURCE: Johns Hopkins Comparative Nonprofit Sector Project

**Figure 7.3.** Volunteers as a share of the
civil society organization workforce, India,
developing and transitional countries, and 36 countries

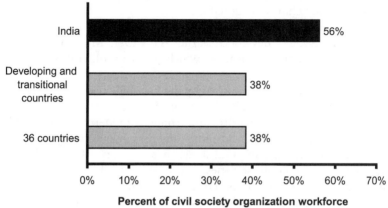

**Percent of civil society organization workforce**

SOURCE: Johns Hopkins Comparative Nonprofit Sector Project

pre-colonial period (1500 BC to the late 1700s AD), philanthropy, voluntarism, mutuality, and the provision of social welfare were based on traditional social institutions, such as religious groups, kin groups, or guilds, and were relatively independent of the state. The colonial period (late 1700s to 1947) brought Western-style philanthropic and charitable institutions affiliated with Christian churches and missions. The post-colonial period (after 1947) was characterized by the growth of development-oriented organizations grounded in the Gandhian movement, social welfare associations promoted by the growing professional class, and empowerment groups linked to socialist movements.

The origins of voluntarism and charity in India can be traced back to the ancient Hindu scriptures *Rig Veda* and *Upanishads* around 1500 BC. The emergence of Buddhism around 600 BC made voluntarism and the provision of social assistance and education key missions of monastic life. As a result, organized religion, especially monasteries, played an important role in providing public services, formal education, public utilities, and services to the poor and needy. Another area influenced by religion was the protection of certain trees and animals — a precursor of modern environmentalism.

However, the key institutions providing social assistance and emergency relief during the pre-colonial period were kin groups (extended families) and guilds. A person's extended family was the most important source of social safety and support in times of distress.

Most Indian craftsmen were also organized into guilds, which rose to prominence during the Buddhist period and became influential in the affairs of local communities. In addition to their regulatory and economic role in determining wages and standards, guilds played an important social function by providing social protections for widows, orphans, and the elderly. Guilds derived their support mainly from voluntary membership dues and fines, but they also received charitable donations.

Islamic influences, dating from the 14th century, tended to weaken the social welfare systems developed earlier. However, Muslim rulers generously supported religious education, which led to a proliferation of religious schools.

British rule in India was launched by the East India Company, which was chartered in 1600. Britain gained control of most Indian territories by the end of the 18th century. The British introduced modern charitable institutions such as schools, colleges, hospitals, and orphanages run by missionaries to promote Christianity. In rural areas, missionaries established self-help groups, cooperative credit societies, and training facilities to promote self-reliance and development. These efforts were emulated by Indian reformers and Western-educated professionals, who established similar institutions.

Christian influences provoked Hindu, Sikh, and Islamic groups to launch their own movements and affiliated organizations including schools, historical societies, and political parties. Another type of organization that emerged during this period was caste associations in South India that sought to raise the status of lower castes within the hierarchy of the Hindu caste system.

The first trade unions were formed in the 1890s in Bombay. Although initially lacking formal structure, they effectively organized workers and presented their demands to the authorities. Organizations promoting professions in arts, culture, and research, such as the Calcutta Phrenological Society, the Society for the Promotion of Industrial Arts, and Bombay Natural History, were formed by the British elite and were initially restricted to Europeans.

Another important 19th-century development among both Hindus and Muslims was the emergence of nationalist movements against British colonialism. These movements created a large number of voluntary associations promoting national education, economic development, self-governance, and self-reliance, as well as social reforms, and led to the formation of the Indian National Congress in 1885.

The culmination of these activities was the advent of the Gandhian movement, which represented a fusion of traditional and Western influences. Gandhian organizations' emphasis on a holistic approach to social problems, rooted in local culture, was similar to traditional organizational forms in India. However, they also strongly emphasized economic development and far-reaching social reforms including education, sanitation, and egalitarianism. After India gained national independence in 1947, Gandhian organizations formed the backbone of the civil society sector, promoting rural development and empowerment.

The post-independence period was also characterized by a greater involvement of the state in social and cultural affairs. The government created and promoted many new organizations, such as the Khadi and Village Industries Commission, the Central Social Welfare Board, schools for the arts, and social welfare and youth organizations. It also extended its control over certain existing private educational institutions. Nonetheless, the activities of many older religious and educational institutions continued without major hindrance.

In 1975, the declaration of a state of emergency by the Indira Gandhi government in response to social unrest briefly suspended the right to associate, but democracy was restored by the 1977 election. The growth of the civil society sector was further stimulated by an influx of foreign funds and government support. The government of India engaged numerous civil society organizations in economic development programs and began providing direct support for their activities.

The policies of economic liberalization and globalization pursued in the 1990s further stimulated the growth and significance of the civil society sector in India. Its activities expanded to include policy advocacy at the national and international level, human rights, women's issues, consumer advocacy, and political education for decentralized local governance.

## 4. Strong presence of service organizations

Given this historical background, it comes as no surprise that services dominate the civil society sector's activities in India. Although only partial data are available on the civil society sector's activities in India,[7] the data suggest that:

- **Service activities most prevalent.** As shown in Figure 7.4, service activities engage about 83 percent of the civil society organization workforce, paid and volunteer, in India. This share is significantly above the developing and transitional and all-country averages (63 and 64 percent, respectively), but is on a par with neighboring Pakistan (83 percent) (see Figure 8.4 in the following chapter).

- **Education dominates.** About 39 percent of all Indian civil society organization workers, paid and volunteer, are concentrated in education.[8] This share of the workforce engaged in educational activities is significantly larger than the developing and transitional country average of 25 percent.

- **Social services significant.** Social services account for about a third of the total civil society organization workforce in India and comprise the second largest activity field. This category includes social welfare services as well as community development and housing, which we could not separate due to data limitations.

**Figure 7.4.** Composition of the
civil society organization workforce, India,
developing and transitional countries, and 33-country average

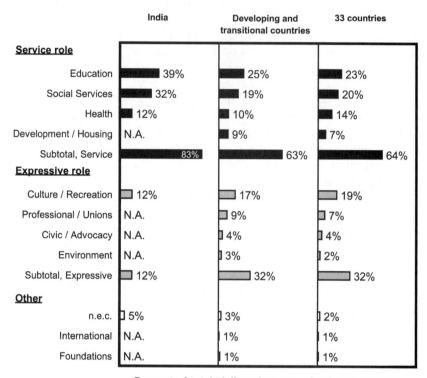

**Percent of total civil society organization workforce**

n.e.c.= not elsewhere classified
N.A.= Not Available
SOURCE: Johns Hopkins Comparative Nonprofit Sector Project

- **Health share similar to elsewhere.** The share of the Indian civil society organization workforce engaged in health service activities is on a par with the developing and transitional and all-country averages (12 percent vs. 10 and 14 percent, respectively).

- **Relatively low share of Indian civil society organization workers engaged in expressive activities.** A rather low proportion (12 percent) of civil society organization workers in India, paid and volunteer, are engaged in activities of an expressive variety. This is well below the developing and transitional and the all-country averages (both 32 percent). However, this may be a result of data limitations that make it impossible to identify civic and advocacy, environment, and professional associations and

**Figure 7.5.** Sources of civil society
organization revenue in India

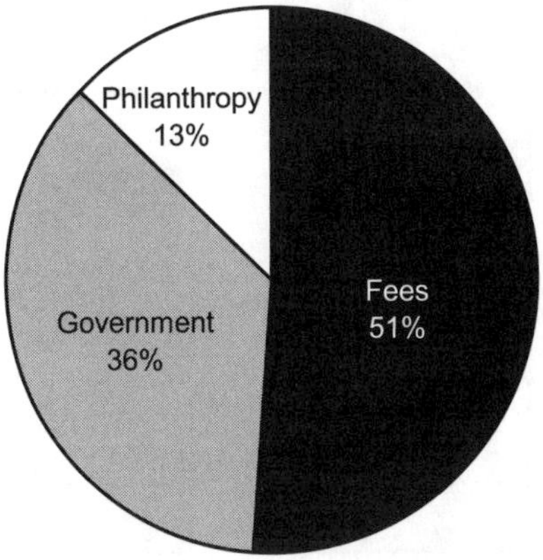

SOURCE: Johns Hopkins Comparative Nonprofit Sector Project

unions separately in the data. What is more, if we were to include community development and social service activities in the expressive rather
than the service activities, then the expressive share would increase to
44 percent. Such an inclusion may be justified by the fact that a very substantial number of organizations in India combine service and community
development with empowerment and mobilization of the rural poor.

## 5. Revenue dominated by fees and charges

- **Fees are the dominant source of civil society organization cash income in
  India.** As Figure 7.5 shows, about 51 percent of all cash revenue received
  by civil society organizations in India derives from fees and other forms of
  self-generated income. By comparison, government payments account for
  36 percent, while private donations comprise the remaining 13 percent.

- **Similar to international pattern.** This pattern of civil society organization
  revenue is quite close to the all-country pattern. Specifically, it closely
  mirrors the all-country average and does not substantially depart from
  the developing and transitional country average (see Figure 7.6). Perhaps
  the only noteworthy difference is that government provides a larger share
  of civil society sector support in India than is common in the developing
  and transitional countries (36 vs. 22 percent), reflecting the long history
  of cooperation between the state and civil society in this country.

- **Volunteers change the revenue structure.** This picture of the support
  structure of the Indian civil society sector changes significantly when the
  value of volunteer input is included. As Figure 7.7 demonstrates, with

**Figure 7.6.** Sources of civil society organization revenue,
India, developing and transitional countries,
and 34-country average

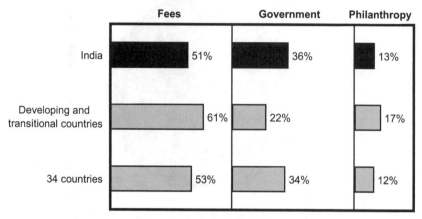

**Percent of total civil society organization revenue**

SOURCE: Johns Hopkins Comparative Nonprofit Sector Project

volunteering included and treated as a form of charitable giving, the philanthropic share of civil society organization support in India increases more than threefold, to 40 percent of the total. This is higher than both the developing and transitional country and the all-country averages (33 and 31 percent, respectively).

## Conclusions and Implications

As this chapter demonstrates, civil society organizations in India employ more workers, paid and volunteer, than a number of key industries. Civil society organization activities concentrate mainly in service areas, especially education. However, the size of this workforce is still relatively small when measured against the country's huge population.

India's broad array of religious, economic, labor, political, and cultural organizations emerged from the social movements that swept the country during the 19th and 20th centuries and reflect the enormous cultural, religious, and ethnic diversity of Indian society. This richness and diversity of associational life in India is often a source of conflict and contradiction. Traditional forms, such as caste, kinship, or ethnic associations, coexist and sometimes vie for power and influence with more modern institutions that encompass development and advocacy organizations, social service organizations, professional associations, and labor unions.

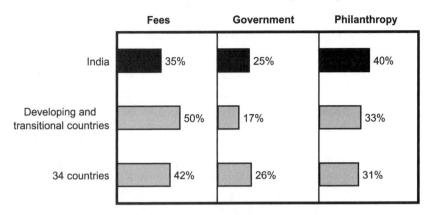

**Figure 7.7.** Sources of civil society organization support including volunteers, India, developing and transitional countries, and 34-country average

**Percent of total civil society organization support**

SOURCE: Johns Hopkins Comparative Nonprofit Sector Project

Because of this vast array of civic initiatives and associations, India does not have a unified civil society sector. Both civic activists and government officials tend to adopt a rather narrow definition of the sector that equates it with development-oriented organizations. All other types of civic initiatives are seen as serving special interests, or even self-interest, rather than society as a whole. As a result, a consistent public policy toward the civil society sector has yet to emerge in India.

Another challenge that Indian civil society organizations face is globalization and the state's fiscal crisis. The latter has reduced the availability of resources and prompted the government to invite private, often foreign, investment to shore up programs in the areas of health, education, environment, drinking water supply, and social services. Although the government usually retains control of the distribution of these private funds, the funding agencies often demand civil society's involvement in the projects they finance.

This cooperation shows the high degree of confidence that both government and donor agencies have in the organizational capacity of the civil society sector in India, and it has had a generally positive impact on the sector. In addition to generating income for civil society organizations, this policy creates an opportunity for civil society organizations to gain first-hand experience working in partnership with state agencies and being involved in large projects.

At the same time, questions have been raised about the proper role of civil society organizations. Many civic leaders question the increasing dependence of their organizations on government and foreign funding. They are often criticized for excessive commercialization and diversion from their original mission. Many organizations resent the subordinate position they are given in the project hierarchy and the bureaucratic requirements imposed on them as a condition of eligibility for government-controlled funding.

Consequently, the civil society sector faces important challenges to promote public policies that will clarify and normalize the sector's relationship with the government and foreign donor agencies and to bolster the sector's internal capabilities and public image. Specifically:

- **Public-private partnership.** The government needs to develop clear guidelines that define the role of civil society organizations in public programs and provide opportunities for partnership and collaboration between these organizations and government agencies.

- **Capacity building.** The leadership of civil society organizations should commit to building their organizational and professional capacity. The government and foreign donor agencies should provide resources to strengthen the organizational capacity of the civil society sector, including professional skill development of civil society organization staff.

- **Building legitimacy through self-regulation.** The development and enforcement of codes of conduct, accountability, and administrative standards are of critical importance. The civil society sector needs to openly endorse and follow such codes and standards, which will allow public accountability of its resources and activities.

- **Information gathering and dissemination.** In order to foster the public's understanding of the civil society sector and its role in Indian society, there needs to be a sustained effort to produce reliable information about the sector's organizational capacity and output, as well as an unbiased assessment of the quality of its services and their social and economic impact.

In conclusion, the civil society sector has proven to be an important agent in facilitating economic development, providing relief and social services, and empowering disadvantaged social groups in India. It is therefore crucial that this role be fully recognized and utilized by both policymakers and foreign assistance agencies. To achieve this goal, however, it is essential to develop an accurate assessment of the civil society sector's capacities and needs. We hope that the work reported here will constitute a useful first step toward attaining this goal.

## Notes

1. The work in India was coordinated by Rajesh Tandon, and S.S. Srivastava served as the Principal Investigator. The research team was aided, in turn, by a local advisory committee (see Appendix D for a list of committee members). The Johns

Hopkins project was directed by Lester M. Salamon, and the work in India was overseen by Leslie C. Hems.

2. The definitions and approaches used in the project were developed collaboratively with the cooperation of Indian researchers and researchers in other countries and were designed to be applicable to India and other project countries. For a full description of this definition, the types of organizations included, and the methodology used, see Chapter 1 and Appendix B. For a full list of the other countries included, see Table 1.1.

3. These results have been released in India in a series of working papers jointly published by the Society for Participatory Research in Asia and the Johns Hopkins Comparative Nonprofit Sector Project: PRIA and Anjaneya Associates, *Exploring the Non-profit Sector in India: Some Glimpses from Tamil Nadu,* Working Paper No. 4 (New Delhi: Society for Participatory Research in Asia, 2002); S.S. Srivastava, Rajesh Tandon, and S.K. Gupta, *Exploring the Non-profit Sector in India: Some Glimpses from West Bengal,* Working Paper No. 6 (New Delhi: Society for Participatory Research in Asia, 2002); PRIA and Society for Socio-Economic Studies and Services, *Exploring the Non-profit Sector in India: Some Glimpses from Meghalaya,* Working Paper No. 8 (New Delhi: Society for Participatory Research in Asia, 2003); Rajesh Tandon and S.S. Srivastava, *Invisible, Yet Widespread: The Non-profit Sector in India* (New Delhi: Society for Participatory Research in Asia, 2003); PRIA and Society for Socio-Economic Studies and Services, *Exploring the Non-profit Sector in India: Some Glimpses from Maharashtra,* Working Paper No. 10 (New Delhi: Society for Participatory Research in Asia, 2003). Other studies include: Charities Aid Foundation India, *Dimensions of Voluntary Sector in India* (New Delhi: Charities Aid Foundation India, 2000). For earlier reports on India produced by this project, see: Helmut K. Anheier and Lester M. Salamon, eds., *The Nonprofit Sector in the Developing World* (Manchester, U.K.: Manchester University Press, 1998).

4. The industry figures used for this comparison come from International Labour Organization data (http://laborsta.ilo.org/) and include only paid employees. Self-employed persons in small shops, whose numbers in India are significant, are not included.

5. Comparative figures do not include religious worship organizations because data on these organizations were not available for all countries. However, religiously affiliated service organizations are included. For more information, see Appendix B.

6. This section draws on the following resources: Siddharta Sen, "The Nonprofit Sector in India," in *The Nonprofit Sector in the Developing World,* ed. Helmut K. Anheier and Lester M. Salamon (Manchester, U.K.: Manchester University Press, 1998), 198–293; PRIA, *Historical Background of the Nonprofit Sector in India,* Working Paper No. 3 (New Delhi: Society for Participatory Research in Asia, June 2001).

7. Except for education and health, the data on the composition of the civil society sector in India reported in this section are not fully compatible with those reported for other countries because of differences in data assembly methodologies.

8. Percentages displayed in figures may not add to 100 due to rounding.

# Chapter 8

# Pakistan

Aisha Ghaus-Pasha, Muhammad Asif Iqbal,
S. Wojciech Sokolowski, and Lester M. Salamon

## Introduction

The civil society sector has a rich history in Pakistan stretching back to its pre-independence, pre-colonial roots in Hindu, Buddhist, Islamic, Christian, and Sikh religious beliefs stressing the obligations of believers to care for the poor and the sick and to promote education. These beliefs manifested themselves in a variety of religions and philanthropic institutions such as Buddhist *stupas,* Hindu *asharam,* Sufi *khanqahs,* Sikh *gurdwaras,* and Islamic *madrassahs.*

Colonialism led to a further institutionalization of voluntary organizations as colonial authorities sought both to promote philanthropy as a way to reduce the demands on government, and to maintain control over the resulting institutions. Christian missionaries contributed further to the development of the civil society sector, establishing numerous schools, colleges, and hospitals that continue to play a significant role.

Following the independence of the country in 1947, civil society organizations experienced another growth spurt, largely in response to the massive migration that occurred. Post-independence governments, both military and civilian, have generally assumed a posture of support or indifference to the gap-filling service role of civil society organizations while opposing their advocacy role.

As a result, the civil society sector in Pakistan remains relatively small. Its activities concentrate mainly in service areas, especially education. Overall, government support of the sector is very limited and directed mainly to one field — community development. But private philanthropy — including money and volunteer work — remains substantial and is the main source of the civil society sector's support.

These findings emerge from a body of work carried out by a Pakistani research team as part of the Johns Hopkins Comparative Nonprofit Sector Project.[1] This work sought both to analyze Pakistani civil society organizations and to compare and contrast them to those in other countries in a

170

**Table 8.1.** The civil society sector* in Pakistan, 2000

---

**$212.3 million in expenditures**
- 0.3% of the GDP

**476,575 full-time equivalent workers**
- 264,251 full-time equivalent paid employees
- 212,324 full-time equivalent volunteers
- 1.1% of the economically active population
- 4.1% of nonagricultural employment
- 18.0% of public employment

---

* Including religious organizations.

SOURCE: Johns Hopkins Comparative Nonprofit Sector Project

systematic way.[2] The result is the first empirical overview of the Pakistani civil society sector and the first systematic comparison of Pakistani civil society realities to those elsewhere in the world.

This chapter reports chiefly on the major descriptive findings of this project relating to the size, composition, and financing of the civil society sector in Pakistan and other countries. Other reports will fill in more of the history, legal position, and impact of these institutions. Most of the data reported here come from surveys designed and implemented by the Johns Hopkins Comparative Nonprofit Sector Project and the local research team. Religiously affiliated service and auxiliary organizations were covered in these surveys, but data could not be collected on places of religious worship such as mosques and churches. For a more complete statement of the types of organizations included, see Chapter 1 and Appendix B. Unless otherwise noted, financial data are reported in U.S. dollars at the 2000 average exchange rate.

# Principal Findings

## 1. A sizeable economic force

The civil society sector in Pakistan (including some auxiliary religious organizations) constituted a considerable, though still relatively modest, economic force as of 2000. More specifically:

- **A $212 million industry.** Civil society organizations in Pakistan accounted for $212 million in expenditures in 2000, or 0.3 percent of the nation's gross domestic product (GDP), as reported in Table 8.1.

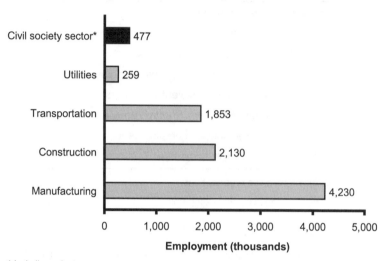

**Figure 8.1.** Civil society organization workforce in context, Pakistan

\* Including volunteers
SOURCE: Johns Hopkins Comparative Nonprofit Sector Project

- **A sizeable employer.** Pakistani civil society organizations employ nearly half a million (476,575) full-time equivalent (FTE) workers. This represents 1.1 percent of the country's economically active population, 4.1 percent of its nonagricultural employment, and 18.0 percent of its public employment (see Table 8.1).

- **Larger than the utilities industry.** Civil society sector employment in Pakistan is thus almost twice that of the country's utilities industry, though it is smaller than a number of other major sectors, such as transportation, construction, and manufacturing (see Figure 8.1).

- **Sizable volunteer presence.** Of the 476,575 full-time equivalent workers in Pakistani civil society organizations, over 40 percent are volunteers.

## 2. Modest in comparative terms

The civil society sector in Pakistan, as measured by its workforce, is smaller than that in most other countries covered by this project.

- **Significantly below the all-country average.** As shown in Figure 8.2, excluding religious worship organizations, the civil society organization workforce — paid and volunteer — varies from a high of 14.4 percent of the economically active population in the Netherlands to a low of 0.4 percent in Mexico, with an average of 4.4 percent overall.[3] The Pakistani figure, at 1.0 percent, excluding all religious worship organizations, is thus well below the all-country average.

**Figure 8.2.** Civil society organization workforce
as a share of the economically active population, by country

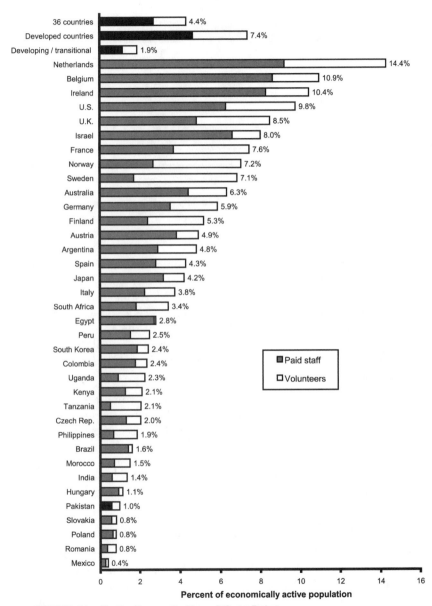

SOURCE: Johns Hopkins Comparative Nonprofit Sector Project

**Figure 8.3.** Volunteers as a share of the
civil society organization workforce, Pakistan,
developing and transitional countries, and 36 countries

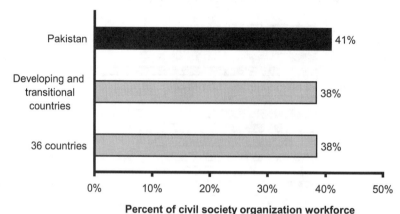

SOURCE: Johns Hopkins Comparative Nonprofit Sector Project

- **Below the developing and transitional country average.** The share of the economically active population employed by civil society organizations in Pakistan is also below the average for developing and transitional countries. Thus, as shown in Figure 8.2, the civil society organization workforce in Pakistan, measured as a share of the economically active population, is roughly half as large as the average for all the developing and transitional countries for which we have data (1.0 vs. 1.9 percent of the economically active population).

- **Volunteer participation.** The full-time equivalent volunteer workforce in Pakistan, at 0.4 percent of the economically active population, is also less than the all-country average of 1.6 percent (see Appendix Table A.1). However, volunteers still constitute a larger share of the civil society organization workforce in Pakistan than they do on average for developing and transitional countries and for all countries (41 percent vs. 38 percent, respectively), as shown in Figure 8.3.

## 3. A conflict-ridden history of civil society development

**Pre-colonial period (before the 18th century).** Philanthropic and voluntary activities date back to early recorded history within the geographical boundaries of modern Pakistan.[4] Religion has been the driving force behind this phenomenon. Islam, Hinduism, Buddhism, Christianity, and Sikhism have provided strong spiritual motivation to their followers to cater to the needs of the poor, sick, and underprivileged in society.

**Colonial period (18th century to 1947).** British rule in South Asia brought about the institutionalization of philanthropic and voluntary activities, which hitherto functioned mainly as individual initiatives. The main focus of these efforts was the delivery of social and humanitarian services such as education, health, and material assistance to the needy. The British introduced Western social welfare institutions to the region and required the legal system to register and regulate philanthropic and voluntary organizations.

A large number of voluntary organizations that emerged in this period provided not only basic social services, such as primary education and healthcare, but also professional and technical education. Secular, Islamic, and Christian organizations established numerous schools, colleges, and hospitals that continue to play pivotal roles in the fields of education and health care. These organizations are still considered to be among the finest in the country.

But service provision was not the only role performed by early Pakistani civil society organizations. These organizations were also prominent in the political activism that grew in the early 20th century as civic leaders began to demand a greater degree of autonomy from British rule. Muslim leaders in the region formed the all-India Muslim League in 1906, which, along with the Indian National Congress Party, pushed for independence.

**Post-independence period.** Following independence and the partition of the subcontinent, the evolution of the civil society sector in Pakistan by and large coincided with the changing sociopolitical environment of the new country. In the immediate aftermath of partition, the civil society sector was key to addressing the social welfare needs of the millions of displaced people. During the 1950s, voluntary organizations continued to focus on reconstruction, rehabilitation, and provision of social services. In addition, the All Pakistan Women's Association began advocacy work supporting women's rights, and another prominent civil society organization, the Family Planning Association of Pakistan, was established to promote reproductive health services.

During the martial law period that began in 1958, voluntary organizations were encouraged to play a supplementary role in the provision of social services, and the National Council for Social Welfare was formed in 1956 to provide these organizations with technical and financial assistance. At the same time, the government took steps to diminish the role of organized religion but targeted mainly Sufi shrines, which are a small segment of organized religion in Pakistan.

The rise to power of a democratic government under the Pakistan People's Party (PPP) led by Zulfiqar Ali Bhutto subsequently energized the civil society sector. Trade unions and organizations focusing on women's rights entered the political scene.[5] However, in 1972 the PPP nationalized private schools, colleges, and other educational institutions that had been established and run by voluntary organizations.

During the 1980s, the civil society sector in Pakistan experienced a significant and multidimensional expansion resulting from the liberal flow of foreign funds that accompanied the Afghan War (1979–89). The government's failure to provide basic social services led to the creation of large private organizations working in rural and urban development (such as the Aga Khan Rural Support Program and the Orangi Pilot Project) and in the field of social welfare (such as the Edhi Trust). Following the Aga Khan Rural Support Program model, the government established national and provincial rural support programs and provided endowment funds to these programs to develop networks of small community-based organizations. Due to the influx of refugees from Afghanistan, many relief and emergency-oriented international donors and nongovernmental organizations also set up headquarters in Pakistan,[6] as did many Islamic organizations that had fought against the Soviet Union in Afghanistan.

Advocacy organizations focusing mainly on human rights and women's issues — such as the Human Rights Commission of Pakistan, the Women Action Forum, and the Pakistan Institute of Labor, Education, and Research — also became stronger and more visible during this decade. Their growth created tension between the government and the civil society sector as well as between secular and religious organizations that persists in the Pakistani civil society sector to this day. In the 1990s, policy shifted in favor of civil society organizations involved in the delivery of social services. Financial assistance from the government and donor agencies increased significantly during this period.

## 4. Strong presence of service organizations

As a result of these social and political forces, service delivery clearly absorbs the largest share of civil society sector activities in Pakistan.

- **Share of service activities larger than elsewhere.** As shown in Figure 8.4, the service share of civil society activities in Pakistan, at 83 percent of the total civil society organization workforce, exceeds the developing and transitional country and all-country averages (63 and 64 percent, respectively).

- **Education dominates.** Especially prominent is the civil society organization involvement in education in Pakistan. More than half (57 percent) of all Pakistani civil society organization workers — paid and volunteer — are involved in education.[7] This is the highest among the 33 countries for which there are comparable data (see Appendix Table A.3).

- **Relatively small share engaged in expressive activities.** Only 17 percent of paid and volunteer civil society organization workers in Pakistan are engaged in expressive activities. This is well below both the developing and transitional country and all-country averages (32 percent each).

**Figure 8.4.** Composition of the
civil society organization workforce, Pakistan,
developing and transitional countries, and 33-country average

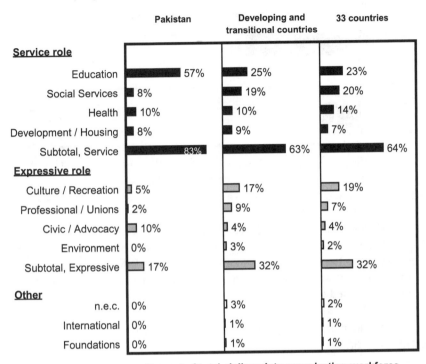

Percent of total civil society organization workforce

n.e.c.= not elsewhere classified
SOURCE: Johns Hopkins Comparative Nonprofit Sector Project

- **Civic and advocacy activities significant.** While the expressive role of the civil society sector overall in Pakistan is relatively small, the civic and advocacy role is still relatively large, accounting for 10 percent of the Pakistani civil society sector workforce. This figure is more than twice the developing and transitional country and all-country averages (both 4 percent). A great majority of these workers are involved with community-based organizations engaged in lobbying at the local level, conveying day-to-day problems to various levels of government, and assisting their communities in resolving issues like water supply, electricity, or sewerage. Human rights advocacy, by contrast, is more limited.

- **More volunteers than paid staff engaged in expressive functions.** As in many other countries, the paid and volunteer staff of Pakistani civil society organizations are distributed quite differently. While service functions

**Figure 8.5.** Distribution of paid employees and volunteers between service and expressive activities in Pakistan

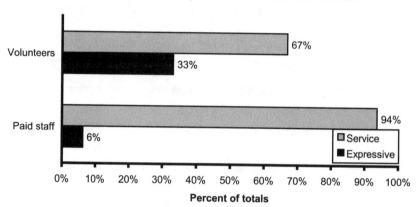

SOURCE: Johns Hopkins Comparative Nonprofit Sector Project

absorb the majority of both paid and volunteer staff time, considerably more of the volunteer effort goes into expressive activities than does paid staff effort (33 percent vs. 6 percent), as Figure 8.5 demonstrates. Clearly, the expressive and advocacy activities of Pakistan's civil society sector are heavily carried by volunteers.

## 5. Revenue dominated by fees and philanthropic contributions

Fees and charges constitute the largest source of civil society organization income in Pakistan, as in most of the other countries for which data are available. However, Pakistan departs from the other countries in the share of its civil society sector revenue that comes from private giving.

- **Fees and philanthropy the major revenue sources.** Just over half (51 percent) of all civil society organization revenue in Pakistan comes from fees, charges, and membership dues; but, private philanthropy from individuals, foundations, and corporations is a close second, accounting for 43 percent of the revenue. By contrast, public sector support is a distant third, providing only 6 percent of the support, as shown in Figure 8.6.

- **Differs from international pattern.** This pattern of civil society organization revenue differs significantly from that evident internationally.

  – Perhaps the most distinctive feature of Pakistan's civil society sector is its significant reliance on philanthropic contributions (see Figure 8.7). Philanthropy's share of civil society organization revenue in Pakistan is over two times the average for developing and transitional countries, and over three times the average for all countries (43 percent vs. 17 and

**Figure 8.6.** Sources of civil society organization revenue in Pakistan

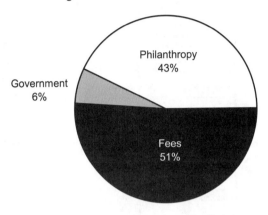

SOURCE: Johns Hopkins Comparative Nonprofit Sector Project

**Figure 8.7.** Sources of civil society organization revenue, Pakistan, developing and transitional countries, and 34-country average

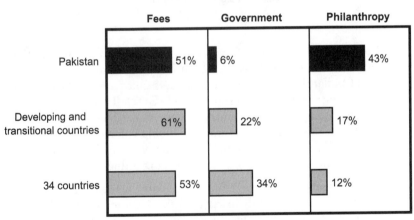

**Percent of total civil society organization revenue**

SOURCE: Johns Hopkins Comparative Nonprofit Sector Project

**Figure 8.8.** Sources of civil society organization revenue, Pakistan, by field

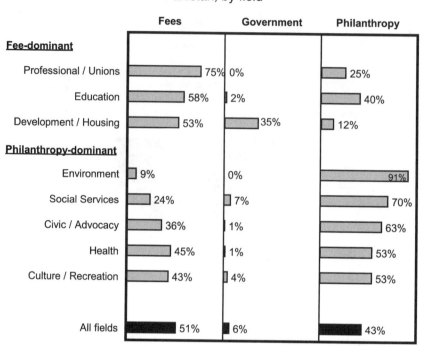

Percent of total civil society organization revenue

SOURCE: Johns Hopkins Comparative Nonprofit Sector Project

12 percent, respectively). However, this outcome reflects the relatively small size of the civil society sector in Pakistan. In absolute terms, the level of philanthropic giving in Pakistan is quite modest, 0.22 percent of the country's gross domestic product (GDP). This is below the developing and transitional country average of 0.30 percent of the GDP, albeit higher than that in several developing countries, such as South Korea (0.18 percent), Brazil (0.17 percent), Mexico (0.04 percent), and the Philippines (0.04 percent) (see Appendix Table A.5).

- By contrast, the level of government support for the Pakistani civil society sector is considerably lower than the developing and transitional country and all-country averages (6 percent of total revenue vs. 22 and 34 percent, respectively), as shown in Figure 8.7. In fact, Pakistan has the lowest level of government support for the civil society sector among all 34 countries studied — 0.03 percent of the GDP, compared to the all-country average of 1.80 percent (see Appendix Table A.5).

**Figure 8.9.** Sources of civil society organization support including volunteers, Pakistan, developing and transitional countries, and 34-country average

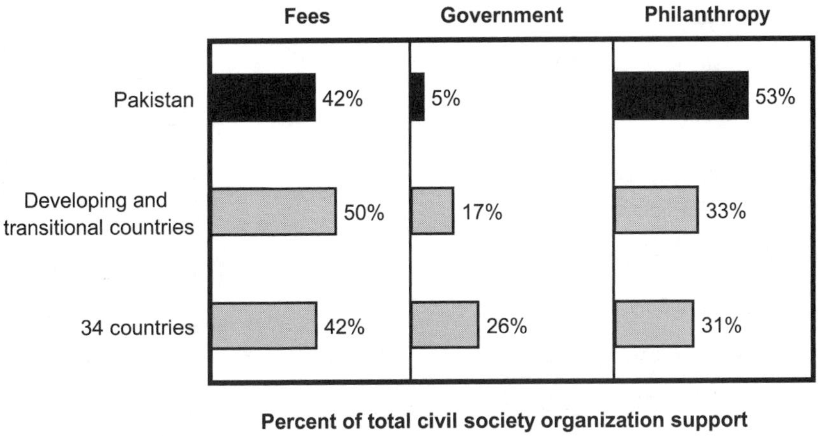

**Percent of total civil society organization support**

SOURCE: Johns Hopkins Comparative Nonprofit Sector Project

- The service fee share of civil society sector income in Pakistan is on a par with the all-country average (51 percent of total revenue vs. 53 percent), but somewhat lower than the developing and transitional country average of 61 percent (see Figure 8.7).

- **Revenue pattern varies among fields.** The Pakistani civil society sector's heavy reliance on private philanthropy also finds reflection in specific fields, although there is considerable variation. As shown in Figure 8.8, philanthropy is the dominant revenue source in five fields: environmental protection (91 percent of all revenue), social services (70 percent), civic and advocacy (63 percent), health and culture/recreation (both 53 percent). By contrast, fee revenue dominates in three fields: professional associations and unions (75 percent), education (58 percent), and community development (53 percent). The latter is the only field that receives substantial government support (35 percent).

- **Volunteer input increases philanthropy's share.** The sizable presence of philanthropy in the revenue structure of Pakistani civil society organizations increases even further when the value of volunteer input is included and treated as a form of philanthropy. As Figure 8.9 demonstrates, the inclusion of volunteer time makes private philanthropy the dominant source of support of the civil society sector in Pakistan, outdistancing fees and charges 53 to 42 percent. This is substantially higher than the developing and transitional country and all-country averages (33 and 31 percent, respectively).

**Figure 8.10.** Sources of civil society organization support
in Pakistan, including volunteers, by field

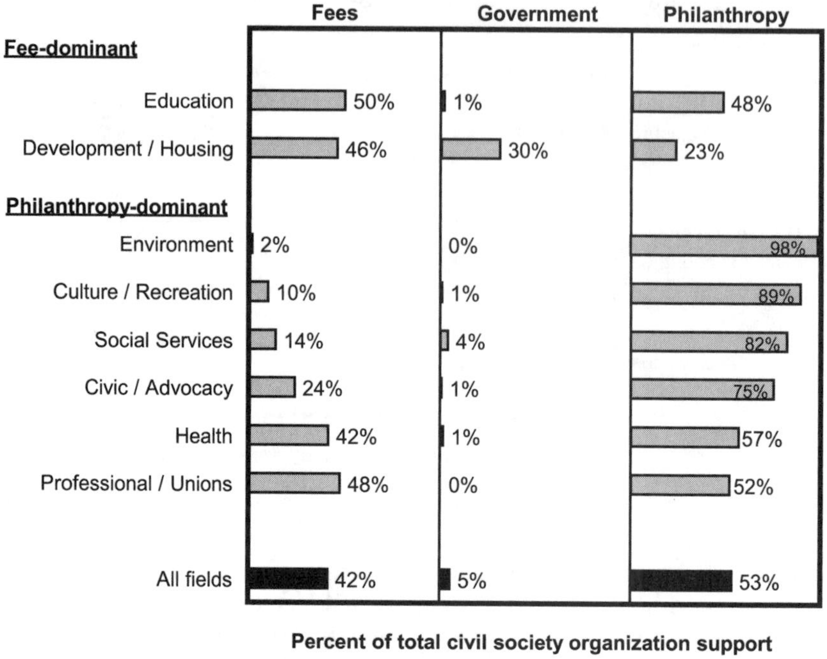

| | Fees | Government | Philanthropy |
|---|---|---|---|
| **Fee-dominant** | | | |
| Education | 50% | 1% | 48% |
| Development / Housing | 46% | 30% | 23% |
| **Philanthropy-dominant** | | | |
| Environment | 2% | 0% | 98% |
| Culture / Recreation | 10% | 1% | 89% |
| Social Services | 14% | 4% | 82% |
| Civic / Advocacy | 24% | 1% | 75% |
| Health | 42% | 1% | 57% |
| Professional / Unions | 48% | 0% | 52% |
| All fields | 42% | 5% | 53% |

**Percent of total civil society organization support**

SOURCE: Johns Hopkins Comparative Nonprofit Sector Project

- With the value of volunteer input included, private philanthropy is
  the main source of civil society organization support in Pakistan in
  six fields (see Figure 8.10). Only education and development rely
  predominantly on other sources of support, specifically fee payments.

## Conclusions and Implications

As this chapter demonstrates, the civil society sector in Pakistan remains
relatively small by international standards. Its activities concentrate mainly
in service areas, especially education. Private donations of money and time
are the sector's main source of support.

However, despite its small size, the Pakistani civil society sector has diverse origins and plays important service and advocacy roles.[8] It includes
age-old welfare organizations, as well as modern development-oriented nongovernmental organizations. Major types of organizations include voluntary
and social welfare organizations, societies, trusts, foundations, and nonprofit companies. While the traditional role of civil society organizations has

been the provision of social services, in the 1980s and 1990s new advocacy organizations emerged.

The diversity and evolution of the civil society sector in Pakistan reflect the sector's strong links with the diverse and vibrant cultural traditions of Pakistani society. This is demonstrated by the presence of ethnic, denominational, sectarian, and clan organizations that espouse traditional religious values as well as by the emergence of modern secular organizations.

Over the years, constraints on financial resources, the public sector's limited institutional capacity, and declining confidence in the government's ability to deliver basic services, have led to the emergence of civil society organizations funded by both private philanthropy and international donors. The attitude of both the government and most political parties towards the civil society sector, however, has been inconsistent.

The events of September 11, 2001, and the subsequent American attack on the Taliban and al Qaeda in neighboring Afghanistan, have further complicated the relationship between the government and the civil society sector in Pakistan, and between secular organizations and religious ones. This is so because some civil society organizations are suspected of aiding and abetting terrorist activities inside Afghanistan, increasing the pressures on the government to crack down on them and straining the relations between government and civil society organizations more generally.

Given this background, the civil society sector continues to face a number of important challenges. For one thing, the legal status of civil society organizations remains unsettled. Pending legislation introduced in 1996 would require all civil society organizations to re-register with the Ministry of Social Welfare within a specified period; grant arbitrary powers of government to de-register, suspend, or dissolve an organization, or to remove any provisions of an organization's constitution; and require external audits.

Fortunately, the government initiated a reform process in 2001 to review the legal, fiscal, and institutional framework for civil society organizations. Called the Enabling Environment Initiative, this process involved nationwide consultations with a variety of stakeholders. Although the recommendations of this initiative are still pending, it is our hope that this project and its outcomes, which include creating greater public awareness of the civil society sector and its strengths and weaknesses, its contributions to society, and its evolving role vis-à-vis the government and the private sector, will contribute to improving the existing environment and thereby promote the sector's growth in Pakistan.

## Notes

1. The work in Pakistan has been coordinated by the Social Policy and Development Centre in collaboration with the Aga Khan Foundation (Pakistan). The research team was aided, in turn, by a local advisory committee (see Appendix D for a list of

committee members). The Johns Hopkins project was directed by Lester M. Salamon, and the work in Pakistan was overseen by Leslie C. Hems.

2. The definitions and approaches used in the project were developed collaboratively with the cooperation of Pakistani researchers and researchers in other countries and were designed to be applicable to Pakistan and other project countries. For a full description of this definition, the types of organizations included, and the methodology used, see Chapter 1 and Appendix B. For a full list of the other countries included, see Table 1.1.

3. Comparative figures do not include organizations classified under ICNPO Group 7 (religion) because data on these organizations were not available for all countries. However, religiously affiliated service organizations are included. For more information, see Appendix B.

4. The history section draws heavily on A. Ghaus-Pasha and M. Asif Iqbal, *Defining the Nonprofit Sector: Pakistan,* Working Papers of the Johns Hopkins Comparative Nonprofit Sector Project, no. 42 (Baltimore, MD: The Johns Hopkins Center for Civil Society Studies, 2003).

5. NGO Resource Center, *The State of the Citizen Sector in Pakistan* (Karachi: NGO Resource Center, 1999).

6. NGO Resource Center, *The State of the Citizen Sector in Pakistan* (Karachi: NGO Resource Center, 1999).

7. Percentages displayed in figures may not add to 100 due to rounding.

8. This section draws heavily on A. Ghaus-Pasha and M. Asif Iqbal, *Defining the Nonprofit Sector: Pakistan,* Working Papers of the Johns Hopkins Comparative Nonprofit Sector Project, no. 42 (Baltimore, MD: The Johns Hopkins Center for Civil Society Studies, 2003).

Chapter 9

# The Philippines

Ledivina V. Cariño, Rachel H. Racelis, Ramon L. Fernan III,
S. Wojciech Sokolowski, and Lester M. Salamon

## Introduction

The civil society sector in the Philippines has been shaped by colonialism, by
the Roman Catholic Church, and by the Filipino people's struggle for self-
determination against colonial powers, and more recently, authoritarianism.
The colonial powers, first Spain and later the United States, established and
maintained charitable and welfare associations and medical and educational
institutions at least partly to consolidate their respective rule. The Roman
Catholic Church facilitated the formation of civil society organizations to
reinforce its social and political influence. The Philippine people used the
associations and organizations brought to them by the colonial powers to
reinforce their common identity, provide mutual help, struggle for national
independence, and more recently, to promote social justice and democracy.

Sometimes the state and the Church worked in tandem, as during the
Spanish colonial era, to affect civil society. At other times, such as during
the Martial Law Regime of the 1970s–1980s, the church worked alongside
civil society in opposition to the state.

These forces — colonial hegemony, a strong Catholic Church, and the
popular struggle for democracy and self-determination — have created a
civil society sector in the Philippines that is relatively modest in size but with
an unusually large expressive component and significant volunteer involvement. The cash revenues of the civil society sector come almost exclusively
from service fees; however, when the value of volunteer work is included,
philanthropy provides nearly half of the civil society sector's support.

These findings emerge from a body of work carried out by a Philippine
research team as part of the Johns Hopkins Comparative Nonprofit Sector
Project.[1] This work sought both to analyze Philippine civil society organizations and to compare and contrast them to those in other countries in a
systematic way.[2] The result is the first empirical overview of the Philippine
civil society sector and the first systematic comparison of Philippine civil
society realities to those elsewhere in the world.

**Table 9.1.** The civil society sector* in the Philippines, 1997

---

**$1.2 billion in expenditures**

- 1.5% of the GDP

**544,719 full-time equivalent workers**

- 207,025 full-time equivalent paid employees
- 337,694 full-time equivalent volunteers
- 2.0% of the economically active population
- 3.2% of nonagricultural employment

---

\* Including religious worship organizations.

SOURCE: Johns Hopkins Comparative Nonprofit Sector Project

This chapter reports chiefly on the major descriptive findings of this project relating to the size, composition, and financing of the civil society sector in the Philippines and other countries. Other reports will fill in more of the history, legal position, and impact of these institutions.[3] Most of the data reported here were generated from Securities and Exchange Commission records that contain annual reports of all registered entities. Additional research work, including a supplementary survey on giving and volunteering, was conducted by the project team. The year covered in this report is 1997. Unless otherwise noted, financial data are reported in U.S. dollars at the 1997 average exchange rate. For a more complete statement of the types of organizations included, see Chapter 1 and Appendix B.

## Principal Findings

### 1. A modest economic force

The size and economic significance of the civil society sector in the Philippines is on a par with that of other developing and transitional countries. More specifically:

- **A $1.2 billion industry.** In 1997, civil society organizations in the Philippines, including religious worship organizations, account for $1.2 billion in expenditures, or 1.5 percent of the nation's gross domestic product (GDP), as reported in Table 9.1. This is considerably larger than previously reported estimates.[4]

- **A significant employer.** The workforce behind these expenditures numbers over 544,000 full-time equivalent (FTE) workers, of which approximately two-thirds are volunteers. This represents 2.0 percent of the

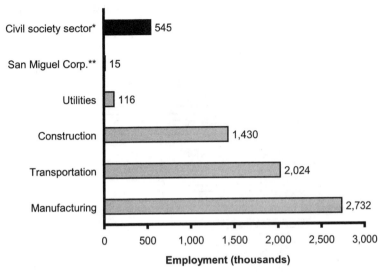

**Figure 9.1.** Civil society organization workforce in context, the Philippines

\*   Including volunteers
\*\*   Largest private firm
SOURCE: Johns Hopkins Comparative Nonprofit Sector Project

country's economically active population and 3.2 percent of nonagricultural employment (see Table 9.1).

- **Larger than many industries.** To put these figures into context, the civil society sector employs 36 times more people than the largest private firm in the Philippines, the San Miguel Corporation, and nearly 5 times more people than the entire utilities industry (electricity, gas, and water) (see Figure 9.1). Its workforce is equivalent to more than a third of that employed in construction, almost a quarter of civil service employment,[5] and a fifth of the manufacturing sector.

## 2. Comparable to other developing and transitional countries

- **On a par with developing and transitional country average.** As shown in Figure 9.2, the civil society organization workforce — paid and volunteer but excluding religious worship organizations[6] — varies from a high of 14.4 percent of the economically active population in the Netherlands to a low of 0.4 percent in Mexico, with an average of 4.4 percent overall. The Philippine civil society sector, at 1.9 percent, excluding religious worship organizations, ranks above nine developing and transitional

**Figure 9.2.** Civil society organization workforce
as a share of the economically active population, by country

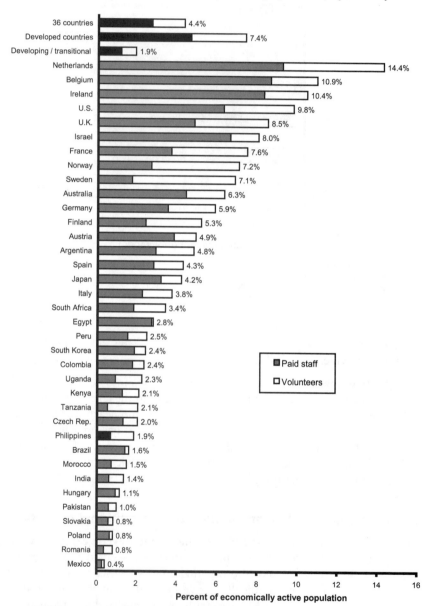

SOURCE: Johns Hopkins Comparative Nonprofit Sector Project

**Figure 9.3.** Volunteers as a share of the
civil society organization workforce, the Philippines,
developing and transitional countries, and 36 countries

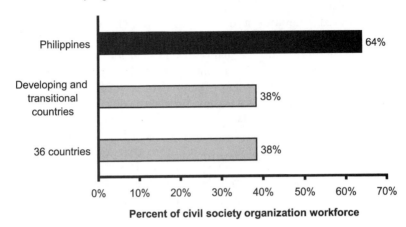

**Percent of civil society organization workforce**

SOURCE: Johns Hopkins Comparative Nonprofit Sector Project

countries, and is equal to the developing and transitional country average. At the same time, this figure is less than half of the all-country average (4.4 percent).

- **Volunteer share of civil society sector workforce higher than elsewhere.** Volunteer participation is unusually high in the Philippines, engaging an estimated 2.8 million people, or 6 percent of the adult population (see Appendix Table A.2). Translated into full-time equivalent workers, this represents 1.2 percent of the economically active population, slightly below the all-country average of 1.6 percent but significantly higher than the developing and transitional country average of 0.7 percent (see Appendix Table A.1). Reflecting this, the volunteer share of the Philippine civil society organization workforce is significantly higher than the developing and transitional country and all-country averages (64 percent vs. 38 percent), as reflected in Figure 9.3.

## 3. The colonial roots of civil society development

Before the Spanish colonization in the 16th century, the Philippine Islands were inhabited by indigenous peoples organized along clan lines with no separate organizations for politics, commerce, or social welfare and philanthropy. The prevailing subsistence mode of production created a deep sense of communalism and mutual cooperation that has survived to modern times in the form of the Filipino value of *pakikipagkapwa-tao*, which denotes sharing one's inner self with the collective.[7]

Spanish colonial rule (1521–1898), and the resulting religious hegemony of the Roman Catholic Church, brought the first social welfare organizations to the islands. Religious orders established a small number of hospitals, asylums, orphanages, parochial schools, and other welfare institutions that primarily served Spaniards and the local elite. The Church also sponsored charities (*obras pias*), which directed personal fortunes to charitable purposes, again serving mostly Spaniards and their local allies.[8]

Local resistance to colonial rule initially took the form of small peasant revolts. This resistance was often organized by *cofradías* (brotherhoods), established by the Catholic Church for the purpose of proselytizing and policing the indigenous population. However, the Church refused to recognize the rebellious associations, and the Spanish government violently suppressed them.[9] Some of these organizations transformed into independent churches that provided mainly spiritual services.[10]

In contrast to these peasant rebellions, the 19th-century struggle for national independence was led by the native intelligentsia, many of whom had received a European education. The movement initially sought reform by spreading its ideals, educating the population, and promoting self-help and cooperation. The reformist movement was represented mainly by *La Liga Filipina* (The Philippine League) established in 1892. However, a more militant mass movement, the *Katipunan,* eschewed reform and called for a popular revolution to win complete independence from Spain. On June 12, 1898, the Philippines gained independence. The *Katipunan* movement was instrumental in this effort, and its legacy remains strong in Philippine society.

However, Philippine independence was short-lived; the retreating Spanish forces ceded their Asian colony to the United States in the Treaty of Paris of 1898. The American rule instituted a separation of church and state and introduced legislation (the Philippine Corporation Law of 1906) that officially recognized private nonprofit organizations. American charitable and religious organizations set up branches in the new colony, and the colonial government subsidized the operations of charitable and welfare institutions to compensate for the reduced capacity of Catholic charities.

The new political environment of tolerance and openness to private civil society organizations allowed new groups to form, including political parties, labor organizations, peasant unions, women's groups, student and youth groups, cooperatives, and other mutual benefit associations. Although the colonial government dealt severely with groups openly fomenting revolt against the American presence, it allowed those advocating purely economic grievances some leeway, including the freedom to strike.

Widespread poverty in the early and mid-20th century ultimately fueled political polarization within the civil society sector, with communist and Catholic organizations competing for influence. This polarization persisted after the Philippines gained national independence in 1946, as rural and urban poverty escalated. As the state increased its repression of communist organizations, the Catholic Church expanded its social action agenda, engaging with workers and peasants to form a federation of anticommunist labor and farm unions to further undermine the communist influence.[11] Protestant churches followed suit and also expanded their services to encompass rural development, cooperatives and credit unions, and practical skills in agriculture. Widespread community mobilization efforts were also undertaken, however, by a variety of other organizations, such as independent churches, Maoist parties, labor unions, peasant associations, and groups of the urban poor.

In response to growing social unrest, President Marcos declared martial law in 1972. The Marcos dictatorship (1972–1986) crushed many activist and advocacy groups and forced others to go underground or at least change tactics. Nongovernmental organizations were tolerated only so long as they appeared nonpolitical or supported Marcos' policies. One popular tactic used by organizations to avoid scrutiny by security forces was to "institutionalize" development work within an academic setting or to join the expanding social action programs of mainstream churches (Catholic and Protestant).

The fall of the Marcos regime in 1986 reestablished the democratic environment that civil society needed to flourish. Facing severe economic problems, the new government welcomed partnerships with civil society organizations to deliver basic services and participate in the policy making process at the local and national levels. Civil society organizations thus participate on local development councils as well as national bodies such as the National Anti-poverty Commission. Nongovernmental organizations were also given the right to negotiate directly with foreign governments to secure funding for projects inside the country. The supportive political environment and availability of new resources has spurred a recent rapid growth of civil society organizations.

## 4. A mix of service and expressive activities

Reflecting this history, most of the Philippine civil society sector workforce is engaged in service functions, such as education or development, although expressive activities, including those of cultural and professional organizations, are also prominent.

- **Service activities, especially education, dominate.** As shown in Figure 9.4, about 60 percent of all Philippine civil society organization workers — paid and volunteer — are engaged in service activities.[12] This share of service activities is similar to that found in other countries. Of these activities, education is the most prominent, absorbing 30 percent of the civil society workforce; this exceeds the developing and transitional country and all-country averages (25 and 23 percent, respectively).

**Figure 9.4.** Composition of the
civil society organization workforce, the Philippines,
developing and transitional countries, and 33-country average

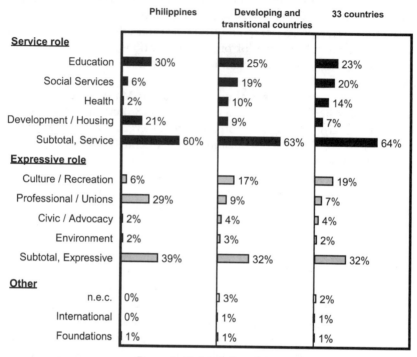

Percent of total civil society organization workforce

n.e.c.= not elsewhere classified
SOURCE: Johns Hopkins Comparative Nonprofit Sector Project

- **Relatively large share of Philippine civil society organization workers engaged in expressive activities.** While most Philippine civil society employment is in service activities, a substantial 39 percent of the workers — paid and volunteer — are engaged in activities of an expressive variety, such as culture, recreation, and professional activities. This is above both the developing and transitional country and all-country averages (32 percent, each).

- **Professional activities especially prevalent.** Among these expressive functions, professional associations are especially prominent, accounting for 29 percent of the Philippine civil society organization workforce. This is more than triple the developing and transitional country average and slightly more than four times the all-country average (at 9 and 7 percent,

**Figure 9.5.** Distribution of paid employees and volunteers between service and expressive activities in the Philippines

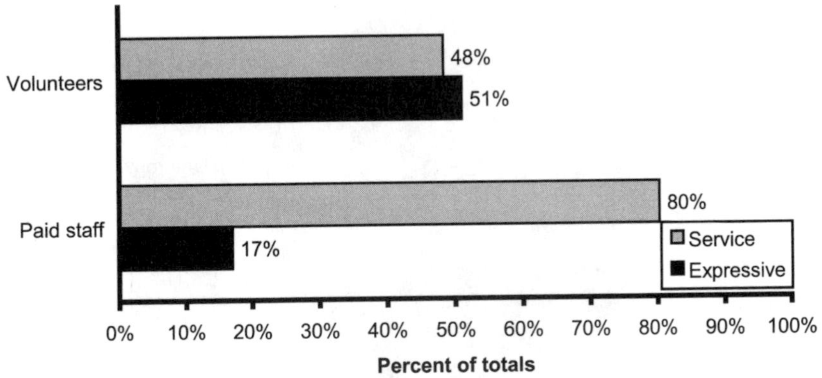

SOURCE: Johns Hopkins Comparative Nonprofit Sector Project

respectively). This figure demonstrates a high level of self-organization among professionals in the Philippines.

- **Expressive activities would dominate if community development were included.** The expressive share of the civil society organization workforce in the Philippines would be even higher (60 percent) if community development–oriented organizations were included in the expressive category. Such an inclusion makes sense in view of the fact that, historically, community development efforts in the Philippines have had strong elements of empowerment and political representation of the rural and urban poor.

- **Paid and volunteer staff distributed differently.** As in many other countries, the paid and volunteer staff of Philippine civil society organizations are distributed quite differently. Volunteer staff time is almost equally divided between service activities and expressive functions (48 and 51 percent, respectively), as Figure 9.5 demonstrates. By contrast, 80 percent of paid employment is engaged in service functions.

## 5. Revenue dominated by fees and charges

Service fees and charges are the dominant source of civil society organization cash revenue in the Philippines. However, when the value of volunteer input is included, private philanthropy becomes a significant source of support.

- **Fee dominance in the Philippine civil society sector.** About 92 percent of all Philippine civil society organization cash revenue comes from service fees, property income, and membership dues, as shown in Figure 9.6. Of the balance, 5 percent comes from the public sector and 3 percent from

**Figure 9.6.** Sources of civil society
organization revenue in the Philippines

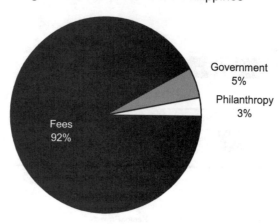

SOURCE: Johns Hopkins Comparative Nonprofit Sector Project

all sources of private philanthropy, including individuals, foundations, and corporations, though this figure would likely be higher if religious worship organizations were included.

– The sizeable presence of fees in the revenue base of the Philippine civil society sector reflects, in the first instance, the inclusion in the sector of numerous large schools and hospitals that finance themselves largely through fees.

– Also contributing to the fee dominance are the dues paid to professional organizations.

• **Differs considerably from international pattern.** This pattern of civil society organization revenue differs from that evident in other developing and transitional countries as well as internationally.

– Philippine civil society organizations rely far more substantially on fees than do those in other developing and transitional countries or internationally (92 percent vs. 61 and 53 percent, respectively), as shown in Figure 9.7.

– Furthermore, Philippine civil society organizations receive far less support from government payments. As shown in Figure 9.7, the 5 percent of civil society organization revenue in the Philippines that comes from public sector payments is only a fraction of the developing and transitional country and all-country averages (22 and 34 percent, respectively).

**Figure 9.7.** Sources of civil society organization revenue, the Philippines, developing and transitional countries, and 34-country average

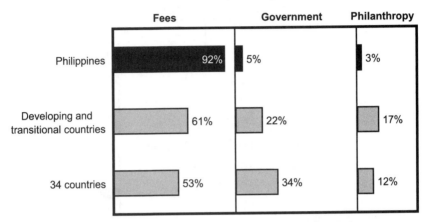

SOURCE: Johns Hopkins Comparative Nonprofit Sector Project

- Philippine civil society organizations also rely on private philanthropy to a much lesser degree than most other countries, especially developing and transitional countries. Private philanthropy accounts for only 3 percent of Philippine civil society organization revenue, compared to the developing and transitional country and all-country averages (17 and 12 percent, respectively).

• **Support structure varies among fields.** Reflecting the prominence of fee income in the Philippine civil society sector, five out of seven fields on which data were collected (education, culture, community development, professional associations and unions, and health care) derive their income predominantly from fees (see Figure 9.8). This reflects the historical pattern of extensive private higher education institutions and hospitals catering to wealthier sections of the population. Government payments, interestingly, dominate revenue in the civic and advocacy field, where they account for 58 percent of all cash revenue. This results from a significant policy shift in the post-Marcos era, which stressed government–civil society partnership. Private philanthropy is the main income source in social services (56 percent). It is also a significant secondary source of revenue for civic and advocacy associations (37 percent).

• **Volunteers significantly change the revenue structure.** The revenue structure of the Philippine civil society sector changes substantially when the value of volunteer work is included. As Figure 9.9 demonstrates, with

**Figure 9.8.** Sources of civil society organization revenue, the Philippines, by field

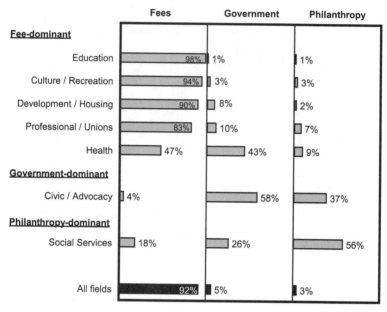

Percent of total civil society organization revenue

SOURCE: Johns Hopkins Comparative Nonprofit Sector Project

**Figure 9.9.** Sources of civil society organization support including volunteers, the Philippines, developing and transitional countries, and 34-country average

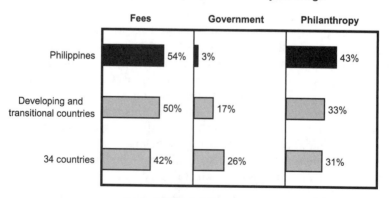

Percent of total civil society organization support

SOURCE: Johns Hopkins Comparative Nonprofit Sector Project

**Figure 9.10.** Sources of civil society organization support
in the Philippines, including volunteers, by field

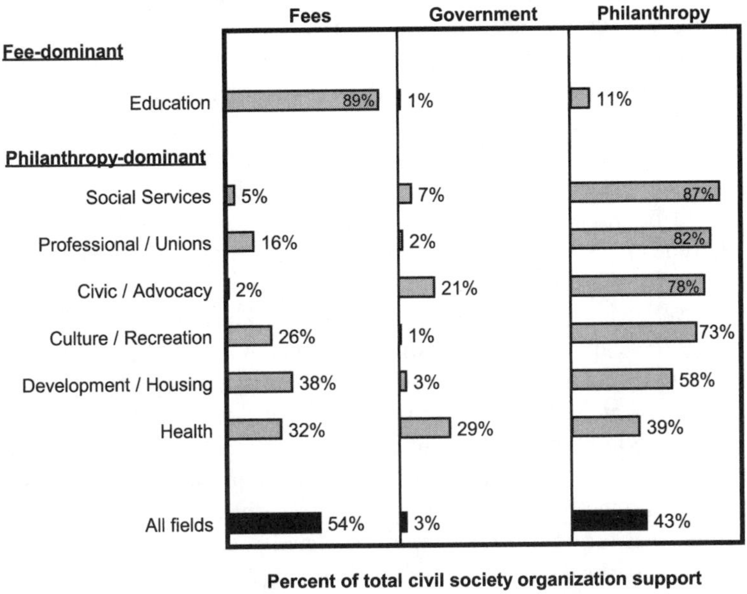

Percent of total civil society organization support

SOURCE: Johns Hopkins Comparative Nonprofit Sector Project

volunteers included, private contributions of time and money swell from
3 percent to 43 percent of total support, while reliance on fees declines
from 92 percent to 54 percent. The addition of volunteers brings the
Philippines closer to the developing and transitional country averages
for philanthropy and fees (33 and 50 percent, respectively). However,
the Philippines' reliance on public sector support remains significantly
below the developing and transitional country and all-country averages
(3 percent vs. 17 and 26 percent, respectively).

– With the value of volunteer input included, private philanthropy becomes the main source of support in six fields. Only education relies
  predominantly on fees, in the form of tuition (see Figure 9.10).

## Conclusions and Implications

The civil society sector is thus a significant force in Philippine society. The
sector provides crucial services, such as education, for better-off segments
of the community, and increasingly serves as a conduit for the empowerment and political representation of disadvantaged groups. Over half of its

workforce is volunteer. Although service fees constitute most of the sector's cash revenue, volunteer input is a significant source of support.

Although the civil society sector is an emerging economic force in the Philippines its significance goes beyond its economic value. The voluntary participation the sector mobilizes shows the continued strength of *pakikipagkapwa-tao* (shared inner self) in the culture. *Pakikipagkapwa* puts a premium on the collective over the individual. This sense of social solidarity has helped many Filipinos through critical times and is especially strong in expressive organizations, where it is manifested as both altruism and mutual self-help.

Philippine civil society organizations cover the entire spectrum of interests present in the society but they draw the most attention in their endeavors to serve social justice and democracy. The Philippine government has recognized the legitimacy of these organizations by encouraging their participation in policy decision making. Beyond this official recognition, volunteers often act as a watchdog of government policy and were instrumental in two non-violent People Power Revolutions which successfully ousted two corrupt presidents. Indeed, government is a point of orientation for civil society organizations, whether they collaborate with it, or heartily oppose it.

Another institutional force shaping the civil society sector in the Philippines has been the Catholic Church. The Church pioneered civil society organizations during the Spanish period, but many of these organizations later turned into a platform for the struggle for national independence. The Church provided a refuge for civil society activities that challenged the autocratic state. It is also the focus of volunteering and giving, since more than half of all philanthropy goes to the small sector of religious organizations. These are not the large bequests of rich citizens, but rather the accumulation of small donations and offerings from the vast majority of Filipinos.

In sum, the civil society sector has been an important social force in Filipino society, one has that received benefits from and in turn has reinforced the people's social solidarity, sense of community, collective interests, self-expression, empowerment, and mutual cooperation. It is an institutional force that provides channels for many interests to be voiced and heard, an arena where some groups may cooperate with the state and Church, while others contest their views. It is an arena where voices of the disadvantaged can be expressed, and where their efforts at assembly and association contribute to building a better society.

## Notes

1. The work in the Philippines has been coordinated by Ledivina V. Cariño. The research team was aided, in turn, by a local advisory committee (see Appendix D for a list of committee members). The Johns Hopkins project was directed by Lester M.

Salamon, and the work in the Philippines was overseen by Leslie C. Hems and later by S. Wojciech Sokolowski.

2. The definitions and approaches used in the project were developed collaboratively with the cooperation of Philippine researchers and researchers in other countries and were designed to be applicable to the Philippines and other project countries. For a full description of this definition, the types of organizations included, and the methodology used, see Chapter 1 and Appendix B. For a full list of the other countries included, see Table 1.1.

3. A further report of these findings can be found in Ledivina V. Cariño (ed.), *Between the State and Market: The Nonprofit Sector and Civil Society in the Philippines* (Diliman, Quezon City, the Philippines: Center for Leadership, Citizenship and Democracy, National College of Public Administration and Governance, University of Philippines, 2002). Some results reported there differ from those included in this report due to differences in data sources and methodologies used. Earlier studies of the Philippines civil society sector have focused on the role of civil society in politics, citizenship, and democracy, including the three-volume study of the University of the Philippines–Third World Studies Center: Ma. Serena Diokno (ed.), *Why a Philippine Democracy Agenda (Vol. 1),* Marlon A. Wui and Ma. Glenda S. Lopez (eds.), *State-Civil Society Relations in Policy-making (Vol. 2),* Miriam Coronel Ferrer (ed.), *Civil Society Making Civil Society (Vol. 3),* (Quezon City, the Philippines: Third World Studies Center, 1997); Ateneo Center for Policy and Public Affairs, *Policy Influence: NGO Experiences* (Quezon City, the Philippines: Institute for Development Research and Konrad Adenauer Stiftung, 1997); and G. Sidney Silliman and Lela Garner Noble (eds.), *Organizing for Democracy: NGOs, Civil Society and the Philippine State* (Quezon City, the Philippines: Ateneo University Press, 1998).

4. The Philippines National Statistical Coordination Board estimated the Philippines nonprofit sector to be only 0.35 percent of GDP as of 1990, but it used a much narrower definition than used here. Republic of the Philippines, National Statistical Coordination Board (NSCB), *Social Accounting Matrix* (Makati, the Philippines: NSCB, 1990).

5. Republic of the Philippines, National Economic and Development Authority (NEDA), "Governance and Institutions Development," in *Medium Term Philippine Development Plan (Angat Pinoy 2004)* (Pasig City, the Philippines: NEDA, 1999).

6. Comparative figures do not include religious worship organizations, because data on these organizations were not available for all countries. However, religiously affiliated service organizations are included. For more information, see Appendix B.

7. Virgilio C. Enriquez, *Indigenous Psychology and National Consciousness* (Tokyo: Institute for the Study of Languages and Cultures of Asia and Africa, 1989).

8. Jaime Faustino, *Traditions in Private Philanthropy* (Manila: Philippine Business for Social Progress, 1997).

9. Renato Constantino, *The Philippines: A Past Revisited (Pre-Spanish – 1941), Vol. 1* (Quezon City, the Philippines: Renato Constantino, 1975).

10. Reynaldo C. Ileto, "Rural Life in a Time of Revolution," in *Filipinos and Their Revolution: Event, Discourse, and Historiography* (Quezon City, the Philippines: Ateneo de Manila University Press, 1998).

11. Wilfredo Fabros, *The Church and Its Social Involvement in the Philippines, 1930–1972* (Quezon City, the Philippines: Ateneo de Manila University Press, 1988).

12. Percentages displayed in figures may not add to 100 due to rounding.

# Chapter 10

# South Korea

Tae-Kyu Park, Ku-Hyun Jung,
S. Wojciech Sokolowski, and Lester M. Salamon

## Introduction

It is not easy to delineate the boundaries of the civil society sector in South Korea, since historically the sector has been overshadowed by the state. Traditionally, efforts to advance common interests took the form of kinship-based self-help activities. Volunteering for organizations was not common. Formal associational groups are a relatively new development, stimulated, in large part, by Western influences and the pro-democracy movement following World War II. In the subsequent years, an abundance of political groups, voluntary associations, and social movements have been formed, though interrupted by a number of distinctive developments, such as the Korean War of 1950–53 and the military coups of 1961 and 1980.

Consequently, the institutional capacity of the civil society sector in South Korea remains rather modest by developed country standards and geared mainly to service delivery, especially education. The sector depends to a substantial degree on service fees and charges, rather than philanthropic donations or government payments. Volunteer participation is also relatively low.

These findings emerge from a body of work carried out by a South Korean research team in cooperation with the Bank of Korea, as part of the Johns Hopkins Comparative Nonprofit Sector Project.[1] This work sought both to analyze South Korean civil society organizations and to compare and contrast them to those in other countries in a systematic way.[2] The result is the first empirical overview of the South Korean civil society sector and the first systematic comparison of South Korean civil society realities to those elsewhere in the world.

This chapter reports chiefly on the major descriptive findings of this project relating to the size, composition, and financing of the civil society sector in South Korea. Other reports will fill in more of the history, legal position, and impact of these institutions. Most of the data reported here

**Table 10.1.** The civil society sector* in South Korea, 1997

---

**$23.1 billion in expenditures**

- 4.8% of the GDP

**702,523 full-time equivalent workers**

- 513,820 full-time equivalent paid employees
- 188,703 full-time equivalent volunteers
- 3.2% of the economically active population
- 4.3% of nonagricultural employment
- 53.2% of public employment

---

\* Including religious worship organizations.

SOURCE: Johns Hopkins Comparative Nonprofit Sector Project

come from surveys commissioned by the Bank of Korea to compile national accounts statistics. Additional research work, including a giving and volunteering survey, was conducted by the project team. The base year for these data is 1997. Unless otherwise noted, financial data are reported in U.S. dollars at the 1997 average exchange rate. It is important to note that we were able to collect data on both religious congregations and religiously affiliated organizations providing various services (e.g., health, social services, and education). For a more complete statement of the types of organizations included, see Chapter 1 and Appendix B.

# Principal Findings

## 1. A sizeable economic force

The civil society sector is a considerable economic force in South Korea, particularly given the country's recent history and level of development. More specifically:

- **A $23 billion industry.** The civil society sector in South Korea expended $23.1 billion on its 1997 operations. This is equivalent to 4.8 percent of the country's gross domestic product (GDP), as reported in Table 10.1.

- **A sizable workforce.** Behind these expenditures lies a workforce that includes over 700,000 full-time equivalent (FTE) staff (including religious worship organizations), both paid employees and volunteers. This represents 3.2 percent of South Korea's economically active population, and 4.3 percent of its nonagricultural employment.

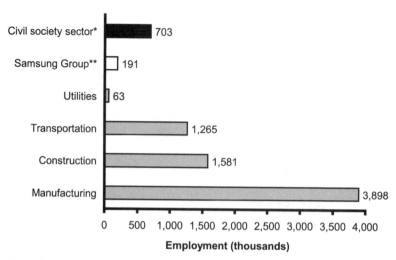

**Figure 10.1.** Civil society organization
workforce in context, South Korea

\* Including volunteers
\*\* Largest private firm
SOURCE: Johns Hopkins Comparative Nonprofit Sector Project

- **More employees than the largest private firm.** To put these figures in perspective, the civil society sector in South Korea employs almost four times as many people as South Korea's largest private corporation, Samsung Group, which employs 191,301 workers (see Figure 10.1).

- **On a par with some whole industries.** The civil society sector in South Korea employs more than ten times as many workers as the country's utilities industry, 60 percent of the labor force in the transportation industry, and half as many as government.

- **Volunteer input.** Of the total civil society organization workforce in South Korea, about one-quarter consists of volunteers (see Appendix Table A.1). Over 1 million people engage in some kind of volunteer work in Korea, which represents approximately 3 percent of the country's adult population (see Appendix Table A.2).

- **Sizable role of religion.** Religion accounts for a sizeable share of the South Korean civil society sector. Religious organizations employ nearly 20 percent of the sector's paid staff and 35 percent of the volunteers. This reflects the fact that traditionally religion and community life in Korea have been intertwined, a pattern that persists with the spread of Western religious organizations in the country.

## 2. One of the largest civil society sectors among developing countries

- **Larger than most developing and transitional countries.** The South Korean civil society organization workforce is one of the largest among developing and transitional countries included in this study. As shown in Figure 10.2, excluding religious worship organizations, for which data are not available for all countries, the civil society sector workforce — paid and volunteer — varies from a high of 14.4 percent of the economically active population in the Netherlands to a low of 0.4 percent in Mexico, with an average of 4.4 percent overall.[3] The South Korean figure is higher than those of 15 other developing and transitional countries included in this project as well as above the developing and transitional country average (2.4 vs. 1.9 percent). Within the developing and transitional group, when religious worship organizations are included, the South Korean civil society sector is surpassed only by those in Argentina and South Africa (3.2 vs. 6.3 and 4.0 percent, respectively).

- **Below the all-country average.** However, the civil society organization workforce in South Korea is much smaller than that in the developed countries (2.4 percent vs. 7.4 percent), and also falls below the all-country average (2.4 percent vs. 4.4 percent). Even with religious worship organizations included, the South Korean civil society organization workforce remains markedly smaller than that in the developed countries, including its Asian neighbor, Japan (3.2 percent vs. 4.7 percent).

- **Volunteer participation lower than elsewhere.** One major reason for the relatively small size of the civil society organization workforce in South Korea compared to the all-country average is the relatively low volunteer participation in the country. Excluding religion, volunteers represent only 0.6 percent of the economically active population in South Korea versus 1.6 percent in all 36 countries (see Appendix Table A.1). Reflecting this, volunteers account for only about 23 percent of the civil society organization workforce in South Korea, compared to 38 percent in our 36-country sample, as Figure 10.3 demonstrates.

## 3. A tradition of state dominance

The South Korean civil society sector reflected in these data was shaped by two forces: the country's Confucian tradition and the combined forces of recent modernization and democratization.[4]

**Confucian tradition.** The Confucian tradition was firmly established in South Korea under the Yi Dynasty, which ruled the country for six centuries, from 1392 to 1910. This tradition created a centralized bureaucratic state that dominated all aspects of social life.

Civic activism and philanthropy under the traditional system were confined mainly to kinship groups or village-based communities and were

**Figure 10.2.** Civil society organization workforce
as a share of the economically active population, by country

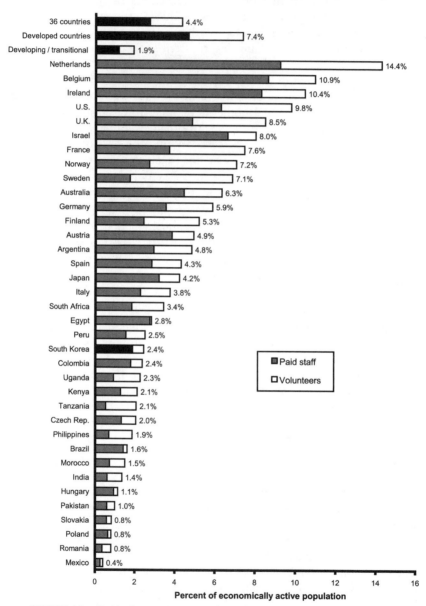

SOURCE: Johns Hopkins Comparative Nonprofit Sector Project

**Figure 10.3.** Volunteers as a share of the
civil society organization workforce, South Korea,
developing and transitional countries, and 36 countries

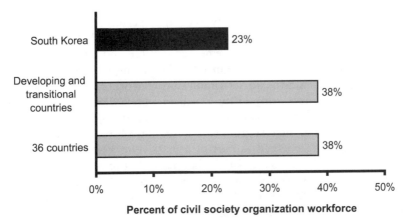

Percent of civil society organization workforce

SOURCE: Johns Hopkins Comparative Nonprofit Sector Project

geared to promoting self-reliance among the poor. Civic activism relied to a substantial degree on the patronage of the wealthy and private voluntary support. The institutional forms of civic activism were less developed and primarily included a state-initiated, social welfare system called *Chang* that aimed to relieve poverty.

**Western influences.** At the end of the 19th century, Western missions, both Protestant and Catholic, established private schools, hospitals, and social welfare associations that become the forerunners of the nonprofit service sector in Korea. Some of these institutions, such as Severance Memorial Hospital, Paik In-Jae Surgical Hospital, and the medical college in the Catholic University of Korea, would later assume a central role in the delivery of health care and educational services.

Western influences also spurred the growth of civic and advocacy organizations in 19th-century Korea. Perhaps the first such entity, the Dongniphuphoe (Independent Association) was formed by a group of intellectuals to promote the modernization of Korean society and gained wide support among youth. Other organizations formed during this period, such as chapters of the YMCA and YWCA, were established with the assistance of American missionaries.

**Japanese rule.** During the Russo-Japanese war (1904–05), Japan established military control of Korea and turned it into a Japanese protectorate. Under Japanese rule, Koreans lost the rights to freedom of speech and freedom of association. Korean resistance to the Japanese occupation took the form of secret associations, such as Shinminhoe or Hungsdan, and culminated in a massive independence movement involving over 2 million students and activists. They proclaimed a Korean Declaration of Independence on March 1, 1919. This movement was brutally suppressed by the Japanese military. However, Korean exiles who escaped persecution formed a provisional government in Shanghai, which provided leadership for subsequent independence movements that re-emerged in 1926 and 1929.

**Liberation from Japanese rule in 1945.** Following an agreement between the United States and the Soviet Union during World War II, Soviet forces engaged the Japanese army in the north of Korea while American troops landed in the southern Korean peninsula on August 11, 1945. A number of political parties and interest groups, representing a broad political spectrum from left to right, emerged as part of a massive movement to re-establish self-governance. Following a United Nations resolution adopted in 1947, the South elected a new government and proclaimed itself a republic with Seoul as its capital. The North responded by proclaiming itself the Democratic People's Republic of Korea. This effectively split Korea into two separate countries.

In addition to the politicized national independence movements, many service-oriented religious groups and charity or enlightening institutions were also founded during this period. These organizations were often assisted by foreign aid or religious organizations.

**Post–Korean War.** Following the Korean War (1950–53), South Korea received substantial foreign assistance from the U.N. Korean Reconstruction Agency (UNKRA), as well as 10 international voluntary organizations. Foreign assistance was instrumental in establishing numerous private social welfare organizations in the country. Nearly half of all social welfare organizations that emerged in South Korea after the end of Japanese occupation were established during the period immediately following the Korean War.

**The primacy of national security concerns by the state until the early 1960s.** After the Korean War of 1950–53, the South Korean state became repressive and undemocratic. Most civil society organizations were service-oriented during this period, providing welfare services or implementing development projects for the poor; and most were supported, if not established, by foreign aid. The revolutionary movement of students and intellectuals that erupted in April 1960 marked the end of this period.

**The economic development stage, early 1960s through 1987.** This revolutionary movement set in motion great changes in South Korean civil society. While the government remained fairly authoritarian and preoccupied with accelerated economic development, rapid growth of the economy resulted in the stratification of society and the development of a middle class. This spurred a rapid growth in the number and activities of civil organizations. The growth was dominated by advocacy organizations that were generally opposed to corruption and the state's broad powers, and education and social service organizations that provided public goods. This period ended with the Great Democratic Movement, when diverse elements of the civil society sector mobilized into a militant pro-democracy force that waged an intense struggle against the authoritarian regime.

**The democratization period from 1987 to 1997.** The democratization period brought about the emergence of increasingly effective and sophisticated civic groups led by a younger generation. They emphasized progressive advocacy functions oriented toward the promotion of open democratic processes, protection of human rights, and safeguards to protect the environment from the pressures of economic growth. During this period, two different kinds of social groups competed with each other: the more radical groups of labor unions, peasants, and students who promoted a broad interpretation of democracy, non-capitalist economic models, and national reunification; and more moderate groups that promoted expanded social welfare protections, environmentalism, consumer rights, and gender equality. By the early 1990s, the moderate groups became increasingly influential. As a result, the South Korean civil society sector developed a cooperative relationship with the state and came to be viewed as a legitimate partner in issues of national governance.

## 4. Strong presence of service organizations

Reflecting the influence of Confucian tradition and Western missions and aid organizations, the South Korean civil society sector has long been distinctly oriented toward service provision, and this remains the case today.

- **Service activities dominate.** As shown in Figure 10.4, about 82 percent of the civil society sector's workforce — both paid and volunteer — is engaged in service activities.[5] Dominant among them is education, which employs 41 percent of the sector's workforce, followed by health (26 percent) and social services (15 percent). Community development activities in South Korea are carried out mainly by social service organizations as a part of their mission, and thus are not reported separately.

- **Significant presence of civic and advocacy activism.** While service functions dominate the South Korean civil society sector, civic and advocacy organizations account for an impressive 10 percent share of the civil society organization workforce. This reflects the importance of the national independence, pro-democracy, and labor movements in the formation of the modern civil society sector in South Korea. However, the overall share of expressive activities is rather low (18 percent), as the other forms of expressive activities, such as culture and professional associations, account only for quite small shares of the civil society organization workforce.

- **Composition different from other countries.** The composition of the South Korean civil society sector thus differs from that found in other countries. While service activities predominate both the all-country and

**Figure 10.4.** Composition of the
civil society organization workforce, South Korea,
developing and transitional countries, and 33-country average

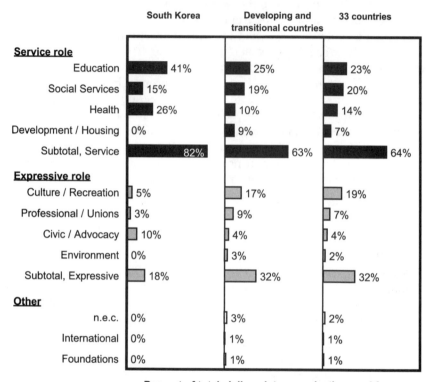

**Percent of total civil society organization workforce**

n.e.c.= not elsewhere classified

SOURCE: Johns Hopkins Comparative Nonprofit Sector Project

developing and transitional country averages (64 and 63 percent of the civil society organization workforce, respectively), that predominance is far more pronounced in South Korea (82 percent). What is more, the education share of South Korea's civil society organization workforce is significantly greater than that of the all-country and the developing and transitional country averages (41 percent vs. 23 and 25 percent, respectively). In only a handful of countries — India, Ireland, Israel, Pakistan, and Peru — does the education share of the civil society organization workforce come close to that in South Korea (see Appendix Table A.3). Although the expressive component of the South Korean civil society sector is far smaller overall than that of other countries, in the field of civic action and advocacy, the South Korean civil society sector exceeds the

**Figure 10.5.** Distribution of paid employees and volunteers between service and expressive activities in South Korea

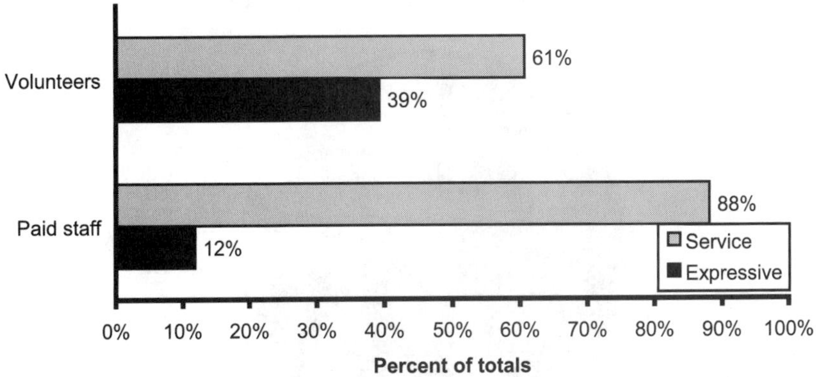

SOURCE: Johns Hopkins Comparative Nonprofit Sector Project

all-country and developing and transitional country averages by a factor of more than 2 to 1 (10 percent vs. 4 percent).

- **Moderate differences in the distribution of paid staff and volunteers.** Although the majority of both paid and volunteer workers in South Korean civil society organizations are employed in service fields, volunteers are more likely than paid staff to work in the expressive fields (39 percent vs. 12 percent of the total workforce) (see Figure 10.5). This reflects the social movement character of expressive activities in South Korea.

## 5. Revenue dominated by fees and charges

Fees and charges are by far the dominant source of civil society sector support in South Korea. This likely reflects the strong presence of fee-based private service organizations, especially higher education and health care, within the South Korean civil society sector.

- **Fees the largest source of cash revenue.** Service fees and dues account for 71 percent of all cash revenue of South Korean civil society organizations. By contrast, private philanthropy and the public sector provide much smaller shares of total revenue. Thus, as Figure 10.6 shows, private philanthropy — from individuals, corporations, and foundations combined — accounts for only 4 percent of civil society organization income in South Korea, while funding from the public sector, which includes grants, contracts, and reimbursements for services, accounts for 24 percent.

- **Financing pattern differs from that found in other countries.** The pattern of civil society finance evident in South Korea differs from that found in other countries. The fee share of civil society organization revenue in

**Figure 10.6.** Sources of civil society
organization revenue in South Korea

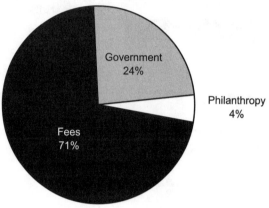

SOURCE: Johns Hopkins Comparative Nonprofit Sector Project

**Figure 10.7.** Sources of civil society organization revenue,
South Korea, developing and transitional countries,
and 34-country average

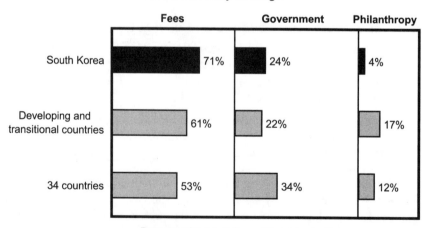

**Percent of total civil society organization revenue**

SOURCE: Johns Hopkins Comparative Nonprofit Sector Project

**Figure 10.8.** Sources of civil society organization revenue,
South Korea, by field

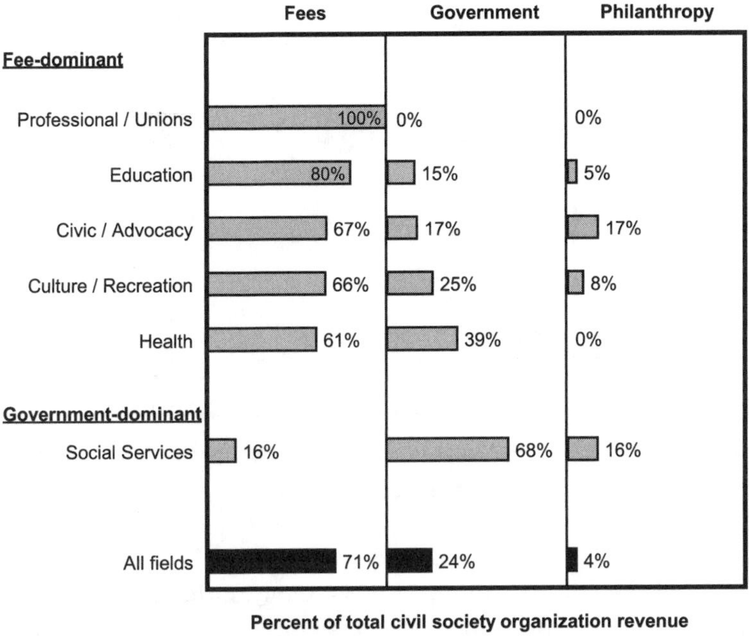

**Percent of total civil society organization revenue**

SOURCE: Johns Hopkins Comparative Nonprofit Sector Project

South Korea is higher than both the developing and transitional country and all-country averages (71 percent vs. 61 and 53 percent, respectively) (see Figure 10.7). On the other hand, private philanthropy in South Korea is proportionately four times smaller than that found in the developing and transitional countries, and three times smaller than the all-country average. While such low levels of philanthropic giving were also found in many industrialized countries, such as Belgium, Germany, Italy, and Japan, the level of government support for the civil society sector in these other countries is generally much higher than that in South Korea (from 37 to 77 percent vs. 24 percent) (see Appendix Table A.4). Public sector support for the civil society sector in South Korea does not exceed the average for the developing and transitional countries, however, even though it falls below the all-country average (24 percent vs. 22 and 34 percent, respectively).

• **Support structure varies among fields.** Given the high share of fee income in the overall financing structure of the civil society sector in South Korea, it is not surprising that fees are a dominant revenue source in all but one field, social services (see Figure 10.8). The fee income share in these fields varies from 61 percent in health to 100 percent in labor unions

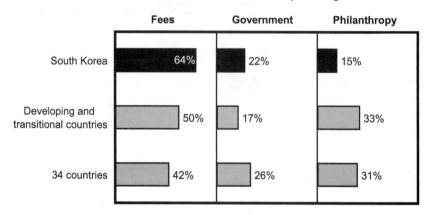

**Figure 10.9.** Sources of civil society organization support including volunteers, South Korea, developing and transitional countries, and 34-country average

**Percent of total civil society organization support**

SOURCE: Johns Hopkins Comparative Nonprofit Sector Project

and professional associations. In social services, the only field in which fees do not dominate, most revenue comes from government payments (68 percent).

- **Volunteers modestly affect the support structure.** Adding the value of volunteer work has a modest effect on the civil society sector's support structure in South Korea. With volunteer time included as a form of philanthropy, the fee income share of total support remains dominant, but drops from 71 to 64 percent of the total, while the philanthropic share increases from 4 to 15 percent (see Figure 10.9).

  – With the value of volunteer input included, private philanthropy becomes the dominant source of support in two fields: civic and advocacy (65 percent of all income) and social services (52 percent), and becomes the second largest source in culture and recreation (29 percent) (see Figure 10.10).

## Conclusions and Implications

The civil society sector, at least in its more formal manifestations, is a relatively new development in Korea. The Confucian tradition, which established the hegemony of a centralized state bureaucracy, was not conducive to the emergence of voluntary associations independent of state control. What

**Figure 10.10.** Sources of civil society organization support
in South Korea, including volunteers, by field.

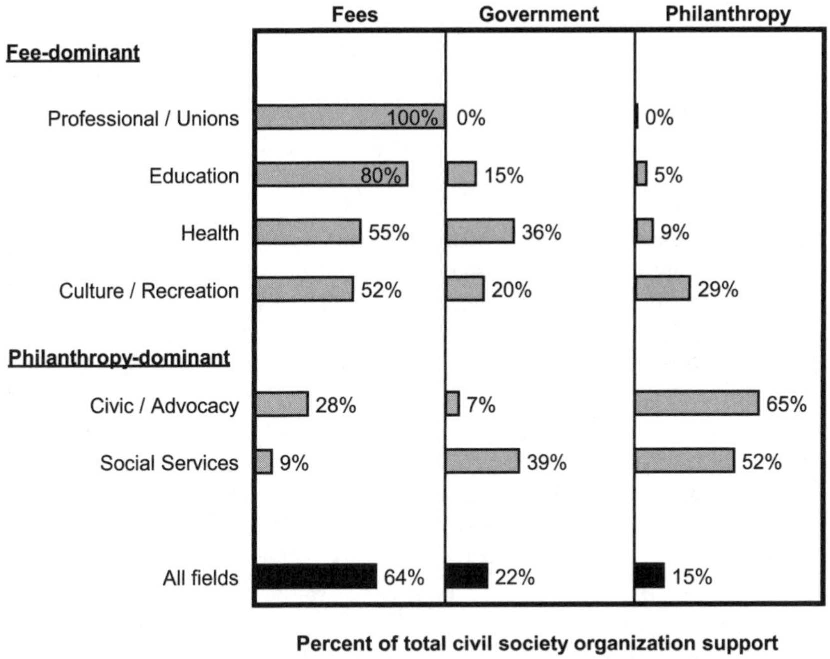

|  | Fees | Government | Philanthropy |
|---|---|---|---|
| **Fee-dominant** | | | |
| Professional / Unions | 100% | 0% | 0% |
| Education | 80% | 15% | 5% |
| Health | 55% | 36% | 9% |
| Culture / Recreation | 52% | 20% | 29% |
| **Philanthropy-dominant** | | | |
| Civic / Advocacy | 28% | 7% | 65% |
| Social Services | 9% | 39% | 52% |
| All fields | 64% | 22% | 15% |

**Percent of total civil society organization support**

SOURCE: Johns Hopkins Comparative Nonprofit Sector Project

is more, traditional poverty-relief efforts emphasized the value of work and self-reliance, rather than philanthropy.

Civic associations in Korea began to emerge only at the end of the 19th century in response to the pressures produced by foreign influences and modernization. While foreign missions and aid organizations were instrumental in establishing service-oriented organizations, the national independence and later pro-democracy and labor movements initiated expressive activities carried out by the civil society sector.

As a result, South Korea, as revealed by the data presented in this chapter, now boasts a rather sizable civil society sector. The South Korean civil society sector is characterized by striking duality, being divided into two contrasting parts. One consists of service organizations active in the areas of education, health, and social welfare services, which have been encouraged to supplement government-provided services. This part includes formally organized and mostly incorporated institutions with well-established ties to government agencies. The other, much newer, consists of civic and advocacy organizations, mostly unincorporated and informally organized, representing human rights, environment, and political democracy organizations, that flourished only after the demise of the authoritarian regimes in the latter 1980s.

Service-oriented civil society organizations have played a major role in serving human needs in South Korean society, but they are facing some criticisms from the general public for lack of accountability and transparency in operation. Public sector support is needed for these institutions to meet the demands of the society more properly. On the other hand, the civic and advocacy groups are at an early stage of their development and still need citizen-based support to expand their role in society.

The levels of giving and volunteering in South Korea still remain low compared to developed countries. The main reason is that their importance is not widely recognized among either the general public or policymakers. Therefore, educating the public about the importance of private philanthropic giving and volunteering is one of the most urgent tasks facing the civil society sector in South Korea. To achieve this goal, however, it is necessary to assess and to popularize the social and economic significance, capacities, and needs of the civil society sector. We hope that this chapter provides a useful contribution toward this goal.

## Notes

1. The work in South Korea has been coordinated by Tae-Kyu Park. The research team was aided, in turn, by a local advisory committee (see Appendix D for a list of committee members). The Johns Hopkins project was directed by Lester M. Salamon, and the work in South Korea was overseen by S. Wojciech Sokolowski.

2. The definitions and approaches used in the project were developed collaboratively with the cooperation of South Korean researchers and researchers in other countries and were designed to be applicable to South Korea and other project countries. For a full description of this definition, the types of organizations included, and the methodology used, see Chapter 1 and Appendix B. For a full list of the other countries included, see Table 1.1.

3. Comparative figures do not include religious worship organizations, because data on these organizations were not available for all countries. However, religiously affiliated service organizations are included. For more information, see Appendix B.

4. The discussion in this section draws heavily on an unpublished report by Chang-Soon Hwang and In Choon Kim, "The History of Nonprofit Organizations in Korea," submitted to the Johns Hopkins Center for Civil Society Studies.

5. Percentages displayed in figures may not add to 100 due to rounding.

Part Four

# THE MIDDLE EAST

# Chapter 11

# Egypt

Amani Kandil, Stefan Toepler,
and Lester M. Salamon

## Introduction

Since at least the beginning of the 19th century, associations, nongovernmental organizations, and other civil society organizations have functioned in Egypt as providers of education, health, and social care. However, over the last two decades, the importance of these organizations has grown tremendously. Both broad economic structural adjustment policies favoring privatization and the state's reduced capability to cope with development issues, social services, and environmental challenges have opened new opportunities for civil society organizations to step into the gap. Additionally, the democratization process and the tendency among citizens to participate directly in public affairs have also energized the development of grassroots nongovernmental organizations (NGOs). These developments, along with significant financial and in-kind support by the government, have allowed the Egyptian civil society sector to emerge as a viable social and economic force with a highly institutionalized base. This development has taken place in the context of an Islamic tradition that has long strongly encouraged philanthropic giving, but in a social and political setting that has historically limited the opportunities for independent organizational activity outside the confines of the state or the market.

These findings emerge from a body of work carried out by an Egyptian research team based at the Arab Network for NGOs (Shabaka) in Cairo, as part of the Johns Hopkins Comparative Nonprofit Sector Project.[1] This work sought both to analyze Egyptian civil society organizations and to compare and contrast them to those in other countries in a systematic way.[2] The work in Egypt is still in a preliminary stage, and the empirical findings remain limited. Nevertheless, the current results represent the first empirical overview of the Egyptian civil society sector and the first systematic comparison of Egyptian civil society realities to those elsewhere in the world. Most of the data reported here were generated from a 1999 survey of civil society organizations sponsored by the Arab Network for NGOs. Additional

**Table 11.1.** The civil society sector* in Egypt, 1999

---

**$1.5 billion in expenditures**

- 2.0% of the GDP

**629,223 full-time equivalent workers**

- 611,888 full-time equivalent paid employees
- 17,335 full-time equivalent volunteers
- 2.8% of the economically active population
- 5.0% of nonagricultural employment

---

* Religious worship organization figures not available.

SOURCE: Johns Hopkins Comparative Nonprofit Sector Project

research work was conducted by the project team. Unless otherwise noted, financial data are reported in U.S. dollars at the 1999 average exchange rate. For a more complete statement of the types of organizations included, see Chapter 1 and Appendix B.

# Principal Findings

## 1. A sizable civil society sector

Perhaps the most salient feature of the Egyptian civil society sector is its significant presence in Egyptian social and economic life. In particular:

- **A $1.5 billion industry.** As of the late 1990s, Egypt's civil society sector accounted for $1.5 billion in expenditures, roughly 2.0 percent of the Egyptian gross domestic product (GDP), as reported in Table 11.1.

- **A significant employer.** Behind these expenditures lies a considerable workforce numbering close to 630,000 full-time equivalent (FTE) workers, which is 2.8 percent of the economically active population. Most of this workforce consists of paid staff (97 percent). However, the true extent of volunteering in Egypt is difficult to determine since much of the volunteering is sporadic and many volunteers work only a limited number of hours. Moreover, a significant amount of volunteering takes place in Islamic and Christian religious settings, and these workers could not be included in the present research. In recent years, official sources have placed the number of volunteers at three million. However, for the purposes of this estimate, volunteering was equated with membership in civil society organizations, although many members do not actively contribute time. Our estimates suggest that approximately 1 percent of

**Figure 11.1.** Civil society organization workforce
in context, Egypt

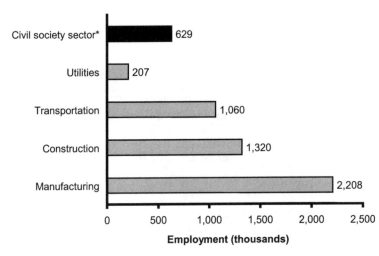

* Including volunteers
SOURCE: Johns Hopkins Comparative Nonprofit Sector Project

the adult population are engaged in volunteer activities (see Appendix Table A.2).

- **Comparable to other industries.** The significant size of Egypt's civil society sector is evident in comparison to other industries. Indeed, as shown in Figure 11.1, civil society organizations employ three times as many people (629,000) as Egypt's utilities industry (207,000). Civil society employment is the equivalent of 60 percent of transportation and nearly half of construction industry employment.

## 2. A comparatively well developed civil society sector

The Egyptian civil society sector is also fairly large when compared to other countries, especially other developing or transitional countries.

- **Above the developing and transitional country average.** As shown in Figure 11.2, the civil society organization workforce — paid and volunteer — varies from a high of 14.4 percent of the economically active population in the Netherlands to a low of 0.4 percent in Mexico, with an average of 4.4 percent overall.[3] The Egyptian civil society sector outdistances most developing and transitional countries in these terms. In fact, there are only two other developing and transitional countries (Argentina and South Africa) where the civil society organization workforce is proportionately

**Figure 11.2.** Civil society organization workforce
as a share of the economically active population, by country

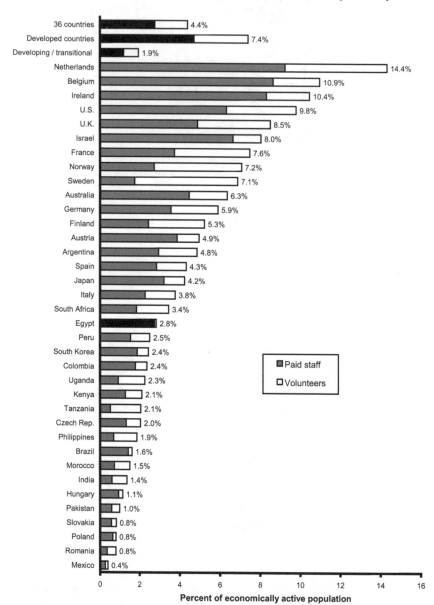

SOURCE: Johns Hopkins Comparative Nonprofit Sector Project

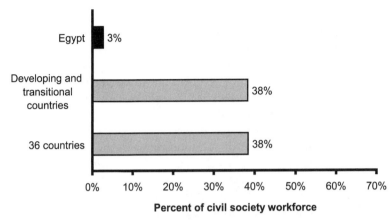

**Figure 11.3.** Volunteers as a share of the
civil society organization workforce, Egypt,
developing and transitional countries, and 36 countries

SOURCE: Johns Hopkins Comparative Nonprofit Sector Project

larger than in Egypt. As shown in Figure 11.2, civil society organization employment in the developing and transitional countries covered in this project averages 1.9 percent of the economically active population, one-third lower than the corresponding Egyptian figure of 2.8 percent.

- **Below the all-country average.** While higher than the developing and transitional country average, the Egyptian civil society sector workforce, as a share of the economically active population, is somewhat below the all-country average of 4.4 percent. However, this may be a result of the lack of reliable data on volunteering in Egypt. When we focus on paid employment only, the Egyptian civil society sector is on a par with the all-country average of 2.7 percent (see Appendix Table A.1).

- **Volunteer participation lags behind the all-country average.** Reflecting the lack of reliable volunteering data, the volunteer staff of Egyptian civil society organizations lags behind its counterparts internationally and in developing and transitional countries. Thus, as Figure 11.3 shows, volunteers, as measured so far, account for only 3.0 percent of the total civil society organization workforce in Egypt, substantially below the developing and transitional and all-country averages.

## 3. A rich and varied history of civil society development

Civil society in Egypt has a long and varied history. As in other Muslim countries, the religious obligation to donate a percentage of one's wealth to the needy (*zakat*) as well as to provide voluntary assistance to the poor (*sadaka*), encouraged by the Holy Quran, are defining features of Egyptian society past and present. Throughout Islamic history, *sadaka* has given rise to religious endowments (*al waqf*) supporting hospitals, schools, orphanages, roads, and general assistance to the poor. These organizations have played important roles in the socioeconomic life of Egypt over time. For instance, a land survey undertaken in 1517 by Sultan Selim Bin Soleyman Pasha revealed that endowments held about 40 percent of all the agricultural land in Egypt.[4] Although socialist policies after 1952 diminished its appeal, religious philanthropy continues to play an important role in supporting associational life as well as social, health, and educational services.

The arrival of the French under Napoleon Bonaparte at the end of the 18th century marked Egypt's first modern exposure to the Western world and led to the establishment of scientific councils, including the Egyptian Scientific Academy in 1798, which is the oldest scientific body in Egypt. Shortly thereafter, Egypt underwent a process of modernization beginning with the rule of Mohamad Ali in 1805. Subsequent reforms in the field of education, including the education of girls, and a continued exchange with the West fostered the development of civil society organizations. The first Western-style association was established in 1821 followed by many other associations concerned with education and culture. Over the next hundred years, the civil society sector flourished. Civil and professional associations, labor unions, congregations, and women's organizations emerged, encouraged by modernization. These organizations also developed in reaction to, and as a means of protecting national values from, the influence of Western religious missionaries and foreign minorities in Egyptian society.[5] This patriotic struggle to combat foreign influences in Egypt gained momentum after the British occupation in 1882 and continued during the liberal period following the collapse of the Ottoman Empire in 1919. The political and legal frameworks of this period accorded full freedom of association, and a diversity of discourses appeared among civil society institutions (Islamic, leftist, liberal, and Arab nationalist).

After the 1952 revolution, this liberal period ended and socialist policies were introduced. Fearful of potential political opposition and the rise of radical Islam and its threat to its secularization goals, the new regime moved to suppress the civil society sector or annex it to the state. Associations, unions, women's groups, and religious civil society organizations were dissolved; special laws were issued to control and dominate associational and religious life; advocacy activities were forbidden; and the remaining civil society organizations had to focus on social care in accordance with national plans. The *al waqf* system was nationalized beginning in the 1950s — leading to a significant drop in religious philanthropy. In addition, Law 32 of 1964 formalized state control over the civil society sector, severely restricted the ability of civil society organizations to receive foreign funds,

**Table 11.2.** Budget sizes of Egyptian NGOs,
in U.S. dollars, 1999

| Size of the budget | Percentage of NGOs |
|---|---|
| Less than $10,000 | 43.7% |
| Between $10,000 - $50,000 | 29.7% |
| Between $50,000 - $100,000 | 7.5% |
| More than $100,000 | 9.4% |
| Not stated | 9.7% |

and granted the government latitude to prohibit the formation of civil society organizations, to replace the leadership, and to suspend or terminate existing organizations at will.[6]

This distrustful relationship began to ease somewhat after 1974 with the general economic liberalization policies that were put in place. Economic policies that encouraged privatization contributed to enhanced state support for civil society organizations to fill gaps in social policies. Moreover, the democratic changes and increasing civil liberties that characterized this period spurred the emergence of new types of organizations, often involving businesses, professional groups, and human rights organizations. During the 1980s and 1990s, the sector also became more efficient in dealing with issues of development and alleviation of poverty. This changed the political discourse concerning the civil society sector favorably.

With Law 32 of 1964 remaining in force until the passage of new legislation in 2002 (Law 184 of 2002), remnants of the distrust between state and civil society continue. This is particularly the case for religious organizations, which reasserted their position using privatization policies in the 1980s to exploit gaps in state coverage in fields such as health and social welfare. In fact, into the 1990s, legal initiatives and increased government control sought to curb growing Islamic control of some civil society groups, and the government–civil society relationship remains precarious.

## 4. Structure and resources

Unfortunately, data are not yet available to document fully the composition and resource structure of the Egyptian civil society sector in detail. However, some broad contours are visible:

**Organizational size.** Most (44 percent) Egyptian civil society organizations are small, with budgets of less than $10,000, although close to 10 percent of the organizations report budgets in excess of $100,000 (see Table 11.2).

**Composition.** The main part of the civil society sector in Egypt consists of associations, literally "indigenous associations" in Arabic. This term is

**Table 11.3.** Profile of the civil society sector in Egypt, 1997

| Sector subcomponents | Estimated number of units | Estimated number of memberships |
|---|---|---|
| Associations or NGOs | 15,000 | 3 million |
| Youth centers | 3,922 | 600,000 |
| Clubs | 931 | 1 million |
| Civil companies | 200 | - |
| Human rights organizations | 27 | 10,000 |
| Professional groups | 24 | 3 million |
| Labor unions | 23 | 3.5 million |
| Business associations | 18 | 30,000 |
| Chambers of commerce, industry and tourism | 3 | 3 million |
| **Total** | **19,347** | **14.1 million** |

officially used in the texts of laws and by the public. Here, the term "indigenous" has a historical connotation and has been used since the creation of associations in the 19th century to denote local voluntary efforts and citizen initiatives.[7] It is worth mentioning that in the 1990s Egypt witnessed the emergence of the concept of NGOs as a synonym for "indigenous associations." However, the use of this term was not restricted to associations active in the field of development. It appeared in the writings of researchers, the media, and conferences as clear evidence of the influence of international discourse, mainly after the United Nations International Conference on Population and Development held in Egypt in 1994. As of 1997, there were about 15,000 associations and NGOs (see Table 11.3).

In terms of the number of organizations, the second largest component of the civil society sector in Egypt consists of a widespread network of close to 4,000 youth clubs and centers. Other important components consist of professional groups (legally referred to as professional syndicates), labor unions, and business associations. Although small in number, syndicates and unions have fairly significant membership (see Table 11.3).

**Funding and revenue.** Associations rely on various sources of funding, both local and foreign. A primary source of local funding is income from the sale of services and products. A secondary source comes from donations and grants offered by individuals, companies, or banks. In addition, there are also governmental subsidies provided by the Ministry of Social Affairs and other ministries. Almost 36 percent of the associations — especially associations active in the field of development — benefit from direct governmental funding, which has reached nearly $10 million. Although this amount is not very large, it is still important to small associations, which make up the majority of the civil society sector in Egypt. Civil society organizations also receive an estimated $60 million from government to carry out national projects.

Finally, the government lends extensive numbers of its own paid workers to the civil society sector — particularly when the organizations are collaborating with the government in the implementation of economic and social plans. In 1997, the Ministry of Social Affairs estimated that approximately 60,000 government workers (the equivalent of 10 percent of the total civil society organization workforce) were "on loan" to civil society organizations.

It is still difficult to assess the exact size of foreign funding granted to associations. The Ministry of Social Affairs declared in its 1999 Annual Report that Egyptian associations have obtained approximately $12 million from foreign sources — a controversial figure that probably understates the full extent of foreign funding.

## Conclusions and Implications

The data reported here reveal a civil society sector in Egypt that is considerably more advanced in scale and capacity than in most other developing and transitional countries. This is due to the gradual liberalization of government policies over the past two decades, as well as the government support of civil society associations particularly in the development arena. The Egyptian civil society sector emerged as one of the key beneficiaries of the democratization process of the 1970s that brought a return to a multiparty system, the sovereignty of law, respect for civil liberties, and economic changes that liberalized the economy by moving towards free market principles. What is more, numerous important social changes, such as increasing disparities in the distribution of wealth, growing poverty, and the social and political marginalization of some social strata, increased the demand for such organizations while developments in communication and information technology made them easier to form.

However, despite these developments, the Egyptian civil society sector until very recently still lacked a supportive legal and regulatory framework due to the fairly narrow and restrictive Law 32 of 1964.[8] Between 1995 and 1999, an organized social and political movement emerged that aimed at changing the existing civil society sector law. The push to change Law 32 of 1964 resulted in several meetings and conferences in closed settings as well as writings in the media and debates in the Egyptian Parliament. In 1998, the government took the unprecedented step of submitting a draft NGO law to representatives of NGOs for public discussion. A number of meetings with the Minister of Social Affairs were organized and a committee was formed to draft and edit the text of the new law. This committee included representatives of the government, public figures, and representatives of the civil society sector. The draft law was edited several times and then approved by the Parliament as Law 153 in 1999. However, this did not last for long. The High Constitutional Court issued a decree in June 1999 that prevented the Law from taking effect on technical grounds because it was not submitted to the Shura Council (an advisory council) prior to its submission to Parliament. It took another three years for the resolution of these procedural issues, and the legislation finally came into force as Law 184 of 2002.

The data reported here were helpful in moving this reform process along. Now that the crucial step of liberalizing the regulatory environment has been taken, this kind of information will prove even more useful in helping to chart and sustain the process of civil society development into the future.

## Notes

1. The work in Egypt has been coordinated by Amani Kandil of the Arab Network for NGOs (Shabaka). The research team was aided, in turn, by a local advisory committee (see Appendix D for a list of committee members). The Johns Hopkins project was directed by Lester M. Salamon, and the work in Egypt was overseen by Stefan Toepler.

2. The definitions and approaches used in the project were developed collaboratively with the cooperation of Egyptian researchers and researchers in other countries and were designed to be applicable to Egypt and other project countries. For a full description of this definition, the types of organizations included, and the methodology used, see Chapter 1 and Appendix B. For a full list of the other countries included, see Table 1.1.

3. Comparative figures do not include religious worship organizations because data on these organizations were not available for all countries. However, religiously affiliated service organizations are included. For more information, see Appendix B.

4. Mohamad Afifi, *Al Auqaf Wal Hayat Al Iqtisadeya Fi Masr [Endowments and Economic Life in Egypt]* (Cairo: Egyptian Public Authority for Books, 1991), 27.

5. Abdel Malek, *Anwar Nahdat Masr [Renaissance of Egypt]* (Cairo: The Egyptian Public Authority for Books, 1983), 84.

6. Amani Kandil, "Egypt," in *The Nonprofit Sector in the Developing World,* ed. Lester M. Salamon and Helmut K. Anheier (Manchester, U.K.: Manchester University Press, 1998), 122–157.

7. Amani Kandil and Sara Ben Nafissa, *Al Gamiyat Al Ahlia Fi Masr [Indigenous Associations in Egypt]* (Cairo: Al Ahram Center for Political and Strategic Studies, 1995), 18–19.

8. Amani Kandil, "Egypt," in *The International Guide to Nonprofit Law,* ed. Lester M. Salamon (New York: John Wiley & Sons, 1997), 88–99.

# Chapter 12

# Lebanon

Hashem El-Husseini, Stefan Toepler,
and Lester M. Salamon

## Introduction

Lebanon is a country with enormous religious diversity that has long been reflected in its religious institutions and in the civil society organizations affiliated with them. Seventeen different sects are acknowledged by the state, and each sect has spawned a multitude of affiliated religious or quasi-religious institutions. Most of these traditionally operated as offshoots of mosques and churches, but many have taken more autonomous form in recent years.

The civil war that raged in Lebanon from 1975 to 1990 played a major role in the development of the Lebanese civil society sector. The civil strife and chaos wrought by the war led to a complete breakdown of state institutions. During this period, civil society organizations — nearly all religiously affiliated — stepped in to provide most of the crucial services needed by the war-torn society. In turn, these organizations were aided by the humanitarian and other foreign support that was flowing into the country at the time. With the end of the civil war, however, foreign aid was largely redirected to rebuilding the Lebanese state. The resulting redirection of outside support has caused significant problems for civil society organizations, which have continued to work on war-related issues and problems.

Unfortunately, even more than a decade after the end of the civil war, Lebanon still lacks the resources and information systems to accurately track and portray the size, scope, and status of its civil society sector. Nevertheless, some broad contours of the Lebanese civil society sector are now visible thanks to the body of work carried out as part of the Johns Hopkins Comparative Nonprofit Sector Project.[1] This work sought both to analyze the Lebanese civil society sector and to compare and contrast it to those in other countries in a systematic way,[2] though the work in Lebanon is still in a preliminary stage as this report goes to press and empirical information remains too limited for cross-national comparison. Unless otherwise noted, financial data are reported in U.S. dollars at the 1997 average exchange rate.

For a more complete statement of the types of organizations included, see Chapter 1 and Appendix B.

## Preliminary Findings

### 1. A sizable presence

Although data are not yet available to portray the overall size, composition, and resource structure of the Lebanese civil society sector with any degree of accuracy, there is little doubt that much of the organizational infrastructure in the fields of health and education is operated by civil society organizations, a reflection of the country's rich diversity as well as the aftermath of the civil war. For example, a 1995 UNICEF survey estimated that civil society organizations maintain 80 percent of all health centers and dispensaries in the country. More recent Ministry of Health data for the year 2000 put the share at about 60 percent. In addition, civil society organizations are thought to operate about 30 percent of all hospitals, or about half of all private hospitals in the country. The situation in the education field is similar. Approximately 70 percent of primary and secondary students are enrolled in private schools, some of which are government subsidized. The estimated 400 subsidized schools account for 20 percent of all private enrollments and are predominantly operated on a not-for-profit basis. Civil society organizations also operate unsubsidized private schools, but their share vis-à-vis commercially run schools is unknown.

Other than health and education institutions, most Lebanese civil society organizations are welfare institutions that are typically established by religious communities and provide a broad range of services. According to a recent study conducted by the Lebanese Ministry of Social Affairs, 4,073 philanthropic associations of all kinds are currently registered in the country, out of which 4,016 are Lebanese, 13 Arab, and 44 international (see Table 12.1). A study by the Social Training Center in Beirut identified 1,302 institutions working in the social field. Of these, 30 percent focused on family care, 26 percent on health care issues, 22 percent on the environment, and another 10 percent on children. Broadly speaking, welfare civil society organizations are particularly interested in specialized services for people with disabilities, drug addicts, the indigent, and juvenile delinquents, as well as the preservation of the environment and the rights of women and children. Civil society organizations are also concerned with human rights because of the large number of prisoners and people missing or kidnapped during the civil war.

Little can be said with certainty about the financial resources and revenue composition of the civil society sector in Lebanon. While the extent of indirect government aid to health and education (e.g., tuition support) remains unknown, direct support, mostly through the Ministry of Social

**Table 12.1.** Number and types of Lebanese NGOs

| Type of association | Number | Percentage |
|---|---|---|
| Political party | 33 | 0.81% |
| Clubs | 153 | 3.76% |
| Philanthropic association | 3338 | 81.95% |
| Scout association | 2 | 0.05% |
| Alumni association | 134 | 3.29% |
| Economic association | 57 | 1.40% |
| Friendship association | 47 | 1.15% |
| Technical league | 167 | 4.10% |
| Scientific association or research center | 111 | 2.73% |
| Other | 25 | 0.61% |
| No answer | 6 | 0.15% |
| **Total** | **4073** | **100.00%** |

Source: Ministry of Social Affairs, Lebanon

Affairs, amounted to $46 million in 2000. In 1999, the European Union and its member states channeled about $10 million to civil society organizations in Lebanon, or less than 5 percent of its total aid to the country. The United Nations Development Program estimated that Lebanese civil society organizations received about $16 million in foreign assistance in 1998. A World Bank survey of a small cross-section of 130 civil society organizations suggests a fairly balanced revenue structure. As Table 12.2 shows, close to 40 percent of the surveyed civil society organizations' income derived from fees, slightly less than 20 percent each from foreign and domestic donations, 8 percent from the government, and the remainder from miscellaneous other sources. While this information is informative, it should not be seen as representative of the Lebanese civil society sector at large.

## 2. A rich and varied history of civil society development

This sizable civil society sector is a product of a long and varied history of civil society institutions in Lebanon. Traditionally, ruling emirs as well as wealthy Muslims donated lands for the establishment of mosques, schools, and social service institutions, typically in conjunction with existing religious institutions. Beginning in the mid-19th century, Lebanon witnessed the emergence of voluntary organizations for relief purposes established by various religious communities. Under the influence of Western missionaries, several organizations were founded to provide educational, health, and residential services to orphans. For example, the first school for the blind in the Middle East was founded in Lebanon by an American in 1868. The

**Table 12.2.** Revenue structure of a sample of
130 Lebanese civil society organizations

| Source | Revenues in USD millions | Percentage |
|---|---|---|
| Government | 13.1 | 8% |
| Foreign | 28.0 | 18% |
| Services Fee | 60.8 | 39% |
| Local Donations | 26.7 | 17% |
| Other | 20.9 | 13% |
| **Total Income** | **149.5** | **100%** |

Source: Omar Traboulsi, *Lebanon Poverty Review. Mapping and Review of
Lebanese NGOs* (Washington, D.C.: World Bank, 1999), unpublished.

increasing number of Christian-based civil society organizations at that time
led in turn to the creation of new Muslim institutions as well.[3] The growth
of these institutions led the Ottoman rulers to institute a law in 1909 that
regulated the establishment of associations in a fairly liberal fashion and
that continues to form the base of the Lebanese legal regulation of the civil
society sector.

France strongly influenced the development of the Lebanese civil society sector in the early 20th century, establishing more than 100 civil society
organizations offering social services and more than 200 schools in Lebanon
and Syria by 1912. With the collapse of the Ottoman Empire at the end of
World War I, the Lebanese territories came under French military administration, and France continued to rule the territories under a League of
Nations mandate until Lebanese independence in 1946. After the formation
of the state of Greater Lebanon in 1920, the French administration favored
the provision of social services and education by French missionaries to
spread Christianity and Western culture and discouraged the formation of
indigenous civil society organizations. The aftermath of the French administration's posture, as well as the absence of any social welfare policies by the
Lebanese government during the 1940s, continued to impact the development of the civil society sector in the first decade after independence, when
very few new organizations were established.

This situation began to change fundamentally when President Chehab
took office in 1958. The following 17 years constituted a period of significant development and growth of the civil society sector in Lebanon. The
state established a special office for social development in which the civil
society sector was represented. With the expansion of the state in the social welfare field, a corresponding expansion of the civil society sector took

place. Social welfare policies attempted to establish access to health care, education, housing, and social security as basic rights. In addition to these new social welfare policies, the growth of the civil society sector was propelled by the increasing industrialization that Lebanon witnessed during this period. Industrialization increased migration from the rural areas of Lebanon to the cities and created densely populated urban areas in need of a growing civil society sector to provide for their social needs.

With the beginning of the civil war in 1975, and the resulting total collapse of the state and its services, the focus of the civil society sector changed from social development to providing emergency relief. Many political parties and armed militias created their own organizations during this period, as did Lebanon's various religious communities to provide for their members' safety and health needs. Consequently, the sector witnessed another jump in numbers. The new organizations were largely health-related and provided services such as distributing medicine and caring for the injured. By the end of the civil war, the number of infirmaries had increased from 250 to 650, two-thirds of which were nongovernmental organizations. The number of institutions assisting people with disabilities similarly increased from 20 to 80. In addition to medical care, these organizations provided food, transportation, and instruction on how to reconstruct war-damaged houses. In addition, some organizations focused on education and the environment. In essence, civil society organizations replaced the state.[4]

The Taef Accord, which ended the civil war in 1990, led to the reconstruction of the state and its institutions. Consequently, the role of the civil society sector shifted again from relief and emergency services to providing care and development assistance. Lebanese civil society organizations now face new challenges. For example, international organizations' direct funding for Lebanese civil society organizations has begun to decline, as resources have shifted to the Lebanese government since the cessation of violence. With less international support, civil society organizations have been challenged to develop ways to help Lebanese society deal with post–civil war traumas and obstacles.

## Conclusion and Outlook

With its rich civil society history, its high degree of religious diversity, and the near absence of a functioning government apparatus during the recent civil war, Lebanon has all the ingredients for fertile development of a civil society sector. It is consequently a fascinating test case for most of our current conceptual understandings of civil society institutions.

Unfortunately, the data situation in the country does not yet make it possible to test these understandings rigorously. Yet the evidence uncovered so far makes clear that civil society institutions are playing a significant role in the social and political reconstruction of this war-torn country.

# Notes

1. The work in Lebanon has been coordinated by Hashem El-Husseini under the guidance of the Johns Hopkins Comparative Nonprofit Sector Project in conjunction with the Arab NGO Network. The research team was aided, in turn, by a local advisory committee (see Appendix D for a list of committee members). The Johns Hopkins project was directed by Lester M. Salamon, and the work in Lebanon was overseen by Stefan Toepler.

2. The definitions and approaches used in the project were developed collaboratively with the cooperation of Lebanese researchers and researchers in other countries and were designed to be applicable to Lebanon and other project countries. For a full description of this definition, the types of organizations included, and the methodology used, see Chapter 1 and Appendix B. For a full list of the other countries included, see Table 1.1.

3. The Center for Social Training, *The Study on Social Services and the Conditions of Those Operating in This Sector* (Beirut: The Center for Social Training, 1980).

4. The Center for Social Training, *The Study on Social Services and the Conditions of Those Operating in This Sector* (Beirut: The Center for Social Training, 1980).

# Chapter 13

# Morocco

Salama Saidi, Stefan Toepler,
and Lester M. Salamon

## Introduction

With the interplay between Berber and Arab cultures since the 10th century and the subsequent influence of both Africa and Europe, Morocco boasts cultural and social traditions that make it as diverse in its heritage as any Muslim country in the world. Though a monarchy, tribal and other forms of informal community organization historically dominated the social and political life of the country and still persist in large parts of rural Morocco. The traditional sociopolitical dominance of such informal organizations was, however, undercut over the past century. Under French influence for the better part of the 20th century, the rise of a highly centralized state administration largely displaced traditional social organization and erected political and legal barriers to formal voluntary association. However, since the 1960s, liberalization has opened new avenues for voluntary participation. Composed of both traditional tribal organizations and modern groups, such as those addressing women's rights and environmental issues, the Moroccan civil society sector is rich and complex yet remains institutionally weak.

These findings emerge from a body of work carried out as part of the Johns Hopkins Comparative Nonprofit Sector Project.[1] This work sought both to analyze Moroccan civil society organizations and to compare and contrast them to those elsewhere in a systematic way.[2] The results reported here are somewhat preliminary and incomplete, but they nevertheless represent the first empirical overview of the Moroccan civil society sector and the first systematic comparison of Moroccan civil society realities to those elsewhere in the world. Most of the data reported here were generated from a 1999 survey sponsored by the Arab NGO Network, supplemented by official government statistics and secondary data sources and analyses. Unless otherwise noted, financial data are reported in U.S. dollars at the 1999 average exchange rate. It is important to note that since Islam is the state religion, data were not collected on religious congregations, though data on religiously affiliated organizations providing various services (e.g., health,

233

**Table 13.1.** The civil society sector* in Morocco, 1999

---

**$274.3 million in expenditures**
- 0.8% of the GDP

**157,878 full-time equivalent workers**
- 74,514 full-time equivalent paid employees
- 83,364 full-time equivalent volunteers
- 1.5% of the economically active population
- 2.8% of nonagricultural employment

---

\* Religious worship organization figures not available.

SOURCE: Johns Hopkins Comparative Nonprofit Sector Project

social services, and education) are included. For a more complete statement of the types of organizations included, see Chapter 1 and Appendix B.

# Principal Findings

## 1. A sizable but economically limited civil society sector

Reflecting its long history, the Moroccan civil society sector boasts some 30,000 organizations in a country of 30 million people. At the same time, the economic contribution of the Moroccan civil society sector is relatively small. In particular:

- **A $270 million industry.** As of the late 1990s, Morocco's civil society sector had expenditures of $270 million, roughly 0.8 percent of Morocco's gross domestic product (GDP), as reported in Table 13.1.

- **A significant employer.** Behind these expenditures lies a sizable workforce numbering close to 160,000 full-time equivalent (FTE) workers, which is almost equally divided between volunteers and paid staff. However, volunteer labor — accounting for 53 percent of the total workforce in Moroccan civil society organizations — remains the driving force in the operations of the civil society sector. Altogether, volunteer and paid work in the sector engages the equivalent of 1.5 percent of the economically active population or 2.8 percent of nonagricultural employment.

- **Comparable to other industries.** Twice as many paid employees work in Morocco's civil society sector (74,514) as in the country's utilities industry (36,000). With volunteers included, the civil society sector workforce is nearly three-quarters as large as that in the transportation industry (217,000) and more than 40 percent of that in construction (367,000), as shown in Figure 13.1.

## Figure 13.1. Civil society organization workforce in context, Morocco

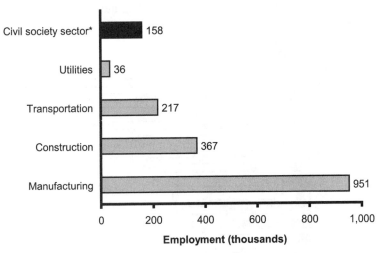

Employment (thousands)

* Including volunteers
SOURCE: Johns Hopkins Comparative Nonprofit Sector Project

## 2. Moroccan civil society in comparative perspective

Although civil society organizations are fairly prevalent in terms of numbers in this country, the workforce of Morocco's civil society sector turns out to be quite small in comparison to those of other countries when expressed as a share of the economically active population.

- **Below the all-country average.** As shown in Figure 13.2, the civil society organization workforce — paid and volunteer — varies from a high of 14.4 percent of the economically active population in the Netherlands to a low of 0.4 percent in Mexico, with an average of 4.4 percent overall.[3] The Moroccan figure, at 1.5 percent, is thus well below the all-country average.

- **Below the developing and transitional country average.** What is more, Morocco's civil society organization employment also falls below that in developing and transitional countries (1.5 vs. 1.9 percent of the economically active population). The Moroccan figure is only about half that in Egypt (2.8 percent), the only other Arab country for which we have data at this time, and it is also lower than the African countries covered, though it is ahead of Pakistan, another predominantly Islamic country.

- **Volunteer participation relatively high.** The relatively small scale of civil society employment in Morocco is largely a function of having comparatively little paid staff, which may be a function of the limited

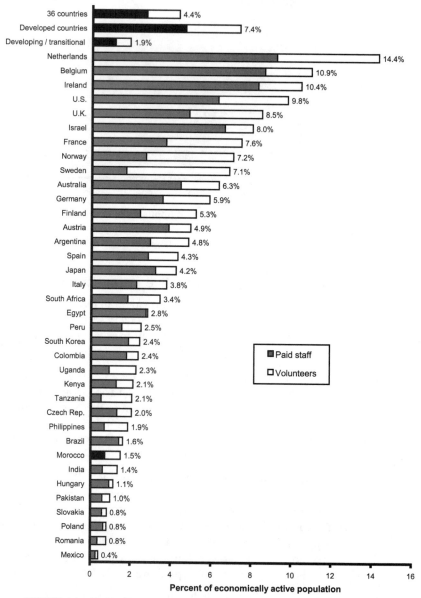

**Figure 13.2.** Civil society organization workforce as a share of the economically active population, by country

SOURCE: Johns Hopkins Comparative Nonprofit Sector Project

**Figure 13.3.** Volunteers as a share of the
civil society organization workforce, Morocco,
developing and transitional countries, and 36 countries

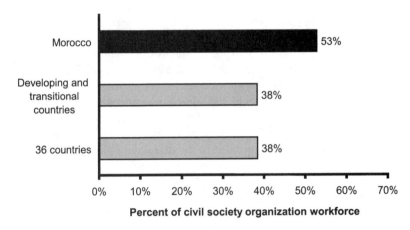

SOURCE: Johns Hopkins Comparative Nonprofit Sector Project

financial support available. Volunteer participation in Moroccan civil
society organizations, on the other hand, is quite significant. Roughly
700,000 individuals (or 4 percent of the adult population) engage in some
kind of volunteer work (see Appendix Table A.2). The volunteer share
of the total civil society organization workforce is 53 percent in Morocco, substantially higher than the developing and transitional country
and all-country averages of 38 percent each (see Figure 13.3).

## 3. A troubled history of civil society development

A number of factors likely account for the sizable presence but relatively
limited economic contribution of the civil society sector in Morocco.[4] Influenced by both Muslim and Berber traditions, Moroccan society used to
be governed largely by tribal and other forms of social organization in a
decentralized fashion. Communal decision-making was done in local assem-
blies (*Jma'a*), and Islamic law (*chariaa* and *waqf*) governed self-help groups
and religious giving, respectively. Most activities of daily life, ranging from
agricultural work, water usage, and crop stocking to education were thus
organized locally, with the monarchy heavily dependent on traditional elites
and communal structures, particularly in rural areas. As a Muslim country,
Morocco was also heavily influenced by the Islamic emphasis on charity,
which gave rise to numerous privately funded religious and other schools
and mosques functioning as *auqaf*, or endowed charities.[5]

During the French Protectorate from 1912 to 1956, however, foreign rule caused a progressive decline in the traditional political system in favor of centralized state power. This led to tighter control by the state over the tribal system in rural areas and limitations on the power and strength of civil society through legal regulation. Although the operating environment was restrictive and oppressive, traditional types of civil society organizations continued to exist in rural Morocco and preserved indigenous traditions, culture, and beliefs. In urban areas, many associations played a significant role in the nationalist movement against the protectorate. Nevertheless, civil society was relegated to the sidelines of political and social development.

After Moroccan independence in 1956, civil society experienced a period of liberalization followed by a renewed restrictiveness between 1973 and 1984 and a subsequent renaissance.[6] In the immediate post-independence period, French legal restrictions were overturned, and the right of civil society organizations to exist was firmly enshrined in a 1958 law, which provided an open and flexible framework accommodating both the deeply rooted traditions of civil society activism and the modern concepts of associative life. Accordingly, a rich associational life emerged during this period, ranging from professional associations, to welfare and charity associations, to those dealing with the provision of traditional human services such as education.

The early 1970s, though, saw a strengthening of state control over all social and political institutions. A decree was promulgated on April 10, 1973, that significantly reigned in the liberalism of the 1958 law by tightening the requirements for legal recognition of associations, regulating dissolution, and introducing sanctions against founding members. Generally, the government, and particularly the Ministry of the Interior, gained substantial discretionary power over associations. Of particular concern to governmental elites was the rise of "political Islam," which posed potential challenges to the prevailing regime. On the theory that no group should be able to proclaim itself more Muslim than the rest of the population, the state since the 1970s has consequently forbidden civil society organizations with religious goals and objectives.

Despite such restrictions, the associative movement continued to progress and play an important role in the social and cultural life of the country, featuring newly emerging groups ranging from theaters and music groups to associations for women, youth, and people with disabilities. The sector truly began to flourish after the mid-1980s due to the changing political and economic landscape in Morocco. The financial crises of the 1980s and the resulting structural adjustment policies led to a realization that the government could not fulfill all the socioeconomic needs of the people. This contributed to a decreased standard of living, and an effort by government to rejuvenate the economy by finding new partners in the private sector, thus creating a point of entry for the civil society sector. The political environment opened new opportunities to political parties and associations, which were encouraged to broaden participation in the democratic process of the country. This was accompanied by an increasing interest in human rights issues at the national level, along with a wider participation by the population in the political, economic, social, and cultural processes of the country.

Government views vis-à-vis the civil society sector began to change as well. Increasingly, the government has come to appreciate the role that the sector can play in the political system and in the socioeconomic development of the country. In recognition of this, the 1958 law was amended again by a new law of July 2002, which made it easier for all civil society organizations to receive foreign funding, a privilege that previously had been reserved for organizations of public utility.

## 4. Structure and composition

Unfortunately, data limitations make it impossible to explore the structure and composition of the Moroccan civil society sector — much less its sources of revenue — with any degree of certainty, particularly from a comparative perspective. Nevertheless, there are at least three areas in which civil society organizations play a vital role in Morocco:

- **Traditional welfare service provision.** Prior to the 1980s, the "first generation" of modern civil society organizations was predominantly active in the provision of traditional social, educational, and health services. Initially operating on their own in fields in which the government proved unable to meet the needs of the people, these organizations have increasingly been brought into partnerships with government. This is particularly true in illiteracy eradication and family planning.

- **Development-oriented nongovernmental organizations.** The "second generation" of civil society organizations emerged during the 1980s, when Morocco became subject to structural adjustment programs enforced by the international aid system. The resulting privatization processes raised awareness of a host of development issues, such as those related to the standard of living, poverty alleviation, and rural-urban gaps in development. In direct response, a large number of local nongovernmental organizations focused on development were established, and many civil society organizations began to focus on improving economic conditions or general living conditions. These organizations were soon recognized by local authorities, which began to rely on them as full partners, especially since civil society organizations proved to be making a difference on the ground. Most of these organizations are local associations established to meet the specific needs of local populations, ranging from electrification, road building, and school construction to local community development, small enterprise, and microcredit promotion. Local development associations generally cooperate with local authorities on an equal footing, and the role they play in the development context has become so fundamental that local authorities arguably cannot achieve much without them.

- **Advocacy and expressive work.** A "third generation" of Moroccan civil society organizations functions in the policy arena, often in cooperation with international networks on issues such as human rights, gender, reproductive health, and the environment. These newer civil society organizations have frequently challenged government policies and have proven to be highly effective. Women's organizations, for instance, pressured for legal changes to the family code following the 1995 United Nations Fourth World Conference on Women in Beijing, and human rights groups successfully lobbied for the establishment of the high-level Advisory Council on Human Rights in the late 1990s, as well as the creation of a dedicated Ministry of Human Rights. Rather than concentrating on social activities, Moroccan civil society organizations are increasingly beginning to influence government initiatives. Overall, the civil society sector is rapidly becoming the principal mechanism for fostering democracy and sustainable development.

## Conclusions and Implications

Overall, the data reported here reveal a civil society sector in Morocco that is sizable in numbers but considerably more limited in economic scale and capacity than sectors in most other countries, including many other less developed countries in the world. This remains the case despite the generally favorable conditions of the past two decades. The longer-term historical view, though, highlights the close connection between the civil society sector and the development and evolution of Moroccan society as a whole. Indeed, the sector has undergone, and in many ways reflects, the broader political, economic, and social changes that have shaped the country.

The policy environment of the civil society sector is currently in flux. No stable and permanent status has been reached that would clearly define respective behaviors and attitudes of the sector and the government. The only matter that has been settled recently is that the government needs civil society organizations to promote the political and socioeconomic changes necessary to develop Morocco. A healthy debate is emerging on the issue of partnership between the government and the civil society sector, and both sides are working to identify and address the real problems that such partnerships involve. This is generally seen as a positive step toward a good governance system, but the debate is just beginning, and more mobilization of effort from all parties is required. Official attitudes have begun to change in favor of the sector, although not necessarily at all administrative levels. There are still significant issues concerning the development of mutual trust, which is impeded in part by prevailing particularism and clientelism in parts of the sector, as well as by governmental concerns about the ideological nature of some civil society organizations, and the civil society sector's fear of loss of autonomy and independence due to increased government funding.

What is more, while still limited in its economic capacity, the sector's rapid and diverse development has impeded coordination efforts. The lack of sector infrastructure organizations, as well as largely unmet training needs, are quickly emerging as crucial challenges, particularly as the sector is increasingly called upon to play a major role in the development of the country. While some organizations are beginning to develop track records as full-fledged partners of the government, the sector largely comprises relatively new and inexperienced organizations, most of them less than 10 years old. Sustainability is therefore still an issue for many, as is the ability to demonstrate their impact and contribution to the socioeconomic development of the country. Hopefully, the kind of data generated within the Johns Hopkins Comparative Nonprofit Sector Project will help overcome these hurdles and allow Moroccan society to fully understand and tap into the potential of its civil society organizations in this period of major social and economic change.

## Notes

1. The work in Morocco has been coordinated by Salama Saidi in conjunction with the Arab NGO Network. The research team was aided, in turn, by a local advisory committee (see Appendix D for a list of committee members). The Johns Hopkins project was directed by Lester M. Salamon, and the work in Morocco was overseen by Stefan Toepler.

2. The definitions and approaches used in the project were developed collaboratively with the cooperation of Moroccan researchers and researchers in other countries and were designed to be applicable to Morocco and other project countries. For a full description of this definition, the types of organizations included, and the methodology used, see Chapter 1 and Appendix B. For a full list of the other countries included, see Table 1.1.

3. Comparative figures do not include religious worship organizations, because data on these organizations were not available for all countries. However, religiously affiliated service organizations are included. For more information, see Appendix B.

4. This section draws on a report by Salama Saidi, "Defining the Nonprofit Sector: Morocco," *Working Papers of the Johns Hopkins Comparative Nonprofit Sector Project* (Baltimore, MD: The Johns Hopkins Center for Civil Society Studies, forthcoming).

5. *Auqaf* indicates the plural of *waqf*, a religious endowment. "Wakf" is also commonly used as an alternate spelling.

6. A. Gahazali, *Projet de Soutien aux institutions démocratiques* (Washington, D.C.: U.S. Agency for International Development, 1996).

Part Five

# OTHER COUNTRIES

# Chapter 14

# Italy

Gian Paolo Barbetta, Stefano Cima, Nereo Zamaro,
S. Wojciech Sokolowski, and Lester M. Salamon

## Introduction

Civil society institutions in Italy have their roots in the social welfare and educational institutions created by the Roman Catholic Church and in the mutual aid societies created by workers at the beginning of the industrial development of the country. During the formation of the modern Italian state in the 19th century, however, these institutions found themselves in the middle of an enormous power struggle. Since neither the Roman Catholic Church, the state authorities, nor the growing socialist movement among the workers was powerful enough to prevail in this contest, the result was a series of compromises that left civil society institutions in a highly ambiguous position.

In the context of an emergent, though incomplete, system of public welfare, private civil society sector institutions focused more on representing interest groups than on providing social and cultural services. Nonetheless, major private providers of social services survived the growth of the public welfare system, although at the cost of some compromise. Thus, for example, while the Church's social welfare institutions were formally absorbed into the state's social welfare system, they continued in many cases to be staffed by religious personnel and to enjoy a degree of practical autonomy. Similarly, while the state extended social protections to workers, it did not do so on a universal basis. And while formerly private social welfare institutions were made eligible for public assistance, they were required to become part of the public system to receive this assistance. This imposed a highly clientelistic pattern on the nascent Italian civil society sector and impeded its development as a powerful independent presence in Italian society.

These and other findings about the current size and scope of Italian civil society organizations emerge from a body of work carried out by the Italian Statistical Office (ISTAT) in cooperation with an Italian research team within the framework of the Johns Hopkins Comparative Nonprofit Sector Project.[1] This work expanded on an earlier assessment of the scope and scale of the Italian civil society sector carried out as part of the Hopkins Project in the early 1990s.[2] Compared to the earlier assessment, this one is based on a much more complete census of Italian civil society organizations. Although it is possible to compare these results to the earlier ones in order to identify trends during the 1990s, the much more complete scale of the survey that underlies the current data makes any such comparisons difficult. Accordingly, this report will focus chiefly on the current data and use the earlier estimates simply as a point of reference.

This chapter reports chiefly on the major descriptive findings of this recent survey focusing on the size, composition, and financing of the civil society sector in Italy and shows how these compare with other countries. Previous reports have examined the history, legal position, and policy environment of the civil society sector in Italy.

The base year for these data is 1999. Unless otherwise noted, financial data are reported in U.S. dollars at the 1999 average exchange rate. For a more complete statement of the types of organizations included, see Chapter 1 and Appendix B.

## Principal Findings

### 1. A sizeable force in the Italian economy

The civil society sector occupies a sizeable role in the Italian economy and society. More specifically:

- **A $36 billion industry.** As of 1999, civil society organizations in Italy, including religious worship organizations, contributed $36.3 billion, or 3.1 percent of the nation's gross domestic product (GDP), as reported in Table 14.1.

- **A significant employer.** Even more impressive is the workforce behind these expenditures, which numbers over 1 million full-time equivalent (FTE) workers, of which just over 40 percent are volunteers. This represents 4 percent of the country's economically active population, and 4.6 percent of the nonagricultural employment.

- **Outdistances many industries.** The civil society sector workforce in Italy is almost five times larger than that of the country's largest private firm, Fiat, and on a par with the transportation industry (see Figure 14.1).

- **Robust growth.** Though earlier estimates were not as complete, it appears that the civil society sector workforce in Italy grew substantially during the 1990s, adding as many as a quarter of a million FTE jobs (paid and volunteer). This represents a growth rate of nearly 5 percent per year between 1991 and 1999.

**Table 14.1.** The civil society sector* in Italy, 1999

---

**$36.3 billion in expenditures**

- 3.1% of the GDP

**1,010,239 full-time equivalent workers**

- 580,109 full-time equivalent paid employees
- 430,130 full-time equivalent volunteers
- 4.0% of the economically active population
- 4.6% of nonagricultural employment
- 29.8% of public employment

---

\* Including religious worship organizations.

SOURCE: Johns Hopkins Comparative Nonprofit Sector Project

**Figure 14.1.** Civil society organization
workforce in context, Italy

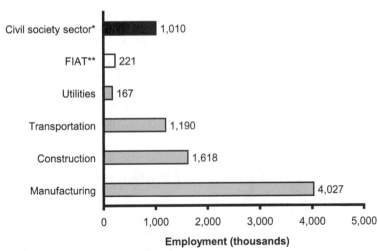

\* Including volunteers
\*\* Largest private firm
SOURCE: Johns Hopkins Comparative Nonprofit Sector Project

## 2. Below the international average

Although the civil society sector in Italy employs a significant number of people, it ranks below the average for the 36 countries for which we have comparable data.

- **Below the all-country average.** As shown in Figure 14.2, excluding religious worship organizations, the civil society organization workforce — paid and volunteer — varies from a high of 14.4 percent of the economically active population in the Netherlands to a low of 0.4 percent in Mexico, with an average of 4.4 percent overall.[3] The Italian civil society organization workforce, at 3.8 percent, is thus slightly below the all-country average, as it was in our earlier estimates.[4]

- **Smaller than the developed country average.** The relative size of the Italian civil society organization workforce falls well below that in the other developed countries for which we have data. Thus, as shown in Figure 14.2, the civil society organization workforce in Italy is only about half the average for the developed countries (3.8 percent of the economically active population vs. 7.4 percent).

- **Volunteer workforce lower than average.** About 4 percent of the adult population in Italy — some 2 million people — report some involvement in volunteer activity (see Appendix Table A.2). This is well below the estimated average of 10 percent among the 36 countries included in this project. Translated into full-time equivalent terms, this yields a volunteer labor force that is 1.5 percent of the economically active population, roughly equivalent to the all-country average of 1.6 percent (see Appendix Table A.1), but well below the developed country average of 2.7 percent (see Figure 1.15). However, because the size of paid civil society organization employment in Italy is also smaller than elsewhere, volunteers account for a slightly larger share of the Italian civil society organization workforce (40 percent) than was found both internationally and in other developed countries (38 and 39 percent, respectively), as reflected in Figure 14.3.

## 3. A long tradition of civil society institutions

Perhaps the first civil society institutions on Italian soil were foundations, which emerged under the Roman legal system.[5] This system provided for the transfer of property to charitable institutions and gave rise to independent non-profit-making institutions. Many of these foundations operated continuously until the 17th century, despite changing economic, social, and political conditions.

Another factor contributing to the emergence of civil society organizations in Italy was the development of city corporations or guilds, which

**Figure 14.2.** Civil society organization workforce
as a share of the economically active population, by country

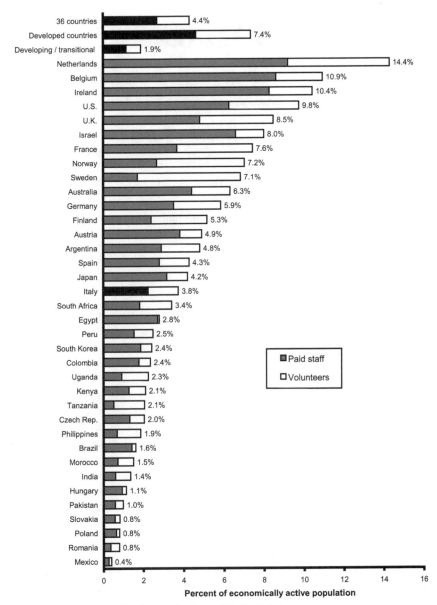

SOURCE: Johns Hopkins Comparative Nonprofit Sector Project

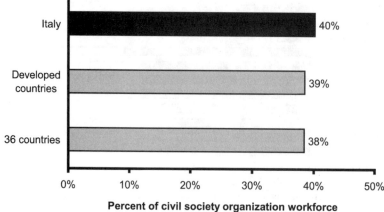

**Figure 14.3.** Volunteers as a share of the civil society organization workforce, Italy, developed countries, and 36 countries

**Percent of civil society organization workforce**

SOURCE: Johns Hopkins Comparative Nonprofit Sector Project

had roots in antiquity. Operating on the principles of solidarity and mutuality, the guilds and corporations provided assistance and aid to members and their families. Such assistance, together with the legal and financial autonomy of the guilds, was instrumental in instilling a sense of self-management.

The real key to the development of charitable institutions in Italy, however, was the Catholic Church. The Church created a wide institutional network of parishes and ancillary organizations that permeated Italian society. This institutional network provided organizational capacity to identify and respond to social needs. It also gave the Church the capacity to supervise and control the operations of each individual institution as well as maintain control over its assets. Religious charitable institutions took many forms, including hospitals for the mentally ill; hospices for the chronically ill; almshouses for beggars and pilgrims; subventions for the handicapped; distribution of free medicines; shelters for abandoned children, orphans, or widows; and workhouses for the poor.

However, starting in the 19th century, provision of social safety net services began to shift to the state. In the 1860s, the Papal State and the Kingdom of the Two Sicilies (parts of southern and central Italy) were militarily annexed to form a new Italian state. Following this change, the new political elite moved to reduce the influence of the Catholic Church and its institutions. Between 1866 and 1890, the state enacted laws confiscating the assets of various Catholic orders, congregations, and charities and forced remaining charities to adhere to state jurisdiction.

The Crispi Law, passed in 1890, established state jurisdiction over health, education, and job training and offered financial assistance to private social service organizations but only on condition that they incorporate under a public charter. The upshot was a curiously ambiguous situation in which many religiously affiliated social service organizations managed to retain their religious character while functioning formally as public bodies.

The beginning of the 20th century witnessed the emergence of the labor movement and affiliated organizations, such as unions and mutual societies, which were particularly strong in the Northern provinces. This movement intensified after World War I and led to electoral victories for the Socialist and Populist parties. This development provoked a reaction by the landed and financial elites that led to the rise of Fascism.[6]

Following the Fascist takeover in 1922, the hostility between church and state eased with the signing of the Concordato in 1929. Religious charities regained their autonomy and became an important conduit for the provision of social welfare, while the state established a compulsory social insurance system and initiated public provision of social and health services. However, Fascist policies were explicitly aimed at restricting the operations of any free associations, especially in the cultural and political areas. As a result, the number of free associations rapidly declined.

With the collapse of the Fascist regime at the end of World War II, a significant expansion of the welfare system occurred, though mostly in the form of state-run services. Two notable exceptions were some social services, which, though publicly funded, were administered primarily by Catholic organizations, and some cultural and recreational services run by organizations connected to labor unions and political parties. Beginning in the 1980s, however, budgetary limitations coupled with dissatisfaction with state-run welfare services led to the rise of new forms of civil society organizations: volunteer-based associations that refused to be represented by the Church hierarchy and a variety of "social cooperatives" that revitalized the mutuality sentiments of the guild, and at the same time sought to merge market means with charitable purpose. The significance of these new trends has been recognized by public policy makers, who have established institutional structures to facilitate cooperation between government agencies and the civil society sector.

## 4. Strong presence of service organizations

Reflecting this history, most of the Italian civil society sector workforce is now engaged in service functions, such as social welfare, health services, and education, as is the case in many other developed countries, as well as internationally. More specifically:

**Figure 14.4.** Composition of the
civil society organization workforce, Italy,
developed countries, and 33-country average

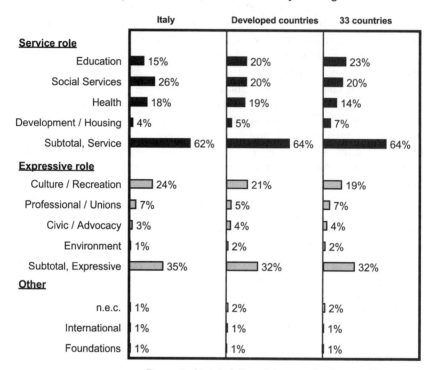

**Percent of total civil society organization workforce**

n.e.c.= not elsewhere classified

SOURCE: Johns Hopkins Comparative Nonprofit Sector Project

- **Service activities dominate.** As shown in Figure 14.4, about 62 percent of all Italian civil society organization workers, paid and volunteer, are engaged in service activities.[7] This share of service activities is comparable to that found in other countries, though it is more than 10 percent lower than that in other European-style welfare partnership states, where it reaches 73 percent (see Table 1.9). The largest proportion of Italian civil society organization workers are employed in social services, which in Italy engages approximately one-fourth of the entire civil society organization workforce, more than in most other countries (20 percent in both developed countries and internationally).

- **Small share of workers engaged in expressive activities.** A considerably smaller proportion (35 percent) of Italian civil society organization workers, paid and volunteer, are engaged in expressive activities. Again, this

**Figure 14.5.** Distribution of paid employees and volunteers
between service and expressive activities in Italy

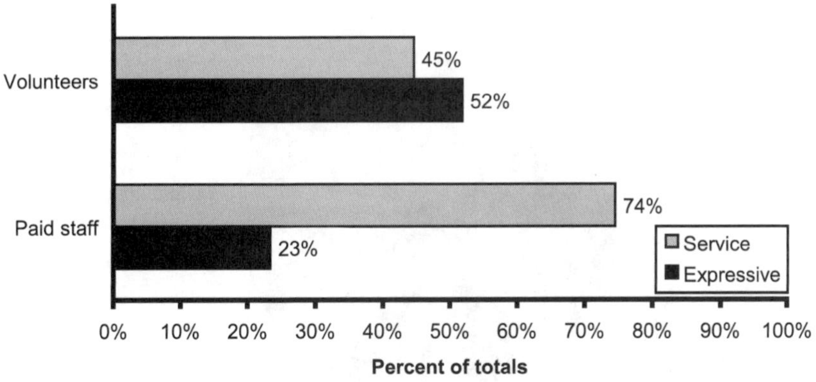

SOURCE: Johns Hopkins Comparative Nonprofit Sector Project

distribution is comparable to that in other countries (32 percent in both developed countries and internationally). However, the share of the civil society organization workforce engaged in expressive activities is higher in Italy than in most Western European countries, except Scandinavia.

- **Culture and recreation activities especially prevalent.** Among expressive functions, culture, sports, and recreation organizations are especially prominent in Italy, accounting for 24 percent of the Italian civil society organization workforce. This share is larger than both the all-country and developed country averages (19 and 21 percent, respectively).

- **Paid and volunteer staff distributed differently.** This picture of the distribution of the civil society organization workforce in Italy changes somewhat when paid staff and volunteers are examined separately. Most of the volunteer staff time is concentrated in expressive functions (52 percent of total volunteer time). However, nearly three-fourths (74 percent) of paid employees are engaged in service functions, as Figure 14.5 shows.

## 5. Revenue dominated by fees and charges

Fees and charges are the dominant source of civil society organization revenue in Italy, outdistancing government support and philanthropy.

- **Fee dominance in Italy.** About 61 percent of all Italian civil society organizations' cash revenue comes from fees for services provided by these organizations, income from property, and membership dues, as shown in Figure 14.6. Only 37 percent of revenue comes from the public sector and 3 percent from all sources of private philanthropy, including individuals, foundations, and corporations.

**Figure 14.6.** Sources of civil society
organization revenue in Italy

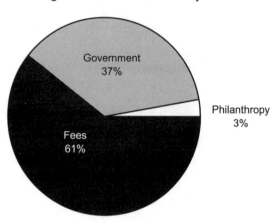

SOURCE: Johns Hopkins Comparative Nonprofit Sector Project

- **Differs from international pattern.** This pattern of civil society organization revenue differs markedly from that evident internationally, especially
  in other developed countries.

  - Italian civil society organizations rely less on government payments than
    their counterparts in other developed countries, especially in European-
    style welfare partnership states, where government payments account
    for 58 percent of the revenue on average, compared to only 37 percent
    in Italy (see Figure 14.7 and Table 1.9 for Europe data).

  - As in most other developed countries, Italian civil society organiza-
    tions receive little support from philanthropic giving. As shown in
    Figure 14.7, 3 percent of civil society organization revenue in Italy
    comes from private giving, which is well below both the all-country
    and developed country averages (12 percent and 7 percent, respec-
    tively). Indeed, at 0.1 percent of the GDP, the rate of philanthropic
    giving in Italy is well below the 0.5 percent for developed countries
    and 0.4 percent internationally (see Appendix Table A.5). This is sur-
    prising in light of the strength of the Catholic and patrician traditions,
    which encourage charity. It likely reflects the substantial reliance on
    the state for social welfare provision in recent Italian history. Also
    at work, however, are the limited tax incentives for charitable giving
    and the fact that churches receive substantial support from a "church
    tax."[8]

  - While relying much less heavily on both government and private phil-
    anthropic support than is the case in other developed countries, Italian

**Figure 14.7.** Sources of civil society organization revenue,
Italy, developed countries, and 34-country average

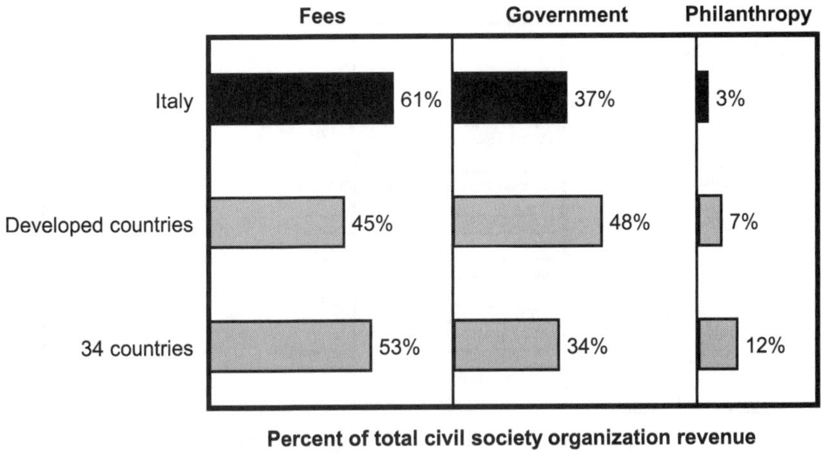

|  | **Fees** | **Government** | **Philanthropy** |
|---|---|---|---|
| Italy | 61% | 37% | 3% |
| Developed countries | 45% | 48% | 7% |
| 34 countries | 53% | 34% | 12% |

**Percent of total civil society organization revenue**

SOURCE: Johns Hopkins Comparative Nonprofit Sector Project

civil society organizations rely much more heavily on fees and charges to support their activities. Such fees account for 61 percent of total civil society organization cash income in Italy, 16 percentage points above the developed country average.

- **Revenue structure varies among fields.** Fees dominate most fields of civil society organization activity in Italy, with the exceptions of health services and development and housing, where government payments dominate (see Figure 14.8), though government support is quite significant in social services as well. Private philanthropy does not account for a significant share of civil society organization revenue in any of the fields studied.

- **Growing fee income.** This pattern of civil society organization support in Italy is comparable to what existed in the early 1990s, but shows a slight overall increase in reliance on fee income.

- **Volunteers change the revenue structure noticeably.** This picture changes noticeably when the value of volunteer input is included and treated as part of philanthropy.

  - As Figure 14.9 demonstrates, with private contributions of time included in the philanthropy total, philanthropy's share of Italian civil society organization support swells to 20 percent, as opposed to the 3 percent represented by monetary contributions alone. Thus, volunteering, not cash donations, is the most important form of philanthropy in Italy. However, even with the value of volunteer time

**Figure 14.8.** Sources of civil society organization revenue, Italy, by field

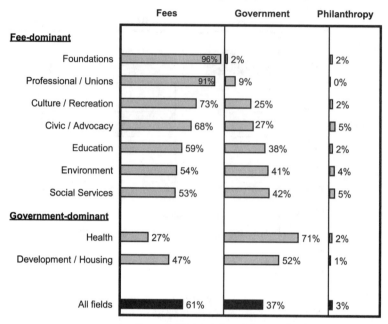

Percent of total civil society organization revenue

SOURCE: Johns Hopkins Comparative Nonprofit Sector Project

**Figure 14.9.** Sources of civil society organization support
including volunteers, Italy, developed countries,
and 34-country average

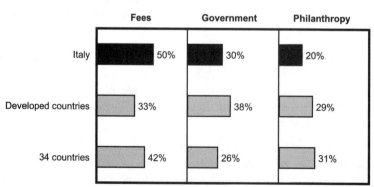

Percent of total civil society organization support

SOURCE: Johns Hopkins Comparative Nonprofit Sector Project

**Figure 14.10.** Sources of civil society organization support
in Italy, including volunteers, by field

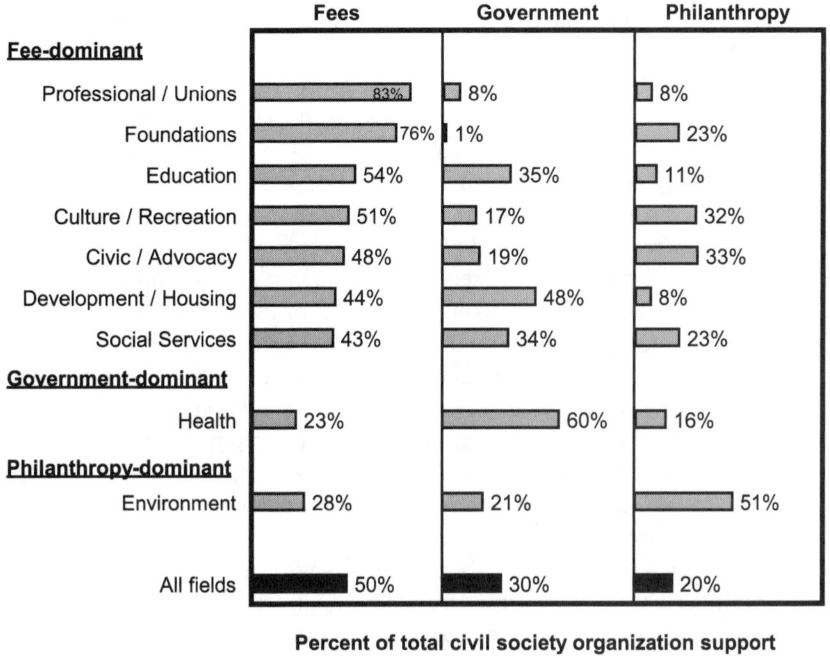

|  | Fees | Government | Philanthropy |
|---|---|---|---|
| **Fee-dominant** | | | |
| Professional / Unions | 83% | 8% | 8% |
| Foundations | 76% | 1% | 23% |
| Education | 54% | 35% | 11% |
| Culture / Recreation | 51% | 17% | 32% |
| Civic / Advocacy | 48% | 19% | 33% |
| Development / Housing | 44% | 48% | 8% |
| Social Services | 43% | 34% | 23% |
| **Government-dominant** | | | |
| Health | 23% | 60% | 16% |
| **Philanthropy-dominant** | | | |
| Environment | 28% | 21% | 51% |
| | | | |
| All fields | 50% | 30% | 20% |

**Percent of total civil society organization support**

SOURCE: Johns Hopkins Comparative Nonprofit Sector Project

included, the share of philanthropic donations in Italy is lower than
that in other developed countries (29 percent) and internationally
(31 percent).

– With the value of volunteer input included, private philanthropy becomes the main source of support in the environmental protection
field (see Figure 14.10). What is more, philanthropy becomes the
second most important source of support in the fields of culture
and recreation, civic and advocacy, and foundations (philanthropic
intermediaries).

## Conclusions and Implications

Although civil society has a long tradition in Italian society, its growth was
limited by the conflictual relations between church and state in the 19th
century, and by the Fascist regime during the first half of the 20th century.[9]
Since World War II, the involvement of civil society organizations in policy-
making in Italy has been mediated by three sets of players: the Catholic

Church and, to a somewhat lesser extent, political parties and labor unions. This situation resulted in the subordination of the civil society sector to the political agendas of these institutional players, which was not conducive to its growth. As a consequence, the scale of the Italian civil society sector has lagged behind that in other countries in Western Europe, though in recent years, the sector has undergone significant growth.

Traditionally, religious institutions have been the main venue for private social service delivery in Italy. Protected by the Church and supported by the state, religiously affiliated organizations gained a de facto monopoly in the provision of private health, social, and educational services. The hegemony of the Church restrained nonreligious organizations from competing with Church-affiliated entities in the service sector. Only in vocational education, where service providers have strong links to labor unions, have nonreligious organizations successfully competed with religious organizations.

Given their attention to direct service delivery, religious organizations played a minor role in the advocacy field. For a relatively long time, this sphere has been dominated by organizations connected to political parties or trade unions whose main task was to mobilize political support for their patrons. As a result, their advocacy role and the capacity to represent genuine public interests were severely limited.

Although this situation has begun to change recently with the rise of new volunteer-based associations outside the Church structures, the capacity of civil society organizations to influence public policy remains limited. Their public image and legitimacy is still strongly connected to traditional institutions, especially the Church, the state, and political parties.

At the same time, privatization policies inaugurated in the 1990s, by reducing the role of the state, have created new demands for private services, and this is producing new opportunities for the civil society sector. But whether civil society organizations can develop stronger partnerships with government agencies, or alternatively, establish themselves as independent service providers, depends on their success at meeting three key challenges: financial autonomy, professionalization, and political legitimacy.

- **Financial autonomy.** The volatility and insufficiency of financial support from public and private institutions may be the most serious problem currently facing civil society organizations in Italy. The absence of legislation encouraging private donations limits fundraising efforts, while the discretionary methods of allocating public funding create extreme volatility in funding availability.

- **Greater efficiency and effectiveness.** There is a marked divide between professionally managed organizations and those that depend mainly on volunteer staff. While the former tend to attract public funding and contracts, the latter often experience difficulty in obtaining public support.

The positive aspect of professionalization is better service quality. However, that may also lead to excessive commercialization and abandonment of the innovative role that civil society organizations have traditionally played.

- **Political legitimacy.** The legitimacy crisis that has engulfed political parties in Italy has created an opportunity for the civil society sector to play a greater political advocacy role. Such political activism is particularly visible in the area of social welfare, in which civil society organizations are lobbying against privatization and reductions in public spending and representing the most vulnerable groups affected by these reductions. Such lobbying by civil society organizations is not limited to defending the organizations' direct interests but encompasses defense of broader social welfare purposes.

The civil society sector in Italy faces a great opportunity for political and professional development by forming a true welfare partnership with the state. However, given the paternalistic tendencies in past civil society–government relations, this partnership will require greater autonomy and a more clearly defined legal status for civil society organizations, as well as greater transparency in awarding public contracts to private institutions. This is therefore an opportune moment in the evolution of the civil society sector in Italy to have available the kind of data presented here.

## Notes

1. The work in Italy has been coordinated by Gian Paolo Barbetta. The research team was aided, in turn, by a local advisory committee (see Appendix D for a list of committee members). The Johns Hopkins Project was directed by Lester M. Salamon, and the work in Italy was overseen by Helmut K. Anheier and later by S. Wojciech Sokolowski. The definitions and approaches used in the project were developed collaboratively with the cooperation of Italian researchers and researchers in other countries and were designed to be applicable to Italy and other project countries. For a full description of this definition, the types of organizations included, and the methodology used, see Chapter 1 and Appendix B. For a full list of the other countries included, see Table 1.1.

2. These early results were published in Gian Paolo Barbetta (ed.), *The Nonprofit Sector in Italy* (Manchester, U.K.: Manchester University Press, 1997).

3. Comparative figures do not include religious worship organizations because data on these organizations were not available for all countries. However, religiously affiliated service organizations are included. For more information, see Appendix B.

4. Our earlier estimates, based on a much smaller sample of agencies, placed Italian civil society employment at 3.2 percent of the nonagricultural workforce, compared to a 22-country average of 4.8 percent. Lester M. Salamon, Helmut K. Anheier, Regina List, Stefan Toepler, S. Wojciech Sokolowski, and Associates, *Global Civil Society: Dimensions of the Nonprofit Sector* (Baltimore, MD: Johns Hopkins Center for Civil Society Studies, 1999).

5. The discussion in this section draws heavily on Sergio Zaninelli, "Historical Developments," in *The Nonprofit Sector in Italy,* ed. Gian Paolo Barbetta (Manchester, U.K.: Manchester University Press, 1997), 80–103.

6. Dietrich Rueschemeyer, Evelyne Huber Stephen, and John D. Stephens, *Capitalist Development and Democracy* (Chicago: University of Chicago Press, 1992).

7. Percentages displayed in figures may not add to 100 due to rounding.

8. About 0.8 percent of income taxes paid by citizens go to churches (or to state activities of public interest) based on the choices of taxpayers.

9. This section draws on Gian Paolo Barbetta (ed.), *The Nonprofit Sector in Italy* (Manchester, U.K.: Manchester University Press, 1997), 226–292.

# Chapter 15

# Norway

Karl Henrik Sivesind, Håkon Lorentzen, Per Selle,
Dag Wollebæk, S. Wojciech Sokolowski,
and Lester M. Salamon

## Introduction

Civic activity in Norway can trace its roots back to the Middle Ages, but its proximate origins lie in the social movements of the early 19th century. These social movements mobilized broad segments of the population to support the revival of local customs and language, promotion of democratic governance, self-help, and community welfare. They also played a role in the country's nation-building process and in the more recent extension of social welfare benefits. As a result, a strong tradition of civic engagement persists in Norway to this day, despite the fact that many of the service and welfare functions once performed by voluntary agencies were integrated into the national public welfare system created in the aftermath of World War II. Indeed, the civil society sector in Norway is quite large by international standards, though it is staffed primarily by volunteers, and its activities are concentrated in expressive fields.

These findings emerge from a body of work carried out by a Norwegian research team as part of the Johns Hopkins Comparative Nonprofit Sector Project.[1] This work sought both to analyze Norwegian civil society organizations and to compare and contrast them to those in other countries in a systematic way.[2] The result is the most encompassing empirical overview of the Norwegian civil society sector to date, and the first systematic comparison of Norwegian civil society characteristics to those elsewhere in the world.

This chapter reports chiefly on the major descriptive findings of this project relating to the size, composition, and financing of the civil society sector in Norway and other countries. Other reports will fill in more of the history, legal position, and impact of these institutions.[3] Most of the data reported here were generated from several organizational surveys designed by the project team and administered by Statistics Norway. In addition, the

**Table 15.1.** The civil society sector* in Norway, 1997

---

**$5.5 billion in expenditures**
- 3.7% of the GDP

**181,472 full-time equivalent workers**
- 66,243 full-time equivalent paid employees
- 115,229 full-time equivalent volunteers
- 8.0% of the economically active population
- 10.0% of nonagricultural employment
- 38.2% of public employment

---

* Including religious worship organizations.

SOURCE: Johns Hopkins Comparative Nonprofit Sector Project

project team conducted a mail survey on giving and volunteering, a survey of local-level associations in the county of Hordaland, and more targeted inquiries of specific organizations not covered elsewhere. The base year for these data is 1997. Unless otherwise noted, financial data are reported in U.S. dollars at the 1997 average exchange rate. For a more complete statement of the types of organizations included, see Chapter 1 and Appendix B.

# Principal Findings

## 1. Significant presence in the Norwegian economy

The civil society sector occupies a prominent role in Norway's economy and society. More specifically:

- **A $5.5 billion industry.** Civil society organizations in Norway accounted for $5.5 billion in expenditures in 1997, or 3.7 percent of the nation's gross domestic product (GDP), as reported in Table 15.1.

- **A significant employer.** Even more impressive is the workforce behind these expenditures, which numbers over 180,000 full-time equivalent (FTE) workers, including religious worship organizations. This represents 8 percent of the country's economically active population, and 10 percent of nonagricultural employment.

- **Outdistances many industries.** Civil society organizations in Norway engage a larger workforce than many industries in the nation. Civil society organization employment exceeds employment in utilities, construction, and transportation, and is nearly 60 percent as great as that in all branches of manufacturing (see Figure 15.1). The civil society sector's

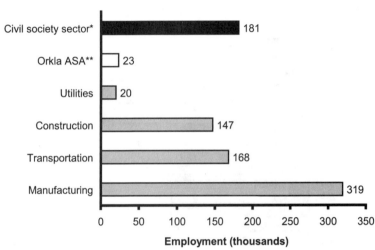

**Figure 15.1.** Civil society organization
workforce in context, Norway

* Including volunteers
** Largest private firm
SOURCE: Johns Hopkins Nonprofit Sector Project

paid employment alone outdistances that of the largest private firm, Orkla ASA, by a factor of 3 to 1 (66,243 vs. 23,378 FTE workers).[4]

• **One of the highest volunteer participation rates in the world.** There are over 115,000 FTE volunteers in Norway, which represents 4.4 percent of the economically active population (see Table 1.8). However, it is estimated that the actual number of people doing some kind of volunteer work is much higher (over 1.8 million) because most volunteers do not work full-time. This represents 52 percent of the adult population, giving Norway one of the highest volunteer participation rates in the world (see Appendix Table A.2).

## 2. One of the larger civil society sectors globally

The Norwegian civil society sector is larger than that in most other countries for which we have data.

• **Above the all-country average.** As shown in Figure 15.2, excluding religious worship organizations, for which data are not available for all countries, the civil society organization workforce — paid and volunteer — varies from a high of 14.4 percent of the economically active population in the Netherlands to a low of 0.4 percent in Mexico, with an average of 4.4 percent overall.[5] The Norwegian figure, at 7.2 percent, is thus significantly higher than the all-country average.

**Figure 15.2.** Civil society organization workforce
as a share of the economically active population, by country

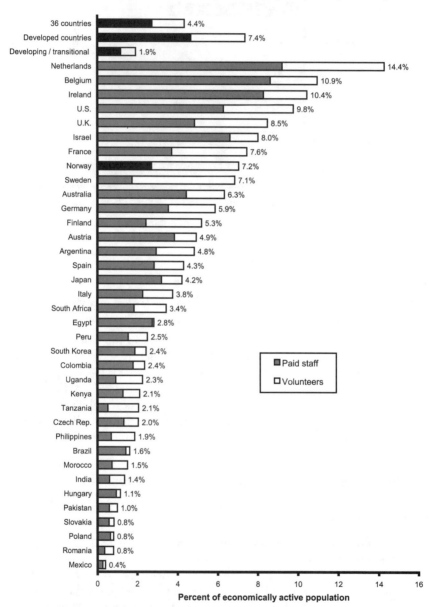

SOURCE: Johns Hopkins Comparative Nonprofit Sector Project

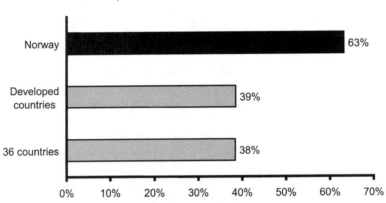

**Figure 15.3.** Volunteers as a share of the civil society organization workforce, Norway, developed countries, and 36 countries

**Percent of civil society organization workforce**

SOURCE: Johns Hopkins Comparative Nonprofit Sector Project

- **Mirrors the developed country average.** Despite a relatively small paid labor force, the overall workforce of the Norwegian civil society sector is on a par with that of other developed countries (7.2 vs. 7.4 percent of the economically active population, respectively).

- **Volunteer participation higher than elsewhere.** The reason for this is the extensive volunteer mobilization in Norway. Expressed in terms of full-time equivalent workers, volunteers represent 4.4 percent of the economically active population in Norway, significantly higher than both the all-country and developed country averages of 1.6 and 2.7 percent, respectively (see Appendix Table A.1). In fact, volunteers constitute 63 percent of the civil society organization workforce in Norway, much higher than the all-country and developed country averages (38 and 39 percent, respectively), as reflected in Figure 15.3.

## 3. A strong tradition of civic engagement

The development of the modern civil society sector in Norway is rooted in the 19th-century nation-building process. Until the beginning of the 20th century, Norway was under foreign rule, first Danish and then Swedish. Beginning in the 1820s, a series of cultural, religious, and societal movements emerged stressing temperance, preservation of local traditions and language, and promotion of sports. As a result, the second half of the 19th century saw the creation of a wide variety of voluntary agencies, such as consumer cooperatives, sports and cultural associations, religious organizations, temperance organizations, and organizations for people with disabilities. These organizations mobilized wide public support for a variety of civic initiatives, from strengthening local traditions and language, to community welfare, to democratic self-governance. In the process, they contributed as well to a strong nationalist movement that ultimately won the country's independence from Sweden in 1905.

Due to a weak aristocratic and merchant tradition, the idea of charity as an independent sphere of activity was never strongly rooted in Norwegian society. Instead, civic, member-based activities gained legitimacy through cooperation with local and central authorities. Local governments generally supported independent citizen initiatives by providing moderate financial support. Local government officials often acted as civic organization leaders. Voluntary agencies, in turn, provided public services in cooperation with those already provided by local public authorities. This close cooperation resulted in a significant integration of public and private service provision.

When government social welfare services were expanded after World War II, many service-providing voluntary agencies were integrated into the public welfare system. Social movement organizations were among the strongest proponents of universal access, but the adoption of the idea of citizen-based rights and universal access to basic human services required a lengthy political struggle involving several parties and political forces. One of the most important steps came in 1967 with Parliament's approval of a social insurance model, which was supported by most political parties. The professional staff of the social services field, for their part, saw integration as a means to modernize and professionalize welfare services and promoted this integration.

While civil society welfare-service providers were slowly absorbed into the national welfare system, new types of organizations emerged during the 1960s focusing on social and leisure activities and advocacy on behalf of disadvantaged groups (e.g., people with disabilities). Sports and cultural associations in particular retained a considerable degree of autonomy from government even though they received considerable government support. In many rural areas, however, traditional social and cultural movement organizations maintained high visibility and support.

A new neo-liberal ideological climate in the 1980s, which challenged the universal social welfare model and centralized welfare planning, created renewed public interest in the civil society sector, and a more results-oriented and instrumental relationship with the service providers. Local authorities took various measures, such as establishing volunteer centers, to promote public participation, and private foundations were used more extensively as tools to achieve public policy goals.

Although the role of civil society organizations has changed over time, Norway clearly has a strong tradition of participation in civic activities.

Associations have traditionally maintained close partnerships with government, in particular through participation in councils, committees, hearings, and corporatist arrangements. These associations still enjoy high legitimacy and trust within political as well as administrative systems and receive considerable government support, which to a large extent is distributed by the associations' own umbrella organizations. However, as shown below, civil society organizations generate an even larger share of their revenue through their own activities, which underscores the vitality of this sector in Norway.

## 4. Strong presence of expressive organizations

Reflecting this history, most of the Norwegian civil society sector workforce is engaged in expressive functions, such as culture and recreation, professions, and advocacy, as is the case in much of Scandinavia and Eastern Europe. More specifically:

- **Expressive activities dominate.** As shown in Figure 15.4, about 61 percent of all Norwegian civil society organization workers — paid and volunteer — are engaged in expressive activities, much higher than elsewhere.[6] This reflects the social movement origins of Norwegian civil society organizations and the absorption of the service components of the civil society sector into the state apparatus with the adoption of social democratic welfare policies after the Second World War.

- **Culture and recreation activities especially prevalent.** Among these expressive functions, culture and recreation organizations are especially prominent, accounting for 41 percent of the Norwegian civil society organization workforce. This figure is almost twice that of the developed country and all-country averages (21 and 19 percent, respectively). However, it is on a par with other Nordic welfare states, where the average is 40 percent (see Table 1.8). This structure of civil society sector employment, which concentrates on culture, recreation, and advocacy rather than on social welfare services, highlights the different role of the civil society sector in social democratic regimes from that found in welfare-partnership and Anglo-Saxon countries.

- **Relatively small share of Norwegian civil society organization workers engaged in service activities.** A considerably smaller 35 percent of paid and volunteer civil society organization workers in Norway are engaged in service activities. This is significantly below both the developed country and all-country averages (64 percent each), though it is on a par with other Nordic welfare states (on average 34 percent of the total civil society organization workforce, as shown in Table 1.8). The main reason for this is that most general welfare service organizations became part of the national social welfare system.

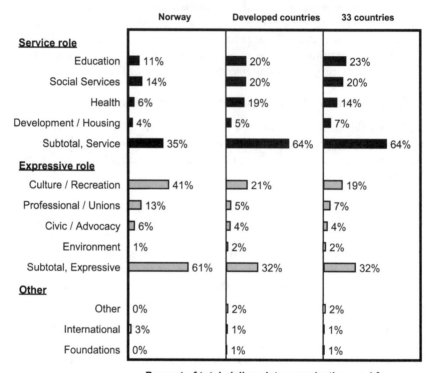

**Figure 15.4.** Composition of the
civil society organization workforce, Norway,
developed countries, and 33-country average

Percent of total civil society organization workforce

n.e.c.= not elsewhere classified

SOURCE: Johns Hopkins Comparative Nonprofit Sector Project

- **Paid and volunteer staff distributed differently.** As in many other countries, the paid and volunteer staff of Norwegian civil society organizations are distributed quite differently. More than three-fourths of the volunteer staff time is concentrated in expressive functions (see Figure 15.5). By contrast, nearly two-thirds of the paid employment is engaged in service functions. This reflects the professionalization of the service fields in Norway.

## 5. Revenue dominated by fees and charges

Fees, charges, and membership dues are the main source of civil society organization revenue in Norway, outdistancing government support and philanthropy. In particular:

**Figure 15.5.** Distribution of paid employees and volunteers between service and expressive activities in Norway

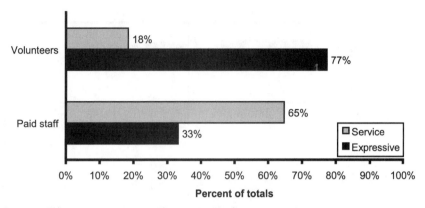

SOURCE: Johns Hopkins Comparative Nonprofit Sector Project

**Figure 15.6.** Sources of civil society organization revenue in Norway

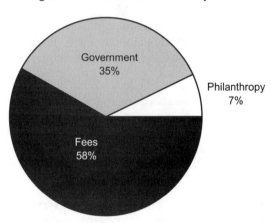

SOURCE: Johns Hopkins Comparative Nonprofit Sector Project

- **Fee dominance in Norway.** About 58 percent of all Norwegian civil society organization cash revenue comes from service fees, property income, and membership dues, as shown in Figure 15.6. Of the balance, 35 percent comes from the public sector and 7 percent from all sources of private philanthropy, including individuals, foundations, and corporations.

**Figure 15.7.** Sources of civil society organization revenue, Norway, developed countries, and 34-country average

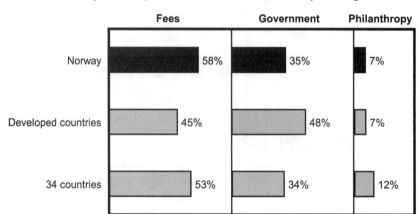

SOURCE: Johns Hopkins Comparative Nonprofit Sector Project

- **Differs from international pattern.** Although this pattern of civil society organization revenue closely parallels that in other Nordic welfare states, it differs significantly from that in other developed countries.

  - The Norwegian civil society sector relies substantially less on government payments than its counterparts in other developed countries, especially in Western Europe. Thus, as shown in Figure 15.7, compared to the 35 percent of civil society organization revenue that comes from public sector payments in Norway, in other developed countries this figure stands at 48 percent. In European-style welfare partnership states it stands at 58 percent (see Table 1.9).

  - Service charges and membership dues represent a larger share of civil society organization revenue in Norway than they do in the developed countries and internationally (58 percent vs. 45 and 53 percent, respectively), as Figure 15.7 also demonstrates.

  - As in most other developed countries, including the other Nordic welfare states, civil society organizations in Norway receive relatively little support from philanthropic giving. As shown in Figure 15.7, the 7 percent of civil society organization revenue in Norway that comes from private giving is below the all-country average (12 percent). It is, however, on a par with both the developed country and Nordic welfare state averages (both 7 percent) (see Table 1.8).

**Figure 15.8.** Sources of civil society organization revenue,
Norway, by field

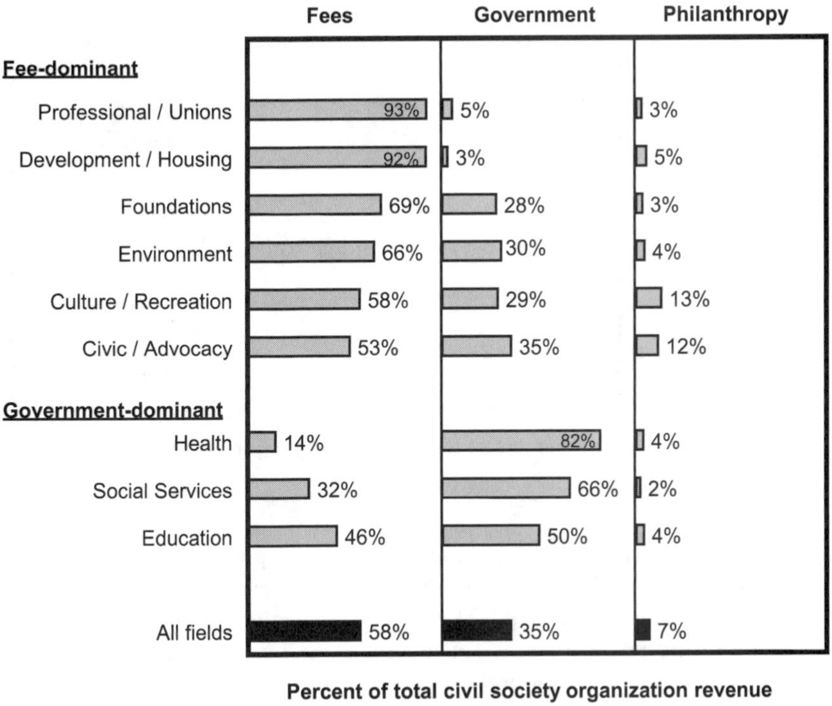

Percent of total civil society organization revenue

SOURCE: Johns Hopkins Comparative Nonprofit Sector Project

- **Support structure varies among fields.** The fee share of total civil society organization revenue is naturally highest among professional associations and labor unions in Norway, where membership dues are the primary revenue source (see Figure 15.8). Fees also dominate in culture/recreation and advocacy. These fees, including proceeds from cafés and rummage sales as well as charges for services rendered to businesses and municipal governments, constitute important sources of income for many volunteer-based organizations in Norway. Government payments dominate revenue in health, social services, and education, though civil society organization involvement in these fields has been limited in the postwar era. As is typical of Nordic welfare states, private philanthropy is not the main revenue source in any field.

- **Volunteers significantly change the revenue structure.** This picture of civil society organization finance changes substantially when the value of volunteer input is included. As Figure 15.9 demonstrates, with volunteers included, private contributions of time and money constitute the largest

**Figure 15.9.** Sources of civil society organization support including volunteers, Norway, developed countries, and 34-country average

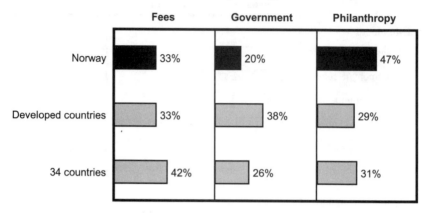

**Percent of total civil society organization support**

SOURCE: Johns Hopkins Comparative Nonprofit Sector Project

source of civil society sector support in Norway, accounting for 47 percent of the total.[7] This is substantially above the developed country and all-country averages (29 and 31 percent, respectively), but on a par with other Nordic welfare states (on average, 45 percent, of the total civil society organization support) (see Table 1.8).

– With the value of volunteer input included, private philanthropy becomes the main source of support in three fields: culture, advocacy, and environmental protection (see Figure 15.10).

## Conclusions and Implications

The development of modern Norwegian civil society is closely linked to the growth of social movements, which were instrumental in mobilizing broad segments of Norwegian society in support of social, cultural, recreational, and political goals. The social movements also provided emerging voluntary associations with a unique identity grounded in notions of social solidarity, local community, and democratic governance rather than philanthropy and charity. While social policy after World War II and the growing professionalization of the social service field resulted in a merger between many voluntary service organizations and the public social welfare system, the social movement principles remained. This time-honored tradition of social movements and grassroots democracy is still visible in the Norwegian civil society sector.

**Figure 15.10.** Sources of civil society organization support
in Norway, including volunteers, by field

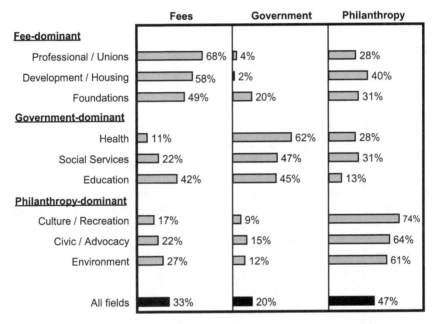

| | Fees | Government | Philanthropy |
|---|---|---|---|
| **Fee-dominant** | | | |
| Professional / Unions | 68% | 4% | 28% |
| Development / Housing | 58% | 2% | 40% |
| Foundations | 49% | 20% | 31% |
| **Government-dominant** | | | |
| Health | 11% | 62% | 28% |
| Social Services | 22% | 47% | 31% |
| Education | 42% | 45% | 13% |
| **Philanthropy-dominant** | | | |
| Culture / Recreation | 17% | 9% | 74% |
| Civic / Advocacy | 22% | 15% | 64% |
| Environment | 27% | 12% | 61% |
| All fields | 33% | 20% | 47% |

**Percent of total civil society organization support**

SOURCE: Johns Hopkins Comparative Nonprofit Sector Project

However, the social movement tradition has been declining steadily since the 1980s. Common values, as an instrument for solidarity and altruistic behavior among members, are diminishing. Many organizations have become professionalized and increasingly commercialized. In a departure from their democratic governance tradition, they are also adopting a leadership-oriented management style that is often at odds with the traditional participatory and grassroots democratic governance structures.

Furthermore, even though many of the older organizations and social movements are still active, their organizational strength and political and cultural influence show signs of weakening. Many of these organizations have departed from the tradition of reliance on ideology, comprehensive political programs, or visions of a "good society" as the means of mobilizing public support and attracting new members. Instead, their appeals are becoming increasingly utilitarian and service-oriented.

Another challenge to the social movement tradition is growing commercialization, which has an adverse effect on volunteer participation.

Associations with broadly defined humanitarian or social goals are gradually being replaced by leisure, sports, and recreational associations, as well as day care centers and community benefit organizations. These newly emerging organizations tend to view their participants as customers rather than members, and activities are perceived as negotiable products. This is, in significant part, a result of new management strategies aimed at increasing the commercial appeal of these organizations at the expense of representing members' interests and values. What is more, the availability of lottery and private funds to civic associations creates competition among civic association leaders and encourages businesslike ways of thinking among the professional staff.

These developments have been encouraged by the neoliberal ideological climate of the 1980s, which transformed the traditional relationship between the government and the civil society organizations providing welfare services from one based on close integration and mutual trust to one infused with a new contract culture focused on competition, time-delimited contracts, legal control, and accountability. However, in culture/recreation and advocacy there is still little dependence on public funding and significant volunteer input, which is a strong reminder, not of a lack of public involvement, but of the vitality of the Norwegian civil society sector in these fields.

How will these challenges affect the civil society sector in Norway? Given its strong social movement roots, the Norwegian civil society sector will not likely surrender its predominantly expressive role. However, if the trend toward commercialization and contract culture continues, this may result in a bifurcation of the civil society sector into a traditional membership-based sphere and a growing pocket of nominally not-for-profit entities providing essentially commercial services to narrowly defined client groups. Although such a bifurcation may have some advantages in the form of increasing service variety, it also poses the danger of compartmentalization and the disappearance of shared values, goals, and overarching ideological projects that have held Norwegian society together. The unintended consequences may be a decline in public participation and citizen connectedness and the weakening of this alternative democratic channel linking citizens through local associations to national public debates.

Perhaps one lesson that may be drawn from this chapter is that while civil society adapts to broader social forces and influences, its strength and resilience strongly depends on its social roots and traditions. The post–World War II social welfare policies transformed the structure of the civil society sector but did not change its essence, which was rooted in the traditions of social movements, grassroots democracy, and partnership with the government. As a result, the Norwegian civil society sector has a strong and distinctive presence on the world "map."

The new challenges posed by commercialization and globalization push the Norwegian civil society sector in a very different direction — that of professionalism and economic efficiency. There are certain benefits associated with this, to be sure. However, it is vitally important to maintain and cultivate the elements of participation and local engagement that gave the Norwegian civil society sector its original strength: a broad membership base, grassroots democracy, expression of shared values, and partnership with government agencies in creating public goods.

## Notes

1. The work in Norway has been coordinated by Håkon Lorentzen, Per Selle, Karl Henrik Sivesind, and Dag Wollebæk. The research team was aided, in turn, by a local advisory committee (see Appendix D for a list of committee members). The Johns Hopkins project was directed by Lester M. Salamon, and the work in Norway was overseen by S. Wojciech Sokolowski.

2. The definitions and approaches used in the project were developed collaboratively with the cooperation of Norwegian researchers and researchers in other countries and were designed to be applicable to Norway and other project countries. For a full description of this definition, the types of organizations included, and the methodology used, see Chapter 1 and Appendix B. For a full list of the other countries included, see Table 1.1.

3. V. Helander and K.H. Sivesind, "Frivilligsektorns betydelse i Norden (The Impact of the Voluntary Sector in the Nordic Countries)," in *Frivillighedens udfordringer (The Challenges of Volunteering)*, ed. L. Skov Henriksen and B. Ibsen (Odense, Norway: Odense Universitetsforlag, 2001), 49–66; K.H. Sivesind, H. Lorentzen, P. Selle, and D. Wollebæk, *The Voluntary Sector in Norway – Composition, Changes, and Causes*, Report No. 2 (Oslo: Institute for Social Research, 2002); D. Wollebæk and P. Selle, *Det nye organisasjonssamfunnet – Demokrati i omforming (The New Organization Community – Democracy in Change)* (Bergen, Norway: Fagbokforlaget, 2002); D. Wollebæk, and P. Selle, "Does Participation in Voluntary Associations Contribute to Social Capital? The Importance of Intensity, Scope and Type," *Nonprofit and Voluntary Sector Quarterly* 31 (2002): 32–61; D. Wollebæk, P. Selle, and H. Lorentzen, *Frivillig innsats (Voluntary Contributions)* (Bergen, Norway: Fagbokforlaget, 2002).

4. Orkla ASA is the largest among firms that have more than half of their workforce in Norway.

5. Comparative figures do not include religious worship organizations because data on these organizations were not available for all countries. However, religiously affiliated service organizations are included. For more information, see Appendix B.

6. Percentages displayed in figures may not add to 100 due to rounding.

7. This figure assumes, of course, that volunteer and paid work are roughly equivalent in value.

# Chapter 16

# Poland

Ewa Leś, Sławomir Nałęcz, Stefan Toepler,
S. Wojciech Sokolowski, and Lester M. Salamon

## Introduction

Civil society in Poland has been shaped by contradictory historical forces
that stymied some of its forms while promoting the development of others.
The loss of national independence in the 18th century, and the long history
of economic underdevelopment that persisted into the 19th century arrested
the development of civic institutions in Poland. At the same time, organized
religion, especially the Roman Catholic Church and Jewish communities,
opened a space for civil society activity and encouraged cultural, self-help,
and charitable organizations to operate, particularly once Poland regained
national sovereignty in 1918.

The German occupation during World War II and the Soviet takeover
afterward destroyed these institutions and led to the development of large,
centralized membership organizations, especially in the fields of culture and
professional associations, but hindered the development of service-oriented
entities. Most private charities and foundations were dissolved, and the
provision of social services was transferred to the state.

At the same time, a strong tradition of relatively independent Catholic clergy kept the flame of independent citizen action alive in Poland,
though with limited opportunities to manifest itself publicly. As a result,
Poles learned to depend more on informal social networks than on formal
institutions in their everyday life, and even in their political affairs.

This situation changed only in the late 1970s and 1980s with the emergence of informal civil society networks and ultimately the independent trade
union movement, Solidarnosc, which then produced the sweeping political
and economic reforms that marked the end of the central planning era.

These aspects of Polish history are reflected in the contours of the civil
society sector as revealed by the data presented in this chapter. Although the
democratic reforms of 1989 unleashed a boom of civil society formation in
the country, the past continues to weigh heavily on the new organizations
that emerged in their aftermath. As a result, the Polish civil society sector

as of the late 1990s remains quite small both absolutely and relative to other countries, with few paid staff, limited volunteer participation, and a focus primarily on cultural and leisure activities. Nevertheless, it remains a significant presence and an important agent of social change and has been gradually overcoming the obstacles to its growth.

These findings emerge from a body of work carried out by a Polish research team in cooperation with the Polish Central Statistical Office and the KLON/JAWOR Foundation, as part of the Johns Hopkins Comparative Nonprofit Sector Project.[1] This work sought both to analyze Polish civil society organizations and to compare and contrast them to those in other countries in Central and Eastern Europe and elsewhere in a systematic way.[2] The result is the first empirical overview of the Polish civil society sector and the first systematic comparison of Polish civil society realities to those elsewhere in the world.[3]

This chapter reports chiefly on the major descriptive findings of this project relating to the size, composition, and financing of the civil society sector in Poland and other countries. Other reports will fill in more of the history, legal position, and impact of this set of institutions. Most of the data reported here were generated from the 1997 census of nonprofit organizations and a 1997 survey of employment carried out by the Polish Central Statistical Office (GUS). These results were supplemented by surveys conducted by the project team and publicly available statistics compiled by GUS. Unless otherwise noted, financial data are reported in U.S. dollars at the 1997 average exchange rate. For a more complete statement of the types of organizations included, see Chapter 1 and Appendix B.

## Principal Findings

### 1. Civil society sector in Poland embryonic, but sizable

Perhaps the most salient feature of the Polish civil society sector is its small size relative to the Polish economy. Nevertheless, these organizations represent a significant presence in Polish social and economic life. In particular:

- **A $1.9 billion industry.** As of the late 1990s, Poland's civil society sector had expenditures of $1.9 billion, or 1.3 percent of the Polish gross domestic product (GDP), as reported in Table 16.1.

- **A sizable employer.** Behind these expenditures lies a sizable workforce numbering over 150,000 full-time equivalent (FTE) workers, including church-affiliated organizations (but not churches themselves), of which approximately 80 percent are paid staff and 20 percent are volunteers. This represents less than 1 percent of the country's economically active population, and 3.2 percent of public employment. However, this may

**Table 16.1.** The civil society sector* in Poland, 1997

---

**$1.9 billion in expenditures**

- 1.3% of the GDP

**156,070 full-time equivalent workers**

- 122,944 full-time equivalent paid employees
- 33,126 full-time equivalent volunteers
- 0.8% of the economically active population
- 1.5% of nonagricultural employment
- 3.2% of public employment

---

* Including religious worship organizations.

SOURCE: Johns Hopkins Comparative Nonprofit Sector Project

understate the scale of the workforce that the Polish civil society sector mobilizes because volunteering is highly sporadic, with volunteers working only a limited number of hours, often only in response to particular appeals. In addition, Polish organizations often hire staff as independent contractors rather than wage employees to reduce their social security tax liabilities. Therefore, these employees may not be fully reflected in our data. While this problem exists in other Central and Eastern European countries, it may be particularly problematic in Poland due to the magnitude of informal networks and the "shadow economy."[4] The total number of people who take some part in the work of civil society organizations in Poland is therefore higher than these data suggest. In fact, our survey data suggest that the actual number of people who do some volunteer work in Poland is quite high, exceeding 3.6 million people, which is about 12 percent of the adult population (see Appendix Table A.2).[5]

- **Smaller than most industries.** Civil society sector employment in Poland is lower than that in most industries, such as utilities (water and electricity supply), transportation, construction, or manufacturing (see Figure 16.1). However, it still outdistances the country's largest private business enterprises. Thus, for example, almost ten times more people work for Polish civil society organizations than for the largest private company, Daewoo-FSO.

## 2. One of the smallest civil society sectors

The size of the civil society sector in Poland is relatively small in comparison to that in other countries.

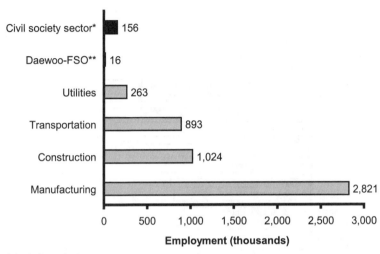

**Figure 16.1.** Civil society organization
workforce in context, Poland

\* Including volunteers
\*\* Largest private firm
SOURCE: Johns Hopkins Nonprofit Sector Project

- **Below the all-country average.** As shown in Figure 16.2, excluding religious worship organizations, the civil society organization workforce — paid and volunteer — expressed as a share of the economically active population, varies from a high of 14.4 percent in the Netherlands to a low of 0.4 percent in Mexico, with an average of 4.4 percent overall. The Polish figure, at 0.8 percent, is thus well below the all-country average.[6]

- **Below the developing and transitional country average.** The Polish civil society organization workforce also lags behind that elsewhere in both Central and Eastern Europe and other developing and transitional countries. Thus, the civil society organization workforce in Poland is below the Central and Eastern European average of 1.1 percent (see Table 1.14) and half the developing and transitional country average of 1.9 percent of the economically active population.

- **Volunteer workforce lower than elsewhere.** The extent of volunteer participation in Polish civil society organizations is also significantly less than both the developing and transitional country and all-country averages. Translated into full-time equivalent workers, the volunteer staff of Polish civil society organizations account for only 0.2 percent of the economically active population, or only a third of the average in the developing and transitional countries (0.7 percent) and one-eighth the all-country

**Figure 16.2.** Civil society organization workforce
as a share of the economically active population, by country

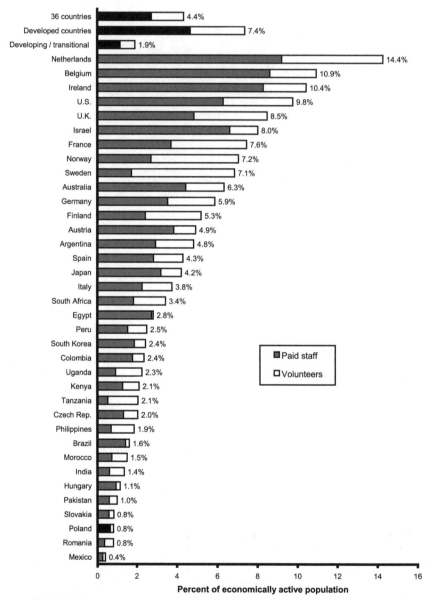

SOURCE: Johns Hopkins Comparative Nonprofit Sector Project

**Figure 16.3.** Volunteers as a share of the
civil society organization workforce, Poland,
developing and transitional countries, and 36 countries

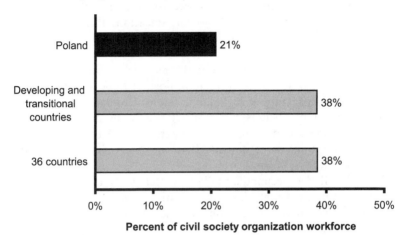

**Percent of civil society organization workforce**

SOURCE: Johns Hopkins Comparative Nonprofit Sector Project

average (1.6 percent) (see Table 1.14). Volunteers represent only 21 percent of the full-time equivalent civil society organization workforce in Poland, substantially less than the developing and transitional and all-country averages (38 percent each), as reflected in Figure 16.3. At the same time, as noted earlier, 12 percent of the adult population engages in some volunteer activity, albeit on a sporadic basis.

## 3. A complex history of civil society development

Several factors account for the relatively modest scale of the civil society sector in Poland. Feudalism and foreign domination, as well as Soviet-controlled state socialism after World War II, were the key forces inhibiting the growth of the civil society sector in this country.

Unlike Western Europe, where the decline of feudalism by the 13th century spurred the growth of cities that fostered self-governance and created fertile ground for civic and professional associations, Poland was saddled with a powerful landed elite that opposed urbanization and efforts at modernization well into the 19th century.[7]

Contributing to this outcome was the fact that Poland lost its independence in the late 18th century and remained under foreign rule until the end of World War I. The ruling Russian and Prussian powers effectively suppressed attempts at Polish self-governance and severely curtailed freedom of association. Many political and cultural activities were restricted or forbidden, so they were often conducted underground under the cover of religious, benevolent, or social associations, including sports or hunting clubs. During this period, a number of formal and informal associations, including foundations, social and economic societies, mutual benefit associations, and cooperatives were formed to take on functions not being performed by public institutions. These organizations also helped to bolster the national spirit, mobilize independence movements, and preserve Polish culture.[8]

Jewish communities, which accounted for a third of the Polish urban population prior to World War II, were an important force in the development of civil society organizations in Poland. These self-governing communities maintained hospitals, shelters, burial societies, schools, and theaters, as well as trade and credit associations and cooperatives.[9] All these communities and their institutions were destroyed by the Nazi occupation of Poland during World War II, however.

World War II also decimated the Polish intelligentsia, which became one of the primary targets of the Nazi extermination campaign, further inhibiting the growth of voluntary associations that had begun to develop during the interwar period.

The Soviet-style central planning, or state socialism, regime that gained power after World War II permitted civic associations to operate in limited areas, such as sports, recreation and culture, and professions, but under tight state controls. Other types of organizations, especially those formed before World War II or created by independent citizen initiative, were either dissolved or denied legal recognition despite a constitutional guarantee of freedom of association. What is more, the relatively generous government social welfare programs put in place by the central planning regime further inhibited the growth of civil society organizations, especially since state authorities rarely contracted out government programs to nongovernmental entities.[10] The few organizations that received government contracts included the Polish Red Cross and associations serving the handicapped. Although these policies gave rise to a new urban professional class, it would take decades before this could translate itself into leadership of civic associations capable of challenging the state socialist regime.

The fall of state socialism in Poland in 1989 led to the lifting of legal restrictions on civil society organizations[11] and the formation of 23,000 new associations and nearly 3,000 foundations between 1990 and 1992.[12] Most of these were independent schools, self-help, or recreational groups aiming to satisfy needs that had not been met by existing state or commercial agencies, or service-oriented organizations formed by professionals to introduce new services such as hospice care, therapy, or rehabilitation. Some were set up as auxiliary mechanisms for collecting fees for nominally free services provided by public hospitals and schools. However, unlike their Western counterparts, these organizations generally received little or no government support. At the same time, the existing leisure, recreational, and cultural organizations formed during the central planning era sought to consolidate their position in the new environment, often laying claim to former state resources in the new era of privatization.

## 4. Strong presence of expressive organizations

Reflecting this history, the Polish civil society organization workforce is almost evenly divided between service and expressive activities. However, in comparison to other countries, an unusually large share of the Polish civil society sector workforce is engaged in essentially expressive functions such as sports, recreation, culture, and professional associations as opposed to service functions such as development, health, social services, and education. More specifically:

- **More civil society organization workers engaged in expressive activities than elsewhere.** As shown in Figure 16.4, 46 percent of civil society organization workers in Poland, paid and volunteer, are engaged in activities of an expressive variety.[13] This is slightly below the overall Central and Eastern European average of 50 percent (see Table 1.14) but significantly higher than the developing and transitional country average and the all-country average (32 percent each).

- **Culture and professional activities especially prevalent.** Among these expressive functions, cultural and professional organizations are especially prominent, accounting for 33 and 11 percent, respectively, of the Polish civil society organization workforce. These figures are roughly comparable to the Central and Eastern European average (34 and 9 percent, respectively) but well ahead of the all-country average (19 and 7 percent, respectively). This structure of civil society organization employment reflects the pattern of civil society development that emerged during the communist era, which sanctioned citizen organizations for essentially cultural, recreational, or professional pursuits. Most of these large-scale organizations split into much smaller locally controlled entities after 1989. This restructuring was closely related to the decentralization of public administration during this period.

- **Fewer civil society organization workers engaged in service activities than elsewhere.** About half of all Polish civil society organization workers, paid and volunteer, are engaged in service activities. This is considerably less than the developing and transitional country average (63 percent) and the all-country average (64 percent), although similar to the Central and Eastern European average of 45 percent (see Table 1.14). This situation very likely reflects the state socialist practice of building a substantial public social welfare system and the limited use that the state has

284   *Leś, Nałęcz, Toepler, Sokolowski, and Salamon*

**Figure 16.4.** Composition of the
civil society organization workforce, Poland,
developing and transitional countries, and 33-country average

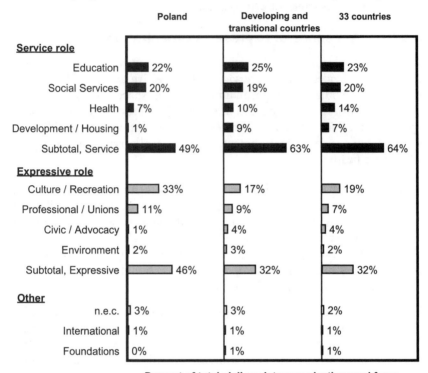

**Percent of total civil society organization workforce**

n.e.c.= not elsewhere classified

SOURCE: Johns Hopkins Comparative Nonprofit Sector Project

made of civil society organizations to deliver state-financed social welfare
services.

- **Little difference in the composition of paid and volunteer staff.** Unlike
many other countries, the distribution of paid and volunteer staff in Polish civil society organizations does not differ much, as both are split
roughly evenly between service and expressive activities, as shown in Figure 16.5. Interestingly, volunteers seem disproportionately attracted to
social service activities (28 percent of volunteer time vs. 17 percent of
paid staff time). This likely reflects the Polish population's responsiveness
to special appeals during natural disasters and the role that civil society
organizations have come to play in compensating for inadequate public
services.

**Figure 16.5.** Distribution of paid employees and volunteers
between service and expressive activities in Poland

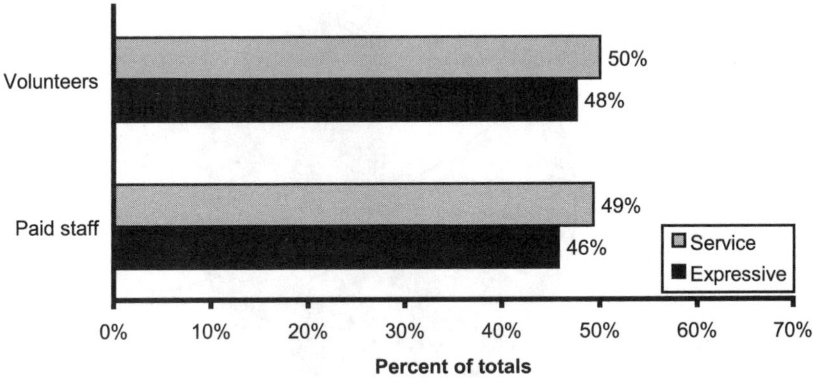

SOURCE: Johns Hopkins Comparative Nonprofit Sector Project

## 5. Revenue dominated by fees and charges

Fees, charges, and membership dues are the main sources of civil society organization revenue in Poland, outdistancing government support and philanthropy. In particular:

- **Fee dominance in Poland.** About 60 percent of all Polish civil society organization cash revenue comes from service fees, property income, and membership dues, as shown in Figure 16.6. Included here are fees for services provided by these organizations. Of the balance, 24 percent comes from the public sector, and 15 percent from all sources of private philanthropy, including individuals, foundations, and corporations.

- **Differs from international pattern.** Although this pattern of civil society organization revenue closely parallels that in other developing and transitional countries, it differs significantly from that evident internationally, and also from that evident elsewhere in Central and Eastern Europe (see Table 1.14).

  - Like other Central and Eastern European countries, the Polish civil society sector relies more heavily on private philanthropy than is common internationally. Thus, as shown in Figure 16.7, the 15 percent of Polish civil society organization revenue that comes from philanthropy is above the all-country average (12 percent). However, it is slightly below the developing and transitional country average of 17 percent and below the Central and Eastern Europe average of 20 percent (see Table 1.14). There are several reasons for this paradoxical pattern of unusually heavy reliance on philanthropy in formerly socialist Poland. Many Polish public institutions, such as hospitals and schools, faced funding

**Figure 16.6.** Sources of civil society
organization revenue in Poland

Philanthropy 15%

Fees 60%

Government 24%

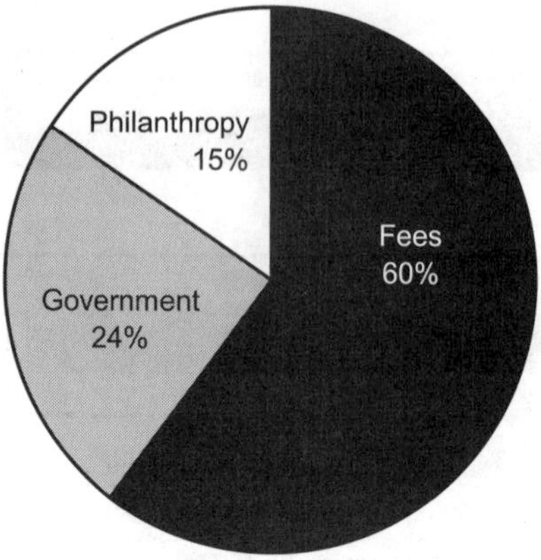

SOURCE: Johns Hopkins Comparative Nonprofit Sector Project

shortages after 1989 but were legally prohibited from charging fees for their services. To supplement their finances, some of these institutions established nominally separate foundations that collected donations in lieu of service fees. Furthermore, nearly half of the private philanthropy reported here is derived from foreign sources, including foundations and government support channeled through private voluntary organizations. Poland received one-third of all European Union Poland and Hungary Aid in Restructuring the Economy (PHARE) grants to Central and Eastern Europe.[14] In 1997, foreign aid accounted for 7 percent of all revenues received by the civil society sector in Poland.[15]

– Like other developing and transitional countries, Polish civil society organizations receive far less public sector support than is common internationally, and certainly less than is common elsewhere in Europe. As shown in Figure 16.7, the 24 percent of civil society organization revenue in Poland that comes from government sources is slightly above the developing and transitional country average (22 percent), but well below the Central and Eastern European average of 31 percent (see Table 1.14), the all-country average of 34 percent, and the European-style welfare partnership country average of 58 percent (see Table 1.9). This relatively low level of government support reflects the heritage of the state socialism era's limits on government contracting with civil society organizations, the neglect of human services by public authorities during the 1990s, and the creeping commercialization of many service fields. In turn, this limited government support helps to explain the relatively small scale of the Polish civil society sector.

**Figure 16.7.** Sources of civil society organization revenue,
Poland, developing and transitional countries,
and 34-country average

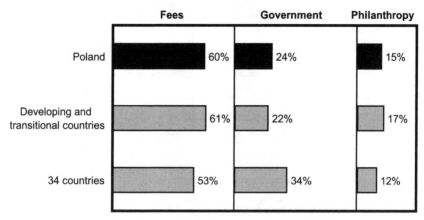

**Percent of total civil society organization revenue**

SOURCE: Johns Hopkins Comparative Nonprofit Sector Project

- With government support limited and private philanthropy also constrained, Polish civil society organizations, like their counterparts in many developed and transitional countries, have had to rely much more heavily on fees than is generally common either internationally or in European-style welfare partnership countries (see Table 1.9).

- **Fee dominance evident in most fields.** This pattern of fee dominance in the revenue stream of Polish civil society organizations is evident in all activity fields except civic and advocacy.

  - The fee share of total revenue is naturally highest among professional associations and labor unions (86 percent), where membership dues are the primary revenue source (see Figure 16.8). But it is also quite high in education (70 percent), housing and development (67 percent), culture and recreation (56 percent), and even social services and health (both 49 percent).

  - In only one field, civic and advocacy, is fee income not the dominant source of revenue. Rather, private donations are the dominant source of support (51 percent) in this field, the only one in Poland's civil society sector where this is the case. The environmental field, where private philanthropy almost edges out fee income (45 vs. 46 percent), is very similar in this respect, but private donations for environmental organizations come mainly from abroad.

**Figure 16.8.** Sources of civil society organization revenue, Poland, by field

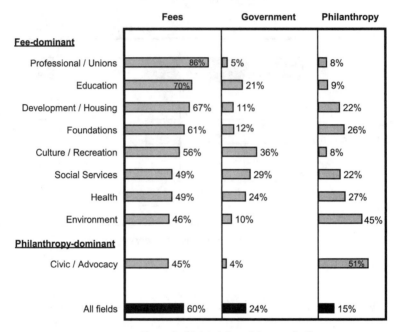

**Percent of total civil society organization revenue**

SOURCE: Johns Hopkins Comparative Nonprofit Sector Project

**Figure 16.9.** Sources of civil society organization support including volunteers, Poland, developing and transitional countries, and 34-country average

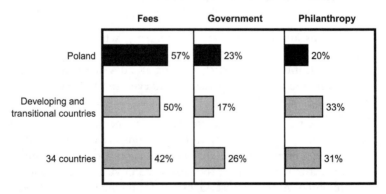

**Percent of total civil society organization support**

SOURCE: Johns Hopkins Comparative Nonprofit Sector Project

**Figure 16.10.** Sources of civil society organization support
in Poland, including volunteers, by field

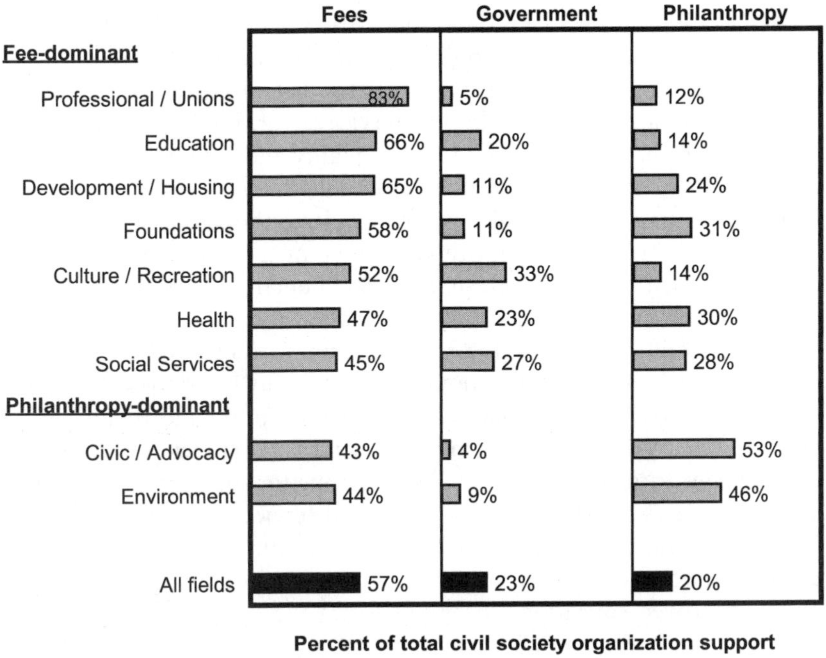

Percent of total civil society organization support

SOURCE: Johns Hopkins Comparative Nonprofit Sector Project

- **Volunteers do not significantly change the revenue structure.** This picture
  does not change much when the value of volunteer input is included. As
  Figure 16.9 demonstrates, with volunteers included, the share of Polish
  civil society organization income that comes from philanthropy increases
  only from 15 to 20 percent. This is below the developing and transitional
  country average (33 percent) and the all-country average (31 percent).

  – Including volunteers moves only one additional field, environment,
    into the philanthropy dominant category. All other fields rely primarily
    on fee support (see Figure 16.10).

## Conclusions and Implications

The data reported here thus reveal a civil society sector in Poland that is
considerably more limited in scale and capacities than in most other countries, including many countries in far less developed parts of the world. That
this is so is due to the continued hold of structures and attitudes that Poland

inherited from its past, and to the ambiguous policies that Polish governments have pursued toward this set of institutions since the dismantling of the central planning system in 1989.

Despite the fact that the Polish civil society sector commands a rather small workforce, however, it would be misleading to conclude that the sector is insignificant. Perhaps its main role has been to provide a venue for innovation in transforming the human service sector. While the state bureaucracy provided basic human services, the quality and range of these services fell far below expectations, creating enormous frustrations on the part of both citizens and human service professionals. Although basic needs, such as education, child care, or health care, were met, though often in an unsatisfactory way, rehabilitation, support, and human services were generally neglected and remained in very short supply.[16]

The democratic reform of 1989 opened unprecedented opportunities for reforming the ossified central planning system. Many health or social service professionals who for years had called for reform of the health and human service sector now had a chance to put their ideas into practice. Civil society organizations turned out to be a valuable venue for such professional innovation. Newly established entities introduced services hitherto absent from the Polish service market such as hospice care, innovative forms of physical therapy, post-surgical rehabilitation, and substance abuse prevention, as well as improved educational offerings for talented youth.[17] Although the scale of these operations was relatively small, they had a significant impact on the Polish service sector as demonstration projects. Unlike their Western counterparts, however, these service organizations were financed mainly by fees and private donations and received very little government support. This helps explain why the civil society sector in Poland remains rather small and includes a relatively large share of sports and recreational activities.

This, in turn, suggests the continuing challenge facing Polish civil society organizations after the 1989 democratic breakthrough, for the various political coalitions in power since 1989 have pursued a highly ambiguous set of policies toward these organizations. To be sure, at the most fundamental level, there was a firm consensus among all political elites that voluntary organizations are an indispensable element of a democratic system. This consensus was enshrined in those parts of the general legal framework that guarantee the principles that underpin civil society organizations, especially the freedom of expression and the freedom of association. After these general principles were put in place, however, there was considerably less eagerness on the part of subsequent governments to establish a sound legal and financial basis for civil society organizations to deliver public services and advocate for public causes.

The evolution of Polish civil society organizations since 1989 thus has not proceeded without paradoxes and, in many ways, remains unfinished.

Among the most striking paradox is that the government continues to over-look these organizations as meaningful social partners in service delivery and in formulating public policy agendas. Also under-recognized is the po-tential capacity of these entities to complement and enhance government service provision. In addition to the often highly unpredictable, and at times chaotic, government policies towards this set of institutions, other crucial external and internal challenges include:

- **Privatization of the state welfare system.** The neo-liberal strategy that dominates the effort to reconstruct the state welfare system has given priority to market and quasi-market institutions at the expense of civil society organizations. While the importance of civil society for democratic development is recognized in general terms, its role as a full-fledged *part-ner* of both central and local governments in service delivery has thus not yet been fully embraced by the political elite.

- **Fostering legitimacy through self-regulation.** Despite some important progress, the development and enforcement of codes of conduct, ac-countability, and administrative standards on the part of civil society organizations remain key tasks facing the civil society sector in Poland.

- **Capacity building and sustainability.** During the first few years after 1989, Polish civil society organizations developed some 300 networks and umbrella groups at both the local and national levels. The National Fed-eration of Non-Governmental Organizations, which represents the entire civil society sector in Poland, as well as the Forum of Non-Governmental Initiatives, the Union of Catholic Associations and Movements, and the Union of Social Service Non-Profit Organizations are the most prominent examples of such national umbrella organizations. Despite this growing infrastructure, however, most civil society organizations in Poland still do not identify themselves as part of a separate "third sector" and have not perceived the need for self-organization. In Poland, as in other countries of Central and Eastern Europe, it is thus crucially important to continue to develop academic training programs and capacity-building efforts to enhance the professionalization of civil society organizations. In addition, constant efforts are needed to promote and strengthen voluntary partic-ipation as well as to build meaningful relationships with the corporate sector.

Taken together, these external and internal challenges limit the ability of civil society organizations to address social issues, meet human needs, and prevent the social marginalization of minority groups as well as the frag-mentation of Polish society. Although these institutions show remarkable initiative and ingenuity in addressing social needs and solving rapidly mount-ing social problems, resource insufficiency and political instability impede the full realization of their vast potential. It is hoped that the kind of data generated within this project will help overcome these hurdles and allow Polish society to tap more fully into the potential of civil society organizations in this period of major social and economic change.

## Notes

1. The work in Poland has been coordinated by Ewa Leś (University of Warsaw), assisted by Sławomir Nałęcz (Polish Academy of Science) with some participation of Jan Jakub Wygnański (KLON/JAWOR). The research team was aided, in turn, by a local advisory committee made up of 14 prominent academics, government and parliamentary officials, and nonprofit leaders (see Appendix D for a list of committee members). The Johns Hopkins project was directed by Lester M. Salamon, and the work in Poland was overseen by Stefan Toepler and S. Wojciech Sokolowski.

2. The definitions and approaches used in the project were developed collaboratively with the cooperation of Polish researchers and researchers in other countries and were designed to be applicable to Poland and other project countries. For a full description of this definition, the types of organizations included, and the methodology used, see Chapter 1 and Appendix B. For a full list of the other countries included, see Table 1.1.

3. Some systematic comparison between the Polish civil society sector and those elsewhere in Central and Eastern Europe is available in the U.S. Agency for International Development's NGO Sustainability Index. However, this source relies chiefly on subjective judgments by teams of country experts and does not seek to generate empirical measures of the scale of civil society activity either in Poland or elsewhere in the Central European region. See: U.S. Agency for International Development, *NGO Sustainability Index for Central and Eastern Europe and Eurasia* (Washington, D.C.: USAID, 2002).

4. Janine R. Wedel, ed. *The Unplanned Society: Poland During and After Communism* (New York: Columbia University Press, 1992).

5. That figure does not include church volunteering, which by some estimates can reach up to 2 million. However, many of the church volunteers also work for lay organizations, and these are included in our estimates reported above. What is more, the number of volunteers was unusually high in 1997 (up to 25 percent of the adult population according to some estimates) as a result of a spontaneous response to a natural disaster (flooding). Subsequent surveys (1999 European Values Survey, Policy 2000, SMA/KRC, KLON, 2001) show much lower participation rates, about 10 percent of the respondents.

6. Comparative figures do not include religious worship organizations because data on these organizations were not available for all countries. However, religiously affiliated service organizations are included. For more information, see Appendix B.

7. Aleksander Gella, *Development of Class Structure in Eastern Europe: Poland and Her Southern Neighbors* (Albany, NY: State University of New York Press, 1989).

8. Ewa Leś, *Zarys historii dobroczynności i filantropii w Polsce* (*Charity and Philanthropy in Poland: An Overview*) (Warszawa: Proszynski i S-ka, 2001), 152–153.

9. Marian Fuks, *Żydzi w Warszawie: życie codzienne, wydarzenia, ludzie* (*Jews in Warsaw: Everyday Life, Events, and People*) (Poznan, Poland: Sorus, 1997).

10. Ewa Leś, "Poland," in *Social Welfare in Socialist Countries,* ed. John Dixon and David Macarow (New York: Routledge, 1992).

11. Ewa Leś, *The Voluntary Nonprofit Sector in Post-Communist East Central Europe* (Washington: Civicus, 1994).

12. Sławomir Nałęcz, "Organizacje społeczeństwa obywatelskiego w III RP" (Civil Society Organizations in the III Republic of Poland), in *Budowanie instytucji państwa: w poszukiwaniu modelu, 1989–2001,* ed. Irena Jackiewicz (Warszawa: Wydawnictwa Sejmowe, 2003).

13. Percentages displayed in figures may not add to 100 due to rounding.

14. Janine R. Wedel, *Collision and Collusion: The Strange Case of Western Aid to Eastern Europe 1989–1998* (New York: St. Martin's Press, 1998).

15. Sławomir Nałęcz, "Organizacje społeczeństwa obywatelskiego w III RP" (Civil Society Organizations in the III Republic of Poland), in *Budowanie instytucji państwa: w poszukiwaniu modelu, 1989–2001,* ed. Irena Jackiewicz (Warszawa: Wydawnictwa Sejmowe, 2003).

16. Magdalena Sokołowska and Bożena Moskalewicz, "Health Sector Structures: The Case of Poland," *Social Science and Medicine* 24, no. 9 (1987): 736–775.

17. S. Wojciech Sokolowski, *Civil Society and the Professions in Eastern Europe: Social Change and Organizational Innovation in Poland* (New York: Kluwer Academic / Plenum Publishers, 2001).

# Appendix A

# Comparative Tables

**Table A.1.** Civil society sector workforce* as a percent of the
economically active population, 36 countries

| Country | Paid staff | Volunteers | Total |
|---|---|---|---|
| Argentina | 2.9% | 1.9% | 4.8% |
| Australia | 4.4% | 1.9% | 6.3% |
| Austria | 3.8% | 1.1% | 4.9% |
| Belgium | 8.6% | 2.3% | 10.9% |
| Brazil | 1.4% | 0.2% | 1.6% |
| Colombia | 1.8% | 0.6% | 2.4% |
| Czech Rep. | 1.3% | 0.7% | 2.0% |
| Egypt | 2.7% | 0.1% | 2.8% |
| Finland | 2.4% | 2.8% | 5.3% |
| France | 3.7% | 3.7% | 7.6% |
| Germany | 3.5% | 2.3% | 5.9% |
| Hungary | 0.9% | 0.2% | 1.1% |
| India | 0.6% | 0.8% | 1.4% |
| Ireland | 8.3% | 2.1% | 10.4% |
| Israel | 6.6% | 1.4% | 8.0% |
| Italy | 2.3% | 1.5% | 3.8% |
| Japan | 3.2% | 1.0% | 4.2% |
| Kenya | 1.3% | 0.8% | 2.1% |
| Mexico | 0.3% | 0.1% | 0.4% |
| Morocco | 0.7% | 0.8% | 1.5% |
| Netherlands | 9.2% | 5.1% | 14.4% |
| Norway | 2.7% | 4.4% | 7.2% |
| Pakistan | 0.6% | 0.4% | 1.0% |
| Peru | 1.5% | 0.9% | 2.5% |
| Philippines | 0.7% | 1.2% | 1.9% |
| Poland | 0.6% | 0.2% | 0.8% |
| Romania | 0.4% | 0.4% | 0.8% |
| Slovakia | 0.6% | 0.2% | 0.8% |
| South Africa | 1.8% | 1.6% | 3.4% |
| South Korea | 1.9% | 0.6% | 2.4% |
| Spain | 2.8% | 1.5% | 4.3% |
| Sweden | 1.7% | 5.1% | 7.1% |
| Tanzania | 0.5% | 1.5% | 2.1% |
| Uganda | 0.9% | 1.3% | 2.3% |
| United Kingdom | 4.8% | 3.6% | 8.5% |
| United States | 6.3% | 3.5% | 9.8% |
| | | | |
| Developing / transitional | 1.2% | 0.7% | 1.9% |
| Developed | 4.7% | 2.7% | 7.4% |
| 36 countries | 2.7% | 1.6% | 4.4% |

* Excludes religious worship organizations.

SOURCE: Johns Hopkins Comparative Nonprofit Sector Project

**Table A.2.** Volunteering, 36 countries

| Country | Value of volunteer work (millions US $) | People volunteering* number (thousands) | percent of adult pop. |
|---|---|---|---|
| Argentina | $2,693.2 | 1,913 | 8% |
| Australia | $4,484.8 | 1,832 | 13% |
| Austria | $1,380.4 | 550 | 8% |
| Belgium | $4,197.7 | 809 | 10% |
| Brazil | $754.1 | 6,483 | 6% |
| Colombia | $229.1 | 1,149 | 5% |
| Czech Rep. | $196.4 | 381 | 5% |
| Egypt | $22.1 | 233 | 1% |
| Finland | $2,657.5 | 326 | 8% |
| France | $41,929.6 | 6,536 | 14% |
| Germany | $48,433.0 | 7,071 | 10% |
| Hungary | $49.7 | 277 | 3% |
| India | $1,355.9 | 16,490 | 2% |
| Ireland | $715.6 | 293 | 11% |
| Israel | $894.7 | 235 | 6% |
| Italy | $8,290.7 | 2,048 | 4% |
| Japan | $23,354.8 | 485 | 0.5% |
| Kenya | $52.0 | 955 | 6% |
| Mexico | $219.6 | 30 | 0.1% |
| Morocco | $98.4 | 699 | 4% |
| Netherlands | $16,991.6 | 1,962 | 16% |
| Norway | $4,255.8 | 1,847 | 52% |
| Pakistan | $68.1 | 133 | 0.2% |
| Peru | $38.2 | 729 | 5% |
| Philippines | $775.9 | 2,833 | 6% |
| Poland | $150.8 | 3,614 | 12% |
| Romania | $155.0 | 325 | 2% |
| Slovakia | $7.3 | 149 | 4% |
| South Africa | $960.5 | 2,659 | 9% |
| South Korea | $2,433.2 | 1,204 | 3% |
| Spain | $7,055.1 | 1,681 | 5% |
| Sweden | $10,206.1 | 2,009 | 28% |
| Tanzania | $289.5 | 2,092 | 11% |
| Uganda | $30.5 | 2,606 | 23% |
| United Kingdom | $21,976.2 | 14,357 | 30% |
| United States | $109,012.6 | 44,564 | 22% |
| Total | $316,415.6 | 131,557 | - |
| Developing / transitional country average | | | 6% |
| Developed country average | | - | 15% |
| All-country average | | - | 10% |

* See Methodological Appendix for estimating procedures.
SOURCE: Johns Hopkins Comparative Nonprofit Sector Project

**Table A.3.** Civil society sector FTE workforce,
by field, 36 countries

| Country | Culture | Education | Health | Social Svcs | Environment | Development | Civic / Adv. | Foundations | International | Professional | n.e.c. | Total (thousands) |
|---|---|---|---|---|---|---|---|---|---|---|---|---|
| | Percent of total civil society workforce* | | | | | | | | | | | |
| Argentina | 13.8 | 31.5 | 9.8 | 13.5 | 1.6 | 15.7 | 1.8 | 0.1 | 0.8 | 8.2 | 3.2 | 659.4 |
| Australia | 22.7 | 17.9 | 14.9 | 23.6 | 1.4 | 10.4 | 2.9 | 0.2 | 0.4 | 3.3 | 2.4 | 579.7 |
| Austria | n / a | | | | | | | | | | | 184.3 |
| Belgium | 11.1 | 30.5 | 23.9 | 22.9 | 0.5 | 8.3 | 0.5 | 0.3 | 0.4 | 1.5 | 0.0 | 456.9 |
| Brazil | 15.1 | 35.1 | 17.5 | 19.2 | 0.2 | 3.0 | 0.7 | 0.0 | 0.4 | 8.6 | 0.3 | 1173.8 |
| Colombia | 7.5 | 20.2 | 15.3 | 18.7 | 0.8 | 18.5 | 1.6 | 1.5 | 0.1 | 14.9 | 0.9 | 377.6 |
| Czech Rep. | 35.8 | 10.6 | 11.9 | 13.1 | 6.1 | 6.7 | 3.5 | 2.2 | 1.4 | 8.6 | 0.0 | 115.1 |
| Egypt | n / a | | | | | | | | | | | 629.2 |
| Finland | 32.6 | 12.4 | 13.1 | 15.5 | 0.7 | 1.6 | 16.8 | 0.2 | 0.4 | 6.2 | 0.4 | 137.6 |
| France | 30.0 | 14.6 | 9.2 | 27.4 | 5.0 | 4.7 | 1.9 | 0.6 | 2.4 | 4.3 | 0.0 | 1981.5 |
| Germany | 19.7 | 7.6 | 21.8 | 27.2 | 2.8 | 4.4 | 3.3 | 1.0 | 1.6 | 4.2 | 6.4 | 2418.9 |
| Hungary | 36.8 | 8.9 | 4.7 | 15.1 | 2.2 | 11.3 | 2.3 | 3.7 | 1.0 | 14.0 | 0.0 | 54.8 |
| India | 12.2 | 39.3 | 12.0 | 31.6 | 0.0 | 0.0 | 0.0 | 0.0 | 0.0 | 0.0 | 5.0 | 6035.0 |
| Ireland | 10.5 | 43.0 | 23.3 | 13.0 | 0.9 | 5.7 | 0.5 | 0.7 | 0.4 | 1.7 | 0.3 | 150.3 |
| Israel | 8.6 | 41.4 | 27.2 | 16.0 | 0.6 | 0.8 | 2.0 | 1.6 | 0.1 | 1.6 | 0.0 | 176.7 |
| Italy | 23.9 | 14.8 | 18.0 | 26.1 | 1.2 | 3.6 | 3.0 | 0.8 | 0.6 | 6.7 | 1.2 | 950.1 |
| Japan | 5.5 | 18.5 | 37.3 | 17.3 | 0.7 | 1.9 | 0.5 | 1.1 | 1.6 | 5.0 | 10.7 | 2835.2 |
| Kenya | 4.7 | 10.8 | 10.1 | 18.6 | 4.0 | 20.2 | 5.3 | 0.3 | 0.0 | 1.5 | 24.5 | 287.3 |
| Mexico | 6.4 | 30.7 | 8.4 | 16.3 | 1.8 | 1.2 | 0.8 | 0.8 | 0.0 | 33.6 | 0.0 | 141.0 |
| Morocco | n / a | | | | | | | | | | | 157.9 |
| Netherlands | 17.2 | 23.1 | 29.5 | 20.3 | 2.0 | 1.7 | 2.9 | 0.2 | 1.2 | 1.8 | 0.0 | 1051.8 |
| Norway | 41.2 | 11.2 | 6.0 | 14.0 | 0.6 | 4.3 | 6.3 | 0.2 | 2.9 | 13.1 | 0.3 | 163.0 |
| Pakistan | 5.2 | 56.6 | 10.4 | 8.0 | 0.3 | 7.8 | 10.0 | 0.0 | 0.0 | 1.7 | 0.0 | 442.7 |
| Peru | 2.5 | 45.2 | 2.6 | 38.3 | 0.4 | 8.8 | 0.5 | 0.9 | 0.0 | 0.9 | 0.0 | 210.0 |
| Philippines | 5.6 | 30.5 | 2.0 | 6.2 | 2.1 | 21.3 | 1.7 | 1.0 | 0.4 | 29.3 | 0.0 | 517.6 |
| Poland | 32.7 | 22.2 | 6.7 | 19.5 | 1.7 | 1.0 | 1.0 | 0.4 | 1.0 | 10.8 | 3.0 | 154.6 |
| Romania | 28.6 | 15.1 | 8.5 | 32.2 | 2.2 | 2.4 | 3.8 | 1.0 | 4.0 | 2.4 | 0.0 | 83.9 |
| Slovakia | 37.0 | 20.4 | 1.9 | 10.1 | 9.0 | 1.1 | 3.8 | 5.6 | 0.9 | 9.1 | 1.1 | 23.0 |
| South Africa | 17.6 | 5.5 | 10.0 | 25.6 | 5.9 | 17.9 | 15.9 | 0.4 | 0.0 | 1.1 | 0.0 | 562.4 |
| South Korea | 4.9 | 40.5 | 25.8 | 15.5 | 0.0 | 0.0 | 9.9 | 0.0 | 0.0 | 3.4 | 0.0 | 535.4 |
| Spain | 15.2 | 20.6 | 10.5 | 30.8 | 3.0 | 9.2 | 5.9 | 0.1 | 2.6 | 1.8 | 0.2 | 728.8 |
| Sweden | 45.5 | 6.8 | 0.9 | 10.5 | 2.1 | 4.4 | 10.2 | 0.2 | 2.3 | 15.4 | 1.7 | 342.9 |
| Tanzania | 10.3 | 11.7 | 10.5 | 16.4 | 10.6 | 12.8 | 7.1 | 7.8 | 3.9 | 3.2 | 5.8 | 330.9 |
| Uganda | 22.7 | 12.8 | 6.7 | 28.8 | 1.0 | 20.2 | 0.5 | 1.0 | 0.2 | 3.3 | 2.6 | 228.6 |
| United Kingdom | 27.5 | 25.4 | 8.0 | 16.0 | 2.4 | 12.5 | 1.8 | 1.3 | 2.4 | 1.5 | 1.2 | 2536.0 |
| United States | 9.0 | 18.5 | 34.2 | 22.1 | 1.0 | 4.0 | 4.9 | 1.0 | 0.3 | 3.9 | 1.1 | 13549.1 |
| Developing / transitional | 16.6 | 24.9 | 9.7 | 19.3 | 2.8 | 9.4 | 3.9 | 1.5 | 0.8 | 8.6 | 2.6 | 12720.2 |
| Developed | 21.4 | 20.4 | 18.5 | 20.2 | 1.7 | 5.2 | 4.2 | 0.6 | 1.3 | 4.8 | 1.7 | 28242.7 |
| 36 countries | 18.8 | 22.9 | 13.7 | 19.7 | 2.3 | 7.5 | 4.0 | 1.1 | 1.0 | 6.9 | 2.2 | 40962.8 |

* Percentages add to 100% across fields.

SOURCE: Johns Hopkins Comparative Nonprofit Sector Project

**Table A.4.** Civil society sector sources of support,
with and without volunteers, 34 countries

| Country | Excluding volunteers Percent share from Govern-ment | Philan-thropy | Fees | Total Millions US$ | Including volunteers Percent share from Govern-ment | Philan-thropy | Fees | Total Millions US$ |
|---|---|---|---|---|---|---|---|---|
| Argentina | 19.5% | 7.5% | 73.1% | $13,321 | 16.2% | 23.0% | 60.8% | $16,014 |
| Australia | 31.2% | 6.3% | 62.5% | $19,810 | 25.4% | 23.6% | 51.0% | $24,295 |
| Austria | 50.4% | 6.1% | 43.5% | $6,262 | 41.3% | 23.1% | 35.6% | $7,643 |
| Belgium | 76.8% | 4.7% | 18.6% | $25,576 | 65.9% | 18.1% | 16.0% | $29,773 |
| Brazil | 15.5% | 10.7% | 73.8% | $11,390 | 14.5% | 16.3% | 69.2% | $12,144 |
| Colombia | 14.9% | 14.9% | 70.2% | $1,719 | 13.1% | 24.9% | 62.0% | $1,948 |
| Czech Rep. | 39.4% | 14.0% | 46.6% | $860 | 32.1% | 30.0% | 37.9% | $1,056 |
| Finland | 36.2% | 5.9% | 57.9% | $6,064 | 25.2% | 34.6% | 40.3% | $8,722 |
| France | 57.8% | 7.5% | 34.6% | $57,304 | 33.4% | 46.6% | 20.0% | $99,234 |
| Germany | 64.3% | 3.4% | 32.3% | $94,454 | 42.5% | 36.2% | 21.3% | $142,887 |
| Hungary | 27.1% | 18.4% | 54.6% | $1,433 | 26.2% | 21.1% | 52.7% | $1,483 |
| India | 36.1% | 12.9% | 51.0% | $3,026 | 24.9% | 39.9% | 35.2% | $4,382 |
| Ireland | 77.2% | 7.0% | 15.8% | $5,017 | 67.6% | 18.6% | 13.8% | $5,732 |
| Israel | 63.9% | 10.2% | 25.8% | $10,947 | 59.1% | 17.0% | 23.9% | $11,842 |
| Italy | 36.6% | 2.8% | 60.6% | $39,356 | 30.2% | 19.7% | 50.1% | $47,647 |
| Japan | 45.2% | 2.6% | 52.1% | $258,959 | 41.5% | 10.7% | 47.8% | $282,314 |
| Kenya | 4.8% | 14.2% | 81.0% | $404 | 4.3% | 23.9% | 71.8% | $456 |
| Mexico | 8.5% | 6.3% | 85.2% | $1,554 | 7.5% | 17.9% | 74.7% | $1,774 |
| Netherlands | 59.0% | 2.4% | 38.6% | $60,399 | 46.1% | 23.9% | 30.1% | $77,391 |
| Norway | 35.0% | 6.9% | 58.1% | $5,640 | 20.0% | 46.9% | 33.1% | $9,895 |
| Pakistan | 6.0% | 42.9% | 51.1% | $310 | 4.9% | 53.1% | 41.9% | $378 |
| Peru | 18.1% | 12.2% | 69.8% | $1,272 | 17.5% | 14.7% | 67.7% | $1,310 |
| Philippines | 5.2% | 3.2% | 91.6% | $1,103 | 3.1% | 43.2% | 53.7% | $1,878 |
| Poland | 24.1% | 15.5% | 60.4% | $2,620 | 22.8% | 20.1% | 57.1% | $2,771 |
| Romania | 45.0% | 26.5% | 28.5% | $130 | 20.5% | 66.5% | 13.0% | $285 |
| Slovakia | 21.9% | 23.3% | 54.9% | $295 | 21.3% | 25.1% | 53.5% | $302 |
| South Africa | 44.2% | 24.2% | 31.7% | $2,386 | 31.5% | 45.9% | 22.6% | $3,346 |
| South Korea | 24.3% | 4.4% | 71.4% | $19,753 | 21.6% | 14.9% | 63.5% | $22,186 |
| Spain | 32.1% | 18.8% | 49.0% | $25,778 | 25.2% | 36.3% | 38.5% | $32,833 |
| Sweden | 28.7% | 9.1% | 62.3% | $10,599 | 14.6% | 53.7% | 31.7% | $20,805 |
| Tanzania | 27.0% | 20.0% | 53.1% | $263 | 12.8% | 61.9% | 25.3% | $552 |
| Uganda | 7.1% | 38.2% | 54.7% | $108 | 5.5% | 51.8% | 42.7% | $139 |
| United Kingdom | 46.7% | 8.8% | 44.6% | $78,220 | 36.4% | 28.8% | 34.8% | $100,196 |
| United States | 30.5% | 12.9% | 56.6% | $566,960 | 25.6% | 26.9% | 47.4% | $675,973 |
| Developing / transitional | 21.6% | 17.2% | 61.3% | - | 16.7% | 33.0% | 50.3% | - |
| Developed | 48.2% | 7.2% | 44.6% | - | 37.5% | 29.0% | 33.5% | - |
| 34 countries | 34.1% | 12.5% | 53.4% | - | 26.5% | 31.1% | 42.4% | - |

SOURCE: Johns Hopkins Comparative Nonprofit Sector Project

**Table A.5.** Sources of civil society sector support
in relation to GDP, 34 countries

**Support as a percent of the GDP by source:**

| Country | Government | Philanthropy | Volunteering | Fees |
|---|---|---|---|---|
| Argentina | 1.00% | 0.38% | 1.03% | 3.76% |
| Australia | 1.69% | 0.34% | 1.21% | 3.39% |
| Austria | 1.40% | 0.17% | 0.61% | 1.21% |
| Belgium | 7.30% | 0.44% | 1.54% | 1.77% |
| Brazil | 0.25% | 0.17% | 0.10% | 1.17% |
| Colombia | 0.32% | 0.32% | 0.28% | 1.50% |
| Czech Rep. | 0.66% | 0.23% | 0.38% | 0.78% |
| Finland | 1.75% | 0.28% | 2.08% | 2.81% |
| France | 2.16% | 0.28% | 2.66% | 1.29% |
| Germany | 2.52% | 0.13% | 1.97% | 1.26% |
| Hungary | 0.89% | 0.60% | 0.11% | 1.79% |
| India | 0.25% | 0.09% | 0.31% | 0.35% |
| Ireland | 6.14% | 0.55% | 1.12% | 1.26% |
| Israel | 8.06% | 1.29% | 1.02% | 3.26% |
| Italy | 1.23% | 0.09% | 0.70% | 2.04% |
| Japan | 2.50% | 0.14% | 0.49% | 2.88% |
| Kenya | 0.18% | 0.54% | 0.48% | 3.07% |
| Mexico | 0.05% | 0.04% | 0.08% | 0.49% |
| Netherlands | 9.04% | 0.37% | 4.13% | 5.90% |
| Norway | 1.32% | 0.26% | 2.76% | 2.19% |
| Pakistan | 0.03% | 0.22% | 0.11% | 0.26% |
| Peru | 0.39% | 0.26% | 0.06% | 1.51% |
| Philippines | 0.07% | 0.04% | 0.94% | 1.23% |
| Poland | 0.44% | 0.28% | 0.10% | 1.10% |
| Romania | 0.16% | 0.10% | 0.43% | 0.10% |
| Slovakia | 0.34% | 0.36% | 0.04% | 0.86% |
| South Africa | 0.79% | 0.43% | 0.71% | 0.57% |
| South Korea | 1.01% | 0.18% | 0.51% | 2.96% |
| Spain | 1.48% | 0.87% | 1.25% | 2.26% |
| Sweden | 1.25% | 0.40% | 4.03% | 2.72% |
| Tanzania | 0.81% | 0.60% | 3.19% | 1.59% |
| Uganda | 0.12% | 0.64% | 0.47% | 0.93% |
| United Kingdom | 3.32% | 0.62% | 1.96% | 3.17% |
| United States | 2.38% | 1.01% | 1.48% | 4.41% |
| | | | | |
| Developing / transitional | 0.43% | 0.30% | 0.48% | 1.33% |
| Developed | 3.35% | 0.45% | 1.81% | 2.61% |
| 34 countries | 1.80% | 0.37% | 1.07% | 1.94% |

SOURCE: Johns Hopkins Comparative Nonprofit Sector Project

**Table A.6.** Share of civil society sector revenue
from government, by country, by field, 33 countries

| Country | Culture | Education | Health | Social Svcs | Environment | Development | Civic / Advocacy | Foundations | International | Professional | n.e.c. | Total (millions) |
|---|---|---|---|---|---|---|---|---|---|---|---|---|
| | Percent* of total cash revenues in each field | | | | | | | | | | | US $ |
| Argentina | 2 | 20 | 27 | 46 | 1 | 8 | 0 | 0 | 100 | 11 | 0 | $2,594 |
| Australia | 3 | 51 | 44 | 51 | 38 | 36 | 25 | 25 | 30 | 7 | 0 | $6,177 |
| Austria | 33 | 73 | 76 | 44 | 48 | - | 65 | - | 40 | 8 | - | $3,156 |
| Belgium | 41 | 97 | 81 | 66 | 94 | 47 | 84 | 1 | 33 | 7 | - | $19,633 |
| Brazil | 5 | 14 | 9 | 48 | 27 | 73 | 28 | - | 0 | 0 | - | $1,761 |
| Colombia | 13 | 17 | 26 | 20 | 27 | 5 | 21 | 14 | 0 | 0 | 13 | $256 |
| Czech Rep. | 42 | 43 | 57 | 50 | 33 | 34 | 51 | 30 | 37 | 2 | - | $339 |
| Finland | 23 | 30 | 66 | 57 | 11 | 4 | 42 | 4 | 30 | 2 | 3 | $2,195 |
| France | 30 | 72 | 80 | 58 | 32 | 37 | 45 | 3 | 43 | 30 | - | $33,144 |
| Germany | 20 | 75 | 94 | 65 | 22 | 57 | 58 | 10 | 51 | 2 | - | $60,753 |
| Hungary | 23 | 23 | 31 | 46 | 11 | 43 | 55 | 25 | 66 | 5 | - | $388 |
| Ireland | 52 | 78 | 89 | 50 | 94 | 96 | 66 | 80 | 24 | 3 | 0 | $3,874 |
| Israel | 43 | 64 | 75 | 33 | 32 | 32 | 25 | 31 | 23 | 14 | 0 | $6,997 |
| Italy | 25 | 38 | 71 | 42 | 41 | 52 | 27 | 2 | 35 | 9 | 4 | $14,406 |
| Japan | 7 | 13 | 87 | 72 | 27 | 37 | 27 | 0 | 19 | 0 | 27 | $117,164 |
| Kenya | 0 | 13 | 0 | 5 | 19 | 2 | 0 | 0 | - | 0 | 0 | $20 |
| Mexico | 12 | 6 | 1 | 9 | 0 | 0 | 0 | 0 | - | 12 | - | $132 |
| Netherlands | 27 | 91 | 96 | 66 | 23 | 7 | 4 | 0 | 45 | 0 | - | $35,640 |
| Norway | 29 | 50 | 82 | 66 | 30 | 3 | 35 | 28 | 35 | 5 | 10 | $1,976 |
| Pakistan | 4 | 2 | 1 | 7 | 0 | 35 | 1 | - | - | 0 | - | $19 |
| Peru | 0 | 6 | 37 | 15 | 62 | 64 | 65 | 0 | 0 | 0 | - | $230 |
| Philippines | 3 | 1 | 43 | 26 | - | 8 | 58 | - | - | 10 | - | $58 |
| Poland | 36 | 21 | 24 | 29 | 10 | 11 | 4 | 12 | 19 | 5 | 17 | $632 |
| Romania | 35 | 47 | 55 | 52 | 59 | 38 | 39 | 49 | 47 | 12 | - | $58 |
| Slovakia | 16 | 73 | 48 | 29 | 13 | 19 | 40 | 18 | 22 | 2 | 4 | $64 |
| South Africa | 6 | 2 | 69 | 57 | 1 | 42 | 82 | 0 | - | 1 | - | $1,054 |
| South Korea | 25 | 15 | 39 | 68 | - | - | 17 | - | - | 0 | - | $4,796 |
| Spain | 24 | 53 | 37 | 49 | 30 | 12 | 30 | 10 | 56 | 28 | 5 | $8,284 |
| Sweden | 25 | 54 | 87 | 71 | 14 | 11 | 23 | 15 | 49 | 5 | 12 | $3,041 |
| Tanzania | 23 | 26 | 33 | 29 | 31 | 26 | 21 | 31 | 31 | 18 | 15 | $71 |
| Uganda | 24 | 12 | 2 | 0 | 0 | 0 | 0 | 0 | 0 | 0 | 0 | $8 |
| United Kingdom | 14 | 63 | 38 | 39 | 27 | 66 | 59 | 29 | 40 | 2 | - | $36,514 |
| United States | 7 | 20 | 41 | 37 | - | 37 | 5 | 0 | - | 2 | - | $173,200 |
| Developing / transitional | 16 | 20 | 30 | 31 | 20 | 26 | 28 | 14 | 29 | 5 | 7 | - |
| Developed | 25 | 58 | 72 | 54 | 38 | 35 | 39 | 16 | 37 | 8 | 7 | - |
| 33 countries | 20 | 38 | 50 | 42 | 29 | 30 | 33 | 15 | 34 | 6 | 7 | - |

* Percentages add to 100% across respective fields in Tables 6, 7, and 8.

SOURCE: Johns Hopkins Comparative Nonprofit Sector Project

**Table A.7.** Share of civil society sector revenue from philanthropy, by country, by field, 33 countries

| Country | Culture | Education | Health | Social Svcs | Environment | Development | Civic / Advocacy | Foundations | International | Professional | n.e.c. | Total (millions) |
|---|---|---|---|---|---|---|---|---|---|---|---|---|
| | Percent* of total cash revenues in each field | | | | | | | | | | | US $ |
| Argentina | 1 | 26 | 1 | 0 | 38 | 0 | 69 | 100 | 0 | 0 | 3 | $2,594 |
| Australia | 3 | 6 | 4 | 11 | 17 | 6 | 9 | 38 | 70 | 3 | 3 | $6,177 |
| Austria | 0 | 0 | 0 | 8 | 16 | - | 0 | - | 55 | 0 | - | $3,156 |
| Belgium | 12 | 0 | 1 | 12 | 2 | 5 | 5 | 66 | 58 | 25 | - | $19,633 |
| Brazil | 5 | 3 | 1 | 52 | 73 | 0 | 0 | - | 0 | 0 | - | $1,761 |
| Colombia | 9 | 8 | 16 | 12 | 43 | 52 | 2 | 25 | 99 | 1 | 13 | $256 |
| Czech Rep. | 13 | 13 | 14 | 19 | 22 | 9 | 24 | 48 | 52 | 3 | - | $339 |
| Finland | 7 | 9 | 3 | 4 | 2 | 1 | 18 | 13 | 8 | 3 | 3 | $2,195 |
| France | 5 | 10 | 6 | 5 | 15 | 2 | 13 | 64 | 40 | 10 | - | $33,144 |
| Germany | 13 | 2 | 0 | 5 | 16 | 0 | 7 | 3 | 41 | 1 | - | $60,753 |
| Hungary | 20 | 25 | 41 | 23 | 21 | 9 | 20 | 30 | 14 | 6 | - | $388 |
| Ireland | 18 | 1 | 8 | 44 | 6 | 4 | 34 | 20 | 76 | 0 | 100 | $3,874 |
| Israel | 17 | 12 | 3 | 28 | 2 | 31 | 46 | 33 | 51 | 24 | 100 | $6,997 |
| Italy | 2 | 2 | 2 | 5 | 4 | 1 | 5 | 2 | 35 | 0 | 0 | $14,406 |
| Japan | 11 | 2 | 1 | 3 | 23 | 13 | 7 | 31 | 27 | 0 | 7 | $117,164 |
| Kenya | 8 | 20 | 0 | 13 | 32 | 7 | 49 | 86 | - | 1 | 11 | $20 |
| Mexico | 1 | 6 | 14 | 38 | 25 | 25 | 25 | 25 | - | 0 | - | $132 |
| Netherlands | 8 | 1 | 1 | 3 | 16 | 0 | 11 | 3 | 35 | 0 | - | $35,640 |
| Norway | 13 | 4 | 4 | 2 | 4 | 5 | 12 | 3 | 24 | 3 | 3 | $1,976 |
| Pakistan | 53 | 40 | 53 | 70 | 91 | 12 | 63 | - | - | 25 | - | $19 |
| Peru | 7 | 6 | 58 | 4 | 29 | 30 | 30 | 0 | 3 | 4 | - | $230 |
| Philippines | 3 | 1 | 9 | 56 | - | 2 | 37 | - | - | 7 | - | $58 |
| Poland | 8 | 9 | 27 | 22 | 45 | 22 | 51 | 26 | 36 | 8 | 11 | $632 |
| Romania | 32 | 22 | 32 | 28 | 26 | 24 | 32 | 38 | 31 | 7 | - | $58 |
| Slovakia | 26 | 5 | 6 | 17 | 13 | 3 | 29 | 66 | 21 | 5 | 6 | $64 |
| South Africa | 42 | 60 | 26 | 11 | 71 | 21 | 11 | 25 | - | 0 | - | $1,054 |
| South Korea | 8 | 5 | 0 | 16 | - | - | 17 | - | - | 0 | - | $4,796 |
| Spain | 35 | 6 | 13 | 20 | 60 | 18 | 60 | 85 | 36 | 2 | 0 | $8,284 |
| Sweden | 12 | 4 | 1 | 10 | 25 | 0 | 21 | 4 | 37 | 3 | 7 | $3,041 |
| Tanzania | 20 | 25 | 21 | 21 | 25 | 13 | 21 | 22 | 22 | 15 | 19 | $71 |
| Uganda | 26 | 44 | 61 | 16 | 99 | 72 | 100 | 16 | 93 | 0 | 9 | $8 |
| United Kingdom | 2 | 3 | 23 | 31 | 45 | 1 | 6 | 24 | 33 | 1 | - | $36,514 |
| United States | 50 | 15 | 5 | 20 | - | 20 | 37 | 29 | - | 10 | - | $173,200 |
| Developing / transitional | 17 | 19 | 22 | 25 | 44 | 19 | 34 | 39 | 34 | 5 | 10 | - |
| Developed | 13 | 5 | 5 | 13 | 17 | 7 | 18 | 28 | 42 | 5 | 25 | - |
| 33 countries | 15 | 12 | 14 | 19 | 30 | 13 | 26 | 33 | 38 | 5 | 18 | - |

* Percentages add to 100% across respective fields in Tables 6, 7, and 8.

SOURCE: Johns Hopkins Comparative Nonprofit Sector Project

## Table A.8. Share of civil society sector revenue from fees, by country, by field, 33 countries

| Country | Culture | Education | Health | Social Svcs | Environment | Development | Civic / Advocacy | Foundations | International | Professional | n.e.c. | Total (millions) |
|---|---|---|---|---|---|---|---|---|---|---|---|---|
| | Percent* of total cash revenues in each field | | | | | | | | | | | US $ |
| Argentina | 97 | 53 | 72 | 54 | 61 | 92 | 31 | 0 | 0 | 89 | 97 | $2,693 |
| Australia | 94 | 42 | 52 | 38 | 45 | 58 | 66 | 38 | 0 | 91 | 96 | $4,485 |
| Austria | 67 | 27 | 24 | 47 | 36 | - | 35 | - | 5 | 92 | - | $1,380 |
| Belgium | 47 | 2 | 17 | 22 | 4 | 48 | 11 | 33 | 9 | 68 | - | $4,198 |
| Brazil | 89 | 83 | 90 | 0 | 0 | 27 | 72 | - | 100 | 100 | - | $754 |
| Colombia | 77 | 75 | 58 | 68 | 31 | 43 | 78 | 61 | 1 | 99 | 74 | $229 |
| Czech Rep. | 45 | 44 | 29 | 31 | 44 | 57 | 25 | 22 | 11 | 95 | - | $196 |
| Finland | 70 | 61 | 31 | 38 | 87 | 95 | 40 | 84 | 61 | 96 | 94 | $2,658 |
| France | 65 | 18 | 13 | 36 | 52 | 61 | 42 | 33 | 17 | 60 | - | $41,930 |
| Germany | 66 | 23 | 6 | 30 | 62 | 43 | 36 | 86 | 8 | 97 | - | $48,433 |
| Hungary | 57 | 52 | 28 | 31 | 69 | 48 | 25 | 45 | 20 | 89 | - | $50 |
| Ireland | 30 | 21 | 3 | 5 | 0 | 0 | 0 | 0 | 0 | 97 | 0 | $716 |
| Israel | 39 | 24 | 22 | 39 | 66 | 38 | 29 | 37 | 26 | 61 | 0 | $895 |
| Italy | 73 | 59 | 27 | 53 | 54 | 47 | 68 | 96 | 30 | 91 | 96 | $8,291 |
| Japan | 82 | 85 | 12 | 25 | 51 | 50 | 66 | 68 | 54 | 99 | 66 | $23,355 |
| Kenya | 92 | 67 | 100 | 82 | 49 | 91 | 51 | 14 | - | 99 | 89 | $52 |
| Mexico | 88 | 88 | 86 | 53 | 75 | 75 | 75 | 75 | - | 88 | - | $220 |
| Netherlands | 65 | 8 | 3 | 31 | 60 | 93 | 85 | 97 | 20 | 100 | - | $16,992 |
| Norway | 58 | 46 | 14 | 32 | 66 | 92 | 53 | 69 | 41 | 93 | 87 | $4,256 |
| Pakistan | 43 | 58 | 45 | 24 | 9 | 53 | 36 | - | - | 75 | - | $68 |
| Peru | 93 | 89 | 5 | 81 | 9 | 6 | 5 | 100 | 97 | 96 | - | $38 |
| Philippines | 94 | 98 | 47 | 18 | - | 90 | 4 | - | - | 83 | - | $776 |
| Poland | 56 | 70 | 49 | 49 | 46 | 67 | 45 | 61 | 45 | 86 | 72 | $151 |
| Romania | 33 | 31 | 13 | 21 | 15 | 38 | 29 | 13 | 22 | 81 | - | $155 |
| Slovakia | 58 | 23 | 45 | 54 | 74 | 78 | 32 | 15 | 57 | 93 | 90 | $7 |
| South Africa | 52 | 38 | 6 | 32 | 28 | 37 | 7 | 75 | - | 99 | - | $961 |
| South Korea | 66 | 80 | 61 | 16 | - | - | 67 | - | - | 100 | - | $2,433 |
| Spain | 41 | 41 | 51 | 31 | 10 | 70 | 10 | 5 | 8 | 70 | 95 | $7,055 |
| Sweden | 63 | 42 | 12 | 20 | 61 | 89 | 56 | 82 | 14 | 91 | 80 | $10,206 |
| Tanzania | 57 | 49 | 46 | 50 | 44 | 61 | 58 | 47 | 48 | 66 | 65 | $290 |
| Uganda | 50 | 44 | 37 | 83 | 1 | 28 | 0 | 84 | 7 | 100 | 91 | $31 |
| United Kingdom | 84 | 34 | 40 | 30 | 28 | 33 | 34 | 47 | 27 | 98 | - | $21,976 |
| United States | 42 | 65 | 54 | 43 | - | 43 | 58 | 71 | - | 88 | - | $109,013 |
| Developing / transitional | 68 | 61 | 48 | 44 | 37 | 56 | 38 | 47 | 37 | 90 | 83 | - |
| Developed | 62 | 37 | 24 | 33 | 46 | 57 | 43 | 56 | 21 | 87 | 68 | - |
| 33 countries | 65 | 50 | 36 | 38 | 41 | 56 | 40 | 52 | 28 | 89 | 75 | - |

* Percentages add to 100% across respective fields in Tables 6, 7, and 8.

SOURCE: Johns Hopkins Comparative Nonprofit Sector Project

**Table A.9.** Civil society sector sources of support,
with and without volunteers, by field, 33-country averages

| Field | Excluding volunteers Percent share from | | | Including volunteers Percent share from | | |
|---|---|---|---|---|---|---|
| | Govern- ment | Philan- thropy | Fees | Govern- ment | Philan- thropy | Fees |
| Culture and recreation | 20.4% | 14.9% | 64.7% | 12.2% | 44.7% | 43.0% |
| Education and research | 38.3% | 12.0% | 49.7% | 34.1% | 19.2% | 46.7% |
| Health | 49.9% | 13.8% | 36.3% | 43.1% | 26.4% | 30.5% |
| Social services | 42.5% | 19.1% | 38.4% | 28.9% | 43.4% | 27.7% |
| Environment | 28.5% | 30.2% | 41.2% | 17.6% | 57.2% | 25.1% |
| Development and housing | 30.4% | 13.2% | 56.5% | 22.8% | 33.5% | 43.7% |
| Civic and advocacy | 33.4% | 26.3% | 40.3% | 18.8% | 57.2% | 24.0% |
| Philanthropic intermediaries | 14.9% | 33.0% | 52.1% | 8.1% | 56.5% | 35.4% |
| International | 33.6% | 38.4% | 28.0% | 25.8% | 59.5% | 14.7% |
| Religious worship | 13.9% | 53.2% | 32.9% | 6.7% | 73.3% | 20.0% |
| Business, professional, labor | 6.1% | 5.1% | 88.8% | 4.3% | 24.8% | 70.9% |
| n.e.c. | 7.0% | 18.5% | 74.6% | 5.3% | 31.9% | 62.8% |

SOURCE: Johns Hopkins Comparative Nonprofit Sector Project

# Appendix B

# Methodology and Data Sources

## A. General Methodology Overview

### Introduction

The Johns Hopkins Comparative Nonprofit Sector Project (CNP), launched in May 1990, has sought to develop a common base of knowledge about a set of institutions referred to in the literature as "nonprofit," "voluntary," or more recently, "civil society" organizations in a disparate set of countries. Accomplishing this task has required attention to five critical conceptual and methodological challenges:

- Selecting a set of countries that differs sufficiently along key dimensions to allow us to detect patterns and trends, and to search for explanations of them;

- Developing a definition of the civil society sector that is broad enough to encompass many different national experiences yet precise enough to distinguish these entities from other social institutions in a consistent way;

- Developing a classification system that could differentiate the various types of civil society entities according to their principal activity;

- Identifying the most meaningful and measurable characteristics reflecting the form and behavior of the institutions under investigation;

- Developing a set of procedures to gather reasonably accurate data on these characteristics in a cost-efficient fashion.

The results reported in this volume were generated in the second half of the second phase of our project, which started in 1997. This Appendix discusses how we went about these five tasks in the countries investigated in this Phase IIB.[1] A more detailed discussion of the methodologies used in previously researched countries can be found in the first volume of *Global Civil Society: Dimensions of the Nonprofit Sector,* as well as online.[2]

### 1. Country selection

This project utilizes an explicitly comparative approach to generate insights into the character and operation of the civil society sector. To do so, we have sought to include countries that differ along dimensions that previous theories have suggested might be relevant for the development of the civil society sector. Those dimensions include:

- The level of economic development;
- The scope of government social welfare spending;
- Religious tradition;
- The legal framework for civil society and philanthropy;
- The degree of social-cultural diversity; and
- Cultural and historical patterns of development.

Whereas the countries studied in the earlier phases of this project were developed or developing and transitional countries in Europe, Asia, North America, and Latin America, Phase IIB extended the focus to developing countries of Africa, the Middle East, and Asia. This has brought a much fuller range of experiences into our analysis, including the experiences of colonialism and a variety of pre-modern social institutions, as well as encounters with authoritarian and openly repressive regimes in the post-colonial period.

## 2. Common definition

A key to our approach has been the formulation and use of a common definition and classification of civil society organizations. To that end, we developed a structural-operational definition that identifies five criteria that define civil society organizations: they are organizations, whether formal or informal, that are institutionally separate from government, non-profit-distributing, self-governing, and voluntary. As outlined in Chapter 1, this definition was developed in collaboration with our local associates and field-tested for its validity. These tests consistently showed that the definition fits reasonably well the realities of diverse countries, although minor adjustments and new "rules of thumb" were often necessary.

The countries investigated in this phase of our project posed unique challenges to the structural-operational definition because of the heavy presence of traditional social institutions and the informal nature of social activities. We concluded, however, that these informal, unregistered activities fit the structural-operational definition as long as they occurred on a regular basis and were governed by culturally sanctioned rules and expectations that define who is a participant and in what role.

Another definitional challenge was posed by the widespread presence of traditional forms of social organization based on kin relations (such as tribes or age-group affiliations in Africa). We differentiated, however, between membership in the tribe or clan, into which one is born, and membership in a tribal association or age-group association, in which membership is ultimately a matter of choice. The former would not meet the voluntary criterion of our definition, but the latter clearly would.

In a similar manner, we distinguished between two different types of cooperatives — those facilitating rural development or empowerment of disadvantaged groups (e.g., *stokvels* — informal credit associations in South Africa) and those that were mainly business ventures for small producers (such as cooperatives of cash crop producers in Tanzania or Uganda). While the former met the non-profit-distributing criterion set by the structural-operation definition, the latter did not and consequently are not included in the data presented here.

We furthermore excluded, to the extent possible, organizations that performed an essentially governmental function (such as tribal councils).

Close collaboration between core staff and local associates resulted in a precise yet flexible structural-operational definition that allowed for a consistent inclusion of most types of civil society organizations found in developing and transitional countries.

## 3. Classification

To provide a way to classify civil society organizations in different countries, we developed the International Classification of Nonprofit Organizations (ICNPO) in Phase I of this project. This classification system emerged through a collaborative process involving local associates from many different regions.

The ICNPO is a classification scheme that groups civil society organizations among twelve major fields, including a not elsewhere classified category, based on their primary activity. The primary activity is the activity that engages the greatest share (in most cases, more than half) of an organization's resources (financial or human). Section C of this appendix shows the full ICNPO.

To ensure some consistency with existing economic classification systems, the ICNPO adheres closely to the service sector classification of the International Standard Industrial Classification system (ISIC), but elaborates on it to provide more detail than ISIC allows. We ascertained that the ICNPO classification worked quite well in the countries brought into the project in Phase IIB. In some of these countries, however, a relatively large number of civil society organizations operate outside of the service sector, mainly in agriculture or small manufacturing. These organizations were assigned to Group 12 under the ICNPO scheme.

ICNPO Group 10 covers places of religious worship (e.g., temples, mosques, churches, and synagogues) as well as organizations carrying out ancillary religious activities, such as choirs and prayer groups. Religiously affiliated service organizations (e.g., hospitals, social service agencies, and schools) are not included in Group 10 but rather are allocated to the respective service field (e.g., health, social services, and education). Because of difficulties in compiling the needed data, coverage of the places of religious worship and of the organizations performing ancillary religious activities was incomplete in many countries. Accordingly, we do not include these organizations in the cross-national comparisons, though they are covered for those countries for which we were able to assemble such data.

## 4. Common sets of variables

One of the key goals of this project is to assess the scale, composition, and funding structure of the civil society sector in each of the project countries. To accomplish this objective, we identified a set of key variables that measure each of these dimensions.

The scale is measured by the size of the civil society organization workforce, which includes both paid employment and volunteers. Because many paid workers and most volunteers work part-time, we had to convert the number of workers into full-time equivalent (FTE) terms. The FTE conversion was accomplished by dividing the total number of hours worked by the paid staff and volunteers, respectively, by the typical workload of a full-time job in the country under investigation (usually 40 hours per week). For comparative purposes, the resulting workforce figures were expressed as a share of the economically active population (EAP). The EAP is the population of working age that is not institutionalized or otherwise unavailable for work, whether they are formally employed, self-employed, producing for their own consumption, or looking for work.[3]

The EAP data came from the International Labour Organization online database.[4] We selected a single source for these data to minimize error due to variations among different sources. These data may differ from those found in other sources available for the target countries. Since volunteers may not always be a part of the EAP (e.g., retirees), we adjusted the EAP figure by adding the estimated number of FTE volunteers outside the economically active population. We did so by calculating the difference between the economically active and the adult populations for each country in this project, expressing that difference as a percent of the economically active population, and computing the unweighted all-country average. This yielded an estimate of 28 percent.

The scale of volunteering was measured chiefly by the total number of volunteer hours worked during the base year period, obtained either via organizational or population surveys. These numbers were then converted into FTE jobs. Since most people volunteer a relatively small number of hours over the period of a year, the number of FTE volunteers and the number of individuals engaged, even if briefly, in some kind of volunteer work differ substantially. While the FTE figure is more suitable for cross-national comparisons, it may not fully reflect the scale of volunteer participation on the national level. Therefore, we also report the total number of people volunteering and express it as a share of the adult population (15 years of age or older). Because people often volunteer in more than one field or organization, the reported number of people volunteering had to be adjusted to reflect this fact.

The composition of the civil society sector is measured by the distribution of the civil society organization workforce (paid and volunteer) by major ICNPO categories, expressed as percentage shares. For analytical purposes, we group these categories into two clusters: service and expressive activities. The service activities are those involving assistance to others, usually of some economic value (e.g., health services, education, social services, and housing and development assistance). The expressive activities are those that aim mainly at the expression of cultural, aesthetic, or political values, or the pursuit of social or collective interests. The ICNPO categories included in this cluster are culture, sports and recreation, environmental protection, human rights and advocacy, and the representation of labor and professional interests. Although religious worship (ICNPO Group 10) should technically be included in this cluster, at least in significant part, gaps in data availability prevented us from doing so. In certain developing countries it also made sense to count development-oriented activities as an expressive rather than service activity, and we discuss that alternative where appropriate.

The funding structure of the civil society sector is represented by the revenue shares (at the field and the sector level) from three major sources:

- Fees and charges, including charges for services performed for individual clients, proceeds from the sale of goods, membership dues, and income on capital investments. It should be underscored that this category does not include service fees paid by government agencies on behalf of service recipients, as these are classified under public sector payments.

- Public sector payments, including public grants, statutory transfers (i.e., payments mandated by law), reimbursements (i.e., third party payments or fee-for-service payments), and public contracts for services. The public sector includes all branches and levels of government and its agencies. This type of payment also includes monies received from foreign governments, inasmuch as the information on such transfers was available.

- Private philanthropy, including individual giving, business donations, and foundation giving. A special case of private philanthropy is volunteer input; we accounted for that input by computing the imputed value of volunteer time by applying average wages for the respective fields of activity.

In many developing countries, transfers from overseas parent organizations constitute a significant portion of revenue for many civil society organizations. The monies so transferred may come either from foreign governments that use transnational NGOs to channel their assistance to recipient organizations, or from private sources. Since the information on the actual source of these funds was usually unavailable, we distributed such transfers between government payments and private philanthropy based on estimates.

Although data were collected at different *time periods* (1995 for the 22 original countries and 1997 to 2000 for the new countries), we have attempted to minimize the consequences of this disparity by relating the size of the civil society sector in a country to the size of the broader economy, particularly the economically active population, and reporting these ratios rather than the absolute numbers. Since these ratios are not likely to change much over the kind of time period we have examined, this approach preserves the basic comparability of the data.

The figures for country groupings represent unweighted averages of the respective figures for the individual countries in these groupings. The use of unweighted averages is justified by the fact that each country is a separate entity and unit of observation which contributes equally to cross-national patterns.

Comparative data are available for 36 countries. However, data were not available for all countries for every variable. Therefore, the data on paid employment by field cover 34 countries; volunteer data by field are available on only 33 countries; revenue data by source are available on 34 countries; revenue data by source and field cover 33 countries; revenue data by source and field including volunteers are available on 32 countries; and religious congregation workforce data cover only 27 countries.

## 5. Data collection and assembly strategy

Our data collection strategy relied on the assumption that the data on civil society organizations are often included in national statistics routinely collected by governmental and para-governmental agencies; however, they are not identified as such and reported separately, but instead are aggregated together with other types of economic activities. Therefore, our data collection strategy typically included a careful survey of existing data sources to identify data that could be extracted from these sources.

However, in most of the developing countries included in this phase of our project, that approach encountered serious obstacles. The main reason was the scarcity of any kind of statistical information in these countries. The existing sources either contained very fragmented and limited information on civil society organizations, or no such information at all. Consequently, we had to rely much more heavily on expressly designed and implemented organizational surveys as the primary data source.

Carrying out such surveys was complicated by the unavailability of the sampling frames from which statistically representative samples could be drawn. To solve this problem, we employed variations of hypernetwork sampling (also known as multiplicity sampling) and "snowballing" sampling techniques.

The essence of this approach was to select a representative sample of regions in the target countries and then to interview all, or a sizable sample of all, residents in these regions to determine the names of the organizations with which they work either as paid staff or volunteers. By carefully tracking the names of all such organizations in the target region, it was possible to build up a roster of all known organizations working in the region. These organizations were then contacted to determine if they met the project definition. A sample of the organizations that satisfied the Project's definition of a nonprofit organization in each region was then selected for detailed organizational surveys. The results of these surveys were then blown up to national estimates using weights based on the relationship that the population in the chosen region bore to the population of all regions of a given type. Where appropriate, administrative records on large organizations were added to these estimates to avoid understating the overall scale of the nonprofit sector in the country.

We utilized a collaborative approach to project definition, data collection, and analysis that involved a core staff at the Johns Hopkins Center for Civil Society Studies and a network of local associates in each of the project countries. Core staff and Local Associates jointly worked out the Project's definitions and data-gathering strategies, and the core staff monitored the implementation of these strategies to ensure consistency from place to place. This allowed the Project to build on the insight and experience of local analysts while still benefiting from the cross-checking made possible by the availability of a consistent body of cross-national data.

## B. Methodology by Country

This section covers only those countries featured in this volume. A more detailed discussion of the methodologies used in previously researched countries can be found in the first volume of *Global Civil Society: Dimensions of the Nonprofit Sector.*[5]

### Egypt

The estimates presented in this report were based on a survey of 1,802 organizations conducted by the Arab NGO Network. The sample was drawn from a listing of civil society organizations, compiled from the Arab NGO Network mailing list, supplemented by "snowballing" (see discussion above in Section 5). The sample was stratified by the size of the organization's budget. The survey instrument was not based on our model questionnaire and was limited to a small number of questions, including the number of paid employees and volunteers. The survey results were then extrapolated to the total known organizational population in Egypt, which consists of 14,748 registered entities.

## India

The data on civil society organizations in India come from an organizational survey administered to entities identified in a multi-stage sampling design. Since an organizational survey of civil society organizations had never been attempted before, our collaborators in India adopted a three-stage sampling design developed by the National Sample Survey Organization. In this design, geographical units were selected as follows:

- In the first stage, the local research team sampled districts of each of the five states selected for this study (Meghalaya, Tamil Nadu, West Bengal, Delhi, and Maharashtra) in proportion to the share of civil society organizations they contained.

- In the second stage, the local research team sampled Census District (CD) blocks from each of the five states selected, again in proportion to the estimated number of organizations we expected to find.

- In the third stage, local researchers sampled either villages (in rural areas) or Urban Frame Survey (UFS) blocks (in urban areas) from the units selected in the second phase.

The local research team subsequently identified and listed all civil society organizations operating in each of the villages or UFS blocks either through registration records obtained from the Office of Registrars in the respective state or through a variation of hypernetwork sampling.

Researchers then sampled a pre-determined number of households in each geographical unit and inquired about civil society organizations known to the respondents. This listing was used as a frame for randomly selecting organizations to be interviewed. The survey instrument was not based on the model questionnaire but used National Industrial Classification codes, which were later re-mapped to ICNPO. The research team projected the results obtained for each state to the national level, with weights proportional to the population of each state.

## Italy

All Italian data on civil society institutions come from the First Census on Nonprofit Institutions,[6] carried out in 2000 by the Italian Institute of Statistics (ISTAT) with the scientific cooperation of Istituto per la Ricerca Sociale and Centro di Ricerche sulla Cooperazione of the Catholic University of Milan. This census stems from earlier studies of the civil society sector in Italy carried out under the umbrella of the Johns Hopkins Comparative Nonprofit Sector Project.[7]

The study was based on the System of National Accounts 1993 definition of "nonprofit institutions," but national legislation was also taken into account to keep within the survey field the "social cooperatives" and any other "not-for-profit organizations of social utility" whose institutional behavior is regulated by Italian law. The list of target institutions for the survey was assembled through matching several administrative archives (private and public) and the operating statistical archives on business enterprises and private institutions. The questionnaire was mailed, and the net response rate was 76 percent.

## Kenya

The data on Kenyan civil society organizations come from existing administrative records as well as from an expressly designed and administered organizational survey. The local research team gathered administrative records from the Central Register of Business Establishments in the Modern Economy (maintained by the Central Bureau of Statistics of the Ministry of Planning and National Development), records of the NGOs Coordination Bureau, records of the Department of Cooperatives in the Ministry of Cooperative Development, and records of the Department of Social Services and Sports within the Ministry of Home Affairs, National Heritage and Sports.

The organizational survey targeted local, regional, national, and international civil society organizations formed or operating in Kenya by the end of 1998 that were still active by the time of the fieldwork. Fourteen administrative districts were selected from different geographical areas arranged according to the level of organizational density (high, medium, and low). High organizational density districts included Nairobi, Kiambu, Nyeri, Meru, and Machakos; medium density districts included Kisii, Siaya, Kisumu, Kakamega, and Nakuru; and low density districts included Mombasa, Kilifi, Isiolo, and Garissa. Both rural and urban districts were covered. The local research team then compiled a comprehensive listing of all civil society organizations operating in those districts, using administrative records that were available. They selected a stratified sample of 718 organizations for face-to-face interviews, using the organizational survey module developed by the CNP core staff. All parameters reported in this publication were derived from this survey and extrapolated to the national level.

## Morocco

The estimates presented in this report were based on a survey of 407 organizations conducted by the Arab NGO Network. The sample was drawn from a listing of civil society organizations compiled from the Arab NGO Network mailing list, supplemented by "snowballing" (see discussion above in section 5). The sample was stratified by the size of the organization's budget. The survey instrument was not based on the model questionnaire and was limited to a small number of questions, including the number of paid employees and volunteers. The survey results were then extrapolated to the total known organizational population in Morocco, consisting of 13,350 registered entities and reconciled with employment data obtained from the National Institute of Statistics.

## Norway

The data mainly come from surveys conducted by Statistics Norway, supplemented by annual reports, targeted organizational surveys, and an expressly designed giving and volunteering survey.

Employment, expenditures, and total revenue figures were derived from the Norwegian Register of Companies and Enterprises data. All other variables included in this report were estimated from surveys. An organizational survey conducted by Statistics Norway covered membership organizations as defined by the International Standard Industrial Classification (Group 91). The survey targeted national level organizations not registered as subsidiaries, and single organizations with a certain level of turnover or employment. A questionnaire was mailed to a stratified sample of 765, which included the 15 largest organizations in the country. The targeted survey, also conducted by Statistics Norway, focused on organizations that received support from the Norwegian Agency for Economic Development (NORAD), grant-making foundations, and local level associations. These surveys were supplemented by information from the organizations' annual reports, the Norwegian Central Bank, the Fund-Raising Control (*Innsamlingskontrollen*), and government ministries.

The expressly designed *Survey on Giving and Volunteering* of spring 1998 provided information about volunteering and membership. The self-administered questionnaire was mailed to a random sample of the Norwegian population aged 16 to 85 (N=4,000). The response rate was 45 percent. The survey results were used to estimate volunteer input and membership.

## Pakistan

The data on Pakistan come from an expressly designed organizational survey targeting both unregistered organizations and those registered under various government statutes (i.e., the Societies Registration Act of 1860, the Voluntary Social Welfare Agencies Ordinance of 1961, and the Companies Ordinance of 1984). The local research team drew a stratified random sample of 2000 registered organizations from the available registries in twelve administrative districts, each containing cities with population of more than one million.

The unregistered organizations were captured by hypernetwork sampling of the population of cities and villages randomly selected from the list based on District Census Reports. These organizations were identified by "snow-balling" (see discussion above in section 5). Only locally based and locally active organizations were included in the sample; those based elsewhere were excluded to avoid double-counting. Religious organizations (such as houses of worship or *madrasas*) were excluded, but auxiliary religious entities (e.g., those managing religious processions and organizing religious events) were included under ICNPO Group 10.

To adjust for possible under-representation of large national organizations that are few in number and thus have a lower probability of being selected in the random sample, such organizations were identified with the help of leading personalities of the sector and national and international organizations.

The survey instrument was administered by trained interviewers who contacted key personnel within every sampled organization. The only exception was national organizations, which received self-administered questionnaires. National estimates were derived from the weighted survey data.

## The Philippines

In contrast to most other countries included in this project, the Philippine data assembly started with an estimate of the civil society sector's expenditures, derived from administrative records of the Securities and Exchange Commission (SEC), to which all registered entities are required to submit annual financial statements. Since the SEC records contained only registered organizations, the local research team launched a supplementary organizational survey targeting 1,302 randomly selected organizations in four major cities. These surveys also provided the basis for estimating the number of volunteers. Employment was then estimated from the expenditure data using the average wage and the expenditure-to-wages ratios obtained from the National Statistical Coordination Board.

## Poland

The data on Poland were collected by the Central Statistical Office and supplemented by information from the National Account System, the Central Statistical Office yearbooks, and Ministry of Justice statistics on registered associations, foundations, labor unions, and other social organizations. A time use survey based on a representative, random sample of 1,000 households with 2,034 adult respondents was carried out by the Central Statistical Office in October 1996, followed by a 1997 census of associations, foundations, labor unions, organizations of employers, political parties, professional and business organizations, and other social organizations; a 1997 labor force census, including nonprofits not covered by the 1997 association census; and a 1998 census of associations, foundations, and other social organizations.

A giving and volunteering survey carried out in June 1998 on a representative, random sample of 1,153 adult respondents was followed by a *Supplementary Organizational Survey* based on a random representative sample of 523 associations, foundations, church-based nonprofits, organizations of employers, professional and business organizations, and other social organizations, conducted by the Polish project team in 1999.

The paid employment, expenditures, wages, and revenue figures were estimated mainly from the 1997 association census data. Volunteering figures come chiefly from the Supplementary Organizational Survey, which produced a much more conservative (and more plausible) estimate than the Giving and Volunteering survey. Data on religious-based social service, health care, and educational institutions were derived from the general labor force census (employment) and Supplementary Organizational Survey (proportion of employment to expenditures, etc.).

## South Africa

The data on South Africa come from expressly designed surveys of two sets of organizations: larger and more formal entities and smaller and less formal community-based organizations. The surveys were carried out by the private consulting firm Social Surveys.

To capture the less formal community-based organizations, the local research team used a variation of hypernetwork sampling. They sampled 40 geographical communities from a commercially available inventory that catalogues South African communities according to their physical, social, and economic characteristics. They then identified, through "snowballing" (see discussion above in section 5), all civil society organizations active in the sampled communities and targeted them with our organizational survey. The resulting sample, serving as the basis for our estimations, consisted of 1,395 entities, of which 755 were active and locally based.

Since the community-based survey was likely to miss larger, centralized organizations we supplemented it by two additional sources. One is the PRODDER database, an official directory of approximately 7,000 larger, voluntarily registered not-for-profit organizations in South Africa maintained by the Human Sciences Research Council (a government-funded research institute). The second source was a supplementary survey of professional associations and unions conducted by Social Surveys. The national estimates were compiled by combining the results obtained from the three sources.

## South Korea

The main source of our estimates for South Korea was data obtained from the Bank of Korea. Expenditures were estimated from the National Account data, which show the final consumption expenditure of nonprofit institutions serving households. These data do not include a major part of medical corporations and other types of nonprofit medical institutions (such as hospitals), treating them as profit-seeking entities. Therefore, the health field was estimated separately from the Bank of Korea data.

Employment data come mainly from the *Report on the Census on Basic Characteristics of Establishments* assembled by the National Statistics Office. The data for education and research came from the *Statistical Yearbook of Education* published by the Ministry of Education and the Korea Educational Development Institute. The main data source for volunteering was a nationwide survey of volunteering administered to 1,533 adults over 20 years of age. The survey was conducted in July 1999 by the nonprofit organization Volunteer 21.

Civil society organization revenues were estimated on the assumption that the amount of total expenditures equals the amount of total revenues. Revenue structure was compiled from various sources depending on the field. For culture and recreation, the data came from the Korea Institute for Culture Policy Development; for education and research, from the Ministry of Education; for health, from the *Statistics for Hospital Management* published by the Korea Health Industry Development Institute; for religion, from the Korea Institute for Culture Policy Development; for civic and advocacy, a survey was administered to a small sample of major organizations; for political organizations, data came from the National Election Committee; and for business, professional, and labor organizations, data came from the Korea Labor Institute.

## Tanzania

The data on Tanzania came from an organizational survey administered by the local research team, and the survey instrument was developed from our model questionnaire. The sampling process involved two stages. First, the local research team drew a sample of administrative districts of thirteen major regions, stratified by the estimated density (high, medium, and low) of civil society organizations. Four districts were selected from each category, while Zanzibar, Unguja, and Pemba were an additional category of their own. The research team then selected at random two regions, one rural and one urban, from each of the selected districts. Finally, they sampled 40 organizations from each of these districts, using the Vice President's 2001 NGO Inventory as the sampling frame. Each of the selected organizations was contacted by an interviewer. The effective sample size (due to non-responses) was 867.

The initial survey results were discussed with local experts, and then used to calculate the national estimates reported in this publication. Supplementary data come from official statistics and the International Labour Organizations' database.

## Uganda

The main source of data on Uganda reported in this publication was the National Social Security Fund (NSSF) data, which contains employment information on larger (5 employees or more) and formally registered organizations. In that set, the local research team was able to identify organizations that meet the criteria set by the structural-operational definition used in the CNP project.

To supplement this source, the local research team launched an organizational survey, using a survey instrument based on our model questionnaire. They first randomly selected two districts, one rural and one urban, from each of the country's four macro-regions — Central, Western, Northern, and Eastern — and added the Kampala District (the capital), which is the most urbanized. In each of the selected districts, they compiled a list of active organizations by using the NGO Board register, which contained 2,521 records, as well as local government sources. A sample of 534 organizations from that list, as well as 903 households in these areas, were selected for the giving and volunteering survey. The national estimates combine the NSSF data (larger organizations) with the organizational survey (smaller organizations) results. The survey results were grossed-up for urban and rural areas separately, using population-based weights, and supplemented by labor and population data from the Uganda Bureau of Statistics.

# C. International Classification of Nonprofit Organizations: Detailed Description

## Group 1: Culture and Recreation

### 1 100 Culture and Arts

*Media and communications.* Production and dissemination of information and communication; includes radio and TV stations; publishing of books, journals, newspapers, and newsletters; film production; and libraries.

*Visual arts, architecture, ceramic art.* Production, dissemination, and display of visual arts and architecture; includes sculpture, photographic societies, painting, drawing, design centers, and architectural associations.

*Performing arts.* Performing arts centers, companies, and associations; includes theater, dance, ballet, opera, orchestras, chorals, and music ensembles.

*Historical, literary, and humanistic societies.* Promotion and appreciation of the humanities, preservation of historical and cultural artifacts, and commemoration of historical events; includes historical societies, poetry and literary societies, language associations, reading promotion, war memorials, and commemorative funds and associations.

*Museums.* General and specialized museums covering art, history, sciences, technology, and culture.

*Zoos and aquariums.*

## 1 200 Sports

Provision of amateur sport, training, physical fitness, and sport competition services and events; includes fitness and wellness centers.

## 1 300 Other Recreation and Social Clubs

*Recreation and social clubs.* Provision of recreational facilities and services to individuals and communities; includes playground associations, country clubs, men's and women's clubs, touring clubs, and leisure clubs.

*Service clubs.* Membership organizations providing services to members and local communities, for example: Lions, Zonta International, Rotary Club, and Kiwanis.

## Group 2: Education and Research

## 2 100 Primary and Secondary Education

*Elementary, primary, and secondary education.* Education at elementary, primary, and secondary levels; includes pre-school organizations other than day care.

## 2 200 Higher Education

*Higher education.* Higher learning, providing academic degrees; includes universities, business management schools, law schools, medical schools.

## 2 300 Other Education

*Vocational/technical schools.* Technical and vocational training specifically geared towards gaining employment; includes trade schools, paralegal training, secretarial schools.

*Adult/continuing education.* Institutions engaged in providing education and training in addition to the formal educational system; includes schools of continuing studies, correspondence schools, night schools, and sponsored literacy and reading programs.

*2 400 Research*

*Medical research.* Research in the medical field; includes research on specific diseases, disorders, or medical disciplines.

*Science and technology.* Research in the physical and life sciences, and engineering and technology.

*Social sciences, policy studies.* Research and analysis in the social sciences and policy area.

## Group 3: Health

*3 100 Hospitals and Rehabilitation*

*Hospitals.* Primarily inpatient medical care and treatment.

*Rehabilitation.* Inpatient health care and rehabilitative therapy to individuals suffering from physical impairments due to injury, genetic defect, or disease and requiring extensive physiotherapy or similar forms of care.

*3 200 Nursing Homes*

*Nursing homes.* Inpatient convalescent care, residential care, as well as primary health care services; includes homes for the frail elderly and nursing homes for the severely handicapped.

*3 300 Mental Health and Crisis Intervention*

*Psychiatric hospitals.* Inpatient care and treatment for the mentally ill.

*Mental health treatment.* Outpatient treatment for mentally ill patients; includes community mental health centers, and halfway homes.

*Crisis intervention.* Outpatient services and counsel in acute mental health situations; includes suicide prevention and support to victims of assault and abuse.

*3 400 Other Health Services*

*Public health and wellness education.* Public health promotion and health education; includes sanitation screening for potential health hazards, first aid training and services, and family planning services.

*Health treatment, primarily outpatient.* Organizations that provide primarily outpatient health services — e.g., health clinics and vaccination centers.

*Rehabilitative medical services.* Outpatient therapeutic care; includes nature cure centers, yoga clinics, and physical therapy centers.

*Emergency medical services.* Services to persons in need of immediate care; includes ambulatory services and paramedical emergency care, shock/trauma programs, lifeline programs, and ambulance services.

## Group 4: Social Services

*4 100 Social Services*

*Child welfare, child services, and day care.* Services to children, adoption services, child development centers, foster care; includes infant care centers and nurseries.

*Youth services and youth welfare.* Services to youth; includes delinquency prevention services, teen pregnancy prevention, drop-out prevention, youth centers and clubs, and job programs for youth; includes YMCA, YWCA, Boy Scouts, Girl Scouts, and Big Brothers/Big Sisters.

*Family services.* Services to families; includes family life/parent education, single parent agencies and services, and family violence shelters and services.

*Services for the handicapped.* Services for the handicapped; includes homes, other than nursing homes, transport facilities, recreation, and other specialized services.

*Services for the elderly.* Organizations providing geriatric care; includes in-home services, homemaker services, transport facilities, recreation, meal programs, and other services geared towards senior citizens. (Does not include residential nursing homes.)

*Self-help and other personal social services.* Programs and services for self-help and personal development; includes support groups, personal counseling, and credit counseling/money management services.

*4 200 Emergency and Relief*

*Disaster/emergency prevention and control.* Organizations that work to prevent, predict, control, and alleviate the effects of disasters, to educate or otherwise prepare individuals to cope with the effects of disasters, or to provide relief to disaster victims; includes volunteer fire departments, life boat services, etc.

*Temporary shelters.* Organizations providing temporary shelters to the homeless; includes travelers aid and temporary housing.

*Refugee assistance.* Organizations providing food, clothing, shelter, and services to refugees and immigrants.

### 4 300 Income Support and Maintenance

*Income support and maintenance.* Organizations providing cash assistance and other forms of direct services to persons unable to maintain a livelihood.

*Material assistance.* Organizations providing food, clothing, transport, and other forms of assistance; includes food banks and clothing distribution centers.

## Group 5: Environment

### 5 100 Environment

*Pollution abatement and control.* Organizations that promote clean air, clean water, reducing and preventing noise pollution, radiation control, treatment of hazardous wastes and toxic substances, solid waste management, and recycling programs.

*Natural resources conservation and protection.* Conservation and preservation of natural resources, including land, water, energy, and plant resources for the general use and enjoyment of the public.

*Environmental beautification and open spaces.* Botanical gardens, arboreta, horticultural programs and landscape services; organizations promoting anti-litter campaigns; programs to preserve the parks, green spaces, and open spaces in urban or rural areas; and city and highway beautification programs.

### 5 200 Animal Protection

*Animal protection and welfare.* Animal protection and welfare services; includes animal shelters and humane societies.

*Wildlife preservation and protection.* Wildlife preservation and protection; includes sanctuaries and refuges.

*Veterinary services.* Animal hospitals and services providing care to farm and household animals and pets.

## Group 6: Development and Housing

*6 100 Economic, Social, and Community Development*

*Community and neighborhood organizations.* Organizations working towards improving the quality of life within communities or neighborhoods, e.g., squatters' associations, local development organizations, poor people's cooperatives.

*Economic development.* Programs and services to improve economic infrastructure and capacity; includes building of infrastructure, like roads; and financial services such as credit and savings associations, entrepreneurial programs, technical and managerial consulting, and rural development assistance.

*Social development.* Organizations working towards improving the institutional infrastructure and capacity to alleviate social problems and to improve general public well-being.

*6 200 Housing*

*Housing associations.* Development, construction, management, leasing, financing, and rehabilitation of housing.

*Housing assistance.* Organizations providing housing search, legal services, and related assistance.

*6 300 Employment and Training*

*Job training programs.* Organizations providing and supporting apprenticeship programs, internships, on-the-job training, and other training programs.

*Vocational counseling and guidance.* Vocational training and guidance, career counseling, testing, and related services.

*Vocational rehabilitation and sheltered workshops.* Organizations that promote self-sufficiency and income generation through job training and employment.

## Group 7: Law, Advocacy, and Politics

*7 100 Civic and Advocacy Organizations*

*Advocacy organizations.* Organizations that protect the rights and promote the interests of specific groups of people, e.g., the physically handicapped, the elderly, children, and women.

*Civil rights associations.* Organizations that work to protect or preserve individual civil liberties and human rights.

*Ethnic associations.* Organizations that promote the interests of, or provide services to, members belonging to a specific ethnic heritage.

*Civic associations.* Programs and services to encourage and spread civic-mindedness.

### 7 200 Law and Legal Services

*Legal services.* Legal services, advice, and assistance in dispute resolution and court-related matters.

*Crime prevention and public policy.* Crime prevention to promote safety and precautionary measures among citizens.

*Rehabilitation of offenders.* Programs and services to reintegrate offenders; includes halfway houses, probation and parole programs, prison alternatives.

*Victim support.* Services, counsel, and advice to victims of crime.

*Consumer protection associations.* Protection of consumer rights, and the improvement of product control and quality.

### 7 300 Political Organizations

*Political parties and organizations.* Activities and services to support the placing of particular candidates into political office; includes dissemination of information, public relations, and political fundraising.

## Group 8: Philanthropic Intermediaries and Voluntarism Promotion

### 8 100 Philanthropic Intermediaries and Voluntarism Promotion

*Grant-making foundations.* Private foundations; including corporate foundations, community foundations, and independent public-law foundations.

*Volunteerism promotion and support.* Organizations that recruit, train, and place volunteers and promote volunteering.

*Fund-raising organizations.* Federated, collective fundraising organizations; includes lotteries.

## Group 9: International

*9 100 International Activities*

*Exchange/friendship/cultural programs.* Programs and services designed to encourage mutual respect and friendship internationally.

*Development assistance associations.* Programs and projects that promote social and economic development abroad.

*International disaster and relief organizations.* Organizations that collect, channel, and provide aid to other countries during times of disaster or emergency.

*International human rights and peace organizations.* Organizations which promote and monitor human rights and peace internationally.

## Group 10: Religion

*Religious Congregations and Associations*

*Congregations.* Churches, synagogues, temples, mosques, shrines, monasteries, seminaries, and similar organizations promoting religious beliefs and administering religious services and rituals.

*Associations of congregations.* Associations and auxiliaries of religious congregations and organizations supporting and promoting religious beliefs, services, and rituals.

## Group 11: Business and Professional Associations, and Unions

*11 100 Business and Professional Associations, and Unions*

*Business associations.* Organizations that work to promote, regulate, and safeguard the interests of special branches of business, e.g., manufacturers' association, farmers' association, bankers' association.

*Professional associations.* Organizations promoting, regulating, and protecting professional interests, e.g., bar association, medical association.

*Labor unions.* Organizations that promote, protect, and regulate the rights and interests of employees.

## Group 12: Not Elsewhere Classified

*12 100 n.e.c.*

## Notes

1. This appendix was prepared by S. Wojciech Sokolowski based on information provided by the local associates in the countries discussed.

2. See: Lester M. Salamon, Helmut K. Anheier, Regina List, Stefan Toepler, S. Wojciech Sokolowski, and Associates, *Global Civil Society: Dimensions of the Nonprofit Sector* (Baltimore, MD: The Johns Hopkins Center for Civil Society Studies, 1999). Information is also available online at: www.jhu.edu/cnp/pdf/method.pdf.

3. See: International Labour Organization, *Current International Recommendations on Labour Statistics* (Geneva: International Labour Organization, 1988).

4. See http://laborsta.ilo.org, *Economically Active Population Estimates and Projections 1950–2010*.

5. See: Lester M. Salamon, Helmut K. Anheier, Regina List, Stefan Toepler, S. Wojciech Sokolowski, and Associates, *Global Civil Society: Dimensions of the Nonprofit Sector* (Baltimore, MD: The Johns Hopkins Center for Civil Society Studies, 1999). Information is also available online at: www.jhu.edu/cnp/pdf/method.pdf.

6. Data are published in ISTAT, *Istituzioni nonprofit in Italia (Nonprofit Institutions in Italy)*, Collana Informazioni n. 50 (Roma: ISTAT, 2001). The results have been analyzed in: Gian Paolo Barbetta, S. Cima, and N. Zamaro, eds., *Le Istituzioni Nonprofit in Italia. Dimensioni organizzative, economiche e sociali.* (Nonprofit Institutions in Italy: Organizational, Social and Economic Dimensions) (Bologna, Italy: Il Mulino, 2003).

7. Gian Paolo Barbetta, ed., *The Nonprofit Sector in Italy* (Manchester, U.K.: Manchester University Press, 1997).

# Johns Hopkins Comparative Nonprofit Sector Project Local Associates

**Argentina**
Mario Roitter
Center for the Study of State and Society

**Australia**
Mark Lyons
University of Technology Sydney

**Austria**
Christoph Badelt
Wirtschaftsuniversität Wien

**Belgium**
Jacques Defourny
Université de Liège

Jozef Pacolet
Higher Institute of Labour Studies
Katholieke Universiteit Leuven

**Brazil**
Leilah Landim
Instituto de Estudos da Religião

**Colombia**
Rodrigo Villar
Confederación Colombiana de ONGs

**Czech Republic**
Martin Potůček/Pavol Frič
Charles University
Institute of Sociological Studies

**Egypt**
Amani Kandil
Arab Network for NGOs

**Finland**
Voitto Helander
Abo Academy

**France**
Edith Archambault
Université de Paris-Sorbonnes

**Germany**
Eckhard Priller
Wissenschaftszentrum Berlin

Annette Zimmer
Westfalische Wilhelms-Universität Münster

**Hungary**
Éva Kuti/István Sebestény
Central Statistical Office

**India**
Rajesh Tandon/S.S. Srivastava
Society for Participatory Research in Asia

**Ireland**
Joyce O'Connor/Freda Donoghue
National College of Ireland

**Israel**
Benjamin Gidron
Ben Gurion University of the Negev

**Italy**
Gian Paolo Barbetta
Istituto de Ricerca Sociale

**Japan**
Naoto Yamauchi/Masaaki Homma
Osaka School of International Public Policy

**Kenya**
Karuti Kanyinga/Winnie Mitullah
University of Nairobi

**Lebanon**
Hashem El-Husseini
Lebanese University

**Mexico**
CEMEFI
Principal Investigator: Gustavo Verduzco
El Colegio de México, A.C.

**Morocco**
Salama Saidi
RAWABIT

**The Netherlands**
Paul Dekker/Ary Burger
Social and Cultural Planning Bureau

**Norway**
Håkon Lorentzen
Institutt for Samfunnsforkning

Per Selle
Norwegian Research Centre in Organization and Management

**Pakistan**
Hafiz Pasha
Social Policy Development Centre

**Peru**
Felipe Portocarrero/Cynthia Sanborn
Centro de Investigación de la Universidad del Pacífico

**The Philippines**
Ledivina Cariño
University of the Philippines

**Poland**
Ewa Leś/Sławomir Nałęcz
Polish Academy of Science

**Romania**
Daniel Saulean
Civil Society Development Foundation

**Slovakia**
Helena Woleková
S.P.A.C.E. Foundation

**South Africa**
Mark Swilling/Hanlie Van Dyk
University of Witwatersrand

**South Korea**
Tae-kyu Park/Chang-soon Hwang
Yonsei University

**Spain**
José Ignacio Ruiz Olabuénaga
Centro de Investigación y Desarrollo – Estadísticas

**Sweden**
Filip Wijkström/Tommy Lundström
Stockholm School of Economics

**Tanzania**
Andrew Kiondo/Laurean Ndumbaro
University of Dar es Salaam

**Uganda**
Bazaara Nyangabyaki/John-Jean Barya
Centre for Basic Research

**United Kingdom**
Jeremy Kendall/Martin Knapp
London School of Economics and Political Science

**United States**
Lester M. Salamon/S. Wojciech Sokolowski
Johns Hopkins University

# Appendix D

# Advisory Committees

## International Advisory Committee

*Farida Allaghi,* AGFUND; *Manuel Arango,* CEMEFI; *David Bonbright,* Aga Khan Foundation; *Mauricio Cabrera Galvis,* Colombia; *John Clark,* The London School of Economics; *Pavol Demes,* The German Marshall Fund; *Barry Gaberman,* The Ford Foundation; *Cornelia Higginson,* American Express Company; *Stanley Katz,* Princeton University; *Miklos Marschall,* Transparency International; *Kumi Naidoo,* CIVICUS; *John Richardson,* European Foundation Centre; *S. Bruce Schearer,* The Synergos Institute

## Local Advisory Committees

### Egypt

*Salwa El Amir,* National Center for Social Research; *Nazli Maoud,* Faculty of Political and Economic Science; *Abd El Monem Said,* Center for Political and Strategic Studies; *Nabil Samuel,* Coptic Angelic Organization for Social Services.

### India

*Indu Capoor,* CHETNA; *Mathew Cherian,* Charities Aid Foundation; *Murray Culshaw,* Murray Culshaw Advisory Services; *Noshir Dadawala,* Centre for Advancement of Philanthropy; *Swapan Garain,* Tata Institute of Social Sciences; *Mr. Jagdananda,* Centre for Youth and Social Development; *Joe Madiath,* Gram Vikas, Berhampur; *Harsh Mandar,* Action Aid, New Delhi; *Ajay Mehta,* National Foundation of India; *Vijai Sardana,* Aga Khan Foundation; *Mark Sidel,* the Ford Foundation; *Pushpa Sundar,* Indian Centre for Philanthropy.

### Kenya

*Patrick O. Alila,* former Director, Institute for Development Studies, University of Nairobi; *Chairperson of the Board of Trustees,* Chandaria Foundation; *Njeri Karuru,* former Project Coordinator, Women and Law in East Africa; *Jaindi Kisero,* Nation Newspapers; *Martha Koome,* former Chairperson, FIDA; *Gibson Kamau Kuria,* Law Society of Kenya; *Betty C.*

*Maina,* former Executive Director, Institute of Economic Affairs; *David S.O. Nalo,* former Director, Central Bureau of Statistics; *Elkana Odembo,* Philanthropic Foundation; *Martin Oloo,* former Regional Programme Officer, Aga Khan Foundation; *Oduor Ongwen,* National Council of NGOs; *Alois Opiyo,* Undugu Society of Kenya; *Kassim Owango,* the Kenya National Chamber of Commerce and Industry; *Aina Tade,* former Programme Officer, Ford Foundation.

## Lebanon

*Muhammad Barakat,* Institutions of Social Welfare; *Role el-Husseini Begdashe,* Lebanese University; *Faheem Dagher,* Pediatrician; *Hasan Hammoud,* Lebanese American University; *Marwan Houry,* Lebanese University; *Naamat Kanaan,* Ministry of Social Affairs.

## Morocco

*C. Ben Azzou,* Statistician, former Moroccan Ambassador to Indonesia; *M. Bennani,* Ministry of Planning; *Ait Haddout,* former Director of the Co-operatives Department; *K. El Madmad,* University of Ain Chock, UNESCO Chair on Migration and Human Rights.

## Norway

*Jon Olav Aspås,* Ministry of Health and Social Affairs; *Erling Berg,* Ministry of Finance; *Paul Glomsaker,* Ministry of Culture and Church Affairs; *Steinar Kristiansen,* Research Council of Norway; *Dag Nissen,* Ministry of Foreign Affairs; *Åsa Steinsvik,* Ministry of Children and Family Affairs; *Ottil Tharaldsen,* Ministry of Labour and Government Administration; *Liv Westby,* Ministry of the Environment.

## Pakistan

*Rolando Bahamondes,* Canadian High Commission; *Kaiser Bengali,* Social Policy and Development Centre; *R. Kamal,* Pakistan Institute of Development Economics; *Mazhar Ali Khan,* Voluntary Social Welfare Agencies; *Munir M. Merali,* the Aga Khan Foundation; *Khawar Mumtaz,* Pakistan NGO Forum; *Mehtab Akbar Rashidi,* Shahrah-e-Kamal Ataturk; *Ghazi Salahuddin,* Journalist; *Sardar Wasimuddin,* Royal Embassy of Japan.

## The Philippines

*Lourdes Casas-Quezon,* Philippine National Red Cross; *David Chiel,* Ford Foundation; *Sheila Coronel,* Philippine Center for Investigative Journalism; *Victoria Garchitorena,* Ayala Foundation; *Emil Q. Javier,* Consultative Group on International Agricultural Research; *Horacio Morales,* La Liga Citizens' Movement for Renewal and Reform.

## South Africa

*Eve Annecke,* Sustainability Institute; *Colleen du Toit,* South African Grant-makers Association; *Nomboniso Gasa,* Centre for Civil Society, University of Natal; *Adam Habib,* Centre for Civil Society, University of Natal; *Firoz Khan,* School of Public Management and Planning, University of Stellenbosch; *Christa Kuljian,* Mott Foundation; *Alan Mabin,* Graduate School of Public and Development Management, University of the Witwatersrand, Johannesburg; *Eugene Saldanha,* Non-Profit Partnership; *Hanlie Van Dyk,* Department of Public Service and Administration, South African Government.

## South Korea

*Hong-sup Cho,* Hangyurae Daily Newspaper; *Kyu-whan Cho,* Angels' Heaven Social Welfare Corporation; *Woo-Hyun Cho,* Yonsei University Medical College; *Ho-jin Jung,* Daesan Foundation for Rural Culture and Society; *Soobok Jung,* formerly at the Korean NGO Times; *Min-young Kim,* People's Solidarity for Participatory Democracy; *Hyung-Jin Lee,* Arche Publishing House; *Chang-ho Lee,* Joongang Daily Newspaper; *Kang-Hyun Lee,* Volunteer 21; *Kwang-Joo Lee,* Bank of Korea; *Eun-Kyung Park,* YWCA; *Yong-Joon Park,* Global Care; *Pyong-Ryang Wi,* Citizen's Coalition for Economic Justice.

## Tanzania

*H. Halfan; Gertrude Mongella,* Advisor to U.N. Secretary General on Gender Issues; *Estomish Mushi,* Deputy President's Office; *M. Rusimi; Edda Sanga,* Radio Tanzania; *Issa Shivji,* University of Dar es Salaam.

## Uganda

*Xavier Mugisha,* Institute of Statistics and Applied Economics, Makerere University; *Tumusime Mutebile,* Ministry of Finance; *Olivia Mutibwa,* Makerere University; *Kiyaga Nsubuga,* Ministry of Local Government.

# Appendix E

# Johns Hopkins Comparative Nonprofit Sector Project Funders*

Academy of Finland
Aga Khan Foundation
Associazione Casse di Risparmio Italiane
Associazione Ricreativa e Cultuale Italiana
Australian Bureau of Statistics
Australian Research Council
Austrian Science Foundation
Banca di Roma
Banco di Napoli
Bank of Sweden Tercentenary Foundation
Canadian Fund (Slovakia)
Caritas Ambrosiana
Cassa di Risparmio delle Province Lombarde
Cassa di Risparmio di Puglia
Cassa di Risparmio di Torino
Charities Aid Foundation (U.K.)
Civil Society Development Foundation (Czech Republic)
Civil Society Development Foundation (Romania)
Civil Society Development Foundation (Slovakia)
Colombian Center on Philanthropy
Deutsche Bank Foundation (Germany)
FIN (Netherlands)
Fondation de France
Fondazione Giovanni Agnelli
Fondazione San Paulo di Torino
Ford Foundation
FORMEZ
Foundation for an Open Society (Hungary)
Fundación Antonio Restrepo Barco (Colombia)
Fundación BBVA (Spain)

---

*Includes only funders for work on countries covered in this book.

Fundación FES (Colombia)
Humboldt Foundation/Transcoop (Germany)
Industry Commission (Australia)
Institute for Human Sciences (Austria)
Inter-American Development Bank
Inter-American Foundation
Juliana Welzijn Fonds (Netherlands)
Kahanoff Foundation (Canada)
W.K. Kellogg Foundation
King Baudouin Foundation (Belgium)
Körber Foundation (Germany)
Ministry of Church and Education (Norway)
Ministry of Culture and Sports (Norway)
Ministry of Education, Culture and Science (Netherlands)
Ministry of Environment (Norway)
Ministry of Family and Children (Norway)
Ministry of Family/World Bank (Venezuela)
Ministry of Foreign Affairs (Norway)
Ministry of Health and Social Affairs (Sweden)
Ministry of Health, Sports and Welfare (Netherlands)
Ministry of Social Affairs and Health (Finland)
Ministry for Public Administration (Sweden)
C.S. Mott Foundation (U.S.)
National Department of Planning (Colombia)
National Research Fund (Hungary)
Open Society Foundation (Slovakia)
David and Lucile Packard Foundation
Productivity Commission (Australia)
Research Council of Norway
Rockefeller Brothers Fund
Joseph Rowntree Foundation (U.K.)
Sasakawa Peace Foundation (Japan)
Swedish Council for Research in the Humanities and Social Services
Swedish Red Cross
U.S. Information Service
Yad Hadaniv Foundation (Israel)

# Also from Kumarian Press...

## *Civil Society and International Development*

**Civil Society at the Millennium**
CIVICUS, edited by Kumi Naidoo

**Creating a Better World:** Interpreting Global Civil Society
Edited by Rupert Taylor

**Global Civil Society:** Dimensions of the Nonprofit Sector, Volume One
Lester M. Salamon, Helmut K. Anheier, Regina List, Stefan Toepler, S. Wojciech Sokolowski and Associates

**Going Global:** Transforming Relief and Development NGOs
Marc Lindenberg and Coralie Bryant

**Nongovernments:** NGOs and the Political Development of the Third World
Julie Fisher

**The Charity of Nations:** Humanitarian Action in a Calculating World
Ian Smillie and Larry Minear

**When Corporations Rule the World,** Second Edition
David C. Korten

**Worlds Apart:** Civil Society and the Battle for Ethical Globalization
John Clark

## *International Development, Humanitarianism, Conflict Resolution*

**Ethics and Global Politics:** The Active Learning Sourcebook
Edited by April L. Morgan, Lucinda Joy Peach, and Colette Mazzucelli

**Human Rights and Development**
Peter Uvin

**Nation-Building Unraveled?** Aid, Peace and Justice in Afghanistan
Edited by Antonio Donini, Norah Niland and Karin Wermester

**Southern Exposure**
International Development and the Global South in the Twenty-First Century
Barbara P. Thomas-Slayter

**War and Intervention:** Issues for Contemporary Peace Operations
Michael V. Bhatia

Visit Kumarian Press at **www.kpbooks.com** or
call **toll-free 800.289.2664** for a complete catalog.

*Kumarian Press, located in Bloomfield, Connecticut, is a forward-looking, scholarly press that promotes active international engagement and an awareness of global connectedness.*